VOLUME 426 JULY 1976

THE ANNALS

of The American Academy *of* Political
and Social Science

Richard D. Lambert, *Editor*

Alan W. Heston, *Assistant Editor*

BICENTENNIAL CONFERENCE ON THE CONSTITUTION: A REPORT TO THE ACADEMY

Special Editor of This Volume

MARVIN E. WOLFGANG

President
American Academy of Political and Social Science
Professor of Sociology
University of Pennsylvania
Philadelphia, Pennsylvania

PHILADELPHIA

Library of Congress Catalog Card Number 76-5778

The articles appearing in THE ANNALS are indexed in the *Reader's Guide to Periodical Literature,* the *Book Review Index,* the *Public Affairs Information Service Bulletin, Social Sciences Index,* and *Current Contents: Behavioral, Social, and Management Sciences.* They are also abstracted and indexed in *ABC Pol Sci, Historical Abstracts, International Political Science Abstracts* and/or *America: History and Life.*

International Standard Book Numbers (ISBN)

ISBN 0-87761-228-5, vol. 426, 1976; paper—$4.00

ISBN 0-87761-227-7, vol. 426, 1976; cloth—$5.00

Issued bimonthly by The American Academy of Political and Social Science at 3937 Chestnut St., Philadelphia, Pennsylvania 19104. Cost per year: $15.00 paperbound; $20.00 clothbound. Add $1.50 to above rates for membership outside U.S.A. Second-class postage paid at Philadelphia and at additional mailing offices.

Claims for undelivered copies must be made within the month following the regular month of publication. The publisher will supply missing copies when losses have been sustained in transit and when the reserve stock will permit.

Editorial and Business Offices, 3937 Chestnut Street, Philadelphia, Pennsylvania 19104.

CONTENTS

BOOK DEPARTMENT   PAGE

INTERNATIONAL RELATIONS AND POLITICAL SCIENCE

ASIA, LATIN AMERICA AND THE MIDDLE EAST

EUROPE

UNITED STATES

SOCIOLOGY

CONTENTS

ECONOMICS

PREFACE

Two years ago the board of the Academy supported Walter Phillips's suggestion that the Academy should plan something to celebrate the Bicentennial in 1976. Our editor, Richard Lambert, recommended in a first written draft that we consider a Constitutional Conference. After several drafts on which we both worked, with helpful suggestions from the board and later our formal organizing committee, a firm proposal was filed with the Philadelphia Bicentennial Commission.

Meanwhile, the Sun Oil Company, also seeking to celebrate the Bicentennial in various ways, discovered our proposal and approached me to determine whether the mutual interests of our two organizations could be merged. The Bicentennial Committee of Sun agreed to the funding of our proposal and the board of the Academy accepted the offer. The president and chairman of the Sun Company at that time, Robert Sharbaugh, Vice-Chairman Robert Donahue, and Dean Chaapel, were most generous with their time and consultations on the planning of the conference.

With help and no hindrance, with encouragement and no impediment, the Sun Company made possible this enterprise and will always be remembered with deep gratitude by the Academy as the facilitator and benefactor of a most successful Bicentennial Constitutional Conference.

Much of that success was due to the months of work performed by the organizing committee. My co-chairman, Richard Lambert, and the other members of the committee helped to formulate the major themes, to select the participants, and to provide constant guidance. They were:

Lee Benson, Professor of History of the American Peoples, University of Pennsylvania
Joseph S. Clark, former U.S. Senator, Philadelphia, Pennsylvania
A. Leon Higginbotham, Jr., Judge, U.S. District Court, Philadelphia
Covey T. Oliver, Ferdinand Wakeman Hubbell Professor of Law, University of Pennsylvania
Louis H. Pollak, Dean and Albert M. Greenfield Professor of Human Relations and Law, University of Pennsylvania Law School
Henry W. Sawyer, III, Partner, Drinker, Biddle & Reath, Philadelphia

As conference chairman, Herbert Wechsler, Professor of Law, Columbia University, and Director of the American Law Institute, steered our movements early on and provided focus for our preliminary thoughts. The late Senior Judge William H. Hastie of the United States Third Circuit Court of Appeals helped me in the ceremony to open the conference formally in Independence Hall. Dean Louis H. Pollak gave us his sterling keynote speech that set the tone for the high caliber of subsequent discussions at the committee meetings.

After the first plenary session on April 5, 1976, at the Hall of the American Philosophical Society, the 90 participants met in four separate simultaneously sitting committees. A previously distributed keynote paper was presented to each committee to provide background facts

and analysis on each specific theme. The originally selected persons
for these roles were as follows:

Committee I—Maintenance of Revolutionary Values. Chair: Patricia
Roberts Harris, Partner, Fried, Frank, Harris, Shriver, and Kampelman,
Washington, D.C.; Keynote: Alfred H. Kelly, Professor of History and
Acting Dean for Graduate Studies, Wayne State University, Detroit,
Michigan.
Committee II—Effectiveness of Governmental Operations. Chair: Henry
W. Sawyer, III, Partner, Drinker, Biddle & Reath, Philadelphia, Pennsyl-
vania; Keynote: Henry J. Abraham, Doherty Professor in Government
and Foreign Affairs, University of Virginia, Charlottesville, Virginia.
Committee III—Shaping of Public Policy. Chair: Elmer B. Staats, Comp-
troller General of the United States, Washington, D.C. Keynote: Charles
E. Gilbert, Professor of Political Science, Swarthmore College, Swarthmore,
Pennsylvania.
Committee IV—The United States and the World. Chair: Adrian S.
Fisher, Frances Cabell Brown Professor of International Law, Georgetown
University Law Center, Washington, D.C. Keynote: Covey T. Oliver,
Hubbell Professor of Law, University of Pennsylvania.

The death of Professor Kelly part way through his keynote paper
was a sad loss for us. His paper was posthumously completed by his
colleague, Professor Richard D. Miles, Wayne State University, and Professor Jack P. Greene, currently Harmsworth Professor of American History
at Queen's College, Oxford, wrote a complementary paper for committee
I. Litigation duties elsewhere prevented Henry Sawyer from chairing
committee II, but Nelson W. Polsby, Professor of Political Science at the
University of California, Berkeley, graciously agreed to accept the chair.

These chairmen and keynoters were of extreme importance in maintaining the excellence of discussions for the three days during which
the committees met at the Powel House. Special tribute should be paid
to the Rapporteurs who so ably synthesized and summarized the committee
proceedings. These members of the University of Pennsylvania Law School
were sometimes creative, often brilliant, always lucid. They added levity
as well as tact to the committee reports. Two Rapporteurs served each
committee:

Committee I—Paul Bender and Martha A. Field
Committee II—James O. Freedman and Frank Goodman
Committee III—Gerald Frug and John O. Honnold
Committee IV—Noyes Leech and Stephen J. Schulhofer

I wish to acknowledge the promotional work of Lewis & Gilman,
Inc., for the media coverage which the conference enjoyed. Palmer
Reed, Howard Burnett, and Joyce Kramer were helpful counselors
from the beginning.
But each member of the board and every participant at the conference
knows that efficiency in the management of the conference, proficiency
in the preparation, solicitude for each participant, ingenuity in providing decor and decorum, intelligence behind many substantive issues
discussed were due to our conference co-ordinator, Varney Truscott.

The grace and dignity which the conference enjoyed were a reflection of her own. Her assistant, Claire Latham, stands with her in the tribute we wish to make to their diligent work.

In this volume we present the first publication produced by the Bicentennial Constitutional Conference. The volume contains a report to the Academy at our 1976 Annual Meeting, including speeches that opened the conference, portions of the committee keynote papers, summaries of the rapporteurs that describe committee proceedings, and the final remarks at the luncheon by the conference chairman. Some of the dialogue of questions from members and response from principal participants at the annual meeting is included.

"The Revolution, the Constitution, and America's Third Century" was the title of our conference. The third century now begins. If the voices of reason and the congenial wisdom of this conference represent the direction ahead, we are safely and well launched.

I remember the softly spoken words uttered by a constitutional historian who stood in awe for the first time in Independence Hall before our opening ceremony: "How wonderful it is to be here—where it all began." I trust that 100 years from now our growing Constitution will continue to protect us all so that we can still say, "How wonderful it is to be here."

MARVIN E. WOLFGANG

The Revolution, the Constitution, and America's Third Century

Participants Present at the
Bicentennial Constitutional Conference, April 5–8, 1976
Philadelphia, Pennsylvania

HENRY J. ABRAHAM
Henry L. and Grace Doherty
Professor in Government and
Foreign Affairs
University of Virginia
Charlottesville, Virginia

JOHN B. ANDERSON
U.S. House of
Representatives
Washington, D.C.

PAUL BENDER
Professor of Law
University of Pennsylvania
Philadelphia, Pennsylvania

LEE BENSON
Professor of History of the
American Peoples
University of Pennsylvania
Philadelphia, Pennsylvania

SAM BROWN
Treasurer, State of Colorado
Denver, Colorado

FLETCHER L. BYROM
Chairman of the Board
Koppers Company, Inc.
Pittsburgh, Pennsylvania

JOSÉ A. CABRANES
Legal Adviser and Director,
Government Relations
Yale University
New Haven, Connecticut

JOSEPH S. CLARK
Former U.S. Senator
Philadelphia, Pennsylvania

TOM C. CLARK
Associate Justice (retired)
U.S. Supreme Court
Washington, D.C.

RUTH C. CLUSEN
President
The League of Women
Voters of the United States
Washington, D.C.

DAVID COHEN
President
Common Cause
Washington, D.C.

JOHN SLOAN DICKEY
President Emeritus and
Bicentennial Professor of
Public Affairs
Dartmouth College
Hanover, New Hampshire

JOHN DIEBOLD
Chairman
Diebold Group, Inc.
New York, New York

HEDLEY DONOVAN
Editor-in-Chief
Time Inc.
New York, New York

DAVID P. EASTBURN
President
Federal Reserve Bank of
Philadelphia
Philadelphia, Pennsylvania

CHRISTOPHER F. EDLEY
Executive Director
United Negro College Fund
New York, New York

GEORGE C. EDWARDS,
JR.
U.S. Circuit Judge
U.S. Court of Appeals,
6th Circuit
Cincinnati, Ohio

THOMAS EHRLICH
President
Legal Services Corporation
Washington, D.C.

DANIEL J. ELAZAR
Director
Center for the Study of
Federalism
Temple University
Philadelphia, Pennsylvania

HEINZ EULAU
William Bennett Munro
Professor of Political
Science
Stanford University
Stanford, California

RICHARD A. FALK
Albert G. Milbank Professor

of International Law and
Practice
Center of International
Studies
Princeton University
Princeton, New Jersey

JOHN D. FEERICK
Representing the American
Bar Association
Partner
Skadden, Arps, Slate,
Meagher and Flom
New York, New York

MARTHA A. FIELD
Associate Professor of Law
University of Pennsylvania
Philadelphia, Pennsylvania

ADRIAN S. FISHER
Frances Cabell Brown
Professor of International
Law
Georgetown University
Washington, D.C.

JAMES O. FREEDMAN
Professor of Law
University of Pennsylvania
Philadelphia, Pennsylvania

HENRY J. FRIENDLY
U.S. Circuit Judge
U.S. Court of Appeals,
2nd Circuit
New York, New York

GERALD FRUG
Associate Professor of Law
University of Pennsylvania
Philadelphia, Pennsylvania

BUELL G. GALLAGHER
Vice Chairman, National
Board of Directors
(Emeritus)
NAACP
New York, New York

RICHARD N. GARDNER
Henry L. Moses Professor
of Law and International
Organization
Columbia University
New York, New York

xii

CHARLES E. GILBERT
Professor of
Political Science
Center for Social and
Policy Studies
Swarthmore College
Swarthmore, Pennsylvania

EDWIN L. GOLDWASSER
Deputy Director
Fermi National
Accelerator Laboratory
Batavia, Illinois

FRANK GOODMAN
Visiting Professor of Law
University of Pennsylvania
Philadelphia, Pennsylvania

JACK GREENBERG
Director-Counsel
Legal Defense and
Educational Fund
NAACP
New York, New York

JACK P. GREENE
Harold Vyvyan Harmsworth
Professor of
American History
Queen's College
Oxford, England

ERWIN N. GRISWOLD
Partner
Jones, Day, Reavis & Pogue
Washington, D.C.

CHARLES V. HAMILTON
Wallace S. Sayre
Professor of Government
Columbia University
New York, New York

PATRICIA ROBERTS
HARRIS
Partner
Fried, Frank, Harris,
Shriver & Kampelman
Washington, D.C.

WILLIAM H. HASTIE
U.S. Senior Circuit Judge
U.S. Court of Appeals,
3rd Circuit
Philadelphia, Pennsylvania

LOUIS HENKIN
Hamilton Fish Professor of
International Law and
Diplomacy
Columbia University
New York, New York

KENNETH HOLLAND
President Emeritus
Institute of
International Education
New York, New York

JOHN HONNOLD
William A. Schnader
Professor of Commercial
Law
University of Pennsylvania
Philadelphia, Pennsylvania

R. GORDON HOXIE
President
Center for the Study of the
Presidency
New York, New York

CHARLES S. HYNEMAN
Distinguished Professor of
Political Science Emeritus
Indiana University
Bloomington, Indiana

ALBERT E. JENNER, JR.
Senior Partner
Jenner & Block
Chicago, Illinois

PHILIP C. JESSUP
Judge
Norfolk, Connecticut

OTTO KAHN-FREUND
Arthur Goodhart Visiting
Professor of Law at
Cambridge University
Cambridge, England

EVRON M. KIRKPATRICK
Executive Director
The American Political
. Science Association
Washington, D.C.

GEORGE B.
KISTIAKOWSKY
Abbot and James Lawrence
Professor of Chemistry
Emeritus
Harvard University
Cambridge, Massachusetts

RICHARD D. LAMBERT
Associate Dean for
Development
Faculty of Arts and
Sciences
University of Pennsylvania
Philadelphia, Pennsylvania

NOYES LEECH
Professor of Law

University of Pennsylvania
Philadelphia, Pennsylvania

SOL M. LINOWITZ
Senior Partner
Coudert Brothers
Washington, D.C.

LEON LIPSON
William K. Townsend
Professor of Law
Yale University
New Haven, Connecticut

JAMES R. MANN
U.S. House of
Representatives
Washington, D.C.

BAYLESS MANNING
President
Council on Foreign
Relations, Inc.
New York, New York

MYRES S. McDOUGAL
Sterling Professor of Law
Emeritus
Yale University
New Haven, Connecticut

CARL McGOWAN
U.S. Circuit Judge
U.S. Court of Appeals,
District of Columbia
Circuit
Washington, D.C.

ROBERT B. McKAY
Director, Program on Justice,
Society and the Individual
Aspen Institute for
Humanistic Studies
New York, New York

MARTIN MEYERSON
President
University of Pennsylvania
Philadelphia, Pennsylvania

CONSTANCE BAKER
MOTLEY
U.S. District Court Judge
Southern District, New York
New York, New York

JAMES L. OAKES
U.S. Circuit Judge
U.S. Court of Appeals,
2nd Circuit
Brattleboro, Vermont

COVEY T. OLIVER
Ferdinand Wakeman
Hubbell Professor of Law

University of Pennsylvania
Philadelphia, Pennsylvania

SUSAN V. PARIS
Member, Administrative
Committee
National Women's
Political Caucus
New York, New York

RICHARD L. PARK
Professor, Political Science
University of Michigan
Ann Arbor, Michigan

J. R. POLE
Reader in American History
and Government
Churchill College
Cambridge, England

LOUIS H. POLLAK
Dean and Albert M.
Greenfield Professor of
Human Relations and Law
University of Pennsylvania
Law School
Philadelphia, Pennsylvania

NELSON W. POLSBY
Professor, Political Science
University of California
Berkeley, California

ROBERT J. PRANGER
Director, Foreign and
Defense Policy Studies
American Enterprise
Institute for Public
Policy Research
Washington, D.C.

SIR LEON RADZINOWICZ
Fellow, Trinity College
Cambridge, England

J. AUSTIN RANNEY
Visiting Professor, Political
Science
University of California
Berkeley, California

MARCUS G. RASKIN
Co-Director
Institute for Policy Studies/
Transnational
Washington, D.C.

GEORGE E. REEDY
Dean and Nieman Professor
College of Journalism
Marquette University
Milwaukee, Wisconsin

SEYMOUR J. RUBIN
Professor of Law
Washington College of Law
American University
Washington, D.C.

HENRY S. RUTH, JR.
Director, Criminal Justice
Research
Urban Institute
Washington, D.C.

STEPHEN I.
SCHLOSSBERG
General Counsel
United Auto Workers
Washington, D.C.

STEPHEN J. SCHULHOFER
Professor of Law
University of Pennsylvania
Philadelphia, Pennsylvania

WHITNEY NORTH
SEYMOUR, SR.
Senior Partner
Simpson, Thacher & Bartlett
New York, New York

CHESTERFIELD SMITH
Partner
Holland & Knight
Lakeland, Florida

ELMER B. STAATS
U.S. Comptroller General
Washington, D.C.

JOHN R. STARK
Executive Director
Joint Economic Committee
U.S. Congress
Washington, D.C.

CLYDE W. SUMMERS
Fordham Professor of Law
University of Pennsylvania
Philadelphia, Pennsylvania

JAMES L. SUNDQUIST
Senior Fellow
The Brookings Institution
Washington, D.C.

HENRY TEUNE
Chairman, Department of
Political Science
University of Pennsylvania
Philadelphia, Pennsylvania

ALPHA TRIVETTE
Past National President
Future Farmers of America
Ladysmith, Virginia

JOAN S. WALLACE
Deputy Executive Director
Program Operations
National Urban League, Inc.
New York, New York

HERBERT WECHSLER
Director
The American Law Institute
Harlan Fiske Stone Professor
of Constitutional Law
Columbia University
New York, New York

CHARLES E. WIGGINS
U.S. House of
Representatives
Washington, D.C.

JOHN MINOR WISDOM
U.S. Circuit Judge
U.S. Court of Appeals,
5th Circuit
New Orleans, Louisiana

MARVIN E. WOLFGANG
Professor of Sociology and
Law
University of Pennsylvania
Philadelphia, Pennsylvania

ESMOND WRIGHT
Director
Institute of United States
Studies
University of London
London, England

J. SKELLY WRIGHT
U.S. Circuit Judge
U.S. Court of Appeals,
District of Columbia
Circuit
Washington, D.C.

OPENING REMARKS AT DEDICATION CEREMONY

I hereby open our Constitutional Conference, which we have entitled, "The Revolution, the Constitution, and America's Third Century."

We are mindful that in this Bicentennial year we celebrate 1776 and the Declaration of Independence. We are also mindful that revolutionary values of that year extended to 1787 and the later adoption of the United States Constitution.

The American Academy of Political and Social Science was founded in 1889 to promote scholarly discussion of political and social issues. It is most fitting that the Academy hold a conference on the revolutionary values that were codified in the principles of the Constitution, and we are gratified that we have been able to bring together a distinguished group whose professional lives, in one way or another, have been concerned with major constitutional issues.

For four days, followed by our annual meeting, we shall meet here and discuss the major issues of the Constitution during our history.

Representatives from law, academia, government, business, industry, labor, and consumer interests will meet here to have a scholarly dialogue to discuss the development of the Constitution historically and its viability for America's next century.

It is indeed my privilege and honor on behalf of the Board of Directors of the American Academy and its organizing committee to welcome the conferees to this momentous meeting.

It is fitting that we are here in the hallowed hall of Independence, where men of much merit made the documents that have been so important to our history. Not since that Constitutional Convention has there been a gathering such as we will be having here this week.

There are differences from that first Constitutional Convention. We represent not political states, but intellectual disciplines and various voices of the public. We are men and, unlike our predecessors, women. We are white and black; our society is composed of free citizens all, not free and slave.

Our function is to discuss and disseminate, not to create an entirely new document. We shall question and remold, and our final voices will be guides for thought and decisions, not binding rubrics. But neither the White House nor Congress nor the Supreme Court can ignore what is said here.

I am indeed proud to present to you, for the purpose of dedicating this Constitutional Conference, the distinguished Senior United States Judge of the United States Court of Appeals from the Third Circuit here in Philadelphia, Judge William Hastie, who will now formally open this meeting on "The Revolution, the Constitution, and America's Third Century."

MARVIN E. WOLFGANG

Dedicatory Ceremony at Independence Hall

This bicentennial year is a time for sober reflection upon our national beginnings that centered on the place in which we are assembled this morning. But a nation's beginning is a proper source of reflective pride only to the extent that the subsequent and continuing process of its becoming deserves celebration.

The lore of our national beginnings contains many anecdotes. A brief one seems apropos here and now. As the draftsmen of our Constitution, their work almost completed, were leaving this building at the end of a long day, a concerned Philadelphia lady stood outside. Addressing a fellow townsman, she asked: "Mr. Morris is it a good Constitution you gentlemen have drafted?" Mr. Morris answered: "That must depend, madam, upon how it shall be interpreted and applied." Today, informed by the experience of two centuries, our appraisal can and should be less Delphic.

As political and social scientists and as citizens largely experienced in the functioning of government, the members of this Bicentennial Conference on the Constitution of the United States bring extraordinary expertise to an examination of the merits and demerits of our 200 years of national becoming and the delineation of paths of constructive change as we enter the third century of our national existence. The elegant brochure prepared for this conference by our host Academy quotes this statement of George Washington to his contemporaries who devised our Constitution: "I do not think that we are more inspired, have more wisdom, or possess more virtue than those who will come after us." We must prove deserving of that expression of confidence.

That will not be easy. Forty years ago, observing the great depression of the 1930s, an eminent British scholar wrote that, under the American constitutional scheme, the powers delegated to the national government were hopelessly inadequate to cope with the economic realities and exigencies of modern industrialized society. Today, although some still question whether Professor Laski has been proved wrong, more voices— certainly the most vociferous ones—are heard decrying the present extent, not to mention abuses, of national power. I cite these polar views merely to suggest the inherent nature and difficulty of many of the matters that will confront this conference. That which has been characterized as "government of the people, by the people and for the people" is as eternally difficult a business as it is an exciting and inciting idea.

I suppose it is human nature on the one hand and the uses of government on the other that make this so. For men will always yearn, and properly so, for both freedom and provision. And in the yearner's mind the relative importance of each will be a variable of time, place, and circumstance. To the extent that there is want in the midst of plenty or the potential of plenty, men will demand that government be more effectively organized and act more aggressively for greater provision. On the other hand, to the extent that governmental impositions prove burdensome or oppressive, there will be outcry for greater

1

freedom. Thus, from generation to generation, it becomes more difficult to satisfy, or even to reconcile, the resulting diversity of deserving, but often contradictory, claims.

Yes, our political legacy includes intractable problems. Yet we continue to believe that the genius of the founders of our nation lay in the devising of political institutions that would both command respect and loyalty because of their decency and exhibit flexibility enough for effective adaptation to the needs of other and different times. For that, we cannot give them too much credit. Yet our belief in the excellence of their work is also the measure of our responsibility to make those institutions serve the people well in our times.

May enthusiasm for participation in that task be the impelling force of this Bicentennial Conference.

WILLIAM H. HASTIE

ANNALS, AAPSS, **426**, July 1976

Introductory Remarks

By HERBERT WECHSLER

ABSTRACT: Two centuries of national existence surely call for the expressions of devotion they will be evoking throughout this year. This meeting focuses on the framing of the polity and government that have endured. In considering the Constitution, we have before us the rich record of the past with its glories and frustrations. We must learn from that record, concentrating on the present and future. To achieve the purpose of this convention, we must feel as free to criticize as to extol the constitutional positions examined. The delegates who signed the Constitution did not consider it perfect, but only hoped that the draft would surmount the weakness of its articles and lead to a "more perfect union." The amending clause represented a significant advance in thought about the nature of organic law. The framers' plan was an innovation in support of adaptation, stringent as its requirements may be.

Herbert Wechsler is currently the Harlan Fiske Stone Professor of Constitutional Law at Columbia University and the Director of the American Law Institute. He was a member of the President's Commission on Law Enforcement and Administration of Justice from 1965–67 and of the Commission on Revision of the Federal Court Appellate System from 1973–75. His publications include Principles, Politics and Fundamental Law *and* The Federal Courts and the Federal System.

PRESIDENT Wolfgang, fellow conferees, distinguished guests, ladies and gentlemen: I approach this conference with the high hope that it may make a useful contribution and deem it a great honor to be asked to take the chair. Before committing myself to the silence and abstention that a chairman must observe, may I venture a brief comment on the task we are assembled to discharge.

THE AMERICAN CONSTITUTION

Two centuries of national existence surely call for the expressions of devotion they will be evoking throughout this year. Our meeting may well be unique in choosing to commemorate the Declaration and the patriots who gave us independence by focusing attention on the sequel to that indispensable achievement, the framing of the polity and government that have endured. Our concern is, therefore, with the Constitution, whose anniversaries it is less customary to observe, though of all the happenings in Philadelphia its formulation has exerted and exerts the largest influence upon the welfare and the destiny of our nation.

In considering the Constitution, we have before us the rich record of the past with its enormous glories and its large frustrations, not the least of which occurred in the election of a century ago. We must learn from that rich record what we can, ambiguous as its instruction often is. That is, however, just the prelude of our task, which is to concentrate upon the present and the future. The Academy, in calling us together, speaks as Antonio, though to a better purpose: "What's past is prologue; what to come/Is your and my discharge."

It is, of course, much easier to call for an assessment of our basic charter in relation to the present and the future than to frame a meaningful response to an assignment of that kind. Such is the human situation that we see the present only through a glass and darkly; our appraisals of the future rarely involve more than the projection of our hopes or our fears. Added to this, the papers that we have before us cover such a range of problems and of speculations that we all would be hard put to do them justice in a period of months instead of days.

In this predicament we must count heavily upon the conferees in each of our committees, guided by their chairmen and keynoters, to focus upon issues that are truly of a constitutional dimension, in the sense that their solution calls for the approval or rejection of specific changes in our fundamental law. This is no doubt to give voice to a lawyer's bias, but as Woodrow Wilson put it long ago, referring to the Constitution: "a written document makes lawyers of us all." I say no more, however, in support of this suggestion than that it will assist us to achieve the most significant conclusions we can reach in the brief time at our command. Think how it helped the Constitutional Convention to agree upon a text that its deliberations started with the 15 resolutions moved by Randolph, constituting the Virginia Plan.

Needless to say, I do not argue that this conference will not fulfill its purpose unless it achieves agreement on a program of amendment. A consensus in this group against the need for change, assuming that defects have been judiciously identified and gains and losses in removing them judiciously appraised, would be a product as important, in my view, as an agenda for reform. In constitutional affairs as in the rest of life, there is wise counsel in the aperçu of Justice Holmes that "imitation of the past, unless we have a clear reason for change, no more needs justification than appetite."

THE CONSTITUTION AND CHANGE

However our task may be defined, and our committees are autonomous as they define it, its performance will require us to feel as free to criticize as to extol the constitutional positions we examine. I should consider this too obvious to say had not my mailbox told me, as yours may have told you, that there is still a sentiment abroad that it is impious or worse to challenge the perfection of our Charter.

That sentiment, however patriotic in its provenance and motivation, is hostile to the spirit of the Constitution and refuted by its text. It is well that we repudiate it now.

The 39 delegates who signed the Constitution did not think the product perfect, not to speak of the 16 who departed or declined to sign or the 18 who stayed away. No more was claimed for the convention's draft than that it would surmount the weakness of the articles and lead to the "more perfect union" that was sought. That "a constitutional door was open to amendment," as Washington put it in his letters to Virginia, so that deficiencies could be eliminated in the future, was the telling argument against the doubters, crucial to securing the approval here and even more so in the state conventions. The Bill of Rights could thus be promised as demand for that security became insistent and provided promptly as the government was formed. So, too, the system chosen for electing presi-

dents could be prevented from collapsing by the Twelfth Amendment, though, as we know today, not all the perils were removed.

To be sure, a great consensus is required for amendment, two-thirds of the Senate and the House and approval in three-quarters of the states of legislatures or conventions as the Congress may elect when resolutions are proposed. A less onerous procedure would, of course, have paid more deference to Jefferson's insistence that the "earth belongs always to the living generation," the premise of the Declaration's proclamation that governments derive "their just powers from the consent of the governed." The revolutionaries in the Constitutional Convention could not have been insensitive to that conception, but neither could they yield to it entirely and create a government that would achieve acceptance by the states and gain sufficient strength to last. They had no choice, therefore, but to impose their present in such large degree upon the future, hoping to obtain its acquiescence by the benefits conferred. We may consider that the hope was not misplaced, for we have had our peaceful revolutions, starting, as Jefferson maintained, with his election as the president but more persuasively, I should suppose, in later years. It is important, though, that we remember that the most transforming changes in the cosmos of the Constitution were produced by civil war.

That cataclysm notwithstanding, we should recognize that the amending clause, which gives this conference its meaning, represented a significant advance in thought about the nature of organic law. In New Jersey, New York, and Virginia, the first constitutions after independence made no provision for amendment, as there was none in Cromwell's Instrument of Government of 1653. Delaware, Georgia, Maryland, Massachusetts, and Pennsylvania did formulate procedures for revision, but only that of Maryland seems viable upon its face. The articles, as is well known, conditioned change on the consent of all the states. The farmers' plan was, thus, an innovation in support of adaptation, stringent as its requirements may be.

That stringency is not without its compensations, for it has contributed to our acceptance of the most distinctive feature of our public law, the scope afforded to revision by interpretation: primarily, of course, interpretation by the courts, with final judgment in the Supreme Court, but also in some part by the Executive and Congress. Bagehot's famous dictum that "the men of Massachusetts could work any constitution," which Wilson properly regarded as a tribute to Americans in general, is supported mainly by the adaptations nurtured in this way. That record is, of course, before us as we move to our deliberations.

There are problem areas in which we may consider that the right solution inheres in interpretative changes as distinguished from revision of the text. Such submissions are, of course, in order, and they have the virtue of reducing or eliminating drafting difficulties that might otherwise be fatal. At the risk of being labeled a misogynist, I refer to the pending Equal Rights Amendment as very possibly a case in point.

INTRODUCTION OF COMMITTEES

I have spoken of the task we have assumed and of the spirit in which I believe we should approach it. That is all an introduction should attempt to say, and I shall say no more. Dean Pollak, who will shortly give the keynote speech, will speak to the substance of the problems that we have before us. Before I call upon Dean Pollak, I would like to introduce the presiding officers of each of our four committees and the authors of the papers that they have before them as a basis for discussion. They are the people who have planned the working sessions of our meeting and will take the lead in their deliberations.

Committee I, with its suggested focus on the "Maintenance of Revolutionary Values," has for its presiding officer Patricia Roberts Harris, and I must confess that I am not quite sure if I should introduce her as Professor, Dean, Ambassador, Commissioner, or something else. All of those titles have been hers in a career of great distinction in legal education, government service, philanthropy, business and community service, as well as in the practice of the law.

The keynote paper for committee I was originally assigned to Professor Alfred H. Kelly of Wayne State, whose sudden and untimely death deprived us of a valued friend and depleted our scholarly resources. Much of his paper had fortunately been completed by the time of his attack, and, thanks to his wife and his associate, Professor Richard D. Miles, the submission is before us. It is buttressed by a second paper by another distinguished historian, Professor Jack P. Greene of Johns Hopkins, presently visiting at Oxford as the Harnsworth Professor of American History. Professor Greene has come to us from England and will make the keynote presentation in committee I.

Committee II will center its attention on "Effectiveness of Governmental Operations." Its chairman is Professor Nelson W. Polsby, a distinguished political scientist, now at the University of California in Berkeley. The author or editor of many works related to our subject and managing editor of the *Political Science Review*, he has thought long and hard about our governmental institutions, with special emphasis perhaps upon a subject that arouses a slight interest in our time, the relationship of president and Congress.

The keynote paper for committee II was prepared by Professor Henry J. Abraham, the Henry L. and Grace Doherty Professor of Government and Foreign Affairs at the University of Virginia. A perceptive student of governmental processes, with special interest perhaps in the judicial, Professor Abraham established his academic reputation at the University of Pennsylvania before succumbing to the gentle graces of Charlottesville.

The emphasis suggested for committee III, "Shaping of Public Policy," may overlap somewhat that assigned to committee II, but that is no disaster. Our chairman is the distinguished Comptroller General of the United States, the Honorable Elmer B. Staats. After important service in the Executive Office of the President, including many years as Deputy Director of the Bureau of the Budget, he was entrusted in 1966 with the immense responsibility of directing the General Accounting Office, established by Congress as an organ of the Legislative branch. If there is such a thing in the United States as a senior career public administrator, surely it is he and we are grateful for his presence.

The basic paper for committee III

was prepared by Professor Charles E. Gilbert of Swarthmore, a political scientist with broad, eclectic interest in the problems of self-government, who has written with great insight on many aspects of the subject. He has attempted to provide in his exhaustive paper a guide to the enormous academic literature bearing on this subject during recent years.

Finally, committee IV has for its subject "The United States and the World." Its chairman, Adrian S. Fisher, was until recently Dean of the Georgetown University Law Center, where he is now Francis Cabell Brown Professor of International Law. Before he took the academic veil, he had had a distinguished career in law and government, including periods of service as General Counsel of the Atomic Energy Commission, Legal Adviser of the Department of State, Deputy Director of the U.S. Arms Control and Disarmament Agency, general counsel to the *Washington Post* and, last but by no means least, Chief Reporter for the Restatement of the Foreign Relations Law of the United States of the American Law Institute.

The issues paper for committee IV was prepared by Covey T. Oliver, Hubbell Professor of International Law at the University of Pennsylvania. Professor Oliver's career also combines distinguished academic contributions and important public service, including two years as Ambassador to Colombia and two more as Assistant Secretary of State for Inter-American Affairs and U.S. Coordinator of the Alliance for Progress. Among his publications, I note with special pleasure that he collaborated with Professor Fisher on the Restatement of Foreign Relations Law.

I wish that time permitted introduction of our conferees, on whom the ultimate success of our venture most depends, but that would plainly be impossible. It is appropriate, however, that I should present the ranking member of the conference, Justice Tom C. Clark, whose 18 years of service as an Associate Justice of the Supreme Court of the United States, not to speak of the manifold good works to which he devotes his retirement, merit the thanks of the Republic.

We come now to the main event of our morning, the keynote of the conference, which will be sounded by Dean Louis H. Pollak of the University of Pennsylvania Law School. Dean Pollak is a native of New York, the son of a distinguished lawyer, much concerned with civil liberty and justice when such concern was not the fashion of our bar. His own career has carried forward that tradition both in practice and in teaching, including almost 20 years at the Yale Law School, five of them as Dean. Two years ago he moved from Yale to Pennsylvania as the Albert M. Greenfield Professor of Human Relations and Law. Then, as if to illustrate the legend of Samarra, the fate that he believed he had escaped in New Haven befell him in Philadelphia, where he again has become Dean.

Louis Pollak is a profound scholar, an able and compassionate lawyer, an ardent citizen and public servant, and withal an unpretentious and delightful man.

ANNALS, AAPSS, 426, July 1976

Keynote Address

By LOUIS H. POLLAK

ABSTRACT: The first order of business should be to consider the Constitution-in-process—how our Constitution has brought us to where we are now. Since we know America's early history only secondhand, we must try to repossess some of our past before contemplating our present and future. I propose a brief survey of the American political enterprise, as Franklin might have surveyed it 100 years after his death in 1790. He would have seen the emergence of 2 instruments of governance of decisive importance, at the beginning of the 19th century—the party system and judicial review. The 3 post-Civil War amendments (Thirteenth, Fourteenth, and Fifteenth) pointed to the horizon of freedom for the slave race and protection of their rights, but the problem facing America was how to achieve these objectives. By 1890, America was coming of age, and the Constitution of 1869, with its protection of the rich and of racist instincts, was obsolete. Today, Vietnam and Watergate are problems overhanging America's future. We continue to look to judges to declare the fundamental values of our nation. The most important cases are those which define the purposes and processes of a free society. The issues build on one another, and so the Constitution builds; therefore, judges must take care to render reasoned opinions.

Louis H. Pollak is currently the Dean and Albert M. Greenfield Professor of Human Relations and Law at the University of Pennsylvania Law School and has served on its faculty for two years. He was previously a faculty member of the Yale Law School, from 1955–65, and served as Dean for 5 years, beginning in 1965. He received his A.B. from Harvard University in 1943, his LL.B. from Yale in 1948, and was admitted to the New York bar in 1949, the Connecticut bar in 1956, and the Pennsylvania bar in 1976. He is vice-president of the NAACP Legal Defense Fund.

I T WAS proper—it was necessary —that the first session of this conference take place at Independence Hall. That spare and tranquil house across the green is a home place not alone for Americans but for all those who "hold these Truths to be self-evident, that all men are created equal, that they are endowed by their Creator with certain Unalienable Rights, that among these are Life, Liberty, and the Pursuit of Happiness."

Jefferson, Franklin, John Adams, and the others who signed the Declaration were not preachers or publicists. They were leaders and doers, persons trained to accountability and action. They knew that it was not enough to assert self-evident Truths and Unalienable Rights, and thereby to proclaim Liberty throughout the land. They knew that "to secure these Rights, Governments are instituted among Men, deriving their just Powers from the Consent of the governed. . . ." So on behalf of the confederation of free states they constructed a Congress which had the appearance of a national government—but on which no effective power to govern was conferred. Congress, assembled in Independence Hall, strove ineffectively, and within a decade the "Articles of Perpetual Union" wasted into inanition. Whereupon, Madison, Franklin, Wilson, Washington, and the rest repaired again to Independence Hall. And there, "in order to form a more perfect Union," they drafted and called upon their fellow citizens "to ordain and establish this Constitution." It is this Constitution—amended, and thereby enlarged, and yet in its central elements intact—which we are assembled to discuss for these four days.

How do we address ourselves to our agenda? We have gathered in reverence at Independence Hall, drawing inspiration from that place and from the moving words of the very great lawyer and judge who dedicated our humble labors to the monumental labors which went before. Listening to Judge Hastie, one remembered that the second purpose of the Constitution, following on the formation of "a more perfect Union," was "to . . . establish Justice." And one felt again the force of Holmes's dictum that "continuity with the past is not a duty, it is only a necessity."

I think our first undertaking today should be to come to terms with that past, to see if we can reach agreement on which the enduring values and structures are that still connect us with the business taken in hand by the American people two centuries ago. But I doubt that we could have pursued that inquiry in an expeditious and effective way if we had begun our working sessions at Independence Hall. It is not simply that for us to deliberate where they deliberated would have been presumptuous. It is that, had we lingered in the house across the green, our search for the past would have been trammeled by the overwhelming symbols. We would have engaged in unequal dialogue with that past. We are better met on ground less hallowed—but venerable enough: in this house where Franklin still presides.

I propose that we take active steps to put ourselves in appropriate relation to our beginnings and our growing years before attempting to assess our present condition. The catalytic Declaration and the lasting Constitution establish the legitimacy of the work we are to undertake. But, unexamined, they shed little light on the paths we can most usefully pursue. The Constitution is with us still, not simply because it has no term of years and no later plebiscite has replaced it with another document. The Constitution is with us because the Declaration summoned it forth to accomplish the Declaration's unfinished purposes. The Constitution, Marshall wrote, was "intended to endure for ages to come. . . ." But, unlike the "perpetual" Articles of Confederation, it has no claim on perpetuity except as it continues to fulfill the "Truths" accepted in 1776 by 3 million white colonists of Western European ancestry. And that continuity of fulfillment, 200 years later and in the century to come, depends on the continuing will to freedom in 1976, and afterwards, of 200 million Americans of all colors and cultures, and 4 billion others with whom we share the Earth.

THE CONSTITUTION-IN-PROCESS

I press the point that as a first order of business we should consider the Constitution-in-process— that is, how our constitutional arrangements have carried us to where we now are—before we can fairly measure the effective congruence of the present Constitution with the vision of those who declared independence. In urging this, I have in mind an admonition voiced by Holmes, speaking for the Court, in 1920—an admonition which, if some greet it as platitude today, merely bears witness that we as a nation are slowly acquiring a better understanding of our dominant legal processes than prevailed before Holmes began to cut away the undergrowth which obscured the path of the law. Herewith, Holmes, in *Missouri* v. *Holland*, laying the foundation for a construction of the treaty power broad enough to achieve the needs of a great nation:

. . . [W]hen we are dealing with words that also are a constituent act, like the Constitution of the United States, we must realize that they have called into life a being the development of which could not have been foreseen completely by the most gifted of its begetters. It was enough for them to realize or to hope that they had created an organism; it has taken a century and has cost their successors much sweat and blood to prove that they created a nation.

Holmes, born in 1841, was in his eightieth year when he wrote those haunting sentences. They move us still because they are instinct with his own experience. His sweat and blood were spent at Ball's Bluff, at Antietam, and at Fredericksburg. Those battlefields were part of the Constitution which he wrought from 1903, when he came to the Court, to 1932, when he gave place to Cardozo.

Holmes and his contemporaries lived the middle of our history. One of that sturdy company—Jeremiah Smith, born when Van Buren was president—came singularly close to linking our century with our nation's beginning. Judge Smith was the erstwhile New Hampshire Supreme Court justice whom President Eliot transformed into a professor in 1890, and who then taught for 20 years. I still recall my father's fond recital of how, one spring morning in the first decade of this century, Judge Smith walked into his classroom in Austin Hall rather more slowly than was his wont, put his books on the lectern, and said gravely: "Gentlemen"—the honorific apostrophe which is today happily obsolete in every American law school — "Gentlemen, I must apologize if I seem somewhat subdued this morning.

This is a sad day in my family's history. This is the one-hundredth anniversary of my brother's death." Judge Smith apparently refrained from burdening the embarrassed young gentlemen with the further information that his father, the *first* Judge Jeremiah Smith, had been wounded at the Battle of Bennington in 1777.

No one at this conference, I think, has memories that antedate this century. We, and the people of this nation generally, know America's prior history only at secondhand. In this bicentennial year, we are nearing what Charles Black has called "the beginning of our third life . . . the day when no one is left who was alive when someone still lived who was born before our Constitution came into being. . . ."

It is against this fact that I ask us to try collectively to repossess some fragments of our past before we contemplate our present and our future. How is this to be done? I wonder if we may take counsel now with Franklin, who so benignly watches over us. I venture the guess that Franklin would be with us in person, if he could, this morning. To be sure, Franklin did not burden posterity, as Bentham did, with the requirement that he be kept in a glass case and produced on ceremonial occasions. But Franklin was equally mindful of the future and equally curious about it. Witness a letter to his friend, Barbeu Dubourg, written in 1773, in which Franklin was responding with interest to Dubourg's speculations about the possibility that people struck dead by lightning could be restored to life. First, Franklin referred to accounts of toads, trapped in sand, revived years and even ages later; next, he wondered whether delicate plants, uprooted for shipment overseas, might

be immersed in mercury and thereby kept alive during a long ocean voyage. Then Franklin said:

I have seen an instance of common flies preserved in a manner somewhat similar. They had been drowned in Madeira wine, apparently about the time when it was bottled in Virginia, to be sent hither [to London]. At the opening of one of the bottles, at the house of a friend where I then was, three drowned flies fell into the first glass that was filled. . . . In less than three hours, two of them began by degrees to recover life. They commenced by some convulsive motions of the thighs, and at length they raised themselves upon their legs, wiped their eyes with their fore feet, beat and brushed their wings with their hind feet, and soon after began to fly, finding themselves in Old England, without knowing how they came thither. . . .

I wish it were possible, from this instance, to invent a method of embalming drowned persons, in such a manner that they may be recalled to life at any period, however distant; for having a very ardent desire to see and observe the state of America a hundred years hence, I should prefer to any ordinary death, the being immersed in a cask of Madeira wine, with a few friends, till that time to be then recalled to life by the solar warmth of my dear country! . . .

Even as a dreamer Franklin was a pragmatist. "A hundred years hence"—except when computing compound interest—was as far a horizon as Franklin cared to look to. But at least this suggests that he would have been willing to meet us halfway. The 100 years he proposed were the very 100 years which, in Holmes's retrospective view, were required to "create a nation." And I put it to you that before we commence the discussion of America in 1976, we ourselves might derive advantage from a perspective taken in middle course. I propose, therefore, that, as predicate for our own bicentennial perspective, we make a brief survey of the American political enterprise, as Franklin might have surveyed it 100 years after his death.

AMERICA 100 YEARS
AFTER FRANKLIN

Franklin died in 1790, one year after Washington was inaugurated and the First Congress set to work. It was almost as if the good doctor had willed himself to stay alive until the Constitution had taken hold. Let us then suppose that Franklin's 1790 casket was a cask of Madeira from which he was to be decanted a century later. Franklin in 1890 might have raised himself on his legs, wiped his eyes, and announced his readiness to finish out the last years of the nineteenth century in the "solar warmth of [his] dear country." And if, to begin his reacquaintance with his countrymen, he had looked back—through a glass, darkly, as it were—on the 10 decades since his initial death, what chiefly would have engaged his scientific scrutiny? The events of the first decade would have interested Franklin, but not greatly surprised him: the establishment of the government departments, and of the federal courts; the adoption of the Bill of Rights; the debate over the First Bank; the Whiskey Rebellion, and the campaigns against the frontier Indians; Washington's ambivalence about furnishing Congress all requested information; the schism between the Hamilton and Jefferson factions, paralleling the war between Britain and France; the reluctance of the judges to advise the government on legal matters, or to become entangled in other nonjudicial responsibilities; the election of John Adams; the Alien and Sedition Acts; and

Madison's Kentucky and Virginia Resolutions.

At the commencement of the nineteenth century, Franklin would have seen the emergence of two instruments of governance which have proved of decisive importance—the party system and judicial review. Neither of these instruments is described in the Constitution, but each serves to carry out its implicit purposes. The party system—or, to be more precise, the *two*-party system—is the instrument for transmuting parochial interest groups (the factions whose dominance Madison, in his Federalist days, had been apprehensive of in a small republic) into coherent, broadly based and enduring majoritarian alliances capable of governing a large and expanding confederation of states. Judicial review is the instrument for curbing legislative and executive acts—at the local or national level—which tend to subvert the allocations of function or the protections of individual rights prescribed by the Constitution.

In 1801 Jefferson took office as president of the United States: he eschewed partisanship—"we are all Republicans, we are all Federalists" —and was the leader of his party. In the same year, Marshall took office as chief justice of the United States: he was the principal leader of the scattered remnants of the other party. Two years after taking office, he announced the Court's decision in *Marbury* v. *Madison* and eschewed politics: "Questions, in their nature political . . . can never be made in this Court." It is perhaps not surprising that Jefferson and Madison and their fellow Republicans saw Marshall's assertion of judicial authority to review and invalidate acts of Congress, and in a proper case to issue orders to cabinet members, in partisan terms: the Federalists, defeated at the polls, would continue to conduct guerilla warfare from the bench.

In conversation with Senator John Quincy Adams, Senator William Giles of Virginia put it this way:

If the Judges of the Supreme Court should dare, *as they had done*, to declare acts of Congress unconstitutional, or to send a mandamus to the Secretary of State, *as they had done*, it was the undoubted right of the House to impeach them, and of the Senate to remove them for giving such opinions, however honest or sincere they may have been in entertaining them. . . . Removal by impeachment was nothing more than a declaration by Congress to this effect: You hold dangerous opinions, and if you are suffered to carry them into effect you will work the destruction of the Nation.

So persuaded, the Republicans impeached that member of the Court who was least restrained about voicing his Federalist opinions from the bench—Justice Chase. But the Senate declined to convict. No justice has been impeached since that day. And Marshall, though he never again struck down a law of Congress, went on to establish federal supremacy over the states, and the Court's arbitrament of that supremacy, in *McCulloch* v. *Maryland*, which sustained congressional power to charter the Bank of the United States and barred states from taxing the Bank out of business; in *Gibbons* v. *Ogden*, overthrowing New York's attempt to close the Hudson and the harbor to steamboats other than those of a single private monopoly; and in the other judicial hammer-blows that built a nation.

Franklin, leader of so many causes, was an early abolitionist. For him the half century which followed the Louisiana Purchase would have been decades of mounting dismay, as the institution which he hated was claiming a vast new dominion and, in the process, threatening to destroy the union of states which he had helped to establish. Taney's opinion in *Dred Scott*, announcing that no descendant of a slave could be a citizen of the United States, and holding Congress powerless to end slavery in the territories, would have been hard reading for the Philadelphian who in 1789, when he was 83, presented a plan "to qualify those who had been restored to Freedom, for the Exercise and Enjoyment of Civil Liberties. . . ," and who in 1790, two months before his death, had called on the First Congress to take the lead in ending slavery in America.

We can suppose that Franklin would have stood with the new Republican, Lincoln, in the great debates with Douglas and the other political campaigns which followed *Dred Scott*, and also in the military campaigns which followed the political ones. But is it not, also, fair to guess that with the onset of the Civil War, Franklin would have urged Lincoln to hold a tighter rein on those of his subordinates, military and civilian alike, who relied on delegations of presidential authority to imprison thousands of suspected Southern sympathizers, to suspend habeas corpus, and on occasion to muzzle particularly virulent elements of the press? Would not Franklin—would not, perhaps, Lincoln himself—have welcomed the Court's ruling in ex parte *Milligan*, decided after Lincoln's death, that military commissions could not try civilians even in time of war if the civil courts were functioning: "The Constitution of the United States is a law for rulers and people, equally in war and in peace, and covers with the shield of its protection all classes of men, at all times, and under all circumstances." And again: "This nation . . . has no right to expect that it will always have wise and humane rulers, sincerely attached to the principles of the Constitution. Wicked men, ambitious of power, with hatred of liberty and contempt of law, may fill the place once occupied by Washington and Lincoln. . . ."

For Franklin, 1865 should have been a halcyon year—the end of rebellion and the end of slavery. But the stillness at Appomattox was broken by the firing of a revolver at Ford's Theatre. With Lincoln dead, Congress and the president were soon at loggerheads about how to rebuild the shattered nation. On paper, the nation's purposes seemed clear enough: the Thirteenth Amendment ended slavery; the Fourteenth Amendment exorcised Taney's dread dictum that blacks could never be citizens; the Fifteenth Amendment granted blacks —*male* blacks, that is—the vote. Taken together the three post-Civil War amendments pointed to the horizon described by Justice Miller, for the Court, in the *Slaughter-House Cases*: "the freedom of the slave race, the security and firm establishment of that freedom, and the protection of the newly-made freeman and citizen from the oppressions of those who had formerly exercised unlimited dominion over him." But how were these objectives to be achieved, and how and on what timetable were they to be squared with plans for readmission of the rebellious states? With these gravest questions of public policy (and sundry others) unanswered and unanswerable, paralysis of government set in. The dominant Republicans tried to use their power base in Congress as a platform for wielding the executive power; but Andrew Johnson, although unable to effectuate his own policies, refused to surrender his authority to Congress. Then the Republicans, turning back the pages to the Republicanism of Jefferson, tried impeachment. But the Senate of 1868 acquitted Johnson, just as the Senate of 1804 had acquitted Chase. Impeachment as an instrument of party conflict disappeared from the constitutional arsenal.

The Court in the late 1860s could do nothing to ameliorate the perilous confrontation between Congress and president. And, in the same era, the Court's expositions of the relationship between the states and the United States showed little understanding of Marshall's great nationalizing judgments, let alone a candid recognition that the Civil War had changed the equilibrium beyond recall. "The general government and the states," said Justice Nelson in 1871, in ordering the federal tax collector to return $61.51 of taxes paid under protest by a Massachusetts probate judge,

although both exist within the same territorial limits, are separate and distinct sovereignties, acting separately and independently of each other, within their respective spheres. The former, in its appropriate sphere, is supreme; but the states within the limits of their powers not granted, or, in the language of the 10th Amendment, "reserved," are as independent of the general government as that government within its sphere is independent of the states.

Little wonder that Henry Adams was later to say, writing of the last year of Andrew Johnson's administration:

The whole government, from top to bottom, was rotten with the senility of what was antiquated and the instability of what was improvised. . . . [T]he whole fabric required reconstruction as much as in 1789, for the Constitution had become as antiquated as the Confederation. Sooner or later a shock must come, the more dangerous the longer postponed. The Civil War had made a new system in fact: The country would have to reorganize the machinery in practice and in theory.

The election of a new president—the soldier-hero who had suppressed the rebellion—promised much: but it only resulted in debacles of a new kind. For the eight years of Grant's presidency, the nation wallowed in multiple malfeasances of a magnitude not even dreamed of by Franklin's most enterprising contemporaries. As Henry Adams wrote of the earliest of the many tawdry episodes: ". . . the worst scandals of the eighteenth century were relatively harmless by the side of this, which smirched executive, judiciary, banks, corporate systems, professions, and people, all the great active forces of society, in one dirty cesspool of corruption."

The election of Grant's successor took place in 1876. Had Franklin observed the American electoral process in the centennial year, he would have had little ground for confidence in the party system. Save only for Watergate, 1876–77 may fairly be viewed as the nadir of American politics. The candidate with the lesser number of popular votes—and, it seems likely, the lesser number of electoral votes—was declared the winner by the 8–7 partisanly divided verdict of a jerry-built electoral commission (5 senators; 5 representatives; 5 Supreme Court justices). Moreover, in exchange for Southern Democratic acquiescence in the installation of Governor Rutherford B. Hayes as president, the Republican leaders agreed to withdraw federal troops from Louisiana and South Carolina, which, in effect, marked the end of popular concern for the great national purpose charted in *Slaughter-House*: "the protection of the newly-made freeman and citizen from the oppressions of those who had formerly exercised unlimited dominion over him."

But did not *Slaughter-House* suggest that at least the judges would keep faith with the commitment made at Bull Run and Gettysburg and then written into the Constitution? In *Slaughter-House*, appellant's counsel—John Campbell of Alabama, the erstwhile justice who resigned from the Court at the outset of the rebellion—had unabashedly relied on the Fourteenth Amendment for the proposition that the Louisiana Legislature lacked power to confer on a single butchering syndicate the exclusive right to operate an abattoir outside of New Orleans. Four justices agreed with Campbell. But the five justices of the majority did not: they found that the Fourteenth Amendment provided no footing for a claim to constitutional protection from state interference with pursuit of a common calling, since the Fourteenth Amendment and the other post-Civil War amendments were so clearly oriented toward what the Court called "the one pervading purpose" of bringing slaves into full freedom.

But in the decade following the centennial, the Fourteenth Amendment underwent a sea-change. In 1883 the Court held that the amendment gave Congress no power to require railroads, theatres, and hotels to desist from segregating or excluding blacks. However, the decision in the *Civil Rights Cases* was not to mean that the amendment was to become a dead letter. Rather, the amendment was to be put at the service of a different constituency. Thus, three years after the *Civil Rights Cases*, the Court ruled that a corporation was a "person" within the meaning of the Fourteenth (and, correspondingly, the Fifth) Amendment, and thereby ushered in the era of constitutional protection of free enterprise from government regulation adumbrated by the *Slaughter-House* dissenters. Blacks seemed to be falling out of constitutional favor, to be replaced by businessmen.

Surveying America in 1890, and in the ensuing decade which closed out the century, Franklin might have noted certain other data and pondered their significance for the future:

1. In 1887 Congress passed the Interstate Commerce Act, establishing a federal commission to govern interstate railroad rates. In 1890 Congress passed the Sherman Anti-Trust Act. Congress was taking the first steps toward national regulation of a national economy and was beginning to improvise new forms of administrative governance. But the Constitution had lagged far behind Congress. The Court's first case under the Sherman Act affirmed dismissal of the suit brought by the United States to set aside corporate acquisitions which gave one company control over 98 percent of the sugar-refining capacity of the United States:

Slight reflection will show that if the national power extends to all contracts and combinations in manufacture, agriculture, mining and other productive industries, whose ultimate result may affect interstate commerce, comparatively little of business operations and affairs would be left for state controls.

2. The census taken in 1890 disclosed that the American frontier was a thing of the past. The continent was beginning to fill up. And America was beginning to look outward: Hawaii was soon to become American territory, to be followed in a few years by Puerto Rico and the Philippines. Shortly, the Court would consider whether, and in what respects, the Constitution followed the flag.

3. In 1890 the Louisiana Legislature passed a law requiring railroads to provide "equal but separate accommodations" for the two races. The Jim Crow statute was sustained six years later in *Plessy* v. *Ferguson*.

4. In 1894, Congress adopted an income tax. In 1895, the Court held the tax unconstitutional.

America, Franklin might have concluded in 1900, had lost her innocence and was coming of age.

The America which came of age in 1900 was an anomolous polity. The Constitution which Henry Adams thought antiquated in 1868 was at last obsolete. It was a Constitution sedulously protective of the racist instincts of the many and the acquisitive instincts of the few. It was a Constitution with little feeling for the "Truths" proclaimed in 1776 or the structure blueprinted in 1787. And it was a Constitution unfitted to help a modern state govern its own increasingly dynamic economy or its ever-more complex relationships with other nation-states.

With the beginning of the new century, we no longer require Franklin to serve as guide. We enter the years of firsthand recollection of some members of this conference. They can recall for all of us the highlights of the long struggle in this century to restore the Constitution to sensible connection with the needs and purposes of the United States: the Sixteenth Amendment;

Holmes and Brandeis dissenting; depression and FDR's fight with the Old Court; World War II and the subsequent deployment of the treaty power; and, last and foremost, the new constitutional era shaped by the Warren Court—ushered in by the rejection of *Plessy* v. *Ferguson* and the acceptance of the oneness of the American people.

We come finally to Vietnam and Watergate—events which (to use Justice Miller's phrase in *Slaughter-House*, as he sketched the background of the post-Civil War amendments), are "almost too recent to be called history, but which are familiar to us all." They are the brooding omnipresences overhanging this and every conference on America's future. They are the two Banquos at every bicentennial celebration.

THE CONSTITUTION TODAY

One could reasonably have expected Lyndon Johnson and Richard Nixon to be more adept than all other elected presidents at understanding and working with Congress, for of all the elected presidents only they had served in the House, the Senate, and the vice-presidency.

In domestic matters, Johnson indeed knew how to induce Congress, miniaturized since Roosevelt's time, to grow again to life-size—to be the equal partner of the president in the shaping of major national policy. Of this partnership, the Civil Rights Act of 1964 is a triumphant example, and there are others. But when it came to Vietnam, Johnson, from Tonkin Gulf on, induced Congress to grow small again and abdicate the adult exercise of its awesome responsibilities. With respect to the Johnson policies which took us into, and kept us in, that longest of

American wars, I am persuaded that they were wrongly conceived, badly executed, and profoundly damaging to America's inner fiber and her effective leadership of the free world. Some whom I respect regard this assessment as largely or wholly in error. Whatever verdict history renders on the merits of Johnson's Vietnam policies, I am bound to acknowledge that the president had the courage of his convictions. By contrast, at least at the outset of the war, Congress, taken as a whole (of course there were illustrious exceptions: such as Wayne Morse, a double maverick; and Ernest Gruening, the aging New Dealer who kept forgetting that loyalty to party and president and concern for reelection normally take precedence over unswerving fidelity to the nation's welfare), had at the outset of the Vietnam War no courage and no convictions. Johnson is to be faulted for fostering congressional inattention to duty. But the duty and the inattention belonged to Congress. At its doorstep lies the decisive institutional failure.

Nor is that failure to be explained away on the basis of some constitutional meta-principle that disagreement with presidential leadership in matters of foreign and military policy is unwise and perhaps even unpatriotic. As a matter of law, the president is of course the negotiator-in-chief and the commander-in-chief, but in both roles the president is subject to legislative constraints even more powerful than those which a sovereign Parliament can readily impose on the Queen's ministers. Nor did the proposition—of which the late Senator Vandenberg was the embodiment—that politics stops at the water's edge amend the Constitution. Indeed, to look at the American experience through the prism of that proposition is not merely to misperceive the Constitution's deliberate separation of functions and authorities, it is to misunderstand our history: America's politics *began* at the water's edge, when Hamilton and Jefferson divided the cabinet and the nation on the proper American response to the outbreak of war between Britain and France.

Nixon came to the White House seeking peace with honor. Two months later, he determined that the way to peace in Vietnam lay through neighboring Cambodia, where North Vietnamese reserves were massed, and he sent in bombers to blaze the trail. But the new war needed to be unacknowledged: public disclosure that Prince Sihanouk's realm was being bombed, and that he was not objecting, might have tended to embarrass the prince's studious neutrality. Nixon's potential embarrassment—waging a new war without asking leave of Congress—was taken care of by his field commanders in a very graceful way. As later described by the House Judiciary Committee, in laying the factual predicate of a draft article of impeachment which the committee did not approve: "On March 18, 1969, the bombing of Cambodia commenced with B-52 strikes under the code name MENU OPERATION. These strikes continued until May 26, 1970. . . . The operational reports prepared after each mission stated that these strikes had taken place in South Vietnam rather than in Cambodia."

Save for a few senior members in whom the Pentagon confided, Congress was not advised that the targets listed in the operational reports were a little wide of the mark. But the official dissemination of these somewhat uninformative reports was not unlawful. We have been reassured on this point of law by the general who was then Air Force chief of staff: "For falsification to constitute an offense, there must be proof of 'intent to deceive.' This is a legally prescribed element of the offense and is negated when the report is submitted in conformity with orders from a higher authority in possession of the true facts." With this aspect of the matter clarified, the only remaining legal question was a technical one: by what constitutional warrant had the president unilaterally initiated and pursued a year-long air war in a neutral country? After the fact, one might even have called it an academic question. But it was a question which continued to worry Congress—the more so, perhaps, because it was the sort of question the federal courts were disposed to term "political," and hence nonjusticiable. And the possibility that the question might arise again, in other guises, led at last to the enactment of the War Powers Resolution of 1973—the first major step in the reestablishment of Congress as one of the three co-equal branches of government. The resolution directs the president, absent a declared war, to report to Congress any significant commitment of armed forces in foreign territory, and to withdraw such forces by a date certain. Nixon vetoed the resolution, but Congress passed it over his veto. In rejecting Nixon's veto, Congress must be taken to have rejected a chief argument contained in Nixon's veto message—namely, that the War Powers Resolution is unconstitutional. Congress must have been very sure of its own constitutional ground, because it well knew that Nixon was a lawyer (at that time), and indeed a very accomplished one. Moreover, Congress also knew that Nixon was a "strict constructionist," which presumably meant that it was not his wont to conclude that an act of Congress was unconstitutional. On the other hand, Congress may have felt that Nixon was apt to be a more flexible constructionist in judging federal laws imposing constraints on the president. Nixon has always set great store on maintaining unfettered the plenary authority of the president—for example, Watergate.

The framers contemplated the dread possibility that some day a president sworn to preserve, protect, and defend the Constitution might find it irksome and might seek to reign under a legal code of his own composition. "This nation," as the Court said over a century ago in *Milligan*, "has no right to expect that it will always have wise and humane rulers, sincerely attached to the principles of the Constitution. Wicked men, ambitious of power, with hatred of liberty and contempt of law, may fill the place once occupied by Washington and Lincoln. . . ."

And so in the end, Nixon, corrupt and sick, quit "the place once occupied by Washington and Lincoln." He yielded to the convergence of two inexorable constitutional mechanisms: impeachment, the great engine intended, not for the exorcism of political foes, but for the trial of those charged with betrayal of the public trust; and the subpoena power of a court of the United States.

THE SUPREME COURT AND THE CONSTITUTION

It will be recalled that Nixon, in *United States* v. *Nixon*, had contended that no court had power to determine the president's obligation to comply with a subpoena requiring the production of presidential re-cords—in that instance, tapes of conversations between the president and his advisers—deemed by the president to be confidential. The president's assertion of executive privilege posed a question, so it was argued, committed by the Constitution to the president alone—in lawyer's parlance, a "political question." And the argument was not without some force. After all, in *Marbury* v. *Madison*, Marshall, in giving assurance that "questions in their nature political . . . can never be made in this Court," had been at pains to abjure any claims to judicial authority "to intrude into the cabinet, and to intermeddle with the prerogatives of the executive." But Chief Justice Burger and his brethren were unpersuaded. They saw the claim of executive privilege as posing a legal question, not a political one. And, therefore, a different sentence in *Marbury* v. *Madison*— "It is, emphatically, the province and duty of the judicial department, to say what the law is"—controlled the result in Nixon's case.

As the last chapter of Nixon's downfall shows, the most extraordinary fact about the American governmental process is the range and magnitude of the public issues which lawyers transpose into litigation and which judges then resolve by saying "what the law is." But the fact is not a new one; it is firmly rooted in Marshall's era, and it was clearly perceived by thoughtful observers dating as far back as Tocqueville. Moreover, criticism of spacious judicial intervention in the formation of fundamental public policy is no new thing. Billboards urging "Impeach Earl Warren" seem almost deferential in contrast to the attacks leveled at Marshall and his brethren: "If, Mr. Speaker, the arch-fiend had in . . . his hatred to mankind resolved the destruction of republican government on earth, he would have issued a decree like that of the judges."

Marshall survived his critics. So did Warren. We continue to look to judges to declare the fundamental values of our nation. In our own time, we have not been disappointed. Jim Crow and its monstrous derivatives—such as the incarceration of Japanese-Americans in World War II—were overthrown by what Richard Kluger has called the "simple justice" of *Brown* v. *Board of Education*. That single judgment connects our America with Lincoln, and with what Lincoln saw at Gettysburg to be the necessary and proper intendment of the Declaration. The nine justices who achieved the decision in *Brown* v. *Board of Education* have given us the opportunity and obligation at last to fulfill our nation's covenants. We are honored today by the presence in our midst of one of the members of that Court, Justice Clark.

The cases which matter most are those, like *Brown*, which define the fair purposes and processes of a free society and trace the contours of human dignity. The issues build upon one another, and so the Constitution builds. When, last week, the justices heard Anthony Amsterdam and Robert Bork argue the death penalty, they were working within a framework reared, in part, by an intrepid Louisiana lawyer— our distinguished fellow-conferee, Judge J. Skelly Wright—who 30 years ago failed by the margin of one vote to persuade the Court that it was unconstitutional to electrocute a man twice. And perhaps the justices, now closeted with these fateful issues, will see relationships to the issues addressed last Wednesday by the New Jersey Supreme Court, when it held that the parents of Karen Ann Quinlan were entitled to help liberate their daughter from an existence which is no longer life.

In similar fashion, but in another part of the constitutional forest, the justices will have the opportunity next year to consider *Brown* v. *Board of Education* in a different context. Does *Brown* apply—or does *Plessy's* "separate but equal" doctrine have continuing dominion—with respect to a school board policy of assigning students who seek a curriculum of academic excellence to high schools segregated on grounds of sex. The court of appeals in this circuit, finding the two schools to be of equal academic quality, a fortnight ago sustained Philadelphia's quaint atavism. The court of appeals' view that, "if there are benefits or detriments inherent in the system, they fall on both sexes in equal measure," seems less than compelling: the Supreme Court observed as long ago as 1948 that "equal protection of the laws is not achieved through indiscriminate imposition of inequalities." Perhaps, notwithstanding the court of appeals' finding that the separate schools are equal, the Supreme Court will detect a fundamental disparagement of women in a policy which sends females to a school named "Girls" and males to a school named "Central." If the Court shows itself capable of sorting out issues of this kind, case by case, within the rubric of the equal protection clause, the case for ratification of the stalled Equal Rights Amendment would be less compelling.

Some may think it unmannerly of me to use this public occasion to suggest that our court of appeals here in Philadelphia may have fallen into constitutional error and that its judgment should be reviewed, with a view to possible reversal, by the justices in Washington. Perhaps I can make amends by being unmannerly in the other direction—through the indiscriminate imposition of impoliteness on all courts within range. I now put it to you that the Supreme Court took a long backward step three months ago when it reversed our court of appeals in *Rizzo* v. *Goode*. In that case, it will be recalled, the court of appeals, on a record showing numerous instances of police mistreatment of local residents, had sustained Judge Fullam's carefully drawn decree requiring the mayor and high officials of the Philadelphia police department to develop procedures which would facilitate orderly inquiry into citizen complaints of police misconduct. On certiorari, five of the justices disagreed. Unpersuaded "that the behavior of the Philadelphia police was different in kind or degree from that which exists elsewhere"— which, if the justices are right, suggests a general malaise in the legal order which should give all of us pause—they held that the remedy devised by Judge Fullam and approved by the court of appeals was an unwarranted federal judicial intrusion into the governance of local affairs. With all respect, I think the greater wisdom lies with Justice Blackmun and those who joined him in dissent:

It is a matter of regret that the Court sees fit to nullify what so meticulously and thoughtfully has been evolved to satisfy an existing need relating to constitutional rights that we cherish and hold dear.

In voicing these concerns, I am acting on what I conceive to be a citizen duty to monitor the content of decisions affecting important constitutional claims. I believe there is a parallel duty to be concerned about the forms of constitutional adjudication. I think you will agree that careless judging is apt to produce careless judgments. Accordingly, I submit that if, following Marshall's lead, the judicial department is to continue to "say what the law is," and thus to articulate the central values of our society, justices and judges must take the time to hear reasoned argument, and also to render reasoned opinions based on what Professor Wechsler has tellingly called "neutral principles of constitutional law." If I am right in this, I think it follows that serious problems are posed by what appears to be an increasing incidence of summary dispositions in our appellate courts. Last week witnessed a particularly troublesome example of this practice: the Supreme Court had before it an appeal from a three-judge district court which had sustained a Virginia statute criminalizing the homosexual acts of consenting adults. Although a case can certainly be made for the result reached by the district court, one would be hard put to say, in light of *Griswold* v. *Connecticut* and subsequent decisions, that the appeal was frivolous. There is certainly no recent Supreme Court decision which flatly concluded the issue in Virginia's favor. And indeed one member of the district court had found that the state lacked constitutional authority to intrude on the private conduct of its citizens in so coercive a way. With matters in this posture, three of the justices voted to set the appeal down for argument. But the majority of the Court overrode their brethren: they voted to affirm, without argument *and* without rendering an opinion.

Given the seriousness and sensitivity of the issues presented on that appeal, I think the course of adjudication followed by the Court disserved the judicial process. I suppose it may be said in support of the decision not to hear argument that it would have been a waste of precious judicial time to explore issues a majority of the justices were prepared to resolve without benefit of opinion. And I suppose that dispensing with an opinion may be supported on the ground that explaining a decision in writing is hard and time-consuming and unrewarding labor when one is unsure of the grounds for one's decision. But neither line of defense seems very compelling. The short of it is that summary affirmance in a case of this consequence disposes of the particular controversy but gives no guidance to the bench, the bar, or the nation. Dispositions of this kind command obedience to a judicial mandate, but they do not generate respect for it. But respect for a court's mandate is not a resource to be squandered. It is the entire basis of the authority Marshall asserted and we have confidently acquiesced in. Judges must act as judges.

As the members of the judicial department must—and I trust will—continue to perform their tasks in ways calculated to command respect, so, too, they must be treated with respect. Not the respect of robes and honorifics and "May it please the Court," but the respect contemplated by the Constitution—tenure during good behavior; and, most insistently, a compensation which is suitable to the burdens and responsibilities of judging and which is not to be diminished. The responsibility of seeing to these matters lies with Congress. It is a responsibility Congress has shirked, just as, until enactment of the War Powers Resolution, it shirked responsibility on questions of peace and war. The responsibilities are of comparable dimension. Momentous as they are, the constitutional imperatives to "provide for the common defense" and to "insure domestic tranquility" are of no higher dignity than the constitutional imperative to "establish justice." I thought it a mistake to try to litigate the "legality" of the Vietnam War, for it was a tactic calculated to withdraw accountability from Congress. With all respect, I feel the same way about the pending litigation asserting the unconstitutionality of current judicial salaries, eroding under inflation. They are not unconstitutional, they are inadequate, grossly inadequate, and Congress is to blame. The proper venue is in the Capitol, not in the court of claims.

An extraordinary thing is happening in our bicentennial year. A few leading English lawyers are beginning to wonder whether English law would not be well served if England were in some manner to adopt a judicially enforceable bill of rights. One of the foremost champions of the idea is Sir Leslie Scarman, the very eminent judge of the Court of Appeal. In his Hamlyn Lectures two years ago, the learned judge even argued that the idea is not quite the constitutional heresy it would appear to be to English lawyers trained on conventional notions of parliamentary supremacy. He pointed out that neither Holt nor Coke was fully persuaded that Parliament's authority was without limit. And most insistently he quoted Cromwell:

In every Government there must be Somewhat Fundamental, Somewhat like a Magna Charter, which should be standing, be unalterable. . . . That Parliaments should not make themselves perpetual is a Fundamental. Of what assurance is a law to prevent so great an evil, if it lie in the same legislature to un-law it again?

In this spirit, and to conclude this prologue to our agenda, I recall us once again to our constitutional beginnings—to Franklin's words on the last day of the convention. I hope they may also serve as epilogue:

. . . Sir, I agree to this Constitution with all its faults, if they are such; because I think a general Government necessary for us, and there is no form of Government but what may be a blessing to the people if well administered, and believe farther that this is likely to be well administered for a course of years, and can only end in Despotism, as other forms have done before it, when the people shall become so corrupt as to need despotic Government, being incapable of any other. . . . Thus I consent, Sir, to this Constitution because I expect no better, and because I am not sure, that it is not the best.

Maintenance of Revolutionary Values

By ALFRED H. KELLY AND RICHARD D. MILES

ABSTRACT: Though the values and institutional structure of the American system of constitutional liberty have to some extent exhibited extraordinary continuity, it has evolved with the growth of the American social and political order and successive political crises. The Revolutionary era saw the emergence of 2 or 3 closely related ideas about man and his relation to the state, which served as the foundations of America's constitutional democracy—the ideas of limited government, natural rights, and the concept of an open society. It is the theory of natural law, natural right, the compact theory of the state, and limited government that Jefferson incorporated in the Declaration of Independence. But it cannot be assumed that the Declaration and the Revolution completed the union between natural rights and human equality. In many respects the sociopolitical structure out of which they came was not democratic at all. For instance, it still tolerated slavery. The Bill of Rights provided a statement of natural and historical rights translated into law. Today, constitutional rights in the areas of equality, the dimensions of an open society, and nationalization of constitutional liberty have changed substantially from those of the Revolutionary era.

Alfred H. Kelly, recently deceased, was Acting Dean of Graduate Studies and Professor of History at Wayne State University, Detroit.

Richard D. Miles, who completed this issues paper, is currently Professor of History at Wayne State University.

THE American system of constitutional liberty, which first flowered in the era of the American Revolution, has roots buried deep within the colonial, English, and Western cultural heritage. Its values and institutional structure have to some extent exhibited an extraordinary continuity; nonetheless, the system has evolved and developed with the growth of the American social and political order and with the successive political crises through which the United States has passed. Paradoxically, as American constitutional liberty enters its third century of national identity, it has not only flowered magnificently once more, it also has entered a new era of crisis which again threatens its existence and which almost certainly will result in profound changes both in the system's values and in its institutional structure.

The Revolutionary era of two centuries ago saw the emergence for the first time of two or three closely related ideas about man and his relation to the state which were to serve as the foundations of the American system of constitutional democracy. Put too briefly, these were the idea of limited government or constitutional supremacy, the idea of natural rights, and the concept of an open society. All were closely associated both in theory and practice; all had venerable origins, some of which in fact went back to the ancient world.

If the modern reader will turn to the first book of Plato's *Republic*, he will find a dialogue between Socrates and Thrasymachus the Sophist upon the nature of law and the state. Thrasymachus, in a direct anticipation of an argument that Marx would invoke more than 2,000 years later, adopts a totally cynical view of the nature of law. The dominant classes in any society, he says, get control both of the priesthood and the instruments for law-making; thereupon they fashion both the law and religious belief to suit their own interests, persuading the populace that what they wish to be secular and profane law is, in fact, the command of the gods. But Socrates, whom Plato sets up as Thrasymachus's antagonist, will have none of this. Admittedly, he says, men in power may seek to corrupt law to their interests. But true law is something much more than that; it reflects certain eternal truths which flow from the nature of the gods themselves. Thus, for the first time the idea of natural law was explicitly stated: that there is a certain natural harmony in the universe which reflects the nature of God himself and which certainly God cannot and would not change. Further, the fundamental principles of natural law can be discovered by the application of human reason, to serve as the foundation of a rational and moral legal system. A few centuries later, Cicero, the great Roman lawyer-philosopher, would give expression to the same idea in his *De Legibus*, proclaiming that man-made law must so far reflect the natural harmony of the Universe that if the Senate and the Roman people themselves (the highest source of sovereignty he could conceive of) should make robbery, adultery, or the falsification of wills law, such pronouncements still would not be such, for they would defy the natural harmony of the gods.

This notion of a natural harmony in the Universe which men could discover by reason and incorporate in a system of rational positive law passed down into the medieval era, where it reappeared in the writings of Aquinas and the other great churchmen. And in the late sixteenth, seventeenth, and eighteenth centuries, it came to maturity in an extraordinary flowering of political theorists, virtually all of whom seized upon the idea of natural law as the theoretical foundation upon which to erect a theory of sovereignty and the parameters of the power of the state. There were a great many such, from Richard Hooker and John Milton to John Locke, Algernon Sidney, John Harrington, Emmerich de Vattel, Samuel Pufendorf, Jean Jacques Burlamaqui, and a host of others. By far the most important of these writers for subsequent American history was John Locke, the theorist of the Glorious Revolution of 1688–89, whose *Second Treatise of Government* by the eve of the American Revolution was so well known as to serve as a kind of bible of political theory for the American colonists.

Like several other natural law writers, Locke began by formulating the idea of a state of nature—a hypothetical time in the remote past, antecedent to the creation of the state, when men had existed in "a state of nature." The state of nature, Locke held, was not one of chaos and anarchy; on the contrary, it was one in which natural law prevailed and under which men recognized certain fundamental principles of right and justice, which determined the relations of men with one another.[1]

Locke thereupon argued that because some men would not obey the dictates of natural law, it had become necessary for good men to covenant together to erect the state, into whose hands they surrendered the protection of natural law and the concomitant body of natural rights that now were recognized as derived ultimately from natural law.[2] Thus Locke adopted for himself the compact theory of the state, which, in fact, certain radical Calvinist writers had formulated a century earlier. The concept solved at one stroke both the problem of the legitimate origins of the state itself (a difficult one for political theorists after the disintegration of the idea of divine right) and the problem of the theoretical limits upon state power.

The state, in other words, legitimized by its origins in natural law and by a political compact that brought it into being, in the final analysis existed solely to protect the rights derived from natural law. Thus, the state was obliged to guarantee all men certain fundamental rights, both against one another and paradoxically against government itself. It was this concept of natural law, natural rights, and limited state power to which virtually all the great political theorists of the age subscribed.

Locke was very certain what the fundamentals of natural rights amounted to. They were the basic guarantees of life, liberty, and property which were to be found incorporated in successive great

---

1. Thomas Hobbes, who published his *Leviathan* in 1651, disagreed with Locke; to him, the state of nature had been one of endemic war of "every man against every man," in which life was "poor, mean, nasty, brutish, and short." But Hobbes, who thus disagreed with the great majority of natural law writers, had virtually no influence upon the development of early American political theory.

2. Or as Tom Paine would have it in the opening pages of *Common Sense* 100 years later, "Governments are founded upon the ruins of the bowers of paradise."

charters of English liberty from the time of King John: Magna Charta, the various confirmations of the charter, and so on. By the time Locke's *Second Treatise* was published, certain of the most fundamental guarantees of liberty and natural rights had been reduced to positive law in the so-called Bill of Rights of 1689.

In reality, the English common law courts had for some centuries been engaged in formulating certain fundamental rights of Englishmen, which the law guaranteed against the state. Over a long period, these courts had developed a series of procedural guarantees for defendants in criminal prosecutions and for the parties in civil cases, which one day would be described under the rubric of procedural due process. Originally, such guarantees had been developed with little or no reference to natural law or natural right; they were, instead, merely the "rights of Englishmen." But in the early seventeenth century, Sir Edward Coke of King's Bench had on at least two occasions invoked common law guarantees with language which at least implied a certain link between the rights of Englishmen and natural rights. It was an association which would become very familiar to the pamphleteers and political spokesmen of the American Revolution more than a century and a half later.

It is necessary to add here only that the idea of the rights of Englishmen as embodied both in common law decisions and in the great charters, along with both natural law and natural rights theory and the compact theory of the state, made their way to the American colonies in the course of the seventeenth and eighteenth centuries, where in intimate association with one another they provided the foundation for the political ideas of the American Revolution. The basic American Revolutionary argument as first stated was that the British government, in the Sugar Act, Stamp Act, and Townshend Act, was violating the fundamental rights of the colonists, who, as Englishmen, were entitled to all those rights commonly extended to Englishmen in Britain. After about 1769 or 1770, the colonists tended to broaden their argument to include the notion that the rights of Englishmen were derived ultimately from natural law and natural right, so that the charters, the critical parliamentary statutes such as the Habeas Corpus Act of 1679, and the great guarantees developed in the common law courts were no more than expressions of positive law of the great fundamental guarantees inherent in natural law and natural right.

JEFFERSON'S REVOLUTIONARY IDEAS

It was this theory of natural law, natural right, the compact theory of the state, and limited government that Jefferson incorporated in the Declaration of Independence, with its affirmation of the "self-evident" truth that "all men are created equal," and that "they are endowed by their Creator with certain unalienable rights," and that "among these are Life, Liberty, and the pursuit of Happiness." There were, however, two rather revolutionary ideas in the concept of natural rights as Jefferson set forth the theory in the Declaration: first, that natural rights somehow were associated with a principle of human equality, and second, that there was a more fundamental human right than that of property—"the pursuit of Happiness."[3]

To grasp how revolutionary Jefferson's ideas were in their immediate meaning as well as in ultimate impact, one needs only to reflect that all governments everywhere up until that time, even in Britain, had been based upon what the historian Edward Channing (speaking of London's attitude toward her colonies) called "the great plum pudding" principle: the government and the social order at large existed for the benefit of the privileged classes, whose superior wisdom, virtue, and social position entitled them to exploit the state for their own ends. It was this principle which Jefferson now was repudiating. His repudiation was inherent, also, in his rejection of property as the most fundamental human right after life and liberty and in his insistence that there was a greater right: the right of every individual to pursue his self-interest free of the restrictions of class privilege or unreasonable restrictions upon liberty imposed by the state.

To put it differently, the Declaration gave expression to a nascent American idea of equality of opportunity in an open society. It was an idea which de Tocqueville would hail some 60 years later as a fundamental operative principle of the American social order. Jefferson did not invent the idea; on the contrary, the growth of fluid class systems and of a measure of political democracy had been distinctive phenomena in several of the American colonies for decades. The Revo-

lution strengthened the democratic thrust of these forces and others already at work along the Atlantic seaboard. It destroyed established churches (only three, all in New England, survived beyond 1785, and they died out in the next 40 years), liberalized criminal codes, opened the West to mass acquisition of land by the middle class, and liberalized somewhat the franchise requirements. And while the Revolution did not destroy aristocracy anywhere, it shifted its base, ruining many old Tory families and weakening others, thrusting former petty bourgeoisie into new positions of influence, prestige, and power, and generally weakening the hold of the old aristocracy, in particular in the North, upon the social and political order.

THE MAGISTERIAL TRADITION IN AMERICAN SOCIETY

But it must not be assumed from any of the foregoing that the Declaration and the Revolution completed the putative union between the doctrine of natural rights and the idea of human equality. The courtship had begun, but the marriage had by no means yet been celebrated. In a great many critical respects the sociopolitical structure out of which the Declaration and the Constitutional Convention of 1787 came was not democratic at all; indeed, from our point of view, even the impulse to a society in which all men and women were to be conceded real equality of opportunity was only a modest one. Most important, this was a society which still tolerated slavery. It is true that the Revolution itself released a substantial antislavery impulse in the United States, which in New England and the

3. It is true that George Mason had used a similar phrase a month earlier in the Virginia Bill of Rights, but it was left to Jefferson to give the idea its universal appeal.

middle states resulted either in the outright abolition of slavery by court decision (Massachusetts) or in the passage of gradual emancipation laws, as in Pennsylvania, New York, and New Jersey. And in response to the same anti-slavery impulse, the Confederation Congress in 1787 incorporated in the Northwest Ordinance of that year a provision forever banning slavery and involuntary servitude from the region north of the Ohio and west of Pennsylvania. But most of the Revolutionary leaders were only mildly disturbed, it would appear, at the continued existence of black slavery among them. Either they were blinded by self-interest to the incongruity of their position, or— as some southerners would presently declare—they simply did not believe that natural rights applied to black people.

As further testament to the very limited role which the idea of equality and universal human rights played in the early American Republic, it is necessary only to recall that the aristocratic tradition in politics was still extremely powerful. Most white males now had the vote, but landed and mercantile aristocrats, together with the more prosperous smaller merchants and small landed gentry along with their lawyer-spokesmen, were expected as a matter of course to take the lead in the political process. Since the early colonial era, there had been a powerful magisterial tradition in colonial politics, in which the magistrates were conceived of as holding power in a kind of trust bestowed upon them through the social compact but which nonetheless left the magistrates free to rule as they thought best. For at least a generation or so after the Revolution, the magisterial tradition

continued almost uninterrupted in the state and federal politics of the new Republic.

Thus, the convention which met at Philadelphia in 1787 and which drafted the Constitution of the United States was very much in the magisterial tradition. The convention has on occasion been viewed by certain historians as something of a counterrevolution, which reversed the egalitarian thrust of the Declaration of Independence and restored the idea of magisterial authority. We believe that is almost certainly an incorrect view of the matter. The men who assembled at Philadelphia were, by and large, drawn from the same class as those who had sat in the Second Continental Congress and put their names to the Declaration. (The names of six of the signers of the Declaration, in fact, are to be found among those of the 39 men who signed the Constitution in 1787.) It was not that a counterrevolution was in progress; rather the convention's objective was, of necessity, a radically different one from that of the Continental Congress 11 years earlier. The task of the Continental Congress had been to formulate a rationale for revolution, that is, for the destruction of an outworn and unacceptable system of sovereignty. The convention's task was an almost precisely opposite one: to establish a new system of sovereignty, to describe, validate, and confine its mechanisms, and to describe, validate, and confine its sweep of power. This task the convention performed with extraordinary wisdom, insight, and success.[4]

4. William Gladstone, as every student of the Constitution knows, a century later was to describe the Constitution as "the most wonderful work every struck off at a given time by the brain and purpose of man."

But the fact that the Constitution in no sense was a counterrevolution should not obscure the generally magisterial character of the gathering. The aristocratic tradition in the convention was very strong, as the names of George Washington, Edmund Randolph, Alexander Hamilton, Gouverneur Morris, Robert Morris, George Mason, Charles Cotesworth Pinckney, Rufus King, John Rutledge, John Dickinson, and John Langdon attest. Most of these men had been born to the purple; a few, like Dickinson, Hamilton, and Franklin, had risen to the top of the social order through fortunate marriages, successful business enterprise, or sheer brilliance. But with one or two possible exceptions, they thought and acted within the magisterial tradition; the word "levellism" (the seventeenth-century Puritan Revolution equivalent of advocacy of egalitarian democracy) was a hateful term to them.

Moreover, the document which they drafted, while it was an extraordinarily liberal and enlightened document for its day, reflecting as it did the best Enlightenment and Republican thought of the time, was nonetheless essentially a magisterial document. Very cleverly, the framers recognized and fitted the new constitutional system into the prevailing state distributions of political power, as indeed they were obliged to do if the document they were drafting were to have any chance of acceptance by the prospective state conventions. Thus, they equated the electoral franchise for

the House of Representatives with that of the most numerous house of the various state legislatures, while in effect they allowed the legislatures of the various states to establish any system they wished for the choice of presidential electors. But in the resultant system, only the House was drawn directly from the electorate, however limited, of the several states. The Senate, chosen by the several state legislatures, was two steps removed from the people. The president, chosen by electors who conceivably might themselves be elected by the state legislatures, was at least two steps removed from the people; if the electoral college failed to cast a majority for a presidential candidate so that the final election was thrown into the House of Representatives, the chief executive was three steps removed from the people. And the members of the prospective new federal Judiciary, nominated by the president and confirmed by the Senate, would in turn be three or four steps from the people.

The result was most emphatically a magisterial Constitution, highly intelligent and enlightened, but in no immediate sense democratic. The saving grace in all this, it would eventually turn out, was that virtually all the critical provisions involved were sufficiently flexible to be adaptable to the rise of political democracy. Without that flexibility and adaptability, the Constitution hardly could have survived.

THE BILL OF RIGHTS

The amendments submitted to the states in 1789 by the First Congress under the new Constitution, 10 of which were to be ratified and to become known collectively as the

---

Of course, the Constitution, while a brilliantly creative work, was not simply "struck off"; it was the end product, rather, of political philosophy of the Enlightenment in which the framers for the most part were steeped.

Bill of Rights, represented a return once more to the problem attacked in the first portion of the Declaration: a statement of natural and historic rights, which now were to be translated into positive law. The authors of the Constitution had not believed a Bill of Rights to be necessary. As James Wilson put it, the new government, unlike that of the states, was to be one of limited and derived powers rather than residual sovereignty; therefore, under a familiar common-law principle, it would be unnecessary to enumerate the limitations upon that government or to state the things it could not do. Such an enumeration, Wilson argued, might even be dangerous; enumeration of specific prohibitions and guarantees imposed on the national government might imply that it possessed other powers not specifically denied it. But this argument had yielded to the exigencies of the ratifying process: the proponents of the Constitution had used the promise of a Bill of Rights to win waverers over to ratification, and the First Congress considered itself to be morally bound to carry out the promises of the Constitution's advocates.

The guarantees the new Bill of Rights imposed upon the national government fell generally into four categories. Most important for the great growth of constitutional liberty in the twentieth century were those laid down in the First Amendment, setting forth what were to be considered the great fundamental guarantees of an open society: the prohibition upon any "establishment of religion"; the "free exercise" clause; and a prohibition upon any abridgment by law upon freedom of speech, press, assembly, and peaceable petition. Every one of these guarantees had a century or more of history behind it; and their original meaning has been the subject of very considerable controversy among historians in the late twentieth century. Thus E. S. Corwin thought the establishment clause prohibited only a state church in the formal European sense but not at all other accommodations between state and church, while Leonard Levy has argued that the Jeffersonian "wall of separation" theory was historically correct. And Zechariah Chaffee was to argue that the guarantees of freedom of speech and press radically altered the English common-law meaning of these guarantees, literally prohibiting all or very nearly all restraints upon speech, a stance adopted also by Alexander Meiklejohn; while Leonard Levy was to argue with equal conviction that the speech and press provisions of the amendment did no more than incorporate the prevailing English common-law guarantee of no prior restraint, leaving the English law of seditious libel still in force. What is certain is that the amendment, except for the little flurry at the time of the Alien and Sedition Laws, was to sleep almost undisturbed into the twentieth century, in part because of the obvious fact that the amendment's restrictions applied only to a government already limited by enumeration in its specific powers, in part because of the restricted and cautious role played by federal sovereignty in state-federal relations until nearly the end of the nineteenth century. Until 1925 there was almost no hint of the constitutional "explosion" which has surrounded the amendment since that time, either in church-state relations, sedition law, or censorship.

The second great set of guarantees, those of the Fifth, Sixth, Seventh, and Eighth Amendments, set down in positive law the ancient common-law guarantees of the rights of Englishmen in criminal and civil procedure in the courts. Taken all together, they added up to the great fundamental guarantees of the fair trial which had been growing and developing since Magna Charta: due process, a prohibition upon double jeopardy and compulsory self-incriminating testimony, jury trial, venue in the vicinage, confrontation of witnesses, compulsory process for defense witnesses, the right to be informed of the nature of a criminal charge, and a prohibition upon excessive bail, excessive fines, and cruel and unusual punishment. Lurking behind all these guarantees, also, was a further one scarcely hinted at in the Fifth Amendment but fundamental to constitutional liberty: the subordination of military to civil power and a severe restriction upon the former's legitimate sphere of authority. Significantly, several of the procedural guarantees involved had only lately been the subject of controversy during the Revolutionary quarrel with Britain; thus the Administration of Justice Act of 1774 had grossly violated the guarantee of vicinage trial found in the Sixth Amendment.

The Second, Third, and Fourth Amendments stated certain traditional guarantees of the rights of Englishmen running back to the quarrel between Crown and Parliament in the seventeenth century. Significantly, several of these had also been involved in some fashion in the Revolutionary quarrel. The Second Amendment's guarantee of the right of the people to keep and bear arms had arisen out of demands of the Puritan militia trainbands before the civil war of the 1640s,

while the Third Amendment's prohibition upon the quartering of troops upon private houses in time of peace not only antedated the Puritan Revolution but also had been the subject of recent disputes between America and Britain involving the Quartering Acts of 1765 and 1774. And the Fourth Amendment, with its prohibition against unreasonable search and seizure and its stipulation of warrants based upon probable cause, not only stated an ancient English common-law right but called up for most Americans memories of James Otis's celebrated attack upon writs of assistance on the eve of the Revolution, in 1761. Again, also, the Second, Third, and Fourth Amendments carried the flavor of the supremacy of civil over military authority.

Finally, the Ninth and Tenth Amendments fell into a special category: they represented two generalized attempts to guard against the possibility of federal tyranny. The Ninth Amendment sought specifically to counter the Federalist argument that a national bill of rights might, by enumeration, imply a denial of rights which the new amendments did not succeed in listing; it provided that the enumeration of certain rights shall not be construed to deny or disparage others retained by the people. The amendment actually changed nothing and was essentially declaratory, in that it stipulated that which James Wilson and other nationalist lawyers had argued was the case anyway. Not until far down into the twentieth century would the amendment acquire any substantial constitutional importance. The Tenth Amendment also was essentially declaratory: it reserved to the states or to the people powers not delegated by the Constitution to the United States or prohibited by it to the states. Significantly, the Congress at Madison's instance, specifically refused to incorporate the word "specifically" in the amendment. Thus, the proposal left the enumerated powers of Congress potentially open to Hamiltonian and Marshallian construction and thus paved the way for the vast expansion of federal powers, notably through the commerce and taxing powers, which was to take place in the twentieth century. Long afterward, states' rights conservatives, arguing that broad construction was a threat to liberty, would attempt to interpolate the word "specifically" into the amendment, but they were destined to ultimate failure.

The new Bill of Rights, taken in the large, was entirely consistent with the Constitution ratified two years earlier. Its statement of the doctrines of limited government and an open society, and its enumeration of certain traditional common-law guarantees, were like the Constitution itself, entirely within the value system of the Revolutionary era. And just as the Constitution in no sense had added up to a counterrevolution against the values laid down in the Declaration, so the guarantees of the new Bill of Rights were not in any fashion a repudiation of the charter drafted at Philadelphia. The amendments, for the most part, expressed familiar ideas which scarcely altered the limited federal Republic the authors of the Constitution had established.

REVOLUTIONARY VALUES AND CONSTITUTIONAL LIBERTY TODAY

If we now engage in a great leap forward in time and subject this system of constitutional liberty and natural rights as formulated in the Declaration, the Constitution, and the Bill of Rights to a very broad and generalized scrutiny, it is possible at once to see certain very great evolutionary changes in the idea of individual rights (they are not often called natural rights anymore), in the character of such rights themselves, and in the means whereby they are defined, implemented, and guaranteed.

Crucial to any consideration of modern constitutional liberty is the fact that the very concept of self-evident natural rights derived from natural law has nearly died out of contemporary constitutional theory. In reality, the demise of the idea of natural rights began in philosophic theory in the late eighteenth century. At the very time that the Declaration gave the concept its noblest expression, David Hume had already launched a devastating attack upon the conception that man could, by a process of reasoning from a priori premises, discover certain fundamental principles of right and justice inherent in the Universe which could in turn be translated into coherent propositions about human right and human liberty.

The higher law idea lived on throughout the nineteenth century, although with diminishing vitality, occasionally winning overt expression, as it did from William H. Seward at the time of the slavery extension crisis of 1850. Occasionally, also, the Supreme Court gave it some recognition of sorts. In the twentieth century, however, the idea lives on in the writings of only a few Catholic philosophers, such as Leo Strauss. Such thinkers as Roscoe Pound, John Dewey, and Morris Cohen turned away from it completely, recognizing that it was a part of what Oliver Wendell Holmes, Jr., called "the illusion of certainty."

In short, the great "self-evident" truths of the Declaration and the natural rights philosophers are no longer self-evident. In their place are the truths of various ideologies, grounded in many instances in the great propositions about man and society derived originally from the Enlightenment, but which are no longer capable of demonstration except through an overt stipulation of unprovable premises. To put the matter differently, the underlying values of our contemporary explosion in civil rights and civil liberties may appear self-evident upon superficial perusal, but upon close inspection they appear to be compounded of our Enlightenment faith in reason and progress, a latter-day utilitarianism (the greatest good for the greatest number), which is in reality a logical extension of the Jeffersonian-Benthamite approach to social theory, and a latter-day concept of egalitarianism—one which in origin goes back to the Declaration and has been nurtured for two centuries by economic dynamism and class fluidity, but which in our own time has taken on a populistic flavor unknown to earlier generations. To all this, one must add that expressions of so-called rights very often contain a power-relationship component (those associated with the Black Revolution are a good example of this fact) and that they may, on occasion, reflect the half-disguised competition for power of competing pressure and self-interest groups.

There is potential for tragedy in all this, for it means that at the very time when the concept of individual rights in everything from due process to racial equality is receiving unprecedented homage, both from the Supreme Court of the United States and from the society at large, the theoretical underpinning which gave such rights their vitality is gone. Rights have become pragmatic, not natural. What this means ultimately is that the rights so confidently proclaimed in the last generation are in reality the product of the shifting realities of the dynamics of the social process. A "right" which the Warren Court thought to be fundamental may be broken in upon, modified, or become inconsequential at the hands of the Burger Court tomorrow, simply because the ideological and power relationships reflected in the Court's membership have changed.

This does not mean that the justices themselves do not suffer from "the illusion of certainty" in the formulation of the propositions about the nature of right and justice which they proclaim. They do not often refer to natural law in cultivating truth; rather they discover either historical truths or self-evident sociological truths which are formulated out of certain half-hidden ideological assumptions about contemporary society and the nature of the social process. There is nothing very new in this process; indeed the ideological and rational procedures by which the Warren Court arrived at some of its landmark decisions about private right resemble strikingly the fashion in which the Court at the turn of the century translated the economic and social myths of laissez-faire capitalism into conceptions of rights in private property against the state.

The self-evident truths of *Lochner* v. *New York* (1905) with its translation, as Holmes put it, of Herbert Spencer's *Social Statics* into constitutional law are vanished now. But the judicial approach to social reality, while it is a different apparent reality which is approached, and a reality seen through very different judicial glasses, remains unchanged. The most spectacular example of this enduring fact is perhaps to be found in *Griswold* v. *Connecticut* (1965), the celebrated decision holding unconstitutional state legislation regarding the dissemination of birth control information. As Justice Black observed correctly, the Court had resorted in its opinion to essentially the same discovery of a self-evident ultimate reality—in this instance a right of marital privacy—as Peckham had indulged himself in in his *Lochner* opinion 60 years earlier.

All this gives rise to a somewhat disturbing thought: the libertarian-oriented rights which we proclaim so confidently with respect to racial minorities, women, accused persons, "far-out" dissidents, and the like, must be seen ultimately as nothing more than the product of the institutions, social pressures, and values of a certain sector of American society. It is not even certain, in many instances, whether they represent majority-held values. In turn, this may well mean that they will prove just as frail and as vulnerable to the terrible erosive process of time as the link between due process and vested interest once proved to be. The only alternative to such a conclusion is the acceptance of some kind of theory of progressive revelation of social truth as a manifestation of cultural progress. In reality, however, such a notion amounts to nothing more than a disguised version of natural law theory.

The fact remains that, from the standpoint of a latter-day Enlightenment-oriented observer, the Supreme Court since the 1930s and in particular in the Warren era brought about through the decision-making process an extraordinary flowering of the idea of constitutional right and of constitutional liberty. In certain fundamental respects, also, the Court has worked directly within the value system generated by Locke, Coke, Milton, Harrington, Sidney, and the other natural rights philosophers of the seventeenth and eighteenth centuries. Other portions of the Court's decisions, those having to do with search and seizure, for example, are directly within the tradition of liberty formulated by the leaders of the American Revolution.

Moreover, the Court's vast concern with procedural due process and the rights of accused persons which the Miranda, Escobedo, Powell, Wainwright, and Coolidge cases embody hearkens back to the centuries-long English concern with the rights of accused persons, the formulation of which already had been evolving for centuries at the time of the American Revolution. The colonists before 1770, with their reverence for Coke, had considered them to be integral to the rights of Englishmen, and Jefferson alluded to them in the third portion of the Declaration in the course of his charge against George III.

Finally, the present Court is directly within the Revolutionary tradition in its concern for the great guarantees of an open society. Issues having to do with separation of church and state, for example, spring directly out of the Revolutionary movement for the disestablishment of state churches, the Virginia Statute of Religious Liberty of 1785, and the incorporation of the establishment and free exercise clauses within the First Amendment. And the Court's concern for free speech and in particular for the rights of dissident political minorities lies directly within the libertarian tradition of freedom of speech which took its departure from the very limited guarantees of "no prior restraint," but which by the time of the crisis over the Sedition Act of 1798 had progressed to the point where Albert Gallatin and his colleagues in Congress had formulated the first broad American-style guarantees of freedom of expression.

A NEW IDEA: ENFORCEABLE EQUALITY

Nonetheless, the modern Court's decisions on occasion carry within them implicit value systems which the Revolutionary era doubtless would have found foreign or at least strangely distorted. Thus the concept of equality within which the Warren and Burger Courts have operated has altered vastly since Jefferson first gave overt expression to the idea in the Declaration; indeed the idea of enforceable guarantees of equality as the Court has conceived them has altered substantially within the last 30 years.

Since the time of the Declaration, in fact, the American idea of equality, which the modern Court translates into legal right, has gone through four or five distinct stages of evolution. The first stage, which Jefferson undoubtedly had in mind in part when he penned the Declaration, had to do with the centuries-old English idea of procedural justice for accused persons (habeas corpus, jury trial, evidentiary safeguards, and the like). The English caste system had interfered with the perfection of this system, but in America by the time of the Revolu-

tion formal caste as recognized at law had so far disappeared with respect to white persons that procedural equality was everywhere recognized. The second stage in the evolution of American egalitarianism, the extension of equal political rights to all white males, was well under way at the time of the Revolution and was to be consummated almost completely by the time of the Jacksonian era. Significantly, several states between 1820 and 1840 adopted new constitutions which embodied the guarantees of white male political equality.

Meanwhile, a novel idea, which Jefferson may well have had in mind in 1776, was working its way into American society: the idea of equality of opportunity, a notion closely associated with the concept of an open society and a fluid class system. Already in the 1830s de Tocqueville, Dickens, Harriet Martineau, and Mrs. Trollope remarked upon the American sense of social egalitarianism, which did not at all carry any guarantee of equality of condition, but rather merely that all white men were entitled, without regard to prior rank, family, or social status, to participate equally in the economic scramble incident to a highly fluid society. Associated with this was another nascent Jeffersonian idea: that of the utilitarian approach to public policy. The concept of the greatest good for the greatest number assumed that no one social group would be favored overtly by the state without reference to the general public welfare. It is this concept of equality of opportunity along with those of equal justice and equal political rights which dominated the American scene far down into the twentieth century.

With the adoption of the Thirteenth, Fourteenth, and Fifteenth Amendments, the evolution of the American idea of equality entered still another stage: the extension of the guarantees of procedural justice, political rights, and equality of opportunity to a succession of minorities formerly excluded from the American social process. The amendments were, of course, intended principally to liberate the black man and to incorporate him in the body politic. For the first time, the interpretation of the egalitarian ideal became a judicial function. But the Court at first entered this field with extreme caution and even reluctance, refusing to endow the Fourteenth Amendment's "privileges or immunities" clause with any content of consequence, rejecting an interpretation of the equal protection clause which would have allowed Congress to legislate against private discrimination, and reconciling, through the "separate but equal" myth, the idea of a racial caste system with a concept of a constitutional democracy.

Within the last 40 years, however, as everyone is aware, the Court has become a powerful champion of racial equality, first insisting upon a rigorous interpretation of the "equal" standard in the separate but equal formula, then, beginning with Brown I and Brown II, destroying first in education and then everywhere else in public facilities the very concept of separate but equal and legalized caste. The Court, moreover, within the last few years has reached out to extend the benefits of an all-inclusive egalitarian idealism to other minorities hitherto partially or completely shut out from the benefits of an open constitutional democracy and fair system of procedural justice: to women, to illegitimate children, to recipients of public welfare, to impoverished prisoners, and so on. All these are logical and rational extensions of the idea born in the Civil War and Reconstruction era: that it is not logically feasible in a constitutional democracy to exclude any minority from the benefits of an open constitutional society.

Even as this process unfolded, however, a novel conception of the egalitarian ideal entered the marketplace of constitutional ideas and found its way both into legislation and into judicial decision: that it was not merely the duty of the government to remove the caste or other legal restrictions upon an open constitutional society but, in addition, the duty of both the federal government and the states to guarantee equality of position within the educational, social, and economic order through positive intervention by government. This is a novel and extraordinary development in the American egalitarian ideal, which to some extent may fairly be said to stand the old notion of equality of opportunity on its head and to replace it—as far as the concept goes—with an enforced equality of position. Insofar as this has received judicial sanction, it appears to be one major way in which the concept of constitutional liberty is being very significantly altered.

There are numerous manifestations of this tendency, but undoubtedly the introduction of affirmative action by the Court into school desegregation cases beginning with Green v. County Board of New Kent County (1968) and continuing through the Swann, Wright, Keyes, and Bradley decisions is undoubtedly the most dramatic. It now becomes the duty of the state, once a finding of de jure segregation occurs, not merely to prohibit such segregation, but also to pass beyond that to a positive remedial program to correct the consequences of past racial injustice by altering the distribution of the races in the public schools. On occasion this has meant resort to racial quota systems of a kind which Justice Frankfurter, within another context, only a few years ago pronounced contrary to the spirit of American constitutional liberty. Through Title VI of the Civil Rights Act of 1964, moreover, the federal government, through Health, Education, and Welfare, has taken it upon itself to assure the existence of appropriate quotas and salaried equality by race, sex, and cultural origin for university faculties and for student bodies, as well as in the great mass of industries that have any kind of contract status with government. The consequence of all this in many instances has been a curious kind of government-guaranteed equal status altogether at odds with the traditional American conception of an open market equality of opportunity.

Very often, however, affirmative action has gone beyond a mere guarantee of equality for the minority or minorities involved and has embraced attempts at inverse discrimination in an effort to remedy long-standing social wrongs, both public and private. Whether one views such attempts with dismay, in the light of their obvious conflict with the traditional open-opportunity concept of American equality, or considers them to be merely the latest and grandest manifestation of the egalitarian dream released by the Declaration is in considerable part a matter of one's individual value system. The Supreme Court thus far has refused to plunge into the maze of constitutional, legal, social, and political issues involved, preferring instead to dispose of the one major reverse discrimination case it confronted, *DeFunis* v. *Odegaard* (1974), on a technicality.

Sooner or later, however, the Court, and ultimately American society, will have to deal with the inverse discrimination issue. The critical questions are obvious: Does state imposed discrimination as a means of remedying past social injustice or inequalities in the class system purify such policies of the taint of violating the equal protection clause, as Justice Douglas's tortured and contradictory dissent in the DeFunis case at least implied? Or are such programs, at last, hopelessly unconstitutional? The answer, obviously, is tied intimately to the question of whether the Court stays with a traditional de Tocqueville concept of American equality or adopts the guarantee of position concept of the last few years.

Of even greater lasting significance: What are the implications for the long-run structure of American society of a government program of enforced equality of opportunity? Does inverse discrimination penalize superior ability, enforcing a lockstep of position, achievement, and eventually of class position which may ultimately reduce the creativity of American society? Will it alter class relationships significantly, by lifting hitherto suppressed minorities into adequately competitive positions in the American social order? Or will it prove unable to make any real impression upon the distribution of wealth, income, membership in the professions, and lucrative occupations that have traditionally characterized American society? Will it operate to reduce social tensions, or will it, in the long run, prove to have generated so many hatreds and tensions of its own as to have frustrated more or less completely the noble aspirations such policies have embodied? The answers to all of these questions will ultimately have to work their way into the law of liberty. One tentative and highly controversial proposition may be advanced here: in the long run, a populistic conception of rights—one that involves state-enforced equality of position as distinct from the guarantee of equality of opportunity—may break in very gravely upon a system of liberty which traditionally has been highly individualistic in its legal and theoretical foundations.

One notable aspect of the new egalitarianism which calls for particular comment is the proposed Equal Rights Amendment (ERA) for women, which at present writing is at least within striking distance of ratification. No enlightened person can quarrel with the amendment's general objective: presumably the elimination of whatever remains of social and economic discrimination against women in American society. A substantial portion of the criticism directed against the amendment has come from highly conservative traditionalists, who in spite of the major social currents of the twentieth century to the contrary still believe that "woman's place is in the home." It constitutes a line of argument not likely to win many friends among those who have watched and studied with sympathy the long struggle, now more than a century old and which goes back to Lucretia Mott, the Grimke sisters, Carrie Chapman Catt, Susan B. Anthony, and so on, to eliminate discrimination against women in American society.

However, analysis of the matter hardly ends there. To paraphrase Justice Holmes slightly, the amendment rests upon the proposition that there are no biological or psychological differences between men and women which either the law or private social institutions properly can take account of. But, in fact, the statute books of the several states are full of protective legislation for women based upon a contrary premise: that both biology and social structure on occasion impose special burdens upon women which in some circumstances demand special intervention and special classification by the state on their behalf.

Nor has it been merely benighted males who have defended legislation and court decisions of this kind. The Progressive era—between the turn of the century and World War I—was one in which a great many highly intelligent women, among them Grace Abbott, Sophonisha Breckinridge, Jane Addams, and Florence Kelley, fought strenuous battles on the floor of one state legislature after another to get special protective legislation for females: hours of labor laws, factory sanitary facility laws, pregnancy leave laws, statutes creating special civil rights for women in marriage, special protection for female prisoners, and so on. Much of this legislation is still on the books. But as Professor Paul Freund has shown conclusively, ERA if adopted would cast doubt upon the special position of women at law in a great variety of respects, many of them damaging to women's rights. It is an argument that can hardly be disregarded lightly.

There is quite evidently a class element in the debate over ERA. The women who sponsor the amendment most strongly are generally drawn from a professional and business background, for whom the special protective legislation of the Progressive era has little meaning. Thus, Martha Griffiths, lately a representative from Michigan and a principal sponsor of ERA in the House, has directed her fire in considerable part at the discrimination which women encounter in law, medicine, college teaching, and so on. By the same token, some of the opposition to ERA has come from female labor leaders, among them Myra Wolfgang of the Waitresses Union, who sees ERA as menacing the kind of special protection for working women she still deems to be valuable. It is conceivable, of course, that if the amendment actually wins ratification, it will undergo a process of judicial interpretation which eventually will allow women to have the best of two worlds.

THE FURTHER EXPANSION OF THE OPEN SOCIETY

A second major respect in which constitutional rights and the law of liberty have undergone substantial change within the last generation or so is through the vast expansion of the dimensions of an open society. At the time of the Revolution, the concept of an open society already was winning general recognition, but the channels of expression involved were as yet rather limited. So far as the Constitution and the Bill of Rights were concerned, it meant little more than a guarantee of religious liberty and the disestablishment of religion;

certain very elementary guarantees of freedom of speech, press, assembly, and petition; and the implicit subordination of military to civil authority. In actual practice, the dimensions of freedom of expression were extremely limited, as Leonard Levy has shown. Moreover, the unwritten philosophic assumptions of an open society were almost certainly stronger and more important than those involving formal legal guarantees: the notion of maximum freedom of movement, maximum economic discretion in a free market, and so on. These were primarily matters of institutional process and the silent operation of mores rather than of constitutional law.

For a surprisingly long time, the constitutional dimensions of the American open society changed relatively little. In the area of freedom of expression, for example, the Supreme Court, as late as 1919, in defining the permissible constitutional limits of governmental suppression of seditious activity could endorse formally the bad tendency doctrine as an offset to the "clear and present danger" which it had accepted the year before. And while the technical constitutional rationale and limits of the bad tendency concept were very different from the rationale the high Federalists had resorted to in 1798 in defending the constitutionality of the ill-starred Sedition Act, the practical limits which the doctrine set upon freedom of political dissent were not very different from those of a century and a quarter earlier. Much the same thing might be said of the Court's decision in the Dennis case in 1951, in which, by means of the so-called sliding scale doctrine, it managed to rationalize "bad tendency" prosecution of 11 Communist party members convicted, in effect, of a charge of having propagated a series of ideas about government and society alleged to be dangerous to national survival. The practical dimensions of the Smith Act, it appeared, were not very different from those of the Sedition Act of 1798 or the Sedition Act of 1918. It is worth observing, also, that the Court during World War II almost completely abdicated its task of protecting the civil liberties of the loyal Japanese-American population, abjectly surrendering to the argument of military necessity to which the Army, the Executive, and Congress in effect all subscribed. The result was an infamous "concentration camp" stain on the record of American constitutional liberty.

This was a by-product of the gravest of national emergencies, war, as were the suppressions of allegedly seditious activities before and since. But the Cold War era, reminiscent in so many ways of the circumstances of the 1790s which produced the first American Sedition Act, produced even more restrictions on civil liberties. Along with the Smith Act and the wave of prosecutions inspired by the Dennis decision, the McCarran Act (1950) and the Communist Control Act of 1954 provided further effective checks on freedom of speech and political activity. To these legislative enactments was added the action of the Executive branch with the establishment of loyalty programs by Presidents Truman (1946–47) and Eisenhower (1953). All of this raised serious constitutional questions, but for the most part, no important judicial assessments of constitutional liberties were forthcoming for some time. This may

have been in part due to the reluctance of the Judiciary to move against coordinate branches of government, though it may equally be surmised that among the members of the U.S. Supreme Court there was no sure majority of strong devotees of personal liberty. Furthermore, there is ample evidence that determined efforts to strengthen national security, however crude, however abusive of the delicate fabric of constitutional liberty, were popular. Popular will, it seemed, actually supported government power to make the open society somewhat less open.

And yet, in a sequel familiar in the unfolding story of American constitutional liberty, it became clear that the idea of the open society survived the exigencies of war, both hot and cold, and, indeed, received a reaffirmation which carried it to such lengths as to form a major change in our idea of freedom. The role of popular attitudes was important in this, too—quite possibly the decisive factor in the long run, thus testifying to the profound significance of a newly aggressive populistic democracy in the determination of the dimensions of constitutional liberty. But clearly the resolution of the problem of freedom during dangerous times was achieved by the advent of a new U.S. Supreme Court, "the Warren Court," as common usage now has it. That presumably conservative decade, the 1950s, saw a remarkable change in the personnel of the Court, as President Eisenhower, in an exercise of appointive power rare in American history, was able to appoint five new justices to that tribunal. And President Kennedy, in his abbreviated tenure, appointed two more. So by the middle or late 1960s, when the new dimensions of the open society became abundantly apparent, it was indeed a decidedly different court which had accommodated the new thrusts of popular feeling to the law of constitutional liberty.[5]

The central matter of constitutional concern during the Cold War, the civil liberties of alleged subversives, began to receive constructive judicial attention toward the end of the 1950s. The Warren Court, without actually striking down the Dennis opinion, in *Yates* v. *U.S.* (1957) modified its interpretation of the Smith Act so radically as virtually to end prosecutions under that statute, while its opinions on the McCarran Act rendered the registration provisions of that law to all intents and purposes unenforceable. And a whole series of state loyalty program laws and loyalty oath statutes failed to pass the Court's scrutiny, most of them condemned because they suffered from the "vice of vagueness" or, by implication, infringed upon First Amendment rights. Even congressional and state legislative investigations, for a moment in 1957 (*Watkins* v. *U.S.*; *Sweezy* v. *New Hampshire*), were given a sharp check.

Meanwhile, a good many forces were at work in American life to produce an unparalleled growth of egalitarianism: a larger and larger percentage of people were achieving a middle-class standard of living; organized labor became a part of the political and economic establishment; various minority groups (Jews, Poles, and others) were now

well beyond the desperate struggles of the urban slums and became significant elements of the mainstream of American culture; there was a comparative decline of the old "White Anglo-Saxon Protestant" ascendancy; and there was an extraordinary expansion of higher education, which poured into business and the professions a flood of educated men and women, most of whom were libertarian in outlook and aggressively egalitarian in their attitudes toward politics and society. The resulting surge of an importunate spirit, kindled to new heights by the pervasive immediacy of television, wrested striking concessions to the claims of personal liberty from the body of established constitutional ideas. The moderately open society of American Revolutionary tradition was rendered impressively more open.

The accommodations to this movement made by the Warren Court, and in many ways continued by the Burger Court, pertained to a wide range of matters; so wide, indeed, as to raise a serious question in the minds of many, including thoughtful libertarians, as to whether the extremes of openness might threaten to replace the fundamental notion of "ordered liberty" with a liberty so disorderly as at last to shake apart the very system long relied on for freedom's guarantee.

Such a turn of thought was for some time pretty much restricted to extremely conservative opinion, or to those with a palpable self-interest in the status quo. Thus the great movement to open American society to black people seemed to have majority support, at least until the appearance of the more advanced development of the idea of equality of position and affirmative

5. Two of the members of the Court who were not replaced, Justices Douglas and Black, furthermore, were usually among the most ardent advocates of strong restrictions on government efforts to limit constitutional liberty.

action noted above. The next major expansion of the open society became important in the 1960s when the Court saw fit to interfere in state legislative and congressional apportionment. The new activism of the Court in this matter, launched in 1960 in the Gomillion case, was wholly apparent in *Baker* v. *Carr* (1962) and further developed within another two years in the Gray, Reynolds, and Lucas cases, among others. As a result, all voters throughout the United States had something like equal access to representative government, whereas before many had been virtually excluded by the happenstance of residence.

When it came to extending the fullest possible measure of constitutional liberty to persons accused of crime, however, it began to appear that there might be some incompatibility between the spirit of populistic democracy and important American traditions. The rights of the accused, particularly the very explicit ones of the Fourth, Fifth, and Sixth Amendments, have often been misunderstood and misinterpreted in popular thought. The notion that invoking the Fifth Amendment protection against self-incrimination is a confession of guilt has been a painfully obvious example in recent decades. When the Warren Court undertook, in effect, an extensive reform of criminal procedure as evidenced in the Mapp, Gideon, Escobedo, and Miranda decisions, faithful adherence to constitutional guarantees seemed to produce results which were plainly contrary to justice: the "criminal," it was widely assumed, went free because of some esoteric technicality.

This happened at a time when Americans were newly conscious of crime in their lives, for it was dramatized daily, and often quite explicitly, on television; it was prominent on many a page of the newspaper; it was constantly discussed in home, office, and shop; it was summarized in regular announcements of statistical summaries expressing a crime rate; and it invariably summoned up the picture of some repugnant person who was brutal, violent, and probably drunk or drugged. For a great many people, to talk of such a person having constitutional rights strained to the utmost the credibility of the very concept itself.

None of this was lost on those running for political office, including the highest in the land. "Crime in the streets" became a theme of the Goldwater campaign in 1964, and contenders for high office have been obliged to discuss the matter ever since. This has provided an interesting case study of the durability of the judicially-promulgated reform of criminal procedure, for Richard Nixon made the matter, through denunciations of the Warren Court and talk of "law and order," a prominent theme of his 1968 campaign. He was the winner that year, and an impressive winner in 1972; he actually did have the opportunity to make four appointments to the Court, including that of a new chief justice; and the new Court has had ample opportunity to change the tenor of decisions regarding the procedural rights of the accused in criminal trials. By early 1976, it seemed clear that the Burger Court would at least stop the process of strengthening the constitutional protections of such rights and when at all possible would render decisions sympathetic to those engaged in prosecutions. This was especially evident in *Harris* v. *New York* (1971), which limited seriously the Miranda decision, and the reaffirmation of the credibility rule in *Oregon* v. *Hass* (1975). Another strong indication is found in *Kastigar* v. *U.S.* (1972) where the protection against self-incrimination provided by the Fifth Amendment was further weakened.

It would seem, then, that the political process has been successfully employed to check the expansion of constitutional liberty in this area—ominous to some people, heartening to others. It is hard to believe that there are immediate practical consequences in this— that is, that the crime rate has been changed by the new pronouncements of the Court. But there is a reenactment of an ancient problem of constitutional government based on the idea of people as the constituent power: how can we prevent the system which the people have created from diminishing the liberties it was intended to serve, when a current majority wishes to do so? In the matter of criminal procedure, we might say that the Constitution, in the Fourth, Fifth, and Sixth Amendments, seeks to embrace all people in the enjoyment of certain precious rights; but recently it seems that many Americans wish to exclude some from the full access to the protections therein set forth. The eagerness of so many to restrict these rights is distressing to anyone who believes in the enduring value of limited government. No doubt it arises from a sense of crisis about crime in American society, a motive similar to alarm about national security in time of war. The extremity of the danger, then, becomes the justification for the limiting of freedom, or at least for a lack of

interest in making it secure to all. In the case of war, Americans have generally been confident that the war would some day end, and then the freedoms, which have been suspended rather than canceled, might be resumed. With regard to crime, a somewhat less confident expectation is probably in order, unless we can recover the Enlightenment assumption of the benevolence and perfectibility of our fellow citizens. Meanwhile, we might capitalize on the strong tradition we have from the Revolutionary era to create a truly open society, including therein even the poor and underprivileged, even when they are so unfortunate as to be accused of crime.

Anyone who lived as an adult through the 1960s must be impressed with the startling expansion of the dimensions of permissible speech and publication, including movies. When the results are surveyed as of 1976, it seems fair to suggest that American society has accommodated a range of expression in writing, speaking, and pictures which would in some respects astound the Revolutionary generation—though, of course, the content would not really be novel to many of them. More and more people, it seemed, were convinced that there should be virtually no bounds to their utterances and that the First Amendment could be invoked as an absolute bar to legal restraint. The most spectacular controversy was the one over obscenity, still not satisfactorily resolved. It may well continue for some time to be what it was called years ago: "a constitutional disaster area."

There had long been something of a tradition that material which was "lewd and obscene" lay outside the protection of the First Amendment. To a large extent, this had been a widely accepted philosophical premise, a matter of common understanding so well respected as to be generally observed. Review by the U.S. Supreme Court of state laws on the matter had been rather inconclusive when the Warren Court in the late 1950s undertook a decisive effort to reconcile the conflict between the new First Amendment claims of free speech with the imprecisions of tradition. The principal result was the finding in the Roth case (1957) which set forth "appeal to prurient interest" as a test of obscenity; yet this elusive quality, which the Court meant to separate from a mere literary concern with the mysteries of sex, was nowhere defined. To that was added a reliance on "contemporary community standards," which introduced the supple element of fad and fashion in public opinion. Subsequent to Roth, where censorship was upheld, a number of additional decisions seemed to support the First Amendment claim of free expression. Then came the curious Ginzburg decision with its assertion that marketing methods (pandering) had tainted the materials themselves, and a criminal conviction was thus sustained. Yet in the same year, 1966, the Court found that *Fanny Hill*, an eighteenth-century book which some of our founding fathers may have known, was not *"utterly* without redeeming social value," hence protected by the First Amendment.

The Burger Court in the 1970s has tried to grapple with this matter, and has even undertaken once again a definition of obscenity. In the Miller case (1973) there appeared a reliance on some familiar ideas (contemporary community standards), new verbal puzzles (depicts or describes in a patently offensive way), and a revised reference to value (lacks serious artistic, political, or scientific value). Punishment for the sale of obscene matter and for exhibiting obscene movies was sustained in the 1973 decisions (Miller and Davis cases), yet the larger consequences somehow were not consistent with those results. The ensuing proliferation of x-rated films and adult bookstores is familiar enough to anyone who looks around in any city. It may well be that there is a substantial acceptance among the American people that obscenity is more a sin than a crime, hence personal, philosophical, and impossible of legal definition. In some indirect fashion, it may be that private opinion, informally supporting a tradition of an open society will settle this matter more surely than formal constitutional pronouncements can.

Religious freedom is one of the most firmly established features of the American tradition. The very founding of many of the colonies from which the United States grew was related closely to this matter. Well before the Revolution, a generous measure of religious freedom flourished in several places, religious toleration in many others, and religious pluralism was a distinctive feature of American society. Among the most revolutionary things which happened within America after 1776 was the change in public policy regarding religion. To organize a body politic without a preferred state church, which is what happened in all but three states, was a most unusual arrangement, scarcely known throughout Western Christendom, then or now. Following disestablishment in the states, came the Jeffersonian idea of thorough separation of church and state, and then the incorporation of these ideas into the new national Constitution through the First Amendment.

Exactly what was meant by the First Amendment, however, became a matter of continuing controversy after World War II, much of it centering around the relationship between religion and education. The critical question, then and since, has been: how complete must separation of church and state be? The Jeffersonian idea, which is the principal eighteenth-century source of American practice, included a strong emphasis on the privacy of religious thought and practice, the neutrality of the state, and the immunity of the citizen from government compulsion, including involuntary participation in any particular religion indirectly through an activity of his government which either supported or suppressed this absolutely private enterprise. It is hard to avoid the conclusion that this mode of thought, coupled as it was with a strong aspiration for an open society, calls for the wall of separation to be pretty nearly absolute.

Nonetheless, during the last two or three decades, the Court has held otherwise a number of times. The arrangements at issue in the McCollum case (1948), it seems, could hardly have been approved, since public school facilities were plainly being used for religious purposes—a rather common practice at the time. But, this case apart, when the support of religious purposes has been more indirect, the Court for a while acted on Justice Douglas's assertion in the Zorach case (1952) that the wall of separation is not absolute and that to assert that it is would be to demonstrate hostility to religion.

To be sure, Justice Black, who had dissented in Zorach, was able 10 years later to incorporate a reply to that idea in his opinion for the majority who held in *Engel v. Vitale* (1962) that a "Regents' Prayer" in New York violated the First Amendment. The "establishment clause," he said, is not irreligious in spirit; instead it "relied on the belief that a union of government and religion tends to destroy government and degrade religion." And compulsory Bible reading in Pennsylvania met a similar fate when the Court declared the practice unconstitutional the following year.

These decisions, though, prompted a renewal of the bitter controversy over the role of religion in the public schools which had lain uneasily quiescent for some years. There was a formidable drive for a "pro-prayer" amendment, an idea still in the air in the 1970s. As the crisis in school financing became grave, particularly so for parochial schools, in the 1960s, there were renewed demands for federal financial assistance to schools, public, private, and parochial. In 1963, Congress enacted a Higher Education Facilities Act which provided construction grants for institutions of higher education, including church-related colleges; and in 1971, in *Tilton* v. *Richardson*, the Court sustained the law. By 1968 the Court had sustained, in the Allen decision, a New York law which provided for public financing of textbooks in private schools in grades seven through twelve. State laws providing direct subsidies of one kind or another to parochial schools—"parochiaid" —were stricken down by the Court in 1971 and 1973, but the matter is far from settled, for the techniques of indirect aid suggested by the Everson and Allen decisions encourage continuing efforts to find further avenues of support for church schools from public funds.

Of all the areas where efforts have been made to expand American society by an even treatment of all, the tradition of state neutrality where religion is concerned is as clear a heritage of the Revolutionary era as any. Yet, of those discussed above—freedom of speech, apportionment, criminal justice procedures, obscenity (extreme freedom of speech), and religion— it is the last which portends the gravest danger, as the potential for divisiveness and antagonism is so great. The development of constitutional meaning here reflects the ambivalence of the latter twentieth century on the matter. On the one hand, we have the end of required religious exercises in public schools, including prayers and Bible reading; on the other, we have public funds providing support, if often indirectly, for the operation of schools whose purpose is to a considerable extent a religious one. Historically, Americans have been for the most part an unchurched people, for until about the middle of the twentieth century most of them did not profess membership in any church at all.[6] The statistics, of course, have their own peculiar infirmities, but they seem to tell us that in recent

6. According to one set of statistics, church members were less than 35 percent of the total population of the United States in 1890; in all likelihood, the percentage was no larger, and quite possibly was smaller, in earlier years. By 1940, church members were 42.8 percent of the population; by 1950, 56.2 percent. This figure rose to 63.6 percent by 1960. U.S. Bureau of Census, *Historical Statistics of the U.S., Colonial Times to 1957* (Washington, D.C., 1960); and U.S. Bureau of Census, *Statistical Abstract of the U.S.: 1966* (Washington, D.C., 1967).

decades the small majority of church members has increased somewhat. The relationship, if any, of this trend to an apparently rising crime rate and the widely held belief that there is a decline in personal morality is not quite the kind of puzzle with which we are concerned. But a constitution must serve an actual people with actual beliefs. One must assume that the populistic democracy prevalent at the dawn of the third century of national life has on its immediate agenda the reconciling of traditional constitutional values respecting religious freedom and the new, energetic impulse to modify them in important ways.

THE NATIONALIZING OF CONSTITUTIONAL LIBERTY

Finally, a third major change in the nature of constitutional rights is one which has been an integral part of the advent of enforceable equality and the expansion of the open society: it is the virtual triumph of the recent, powerful tendency to nationalize constitutional liberty. The libertarian values of the Revolutionary era have a far greater reach and play a far more conspicuous part in American lives today than ever before. This is in some measure a product of the apparently relentless expansion of the national government so evident throughout American history; but, more important, it is the result of a kind of judicial activism which must have seemed most improbable only 20 years ago.

During the first years of the Constitution, there had been some inclination to assume that constitutional liberty in certain fundamental respects flourished throughout the land, simply as a matter of the inherent purpose and meaning of constitutional government. And lying directly behind that thought was the philosophy of natural rights so recently and repeatedly proclaimed in the Revolutionary era. Certain federal judges in the 1790s, furthermore, assumed that such an abstract principle of justice implied that, under the U.S. Constitution, final authority to articulate such fundamental rights was vested in the federal Judiciary rather than in the state legislatures. Thus, Justice William Paterson found an act of the Pennsylvania legislature invalid in 1795 because it was "inconsistent with the principles of reason, justice, and moral rectitude" and "contrary to the principles of social alliance in every free government." And Justice Samuel Chase criticized an act of a state legislature because it was "contrary to the great first principles of the social compact."

Such rhetoric, and the awesome magnitude of national judicial power it implied, receded in a few years as new issues diverted constitutional development into new channels. Most of the practical concerns for personal liberty were determined by state and local law, presumably limited by the bills of rights and other restraints on government found in state constitutions. While the Fourteenth Amendment provided another kind of restraint on state government, it became clear in the closing decades of the nineteenth century that it had not, in fact, brought about the expansion of liberty which its framers had expected.

It was not until well into the twentieth century that the real potential of the Fourteenth Amendment for constitutional liberty became active. Between 1925 and 1932 the Court found in a number of cases that the federal Bill of Rights was a limitation on state police power by virtue of the due process clause of the Fourteenth Amendment; for the most part, it was First Amendment freedoms which were protected in this manner. A most significant resumption of this idea came in 1937 when Justice Cardozo, while denying that the Fourteenth Amendment automatically protected all the rights found in the first eight amendments, nonetheless said the rights "implicit in the concept of ordered liberty" were so protected. He also spoke of principles of justice "so rooted in the traditions and conscience of our people as to be ranked as fundamental." This was distinctly reminiscent of the language of Paterson and Chase in another era; the eighteenth century was speaking to the twentieth.

By mid-century the Court had incorporated fully the guarantees of the First Amendment within the due process clause of the Fourteenth Amendment, and modernized the meaning of First Amendment freedoms in many ways so that constitutional protection was given to picketing by labor unions, meetings in public parks, parades, pamphlet peddling, and other matters which state and local governments had so often forbidden. And one member of the Court, Justice Black, in *Adamson* v. *California* (1948) plainly asserted that the Court ought at once to declare the entire content of the federal Bill of Rights formally incorporated in the Fourteenth Amendment. This was rejected by his colleagues at the time, and has not yet quite been embraced by the Court. But the Warren Court (of which Black was a member) ultimately performed most of what Black had urged. This was most conspicuous in the field of criminal trial procedures. In the 1960s, in one case after another, the process was evident, making it clear that the states were restrained by the Fourth, Fifth, Sixth, and Eighth Amendments— and they had long been restrained by the First. As Leonard Levy has said, "The Warren Court's criminal-law revolution, then, consisted in nationalizing the Bill of Rights."

In addition, the Warren Court formulated a new constitutional law protecting an extraordinary range of private activities against interference by a state. Notable here were a controversial 1965 decision striking down long-standing state birth control legislation as a violation of a new-found right of marital privacy, a judicial nationalization of the law of libel that made public political criticism virtually immune from either private or criminal libel suits, the development of a new law of obscenity which was quite broadly permissive, and the new reach of separation of church and state which banned prayers and Bible reading from public schools.

The momentum of change has not been sustained by the Burger Court; yet it had its moment of dramatic humanitarian-liberal activism in 1973 when it found state anti-abortion statutes to be an unconstitutional violation of a right of privacy guaranteed by the Fourteenth Amendment. And in a series of cases involving scurrilous, vulgar, and perhaps obscene language provocatively uttered in public, the Burger Court denied state and local authorities the right to prosecute the offenders, very nearly overruling the 1942 decision in *Chaplinsky* v. *New Hampshire* where the punishment of somewhat milder language had been sustained.

The traditional weight of governmental restrictions on civil liberty in the United States had long been heaviest at the state and local level; this was now substantially lightened. However, it had been achieved by the exercise of a newly expanded power in the federal Judiciary. Such activism in the national government would have been shocking and even repugnant to most people in an earlier day, but it now seemed more or less plausible because Americans had for some time witnessed a considerable expansion in government as a whole. Here, then, was a price which had to be paid for the nationalizing of constitutional liberty: the amazing growth in only a generation or two of the national government. If one branch, the Judicial, had done much to enhance liberty, what was the record of the other two?

As to the legislature, the record is extremely complex. Many of the nation's new laws during the last half-century or so have been attempts to enhance the status and prospects of large numbers of people. On the other hand, some of those very laws have had mixed and limited results. The Social Security system, for example, virtually confiscates money from both an employee and his employer (who usually have no choice in the matter) for the sake of an extremely modest, if distinct, improvement in the employee's later life after he stops working. And it is remarkable that we have had three major laws which deal with sedition and subversion (1940, 1950, 1954) in this period and only two important ones (1798, 1918) in the preceding century and a half. Presumably Congress is within reach of the people, though, since most of its members must stand for reelection every two years, and one must assume that over a generation's time any laws which are strikingly unpopular will be changed. Yet there is an important check on that process, for there is one person whose vote is worth that of nearly two-thirds of the members of Congress, namely the president.

Here, it seems, in the growth of executive power is a major potential menace to constitutional liberty. It may well be that the sheer growth of government in general is a great departure from the thinking of the Revolutionary generation; the one part of it which is most striking is surely that of modern presidential power. The central theme of the Declaration of Independence was the assigning of the loss of American liberty to the acts of the king; the first organization of a common government was one which had no executive power at all in any direct sense; even the newly devised state governments often provided only a limited executive authority; and the opponents of the U.S. Constitution in the ratification controversy made much of the potential for tyranny in the office of president, expressed by Patrick Henry when he denounced it by saying, "It squints toward monarchy."

Most of modern presidential power has developed in response to the great national crises of recent generations: depression, war, and quasi-war. There had been intermittent experiences with this along the way, of course: one thinks particularly of Lincoln and Wilson as assuming a virtual war-time dictatorship in the interest of national survival. But it was understood at such times that the extra-ordinary conditions would one day end, and things would return to a less regimented order. Recently, however, there has arisen an un-articulated assumption that we are always going to be menaced with the threat of war or depression, and therefore we must accept great reaches of presidential power in order to preserve the country.

The spectacular events of recent presidential history are too well known at this moment to require repeating here; they are still being kept before us in books and movies. The most disturbing dimension of this is the persistence of the idea that we must expect presidents to exercise great power; that it has been the abuse of power rather than power itself which is the evil; and the faith that this bicentennial year is, happily, also an election year in which we can find a good person to whom this power may be entrusted. A careful reading of the U.S. Supreme Court's opinion in *U.S. v. Nixon* (1974) reveals a good deal of judicial self-restraint; most of the awesome power of the president remains intact. Little has been proposed for the reduction of presidential power. The election, it would appear, is expected to solve the problem by selecting an honorable person to whom such power may be entrusted. Few people seem impressed with the old notion that power corrupts.

In striking contrast, the new reach of judicial power has generated a good number of proposals for its limitation. Those who have been disappointed in recent rulings have felt a bitter resentment that men in distant Washington have allowed offensive conduct to go unpunished. As one controversial decision has followed another, the ranks of the disappointment have grown. Some are angry about crime, others about pornography, many others about abortion, and perhaps the greatest number of Court-haters are those who are upset by court-ordered busing of school children. All this puts a considerable strain on the American political and constitutional system, just at a time when populistic democracy seems ascendant. The dominant thought in many people's minds is that the U.S. Supreme Court has frustrated popular will in many states and communities, where strong majorities have wished to close adult bookstores and x-rated theaters, get tough with suspected criminals, outlaw abortion, establish parochiaid, and send their children to the neighborhood schools which prompted them to take up their current residence in the first place.

Inescapably, this will spill over into the political process even more conspicuously than it has in the recent past. What elected officers of government can do in response to these pressures is not entirely clear. The most serious proposal is for new amendments to the U.S. Constitution which have the effect of overruling the Court. There is something of a precedent for this, of course, in the Eleventh Amendment, which restored a dignity to the states which the Court had destroyed, and perhaps in the Sixteenth Amendment as an example of achieving that which the Court had forbidden. Yet we have been doing a good deal of amending lately. More to the point, no doubt, is the question of whether Constitution-amending is a sound way of formulating social policy. The experience with the Eighteenth Amendment is not reassuring. A constitution should endure, and that of the United States gets much of its veneration because of its durability.

But it is the durability of constitutional liberty which is the more particular concern. The essence of constitutionalism is the limitation of power, the foremost of the principles derived from the Revolutionary era; together with the commitment to natural rights, this made people confident in their expectation of an open society. The growth of constitutional liberty in recent decades is impressive, and it has been in the main guided by the values present at the founding of the nation. While grave problems await Americans in their third century of national life, the ideals of Jefferson, Madison, Adams, and the other libertarian-minded founders may still serve the cause of constitutional liberty.

ANNALS, AAPSS, **426**, July 1976

Values and Society in Revolutionary America

By JACK P. GREENE

ABSTRACT: The original principles and values of the American Republic and how they were rooted in and were reflections of the particular social conditions in early America are the subjects of this paper. The foundation of the "American science of politics" was a hardheaded and realistic view of human nature. The founding fathers saw America as having in its power the ability to begin the world over by discovering the "constant and universal principles" of government. What emerged from America's adaptation of the body of theory and tradition available was a system that was distinctively American. The American system incorporated the concept of the natural rights of man, existing independently of government. The government was limited by constitutions and by its representative nature; it was to be responsive and responsible to the people. The sovereignty resided within the people themselves. America would be safe from the tyranny of a majority faction by its multiplicity of interests. The primary purpose of government, according to the Declaration, was to secure man's inalienable rights—life, liberty, and the pursuit of happiness—and other values sought were unity and public virtue. These values expressed and reflected the social conditions of early America.

Jack P. Greene is the Harold Vyvyian Harmsworth Professor of American History and Fellow at Queen's College, Oxford University, as well as the Andrew W. Mellon Professor in the Humanities at the Johns Hopkins University. He was Visiting Professor at Columbia University from 1973–74 and a Fellow at Woodrow Wilson International Center for Scholars from 1974–75. His publications include Colonies to Nations, 1763–1789: A Documentary History of the American Revolution *and* The Reinterpretation of the American Revolution, 1763–1789.

In Order that a . . . State should long survive it is essential that it should be Restored to its original principles.[1]

EVEN if the Bicentennial of the United States did not suggest, the mood and circumstances of post-Vietnam and post-Watergate America would strongly demand a reconsideration of the relevance of the principles and values on which the country was originally founded. The dispiriting and divisive war in Southeast Asia followed by a humiliating "peace with honor" and the rapid "loss" of Vietnam, Cambodia, Laos, and Angola to the free world; the marginal successes of the federal government in coping with the bewildering difficulties of stagflation; the seeming inability of government—at all levels—to deal effectively with the apparently intractable problems posed by the proliferation of crime and violence, the decay of the cities, the continuation of racial and sexual discrimination, and the pollution of the environment; the corruption of the political system itself to a point that required the resignation of the two highest elected officials in the land and permitted agencies of the federal government to violate at will many of the country's most cherished values and to operate essentially beyond the control of all of the elected delegates of the people —this nearly endless litany of abuses, defects, failures, and, at best, marginal successes over the past two decades seems, from a variety of indications, to have led to a manifest loss of confidence—outside as well as inside the United States—in the capacity of the American political system to solve the nation's problems.[2] This loss of confidence has led, within the United States, to a retreat or alienation from public life and, abroad, to widespread predictions of the death of the liberal state as exemplified for the past 200 years by the United States.

In such an apparently desperate situation, the principal question for a gathering such as this becomes, not whether the principles of 1776 can sustain us for a third or even a fourth century, but whether they still have any relevance at all at this moment, whether social and political conditions have not changed so drastically between 1776 and 1976 as to render the political system hammered out between 1776 and 1789 entirely obsolete or at least in need of fundamental revision. To put the question another way, is the alleged incapacity of the United States to deal with the massive problems now confronting it traceable not merely to the sudden agglomeration of a series of unrelated or only tenuously connected short-term problems that are susceptible to manipulation by changes in policy and/or leadership but also to the long-term disintegration and ossification of the political system itself, to some deeper systemic failure rooted in the very foundations of the American nation?

Yet, the very survival of the American political system for the past 200 years is, at the very least, a powerful testimony to its capacity to respond to the most profound kinds of changes in social and political conditions, while the outcome of Watergate and its associate scandals

---

1. Niccolò Machiavelli, *The Discourses*, ed. Bernard Crick (London, 1970), p. 385.

2. The latest Harris Poll in March 1976 revealed the lowest confidence in American institutions among the American public ever recorded during the 10 years during which such polls have been taken.

and abuses of power provides vivid —and heartening—evidence that the old system may still have some life in it. Even if that system and the principles, values, and institutions on which it rests and through which it finds embodiment and expression should not turn out to be the causes of our present discontents, however, it is certainly desirable, in the spirit of both Machiavelli and the founding fathers, to seize the occasion of the Bicentennial to take a careful look at the viability of "the original principles" on which the Republic was founded. What the original principles and values of the American Republic as they were formulated during the era of the American Revolution actually were and how they were rooted in and were a reflection of the particular social conditions that obtained in early America are the subjects of this paper. Hopefully, a discussion of these subjects will provide a basis for the consideration of the more pressing questions of which Revolutionary values ought to be reaffirmed, strengthened, and maintained and which eliminated as inappropriate and dysfunctional to a vastly different late twentieth-century world.

THE REVOLUTIONARY INHERITANCE

[During the Revolution], every thing in America seemed to operate, to promote political knowledge. The principles of civil liberty, which were but imperfectly considered in the writings of Locke, Sydney, and Montesquieu, occurred every moment to the views and feelings of the whole body of the people: Instead of being any longer barely the discoveries of a few enlightened philosophers, they became the prevailing sentiments of the whole body of the American citizens: And

from that period until now, they have been constantly operating to produce a more natural form of government, a more perfect system of freedom, and a more flourishing state of society in America, than ever had been known before, among all the associations of men.[3]

American understanding of precisely what the principles and values of the American Revolution actually were has fluctuated widely according to changing social circumstances, political exigencies, and cultural orientations. Part of a sweeping new movement toward greater sophistication in historical studies,[4] the analysis of the Revolution over the past quarter century has produced what seems to be a far more accurate and detailed and a far less anachronistic comprehension of most aspects of the era of the Revolution than we have ever had before. In no area is this more true than in the analysis of the principles and characteristics of what Gordon S. Wood has called the emerging "American science of politics," knowledge of which has been enormously enriched by the careful studies of Douglass G. Adair, Bernard Bailyn, Richard Buel, Jr., Martin Diamond, Cecelia M. Kenyon, Perry Miller, Edmund S. Morgan, J. G. A. Pocock, J. R. Pole, Gerald Stourzh, and Gordon S. Wood, to name only the principal contributors.[5]

3. Samuel Williams, *The Natural and Civil History of Vermont* (Walpole, N. H., 1794), p. 310.
4. See Jack P. Greene, "The New History: From Top to Bottom," *New York Times* (8 January 1975), for a brief description of this movement.
5. The works of most of these men are discussed at length in Jack P. Greene, "Revolution, Confederation, and Constitution, 1763–1787," in William H. Cartwright and Richard L. Watson, Jr., eds., *The Reinterpretation of American History and Cul-*

The foundation of the "American science of politics," these new studies have revealed, was a hardheaded and, we would now say, realistic view of human nature. Rejecting the belief of a few of the more radical thinkers of the European enlightenment in the perfectibility of man, the founding fathers were virtually unanimous in their distrust of the human animal. Man was an imperfect creature whose actions and beliefs were often shaped by passion, prejudice, vanity, and interest and whose boundless ambition, though sometimes diverted into socially desirable channels by his craving for public approval and fame, made it difficult for him to resist the temptations of power and vice. Man's feeble capacities for resistance thus turned power and vice into corrupting and aggressive forces, the natural victims of which (in the public arena) were liberty and virtue, those central pillars of a well-ordered state.[6] Yet, this unflattering view of man was counteracted by a belief that, through reason, man could use his own imperfections as a basis for constructing a stable and effective political system that would provide him with all the benefits that could be expected from political society. That politics, to quote David Hume, could "be reduced to a science," that the application of intellect to the problem of human governance could yield, in the phrase of the Society for Political Inquiries, a body established by Benjamin Franklin, Thomas Paine, and others in Philadelphia, in 1787, "mutual improvement in the knowledge of government, and . . . the advancement of political science," was the confident expectation of most of the men who assumed responsibility for working out the new political systems for the United States during the Revolution.[7]

This belief in the efficacy of reason underlay an animated, engaging, and, for the participants, exhilarating search for what the Vermont divine and historian Samuel Williams referred to in the previously quoted passage as "a more perfect system of freedom . . . than ever had been known before, among all the associations of men." There had been no comparable opportunity presented to mankind, said Thomas Paine, "since the days of Noah." Americans had it in their "power to begin the world over again" by discovering what Douglass Adair has called those " 'constant and universal principles' of . . . government in regard to liberty, justice and stability." Yet, Americans did not, as Paine supposed, have an entirely "blank sheet to write upon."[8] "In the estab-

ture (Washington, 1973), pp. 259–96. But see, also, J. G. A. Pocock, *The Machiavellian Moment: Florentine Political Thought and the Atlantic Republican Tradition* (Princeton, 1975), pp. 462–552, and Gerald Stourzh, *Alexander Hamilton and the Idea of Republican Government* (Stanford, 1970).

6. See, especially, Arthur O. Lovejoy, *Reflections on Human Nature* (Baltimore, 1961), pp. 37–65, and Bernard Bailyn, *The Ideological Origins of the American Revolution* (Cambridge, Mass., 1967), pp. 55–93.

7. Douglass G. Adair, "That Politics May Be Reduced to a Science: David Hume, James Madison, and the Tenth *Federalist*," *Huntington Library Quarterly*, 20 (1957), pp. 343–60; Thomas Paine, "The Society for Political Inquiries," 1787, in Philip S. Foner, ed., *The Complete Writings of Thomas Paine*, 2 vols. (New York, 1945), vol. 2, p. 42.

8. See Adair, "That Politics May Be Reduced to a Science"; Paine, *Common Sense*, and "The Forester's Letters," 1776, in Foner, ed. *Complete Writings*, vol. 1, p. 45, vol. 2, pp. 82–3.

lishment of our forms of government," said George Washington in his circular letter to the governors of the states at the conclusion of the War for Independence, Americans were able to draw upon "the treasures of knowledge, acquired by the labours of philosophers, sages, and legislators, through a long succession of years." The classical tradition, the English common law, the writings of seventeenth-century New England Puritans, the political thought of John Locke and other natural rights theorists of the seventeenth and eighteenth centuries, the social and political thought of British opposition writers, and the ideas of both the Scottish and the continental European Enlightenment provided Americans with a plentiful stock of political wisdom to which they could, and did, turn for guidance. But practical experience derived from a century and a half of internal self-government, the lessons of which had been vivified by a decade of intense political interchange with Britain just prior to the Revolution, may have been even more helpful in the quest for an American science of politics. For the men who worked out the major components of the new American system were—almost to a man—experienced politicians. In marked contrast to virtually all later political revolutions, the American Revolution occurred in a society that had already undergone extensive political development and had at its command impressive political resources in the form of experienced and acknowledged leaders, tested institutions, and a politically conscious and socialized electorate.[9]

If Americans had a large body of theory and tradition and a broad range and deep level of experience to draw upon, however, little of it could be applied to the conditions of an independent America without considerable modification. What emerged from this process of adaptation was a political system that was in its working principles, characteristics, and underlying goals distinctively American.

The departures from traditional theory and practice, in relation to most of what may be referred to as the main working principles of government, were in many respects substantial. In the best British tradition, Americans would retain a strong belief in the principle of limited government: they, like Britain, would have a government of laws, not men. But they quickly rejected the contemporary British orthodoxy that the supreme legislative power was omnipotent and could alter the fundamentals of the Constitution as well as ordinary statute law—"the power and jurisdiction of parliament," said Sir William Blackstone in his enormously influential *Commentaries on the Laws of England*, "is so transcendent and absolute, that it cannot be confined . . . within any bounds." To defend themselves against Parliament's efforts to tax them after 1764, Americans had fallen back on the higher law doctrine of Sir Edward Coke and other seventeenth-century interpreters of the common law who had suggested that the fundamental

9. Washington's Circular Letter, 8 June 1783, in ed. Jack P. Greene, *Colonies to Nation 1763–1789: A Documentary History of the American Revolution* (New York, 1975), p. 438; Bailyn, *Ideological Origins*, pp. 22–53; Jack P. Greene, "The Growth of Political Stability: An Interpretation of Political Development in the Anglo-American Colonies, 1660–1760," in John Parker and Carol Urness, eds., *The American Revolution: A Heritage of Change* (Minneapolis, 1975), pp. 26–52.

rights of Englishmen were beyond the reach of a mere legislative body. Over the next quarter century, they incorporated into the American system of government the basic principles that the natural rights of men were not conferred by but existed independently of a limited government and that neither those natural rights nor any other component of the fundamental law, as laid down by the Constitution, were susceptible to change by government. Indeed, Americans developed the "important distinction," a distinction, said *The Federalist* papers, that seemed "to have been little understood and less observed in any other country," between fundamental law and statute law, between "a Constitution established by the people and unalterable by the government, and a law established by the government and alterable by the government." Unlike the British constitution, that amorphous result of a series of discrete actions by the ordinary organs of government, the American constitutions were written documents, ideal designs of government constituted by the people in specially elected conventions and designed to confirm the fundamental rights of the citizenry at the same time that they specified a form of government that would secure those rights.[10]

Governments were, moreover, to be limited not only by constitutions established by the sovereign

power of the people but also by the very character of government itself. For American government was *representative* government and representative throughout, not just in one of its parts. Americans rejected the European idea that society was divided into separate orders or estates and that each order needed its own organ of government to protect its special interests. In America, there would be no "distinction of rights in point of fortune," "no distinctions of titles, families, or nobility," no legally privileged "family interests, connexions, or estates," no "hereditary powers." "*Representative government*," said Paine, "is freedom," and the "floor of freedom" had to be "as level as water." Among *citizens*, at least, there had to be an absolute equality of rights. Thus, in the American conception of politics, government was divided into separate branches, not because each part represented a different social constituency, but simply because it would act as a check upon the others. Because each branch derived its "whole power from the people," moreover, it was directly "accountable to them for the use and exercise" it made of that power, and the chief "security of the people," Samuel Williams pointed out, derived less "from the nice ideal application of checks, balances, and mechanical powers, among the different parts of the government" than "from the responsibility, and dependence of each part of the government, upon the people." Representative government was to be responsive and responsible government.[11]

10. Blackstone, *Commentaries on the Laws of England*, 4 vols. (Philadelphia, 1771–72), vol. 1, pp. 160–62; Bailyn, *Ideological Origins*, pp. 175–98; R. R. Palmer, *The Age of Democratic Revolution: A Political History of Europe and America, 1760–1800*, vol. 1: *The Challenge* (Princeton, 1959), pp. 213–35; ed. Edward Mead Earle, *The Federalist* (Washington, D.C., 1937), no. 53, p. 348.

11. Williams, *History of Vermont*, pp. 342–44; Paine, *A Serious Address to the People of Pennsylvania. . . .* (Philadelphia, 1778) and *Rights of Man, Part Second* (London,

The notion that all power derived from the people was the foundation for still another and, in many ways, the most crucial innovation in the American science of government: the idea that sovereignty resided in the people themselves rather than in any institution of government. Earlier British and European thinkers had been unanimous in their belief that sovereignty was indivisible, and during the 1760s and 1770s British political writers found the American argument that there might be two or more taxing powers in the same political society, a multiplicity of parliaments each with a separate jurisdiction over a specific area, incomprehensible. Such an argument seemed to imply the existence of more than one sovereign power within a single state, but to most Britons the very idea of an imperium in imperio—a sovereign authority within a sovereign authority—was nothing but a solecism, a total contradiction in terms. The colonies were either part of the British Empire and therefore under the authority of the King-in-Parliament assembled, the repository of sovereign power in the Empire, or they were separate states each operating under its own sovereign authority. There was—there could be—nothing in between.

Faced with the same problem of how the essential powers of sovereignty might be divided between the state governments and the national, American political writers solved the problem of the indivisibility of sovereignty and thereby made possible the creation of a workable federal system, perhaps the most important political innovation of the Revolutionary era, by relocating sovereignty not in governments but in the people themselves. If the people were sovereign, as the federal Constitution of 1787 assumed, the "state governments could never lose their sovereignty because they had never possessed it," and the people could delegate the essential powers of sovereignty to any government or governments they wished, giving some powers to one government and other powers to another. According to this theory, all governments at all levels were the agents of the sovereign people. Thus, as James Madison wrote in *The Federalist*, both the state governments and the national government were "but different agents and trustees of the people, constituted with different powers, and designed for different purposes." Such a distribution of power between state governments and the national government, and the countervailing pressures arising from that distribution, would, in fact, be still another device for protecting the people against two great an assumption of power by either.[12]

In many ways, the most considerable departure from traditional political wisdom was the idea that, contrary to the dictum of Montesquieu, public virtue might not be requisite for a popular republican government—especially if such a government extended over a large area. The establishment of republican governments in the states in the mid-1770s had been accompanied by widespread expressions

1792), in Foner, ed., *Complete Writings*, vol 1, p. 390, vol. 2, pp. 282–83, 287; and Gordon S. Wood, *The Creation of the American Republic, 1776–1787* (Chapel Hill, 1969), esp. pp. 519–618.

12. Bailyn, *Ideological Origins*, pp. 198–229; Wood, *Creation of the Republic*, pp. 524–47.

of the conviction that no popular government could long survive without a virtuous citizenry which would eschew vice and luxury and put aside all individual concerns in pursuit of the common good. By the mid-1780s, however, some writers were beginning to sense, somewhat in the spirit of Bernard Mandeville, that private vice might render public virtue unnecessary in a free government, that the clashing of self-interest might in fact provide "the energy of true freedom." How precisely this situation might be achieved was, as Douglass Adair has shown, the special insight of James Madison as derived from David Hume and revealed in *Federalist* no. 10. Whereas earlier republics had invariably fallen prey to the tyranny of a majority faction, the United States, Madison predicted, would be saved from that unhappy fate by its enormous size and the multiplicity of interests that would necessarily result from that size. With so many separate and diverse interests, there could be no possibility of enough of them submerging their differences and getting together to form a majority faction. In a large republic, Madison thus suggested, the struggle of manifold interests would operate, to quote Martin Diamond, as a "safe, even energizing" force that would operate to safeguard the liberty and stability of political society. Not a single unitary interest, then, but a plurality of conflicting interests was the proper foundation for a free government. Traditional hostility to faction and party as the instruments of partial and self-interested men would no longer be functional in the new American regime: within a generation after the ratification of the federal Constitution, in fact, political parties would come to be seen as essential to mobilize the diverse and multiple interests of the country for the purpose of providing effective government.[13]

The new science of politics that emerged in the United States during the Revolutionary era was not, of course, in all ways a departure from the past. Traditional skepticism about the political capacities of the broad body of the citizenry, though sharply mitigated by the already highly inclusive character (in relative terms) of American political society, continued to be manifest in a variety of constitutional checks on the power of the electorate: by bicameral legislatures and such institutions as the council of censors in Pennsylvania and Vermont and the council of revision in New York, at the state level, and by the indirect selection of the president, Senate, and Judiciary at the federal level. Similarly, there was no real revision in traditional criteria of who might be admitted to citizenship: all categories of people thought either not to be free from external control (such as slaves, servants, and propertyless adult males) or lacking in sufficient discretion (such as women and free people of color) were routinely denied the franchise, despite a few proposals for universal manhood and even universal adult suffrage.[14] Finally, political leadership continued to be considered as the preserve of the

13. Wood, *Creation of the Republic*, pp. 65–70, 610–11; Adair, "That Politics May Be Reduced to a Science"; Martin Diamond, "Democracy and *The Federalist*: A Reconsideration of the Framers' Intents," *American Political Science Review*, 53 (1959), pp. 52–68.

14. On this point, see Jack P. Greene, "*All Men Are Created Equal*": Some Reflections on the Character of the American Revolution (Oxford, 1976).

"aristocracy of talent," those people of unusual wealth, education, merit, or talent who were sufficiently expert to provide effective government. American political leadership would, like that in much more traditional societies, designedly continue to be elitist in character and the broad body of electors deferential to their political superiors. The power of the people was still intended not primarily "to facilitate their will in politics but to defend them from oppression."[15]

What Americans wanted their governments to be like, the specific characteristics they expected them to exhibit, was implicit in these many working principles of their political system. Governments were to be representative (popular and responsive), responsible (competent and attentive to the general interests of political society), equal (without any distinctions of rights among citizens), open (subject to review by the citizenry), and concerned with the single end of the "public business" and "not the power, the emolument, or the dignity, of the persons employed" in government. A proper concern with the public interest, moreover, necessarily demanded that government also be mild (in the construction and application of the law), simple (with no more officials in either civil or military capacities than were absolutely necessary), and inexpensive.[16]

But a government exhibiting these characteristics and built upon the principles described above might have been turned to any number of purposes, and the primary question must surely be what goals the American political system as fashioned in the era of the Revolution was supposed to achieve, what values, or larger ends of government, the Revolutionary generation had in mind when it was constructing that system.[17] Most of these values were explicit in the major American state papers.

The primary purpose for which governments were instituted, said the Declaration of Independence, was to secure the inalienable rights of men, of which the Declaration listed three: life, liberty, and the pursuit of happiness. Security of each of these three rights was certainly among the most fundamental values of the Revolutionary generation. Security of life, the first in the trilogy, and liberty, the second, were ancient goals of British government and require little examination here. But the reader should be reminded that in the American Revolutionary context, liberty was beginning to mean something more than a bundle of inherited liberties and rights that were the prescriptive possessions of citizens. During the Revolution, liberty had in fact come to carry a double meaning: it referred to both the right of the citizen to participate in the political process and, as the American conception of

15. J. R. Pole, "Historians and the Problem of Early American Democracy," *American Historical Review*, 67 (1962), pp. 626–46; Richard Buel, Jr., "Democracy and the American Revolution: A Frame of Reference," *William and Mary Quarterly*, 3d. ser., 21 (1964), pp. 165–90.

16. See Williams, *History of Vermont*, pp. 342, 347–59, for a discussion of the attributes of American government.

17. The term "values" is used here and throughout this paper in its general vernacular sense of the larger goals, purposes, or objects which constitutions, institutions, laws, and other political instruments are designed to achieve. See Judith Blake and Kingsley Davis, "Norms, Values, and Sanctions," in Robert E. L. Faris, ed., *Handbook of Modern Sociology* (Chicago, 1964), pp. 456–57.

natural rights discussed above suggests, those inherent rights that pertained to all citizens qua citizens which could not in any way or to any extent legitimately be violated by government.

Implicit in these first two objects of political society were two further ones that were made explicit in the preamble to the federal Constitution—order, variously referred to in Revolutionary state papers as safety or domestic tranquility, and justice. If Americans believed in liberty as an end of political society, it was an ordered liberty justly distributed among all citizens by an impartial government. Liberty was not to be confused with licentiousness, which was liberty carried to such an excess as to produce its direct opposite. The "blessings of liberty," said the Virginia Declaration of Rights, could only "be preserved to any people . . . by a firm adherence to justice . . . [and] moderation." Justice had to be the guiding principle behind all government actions. The list of grievances in the Declaration of Independence bristles with indignation at the many alleged injustices of the British government toward the Americans during the previous 13 years.[18]

"Pursuit of happiness" was certainly the most novel and the most ambiguous of the inalienable rights or fundamental values of political society asserted by the Declaration of Independence. The happiness of individual citizens had not previously been considered a concern of government in traditional European thought and practice: unlike property, the third component of the traditional trilogy of rights as laid

down by John Locke in his *Second Treatise on Government*, happiness, as Cecelia M. Kenyon has pointed out, was not susceptible to objective definition and varied enormously from one individual to another. What Jefferson and his colleagues meant to imply by substituting it for property has been a perennial subject of scholarly debate. Almost certainly, however, they did not mean to assert, as an earlier generation of historians assumed, the supremacy of human rights over property rights. Most of the leaders of the Revolution would probably have agreed with Thomas Paine that liberty should always take precedence over "the defence of property." But in the Anglophone world of the late eighteenth century, few people ever suggested that there might be any conflict between the two. Like most contemporary British political writers, Americans regarded security of property as one of the most important components of liberty, and in the years after 1776 they also assumed a similar link between property and happiness: security of property was, in all quarters, said to be a basic ingredient of happiness.

Upon a close inspection, in fact, happiness, as it was conceived by the Revolutionary and later generations, turns out to have been composed of several such ingredients. Not just security of property, but peace and a situation in which citizens might become prosperous and achieve a state of what was referred to as "competency and independence" were said to be important components of happiness and legitimate goals of political society. Whereas systems of government, in the old world, supported themselves "by keeping up a sys-

18. Most of the major state papers of the Revolution are conveniently reprinted in Greene, ed. *Colonies to Nation*.

tem of war," Thomas Paine told Europeans in *The Rights of Man* in 1792, the system of government in the new world promoted "a system of peace, as the true means of enriching a nation" by enriching the inhabitants that composed it. Peace was thus a means of achieving a still more fundamental objective. True happiness, Paine told his European readers, had been discovered in America to be the product of a situation in which every citizen might "pursue his occupation, and enjoy the fruits of his labors, and the product of his property, in peace and safety, and with the least possible expense." Every citizen should have the opportunity to pursue his happiness in peace and safety, and the pursuit of happiness was the quest for property, prosperity, and independence from control by any other man. Government was thus expected both to facilitate the pursuit of happiness by the citizens who lived under it and to protect them in the enjoyment of whatever fruits their efforts had borne.[19]

If, as Charles Pinckney declared in the Federal Convention in 1787, the "great end of Republican Establishment" was the creation of a government "capable of making" its "citizens . . . happy" by fostering an environment in which they could, in peace and safety, pursue and enjoy prosperity and independence, the Declaration of Independence suggested through the assertion of the "self-evident" truth that "all men are created equal" that equality, in some form, might be a goal of American political society. Whether by this assertion Jefferson and his colleagues were talking about equality in the state of nature, a conventional proposition found in the political theory of Hobbes, Harrington, Locke, and most other natural rights philosophers, or equality in civil society, a potentially radical idea, is still an open question. Given the American tendency, noted by Cecelia M. Kenyon, "to blur the differences which Locke [and others] had either stated or implied between the state of nature and the state of civil society," it cannot safely be assumed, however, that they meant to confine their concern with equality to the state of nature. Certainly, as much of the rest of the Declaration makes explicit, the form of civil equality they had chiefly in mind was equality between Americans and Britons —formerly as subjects of the same empire and thenceforth as members of "separate and equal" political societies.[20]

But the concept of equality was widely recognized to have far broader implications, and during the Revolution a rough consensus emerged as to precisely what equality in civil society did—and did

19. See Cecelia M. Kenyon, "Republicanism and Radicalism in the American Revolution: An Old-Fashioned Interpretation," *William and Mary Quarterly*, 3d ser., 19 (1962), pp. 153–82; Paine, "Thoughts on Defensive War," 1775, and *Rights of Man, Part Second*, in Foner, ed., *Complete Writings*, vol. 1, pp. 363, 388, vol. 2, p. 54; Williams, *History of Vermont*, pp. 337, 359.

20. Pinckney, Speech, 25 June 1787, in Greene, ed., *Colonies to Nation*, pp. 532–33; Kenyon, "Republicanism and Radicalism"; David S. Lovejoy, " 'Rights Imply Equality': The Case Against Admiralty Jurisdiction in America, 1764–1776," *William and Mary Quarterly*, 3d ser., 16 (1959), pp. 459ff.; J. R. Pole, "Loyalists, Whigs and the Idea of Equality," in Esmond Wright, ed., *A Tug of Loyalties: Anglo-American Relations, 1765–85* (London, 1975), pp. 66–92; Robert Ginsberg, "Equality and Justice in the Declaration of Independence," *Journal of Social Philosophy*, 6 (1975), pp. 6–9.

not—imply. It emphatically did not mean that all men were equal by nature, or that all men should have "an *equality of wealth and possessions.*" What it does seem to have meant was equality both of opportunity and of rights—for citizens. Equality of opportunity connoted the equal right of every individual citizen to pursue his happiness, to achieve the best life possible within the limits of his ability, means, and circumstances; equality of rights meant that all citizens— and certainly not all men who were not all citizens—would, as Samuel Williams put it, have "an equal right to liberty, to property, and to safety; to justice, government, laws, religion and freedom." The American belief in equality of opportunity can be witnessed in the widespread insistence that there should "be no monopolies of any kind, that all trades shall be free, and every man free to follow any occupation by which he can procure an honest livelihood, and in any place, town, or city, throughout the nation," while the commitment to an equality of rights is best illustrated by their rejection of all suggestions for the recreation in America of the European system of privileged "orders and degrees." In America, said Thomas Paine, there would be "no other race of men . . . but the people."

How far the Revolutionary commitment to equality extended can be surmised from the treatment of the two issues of established religion and chattel slavery. The commitment extended far enough to permit most states to disestablish formerly legally established churches and to enunciate principles of religious toleration and equality of all denominations. Thenceforth, each American would be left at "full and perfect liberty, to follow the dictates of his own conscience, in all his transactions with his maker" and "all denominations" would "enjoy equal liberty, without any legal distinction or preeminence whatever." But the commitment was not strong enough to force them to abolish chattel slavery wherever it was economically viable or even to extend citizenship to those people who had successfully escaped slavery. Free people of African and Amerindian descent, like women and children, were not thought to have the discretion requisite for the responsible exercise of citizenship. For the time being, the American commitment to equality would be limited to citizens, that is, to white adult independent males.[21]

Another value that was widely manifest during the Revolution was the insistence that American political society encourage public-spiritedness or public virtue. Somehow, George Washington told Americans upon his leaving his command at the end of the war, they had to acquire "that pacific and friendly disposition . . . which will induce them to forget their local prejudices and policies; to make those mutual concessions, which are requisite to the general prosperity; and, in some instances, to sacrifice their

21. Williams, *History of Vermont*, pp. 330, 336–37; Paine, "Six Letters to Rhode Island," 1782, and *Rights of Man, Part Second*, in Foner, ed., *Complete Writings*, vol. 1, p. 281, vol. 2, p. 337; Greene, *"All Men Are Created Equal."* Discussions of American considerations of the meaning of equality may be found in Wood, *Creation of the American Republic*, pp. 70–75, and Willie Paul Adams, *Republikanische Verfassung und bürgerliche Freiheit: Die Verfassungen und politischen Ideen der amerikanischen Revolution* (Darmstadt und Newwied, 1973), pp. 162–90.

individual advantages to the interest of the [whole] community." Despite the insights of James Madison and others concerning the possibility of building a stable state on the clash of self-interest, most members of the Revolutionary generation still believed that public virtue—as principally defined by a concern for and willingness to subordinate individual and local interests in behalf of the common welfare—was necessary to the successful functioning of any republican political society.[22]

One final value that received strong emphasis during the Revolution was unity. Prior to the 1760s, the disunion of the colonies was notorious. For 150 years they had been, in most cases, more directly connected with Britain than with each other, and they had often quarreled over boundaries and even refused aid to one another against enemy attacks. During the long altercation with Britain prior to the Revolution, however, they learned the importance of maintaining a united front, and, from 1774 through the end of the war, American political leaders, acutely aware of the extreme fragility of the extensive union they were trying to establish because of the multiplicity of conflicting interests and traditions it contained, stressed the importance of a firm and steady union, lest division contribute to the failure of the Revolution by permitting the British to divide and rule. Following the war, these same leaders emphasized the necessity for a strong and perpetual union as the only device through which the new American states could achieve either their full potential as repub-

lican polities or their rightful place among the rest of the nations of the world. On "the UNION OF THE STATES," said Paine at the conclusion of the war, "our great national character depends. It is this which must give us importance abroad and security at home. It is through this only that we are, or can be known in the world." In the late 1780s, The Federalist declared hopefully, "the utility of the UNION" was "deeply engraved on the hearts of the people in every State." But it would take another century and a civil war before such a declaration could be applied with full confidence to the United States as a whole.[23]

The Revolutionary generation did not, of course, give each of these values equal emphasis, and a rough system of priorities can be established among them. They may be broken down into four categories according to their importance to the people of the Revolution. Life and liberty were given the highest priority and belong in the first and most important category. Only very slightly behind them, the pursuit of happiness falls into a second category. Of only somewhat less importance, public virtue, justice, order, and peace comprise a third category, while, as least valued by the Revolutionary generation, unity and equality can be assigned to a fourth and last category.

SOCIAL FOUNDATIONS OF REVOLUTIONARY VALUES

In the state of society which had taken place in America, the foundations of her freedom were laid.[24]

22. Pocock, *Machiavellian Moment*, pp. 527–45.

23. Paine, "The American Crisis," 1783, in Foner, ed., *Complete Writings*, vol. 1, p. 232; Earle, ed., *The Federalist*, no. 1, p. 7.

24. Williams, *History of Vermont*, p. 369.

Unity; public virtue; equality of opportunity and rights for citizens; public happiness as represented by peace and tranquility and the ability of all citizens to strive for prosperity and independence, secure in the knowledge that the property acquired as a result of their strivings would be secure; order; justice; liberty as both the sanctity of individual liberties and the right to participate in the political process; security of life—these were the principal values of the Revolutionary generation, the fundamental goals political society was expected to promote. They were values that were expressive of and appropriate to a special combination of social conditions that obtained in early America. "Writers upon American politics" during the Revolution, Samuel Williams accurately observed, learned their political "principles from the state of society in America," and the salient characteristics of that society, at least as it existed for those segments of the population who were of European extraction, were simplicity, openness, relative plenty, relative equality, and activity.[25]

Despite the efforts of the colonists to transplant to the new world as much of the world they had left behind as possible, circumstances of life in the colonies had never been congenial to their success. The easy availability of land and a high demand for labor to exploit it and the resources it contained produced a wide diffusion of property and a society that was more equal and less differentiated than any in the Western world at that time. Every one of the fundamental supports of the traditional society of the old world—the legally sanctioned distinctions of rank and

degree, the scarcity of land and other resources, the psychology of passive dependence among the vast majority of the population, and the feelings "of subordination that property, ancestry or dignity of station . . . naturally excited" in Britain and Europe—all of these were either missing altogether or extraordinarily weak in the new world. The result was that the traditional patterns of family and corporate authority that lay at the heart of the patronage societies of the old world never managed to achieve much vigor in the new. Thus, as Crèvecoeur remarked in his famous *Letters from an American Farmer*, the European coming to America was confronted with a society totally "different from what he had hitherto seen. It is not composed, as in Europe, of great lords who possess every thing, and a herd of people who have nothing. Here are no aristocratical families, no courts, no kings, no bishops, no ecclesiastical dominion, no invisible power giving to a few a very visible one." Instead, he found "a people of cultivators" with but few towns scattered among them, "a pleasing uniformity of decent . . . habitations," and a lexicon "short in words of dignity, and names of honour." As Tocqueville later remarked, free men in America were "seen on a greater equality . . . than in any other country of the world, or in any age of which history has preserved the remembrance."[26]

Along with an extraordinary laxity

25. Ibid., p. 372.

26. Jack P. Greene, ed., "William Knox's Explanation for the American Revolution," *William and Mary Quarterly*, 3d ser., 30 (1973), p. 300. Michel-Guillaumme Jean de Crèvecoeur, *Letters from an American Farmer* (1782), as reprinted in Willard Thorp, Merle Curti, and Carlos Baker, eds., *American Issues*, vol. 1: *The Social Record*

of political control on the part of Britain, the vast opportunities and profuse abundance of the American environment exercised a profound effect upon the development of values and personality. Whereas in the old world, many, probably most, of the colonists had been, in the words of Crèvecoeur, "as so many useless plants, wanting vegetative mould, and refreshing showers" and had been "mowed down by want, hunger, and war," in America as a result of transplantation they had, "like all other plants, . . . taken root and flourished." "From involuntary idleness, servile dependence, and useless labour," they "passed to toils of a very different nature, rewarded by ample subsistence." As Crèvecoeur penetratingly observed, this "great metamorphosis" had "a double effect": first, it extinguished "all . . . European prejudices," encouraged men to forget "that mechanism of subordination, that servility of disposition which poverty had taught" them in the old world, and nourished a jealous sense of personal independence, marked impatience with restraint, and a profound antagonism to any barriers to the pursuit of individual happiness; second, it greatly enlarged their expectations for themselves and their children and prompted them to form "schemes of future prosperity," to marry earlier and produce more children to fill up the vast open spaces, to endeavor to educate their children in preparation for the bright new world they had before them, and to develop "an ardour for labour" unknown in the old world. The ease "of acquiring subsistence, and es-

tate," said Samuel Williams, both produced "a spirit of universal activity, and enterprise" and encouraged men to preoccupy themselves with the pursuit of their own individual interests to the exclusion of all other concerns. Men were "careful and anxious to get as much as they can," said Crèvecoeur, "because what they get is their own." In America, then, "nature and society . . . combined" to raise free men from a state of passive dependence to one of active independence, to produce a "natural, easy, independent situation, and spirit," and to nourish a "spirit of freedom," industry, and economy, a thirst for property, knowledge, and improvement, and—because most free men were free from want and too preoccupied with their own pursuits to have time for dissipation and vice—habits of virtue. "Industry, good living, selfishness, litigiousness, country politics [that is, the politics of skepticism and dissent], the pride of freemen, religious indifference"—these were the personal characteristics that were "produced, preserved, and kept alive, by the state of society" in America.[27]

The political system established in the United States during the Revolution was thoroughly compatible with this "state of society" and the character and values of the men who composed it. Government in America was to be the servant of the individual citizens who created and lived under it; they were not to be the servants of the government. Independence from Britain and the establishment of a more perfect union through the federal Constitution were not ends in themselves but means through

(Philadelphia, 1941), pp. 104–06; Alexis de Tocqueville, *Democracy in America* (New York: Vintage Books, 1954), vol. 1, p. 55.

27. Crèvecoeur, *Letters*, pp. 104–06; Williams, *History of Vermont*, pp. 324–33, 372–76.

which the citizenry could help to make sure that neither external interference nor internal divisions would prevent political society from achieving its most fundamental purpose: the promotion of the liberty, prosperity, and happiness of individual citizens. The main object of concern to most Americans, Charles Thompson complained in 1786, was their own "individual happiness," and this strong predisposition among individuals to preoccupy themselves with their own private concerns at the expense of public obligations was productive of a powerful tension between the pursuit of happiness and public virtue, between the insistence upon personal independence and the need for public-spiritedness. This tension, strongly manifest during the War for Independence, was temporarily resolved in the early nineteenth century by giving precedence to the pursuit of happiness over public virtue, by defining the public good as the sum of private happinesses. Except in times of war and public distress, this resolution was workable so long as resources were plentiful and private interests did not interfere excessively with the welfare of the whole society.[28]

Government, Thomas Paine wrote with the American model firmly in mind, was thus *"nothing more than a national association acting on the principles of society."* That those principles were not universal, that the "form of government which was best suited to . . . one stage of society" might cease "to be so, in another," was widely recognized by the men of the Revolution. They also understood that unless a government could adapt to changes in the nature and circumstances of society it would "lose much of its respectability, and power; become unsuited to the state, and injurious to the people." Not just the dangers of corruption, but also the changing character of society itself made a "frequent recurrence to fundamental principles" desirable. What was "written upon paper respecting government," said Samuel Williams, was not sacred and not "otherwise good or bad, than as it is applicable to mankind, and may be beneficial, or disadvantageous to them."[29]

CONCLUSION

No policy would appear more puerile or contemptible to the people of America, than an attempt to bind posterity to our forms, or to confine them to our degrees of knowledge, and improvement: The aim is altogether the reverse, to make provision for the perpetual improvement and progression of the government itself.[30]

That the values of the Revolution and the system of government through which they were expressed would eventually have to be modified to meet changing social conditions was clear to most men of the Revolution. For the first century of the Republic, however, there were no *social* changes sufficiently profound to demand fundamental changes in either the political or the value systems that had been articulated during the Revolution. Such changes as occurred tended simply to remove or modify existing anomalies discovered to have been incompatible with the

28. Wood, *Creation of the American Republic*, p. 610.

29. Paine, *Rights of Man, Part Second*, in Foner, ed., *Complete Writings*, vol. 1, pp. 360–61; Williams, *History of Vermont*, pp. 345–46, 358.

30. Williams, *History of Vermont*, p. 346.

original values of the Republic. Thus, it is hardly surprising that the principle of equality should have been given ever greater emphasis in the most egalitarian society in the Western world. The substitution of faith for skepticism in the political capacities of the broad body of citizens, the expansion of the suffrage to include all adult white males, and the growing insistence upon equal access to public office for all citizens both undermined the last vestiges of traditional political mentality in the American political system and testified to the increasing importance of equality as a political value within American society. Similarly, the abolition of slavery and the adoption of the Thirteenth, Fourteenth, and Fifteenth Amendments to the Constitution committed that society to the eventual destruction of the racial limits within which liberty had hitherto been confined.

If American society underwent few basic alterations during the first century of the American Republic, it has changed profoundly during the second. It has moved from simplicity and (relative) homogeneity to complexity and (relative) heterogeneity: from a country of mostly independent rural proprietors of British and/or North European stock, it has become a nation largely composed of urban dwellers of extraordinary ethnic diversity who, to a very great extent, depend for their livelihood, either directly or indirectly, upon large-scale business, industrial, and political organizations. As concentrations of wealth have become greater, so has poverty and social inequality. Relative plenty, vast open spaces, and an optimistic sense of boundlessness and activity have been replaced by impending scar-

city and anxious fears of constriction and passivity. The new state of dependence in which most Americans have come to live over the past century has produced a widespread and a totally new value: economic security or freedom from want. Government has long since ceased to be inexpensive and—for some segments of society—even mild. The isolation and reliance upon a pacific disposition in foreign affairs has been replaced by involvement and reliance upon the threat of force.

Given the fundamental character of these and other changes, it is perhaps surprising that Revolutionary values have proved as viable as they have. Many restraints have had to be imposed upon the pursuit of happiness as Americans discovered early in the twentieth century that in a society with resource limitations private vices were not always public benefits, but there has been an enormous expansion of the ideals of liberty, justice, equality (racial and sexual), and privacy—a value that had received little emphasis in the Revolutionary era—to the point, some commentators have argued, that they threaten their companion values of order and stability. The adaptibility of these values strongly argues, in fact, that they are still laudable and appropriate goals for American society. But changing social and political (especially international) conditions may make it necessary to revivify and to reorder priorities among them, perhaps even to reconstruct the American science of politics so that it may be better able to secure them in a more complex world. Such an effort would be entirely commensurate with the expectations of the founders of the American Republic.

Report on Committee I

By PAUL BENDER AND MARTHA A. FIELD

ABSTRACT: It was suggested that a way of clarifying constitutional values might be to look closer at the framers of the Constitution—what were their views and background. They were elitists, from diverse backgrounds, representing a relatively broad spectrum for the time. Particular revolutionary values were discussed, beginning with equality. Discussion particularly centered on whether equality referred to "equality of opportunity" or "equality of result." It was expressed that equality of result was not in conflict with equality of opportunity but a necessary tool to achieve it. Generally, equality of opportunity was preferred to equality of result, except that there should be a certain amount of result equality in order to ensure real equality of opportunity, and it was agreed that quotas were sometimes necessary to correct past discrimination. Other values were discussed briefly, including domestic tranquility, exporting democracy, free speech, constitutional respect for individual autonomy and privacy, and fairness of treatment by government. Revolutionary values were summarized as falling into 3 categories: freedom of expression, equality, and protection from government arbitrariness.

Paul Bender is Professor of Law at the University of Pennsylvania. He previously served as Law Clerk to U.S. Appeals Court Judge Learned Hand and to Supreme Court Justice Felix Frankfurter and was Assistant to the U.S. Solicitor General and General Counsel to the Federal Commission on Obscenity and Pornography. He is co-author of the 4th edition of Political and Civil Rights in the U.S.

Martha A. Field is Associate Professor of Law at the University of Pennsylvania and was Law Clerk to Supreme Court Justice Abe Fortas and to U.S. Appeals Court Judge John Minor Wisdom. Her publications include "Problems of Proof in Conscientious Objector Cases" and "Abstention in Constitutional Pullman Cases: The Scope of the Truman Abstention Doctrine," University of Pennsylvania Law Review.

OUR task as reporters is to summarize 15 hours of discussion in 20 minutes. Since our task on the committee was to discuss the Maintenance of Revolutionary Values, it was suggested at the outset that we ought to determine what those revolutionary values were. It was pointed out that there were several distinct sources of revolutionary values and that they differed markedly in tone—that is, the Declaration of Independence should not be confused with the Constitution itself. The Declaration has much more ringing phrases concerning rights, particularly the right of equality on which the committee spent a great deal of time, but the Declaration is a series of impieties, as one member of the committee put it; it's a statement of revolt against the system.

The Constitution by contrast, is a sober, responsible document designed to work, to create a stable system that could last. Moreover, the Constitution of 1787 did not contain the Bill of Rights, which some suggested as a third possible constitutional source of revolutionary values. And finally the system underwent fundamental change three-quarters of a century later when the Civil War Amendments became part of the Constitution. So different constitutional values derive from each one of these developments, and we were not always totally precise about *which* "Constitution" we were discussing when we were talking about constitutional values.

THE FRAMERS OF THE CONSTITUTION

It was suggested that a way of clarifying what the constitutional values were might be to have a fuller picture of what kind of men the framers of the Constitution were—what were their views and what was their background. Knowing this might give us a better perspective as to which of the expressed values were really to be taken seriously and which were simply felicitous phrases, thrown in for their good sound and perhaps for the remote future.

The conclusion drawn in response to this seemed to be that the framers were elitists but perhaps were less so than ruling groups in other countries at the time. They came from diverse backgrounds and they represented a relatively broad spectrum, for the time at least. The background and views of the framers were not pursued at very great length in the committee, however, largely because committee members generally agreed that constitutional interpretation today was not governed by what the framers as individuals had meant.

There was much discussion of the degree to which we should regard the Constitution as a "living document," independent of the intention of its creators. One reason people thought the Constitution had to carry the quality of incorporating meanings other than the meanings that the framers had originally intended for it was that the problems facing us today differ in many respects from those of the past. For example, today we have limited resources, not an open frontier. Today a union of church and state may seem less threatening than a union of state and corporate power. But though all seemed to agree that judges were flexible to some extent concerning constitutional interpretation, and that the American system, in comparison with European systems, was one that favored and encouraged judicial activism, there was a difference of emphasis among the participants. Some stressed the freedom of the Judiciary to choose while others were careful to point out that there are considerable constraints upon the Judiciary. I suppose the most notable of these restraints is the Judiciary's inability to enforce its own judgments and hence its ultimate dependence upon popular acceptance. Moreover all agreed upon the importance of Congress joining with the courts in furthering constitutional development and implementation. It is only a recent phenomenon, it was pointed out, a development of the 1950s really, that the Court has assumed the role of leader in the area of individual liberties. Even then important decisions, such as the school desegregation decisions, did not win popular acceptance and were not effectively implemented until backed up by congressional legislation.

REVOLUTIONARY VALUES

Equality

At this point in the committee's deliberations, the discussion turned to substance and to particular revolutionary values. The first revolutionary value we talked about, and really the only one we ever covered in any great depth, was the value of equality. The irony of this being treated by the committee as the central value of the day was noted, for equality was clearly not a top priority value of the framers. Indeed, the central statement pertinent to equality in the Declaration referred simply to "all men," and even there *all* men were not included. Slaves clearly were excluded, even freed blacks may well have been excluded, and nonpropertied men were excluded, at least for some pur-

poses. Nevertheless, equality seems to have been a revolutionary value in the sense that there was a principle favoring equality among that group of persons who did count as first-class citizens. The development of equality since has come more easily because, as groups of persons are added to the list of first-class citizens, the revolutionary principle of equality seems to carry over to them.

Little attention was given in our discussions of equality to the state action limitation in the Equal Protection Clause of the Constitution. There seemed to be an underlying feeling among committee members that private discriminatory action really raised the same problems as action by the government. Part of the explanation for failing to distinguish between state and private action may have been that the committee discussions concerned congressional action enforcing the Fourteenth Amendment as much as it concerned judicial interpretation of the Constitution, and often no distinction was drawn between these two forms of equality decision-making.

The issue that we did discuss the most in relation to equality was whether it referred to "equality of opportunity" or to "equality of result"—that is, must we to enforce equality simply give every person the same chance to better him or herself, or must we instead see that people end up in the same position. The view was expressed that equality of result, which was also sometimes referred to as "equality of status" or "equality of position," was a necessary part of equality of opportunity in a society where economic goods are limited. It was not in conflict with equality of opportunity but was a necessary tool to achieve it. A child born into a poor, uneducated family, for example, cannot in reality have the same opportunity as a child born into a rich, educated family unless equality of result is afforded at least at some stage. On the other hand, committee members resisted the notion that total equality of result, which would include equality of economic status, was possible or was even desirable.

After much discussion of the seeming tension between the concepts, it seemed to be resolved that they fit together to demand, as a constitutional value, certain minimal standards of decency for every person. These minimal standards would cover, among other things, food, housing, health, education, and generally opportunities for human self-fulfillment. This may have been the single most important constitutional idea emerging from the three days of discussions. The constitutional basis for ensuring to all the minima for a decent life was not agreed upon, but all seemed to agree that this constitutional right was necessary in order to ensure adequate opportunity for every person. A minimal equalization of result or status would be provided in order to ensure some equality of opportunity. Diversity would be permitted above the minimum, but the minimum would be provided for all.

This compromise between equality of opportunity and equality of status seemed, as well, to help us out on another major concern that ran through our discussions of equality in the conference—that is, a concern that there might be a tension between equality and liberty. The overall position seemed to be that the tension between liberty and equality was less serious than it first appeared, because the constitutional value of affording all the minima of a decent life adequately protected both interests. That is, what liberty had to be given up to achieve this measure of equality was not a serious loss. It should be looked upon not as a loss of liberty, but as a redistribution of liberty, a sharing of it.

Despite the need to compromise to some extent, the committee generally did seem, however, to prefer equality of opportunity to result equality as the basic constitutional value which should be recognized. There were only two exceptions to this preference, or there were only two that had general acceptance among committee members. The first was the one already described: that there should be a certain amount of result equality in order to ensure some real equality of opportunity. The second situation arose in a discussion of quotas. Although the committee expressed its distaste for quotas, it seemed to accept them as an appropriate remedy to redress past discrimination, or past discrimination against a class at any rate. The apparent theory for requiring result equality here, was that only this remedy would render the situation as it would have been had the discrimination not occurred. Moreover, by thus remedying the situation, equality of opportunity would come more readily.

Although in principle, then, it seems that quotas were endorsed, though reluctantly, as a means of redressing past discrimination, some people seemed to think that the legitimacy of quotas depended upon the position to be filled. For police and firepersons, quotas were legitimate. A discussion of quotas in bar exams followed, however, and the participants (who were largely lawyers) seemed to be significantly more troubled. A discussion of quotas in academia ensued, where a real division took place within the committee. As may or may not surprise you, the academics generally took the position that in their discipline, only they could judge the capabilities of applicants, while members of the Judiciary, by contrast, took the position that they were not disabled from finding and redressing discrimination in academia as in other areas. Perhaps if police or firepersons had been represented on the committee, the same debate would have ensued there.

There were, then, limited situations in which equality of result was endorsed as an appropriate constitutional value. In those situations, there was a concern who should pay the price of equalization. The Supreme Court's decision which granted retroactive seniority rights to blacks discriminated against in past hiring, was the subject of much discussion. It was pointed out that those who paid the price of retroactive seniority were neither those responsible for the discrimination nor those best able to pay. Instead, the people who paid the price were those who were only one rung higher on the economic ladder. An analagous problem, I suppose, is the insulation of those in the suburbs from any proportionate economic burden for the problems of the cities. That was an inequity that was also frequently noted in the committee discussions, and it was noted that Congress has much more flexibility in solving both these problems and in devising the most appropriate remedy than the courts do. Courts must simply choose between the remedies available under the statute or other provision the court is enforcing in the particular case. There was sentiment that Congress should

look into making available a more appropriate remedy in the retroactive seniority situation.

Other values

Finally, the discussion turned to revolutionary values other than equality. As I said earlier, by the time we reached the discussion of other values, there really was little time left to discuss them in any detail. The format we followed was simply for members generally to contribute a list of those values that they considered the most important.

The value first discussed was domestic tranquility, and the main question raised in conjunction with that was whether it was a revolutionary value or whether it was, instead, an expected result of other values, a result that would follow from having a fair and open society. The question was raised, if it was a revolutionary value in itself, how was it to be enforced consistent with other values.

Discussion next turned to the possible revolutionary value of exporting democracy. While the framers may have thought of themselves as a model for the world, there was great concern that any statement on the committee's part that democracy should be so viewed was needlessly smug and perhaps somewhat inaccurate. At the same time, concern was expressed that, through our foreign policy, we have done much to undermine democracy, rather than to promote it, by supporting dictatorships over democratic movements. The suggestion was made that we should speak out against this practice as inconsistent with the revolutionary value of serving as a democratic model.

This issue was finally resolved by deciding that the issue was outside of our jurisdiction and was instead within the jurisdiction of committee IV.

Another value that was mentioned a great deal was the value of free speech, although there was little extended discussion of it.

Perhaps the most significant innovation proposed respecting free speech was that more effective platforms be provided for the ordinary citizen. The point was made that the chief platform available now, demonstration under the watchful eyes of an often hostile police force, is not a sufficient medium for the ordinary citizen to air demands.

Another value noted was a constitutional respect for individual autonomy and privacy. It was thought that this value should lead the government to let persons do as they would as long as they were not harming other individuals in any tangible way. Among other things, this would require an end to legislation punishing truly victimless crime. There seemed to be some consensus that this privacy right was indeed a revolutionary value. Unfortunately, there was not time for an extended discussion around it to develop.

Another frequently mentioned value which all agreed to be extremely important was fairness of treatment by government—a lack of arbitrariness on the part of the government in treating individuals.

Finally, one person summed up the constitutional values by saying that there was a triad of the most important values. The first is freedom of expression—political, religious, and aesthetic. The second is equality, in its total range. The third is protection from governmental arbitrariness. This triad may actually include all the revolutionary values. Indeed, he then reduced all of those values to one value, which was promotion of individual fulfillment. I think there was no dissent from that on the part of anyone on the committee.

The committee asked its rapporteurs to end on an optimistic note, although it recognizes that optimism is not totally justified. Optimism, in the committee's view, flows from the fact that, although the committee does not wish to give the impression that the fight is over, that justice reigns throughout the land, that we may lay down our oars, we do wish to mention and to pay tribute to the enormous accomplishments that have been made. We wish to do this, if for no other reason, because we wish to encourage people to attempt further accomplishments. It is important to note that past efforts have succeeded and there is no reason to think that future efforts will not succeed as well.

We do note, however, that most of these accomplishments have come relatively recently, since 1950. There was some comfort taken by the committee in the fact that it was not just a racial question any more, that race and sex were now marching side by side, and that that significantly changed the atmosphere for the better. It was also said that it is a very good sign of where we are that there is increased voluntary compliance with constitutional values, that the mark of a society which has adherence to values is that they adhere to those values voluntarily, and that you could note a very distinct improvement in the society in that area.

It was also noted that one mark of our improvement is that we are capable of getting rid of our leaders when they fail us, as happened fairly recently. On the other hand, the view was expressed that Watergate indicated weakness, rather than strength, since mismanagement and accident seemed to play as much of a role as a spirit of vigilance in the ultimate outcome.

The shadows across the note of optimism with which we leave you are as follows:

A feeling of growing apartheid in the country, perhaps growing primarily out of the school segregation situation and the fact that efforts to end segregation seemed to be driving people into the suburbs, while the Supreme Court refuses to break the line between the inner city and the suburbs for these purposes. This was an alarming thing to many people on the committee.

The increased amount of crime in the country, especially in the inner cities, where segregation was most prevalent, was also noted with alarm. And also noted was the Supreme Court's apparent recent tendency to stay out of these areas, to reduce its jurisdiction, not to get involved with some of the most serious current problems.

So, although we do end on a note of optimism, it is optimism tinged with some reservations and feelings that at least in the coming months or years the optimism may not prove founded, but we all hope that it will.

*   *   *

QUESTIONS AND ANSWERS

Q: I'm Professor Harold Blostein, the chairman of the Political Science Department of Kearney State College in Kearney, Nebraska. You did not grapple with what appears to be a negative state assumption in the Constitution. Was this viewed as a constitutional value? The system of separation of powers and checks and balances, as reflected in our Constitution, comes close to an assumption that the least government is the best government, and that, perhaps, some measure of government by paralysis is more desirable than not.

A (Greene): It depends on what one means by the term "values." The principle of separation of power is what I would call a working principle of government, and not one of the objectives of government.

It is an objective of government to limit power, but for other ends— for rather larger objectives, so that

individuals will not be hampered by government in the pursuit of happiness or liberty. The notion of separation of powers rests upon a belief in the imperfectability of man, and the limitation of government. The separation of powers is, of course, the principal device in the Constitution for limiting the powers of the federal government, just as the Bill of Rights and the Declaration of Rights in the states, when subsequently added to the Constitution, were principal means for limiting the power.

A (Field): I just want to make a small addition to the concern expressed. While I think the separation of powers is relevant to the question of whether we have too much government, it seems to me that the separation of powers relates primarily to distribution of government power among the branches, and does not speak to the question of how much power there is. It seems to me that the most appropriate place for that to be taken up is in a discussion of the constitutional right of privacy. I think it is a revolutionary value that there should not be too much government and that individuals keep a private sphere of decisions.

Q: I'm Kenneth Abel from Huntsville, Alabama. I wonder whether there was any evidence of the type of wisdom exhibited by the founding fathers applying the rule of common sense to the discussion of revolutionary values? It would appear to me that we did have a free discussion without much recourse to what is practical. What is a possible dream and what is an impossible dream?

It seems that some are urging that we have a no-merit guarantee of the free offerings of the economy at the expense of those who are productive participants.

A (Harris): I think that the question is, did we deal with the practicality of the commitment to such values as we identified as revolutionary values? I would think that, if there was any major disappointment among us, it was that every judgment was tempered by a concern for very present and immediate reality. Now, what was for me the most surprising and the least controversial agreement among us as a committee was that it is an obligation of the society of which we are a part, the society of the United States, to guarantee a floor of decent life for every member of that society. That was almost thrown out and forgotten, and what struck the chairman was that what, for me, seemed

to be almost a newly revolutionary value of society's obligation to its members was accepted by the committee I members.

What we were unable to deal with, for reasons you suggest, was the definition of the word "decent," and it is here of course that the debate of the next 100 years apparently is going to take place. While there are those who would debate the obligation, there was an assumption of the validity of this value of a baseline equality of opportunity for all members of the society.

I would say we thought we were being eminently practical, and it took us to positions that some of us, perhaps, prior to the discussion, would not have expected. The acceptance of the validity of something denominated as quotas was the direct result of the understanding that there cannot be equality of opportunity if some people are excluded from participation in the context in which opportunity is relevant, and therefore it may be necessary to require police departments and, despite unanimous disagreement of my academic colleagues, university faculties in order for persons to begin to have the opportunity of competition on the basis of merit that we have in mind.

Q: I am Dan Alexander from the University of Tennessee of Nashville. I seem to detect from the committee's report that you sense there is a disease in society now, in the sense that there is no equality of opportunity because there is no equality of result as the system is now. I want to take issue with that to the extent that I think that a government that is large enough to give you everything that you need is also large enough to take everything that you have. If the government could grow to the extent that it could ensure for us equality of result by ensuring equality of opportunity, then, I think, the cure is much worse than the disease. When can we expect this government to lay dormant that authority that it used to cure that disease? It frightens me to have a government large enough to accomplish these things.

A (Harris): The tension between particular goals espoused in the revolutionary values was expressed throughout the meeting, and there was one expressed reservation and concern almost identical to the one you have expressed. Perhaps the conclusion was best expressed by Professor Field, that one of the values should be the protection of as much autonomy in the individual as is possible; and one of the ways, to achieve this, of course, is the limitation of the arbitrary and unnecessary intrusion of government.

Q: I'm John W. Hopkirk, professor of political science at Widener College in Chester, Pennsylvania.

In Watergate, there was a very sweeping claim of executive privilege presented by the lawyers for Richard Nixon. I wonder if one can say that separation of powers wasn't really present in the minds of the revolutionary era.

A (Greene): I didn't say that at all. I tried to make an intellectual distinction between what I call "working principles" and what I call "revolutionary values."

By working principles I meant those devices and/or theories which are customary ways of doing things and, in fact, would accomplish the values. The limitation of power was the preeminent concern in the Declaration of Independence, and it is obviously a continuing concern. That is also what motivated the Constitutional Convention; one way in which the Second Continental Congress, which adopted the Declaration of Independence, and the Constitutional Convention in Philadelphia in 1787, were in fundamental agreement was that power was the primary threat to liberty and that power had to be curtailed. What they were talking about was not the power of private individuals, not corporate power which would concern us now, but, fundamentally, public powers incorporated into public institutions which might and would, if they had the opportunity, behave extra-constitutionally and engage in arbitrary exercises.

The meaning of power was so corrosive because human beings were weak and couldn't resist it if they had the opportunity to take it. You couldn't rely on men. You had to have a government of laws and constitutions which restricted those men; and they were not talking about just George III, they were also talking about themselves. They wanted themselves restricted as much as somebody else. The separation of powers was a device for achieving those larger aims of political society: liberty, life, the pursuit of happiness, justice, and later, equality.

Q: I'm John W. Davis, and I am the director of the Herbert Lehman

Education Fund of New York. I want to ask a question about three words, "We the people." Who were they and for whom did they speak?

A (Harris): First of all, I'm not sure that we have made it as clear as we might or that there was agreement among us as discussants that we were talking about developing documents as well as concepts and values. "We the people," as Miss Field's report indicated, certainly did not include you and me, Dr. Davis, because we are black, did not include Professor Field and me because we are females, and did not include unpropertied males who were white; but the developmental process, particularly the Civil War Amendments, but also the almost contemporaneous adoption of the Bill of Rights, indicated a kind of concern for the possibility that even those persons would be included in protections. Due process even under the Fifth Amendment might well be construed to go beyond.

We were in agreement that, whatever "We the people" meant at the time, developing concepts of equality moved it from a lower place in the hierarchy of governing values to an upper if not primary place in the hierarchy of values at the present time because of the development of both our concept of the value and the documents on which we base the responsibility of government, and to some degree society, with respect to who "We the people" included.

Q: I'm Jeffrey Kimble, associate professor of history, Miami University, Oxford, Ohio. I was personally pleased by the generally democratic tone of the committee's words, but it seems to me that there was one serious omission in the analysis of inequality, and that was the relationship between inequality and the distribution of wealth and power in the way that decisions are made—in other words, the relationship between inequality and the socioeconomic system, a system which treats people as commodities and makes private decisions for profit which affect people's lives.

A (Harris): Exactly the point that you made was noted early in our discussion. And, indeed, the context in which the discussion of the inequality of the burdens placed upon those one rung above those being protected was made in a discussion which pointed out that there was inadequate attention to questions of economic privilege and assumptions that one did not touch anybody but the worker who had taken the job that should have gone to the black protected by the recent decision.

I cannot say what would have happened had we probed that more deeply. I suspect that, regardless of the relationship of the Sun Oil Company to this conference as its patron, the result would have been identical. The assumption that equality of opportunity was the basic equality that still motivates us, was accompanied in some instances by the assertion that this did not deny the opportunity for some people to have substantially more in the way of power of economic resources, that, indeed, it is impossible to conceive of any society, because none has existed, in which the inequality of position and of ability to manipulate the resources of the society has not been present, and that the pre-eminent value, even if we had approached it as you did, probably would have come out as equality of opportunity.

———————

Q: My name is Ted Dahl. I am an economist with the Lincoln First Bank in Rochester. In the earlier discussion, the pursuit of happiness and private property were considered not to be at odds with each other, yet the conclusion that seemed to be reached by the committee was that the creation of wealth and the defense of private property were not as important as the redistribution of the wealth that was in existence, and I wonder if you are not preaching courses that would be counterproductive to actually aiding the people that you want to.

A (Field): When we talked about a mandatory minimal income that would be available for all people as the only way of assuring equality of opportunity, the question came up of what degree are you going to redistribute. That is, is there going to be overall equality? Members of the committee would have sharply differed with each other on questions of degree, but what was said is simply that we haven't started redistributing at all. We don't assure minimal standards of decency at all. We don't have to decide how far we have to go in order to do that; we just have to start, and the problems will be solved later. I think that's responsive to your concern and also several other concerns that have been raised by other persons.

A (Harris): There were two brief flurries of discussion around that issue. There was, however, an insertion by one of our members that all assumptions of equality in the past had been based upon assumption of growth in the economy, and not really a redistribution but a share in a larger pie.

Effectiveness of Governmental Operations

By HENRY J. ABRAHAM

ABSTRACT: The Judiciary has always received a higher rating of esteem and regard than the other two branches of government. However, it is not free from pragmatic or philosophical operational problems. Two of these are finding a line between judging and legislating and court reform. Suggestions for reform fall into three categories: (1) those dealing with the institution and modus operandus of the courts, (2) those concerned with court staff, and (3) those dealing with the legal framework mandated by lawmakers and the Constitution. A matter of infinitely more pressing concern is how to confine judges to judging rather than legislating. The Supreme Court must possess the power to interpret legislation, but a line must be drawn between the imposition of judicial judgment and the exercise of judicial will. Our federal system underlies both the disappointments and the accomplishments of the American government. The apparent trend toward centralization of federal power is both an axiom of modern American federalism and irreversible. However, since excessive rigidity of centralization is a weakness, regional, state, and local governments should retain a substantial sphere of independence.

Henry J. Abraham is the Henry L. and Grace Doherty Professor of Government and Foreign Affairs at the University of Virginia. He previously served as Professor of Political Science at the University of Pennsylvania, Visiting Professor in Government at Columbia, and Fulbright Lecturer in American Political Science and Constitutional Law. In 1960–61 and 1970–71 he was an American Philosophical Society Fellow. His publications include: The Judicial Process: An Introductory Analysis of the Courts of the U.S., England, and France, Freedom and the Court: Civil Rights and Liberties in the United States, *and* The Judiciary.

Part of this issues paper has been dropped since the material is covered in other papers.

IF IT has perhaps not been universally efficient, there is but little doubt that our Article 3 branch, the Judiciary, has been the most effective operationally. In any event, despite the winds of fortune that have buffeted it, and despite its posture as an easy target for public criticism and blame, it has—with but rare exceptions—always received a higher rating of esteem and regard from the body politic than either of the other two branches. Concededly, the percentage of voiced approbation is rarely, if ever, much higher than one-third of those polled among the electorate, yet that figure has been consistently higher than that accorded the Legislative or the Executive branch. This is hardly an astonishing fact of governmental life, for, in the main, it has been the judges who have kept the American Constitution alive—by, in Anthony Lewis's words, "giving its eighteenth-century phrases the flexibility to meet new conditions while at the same time applying its broad language of freedom to meet new dangers. They have articulated our ideals."[1] Whether reliance on that judicial power is wise or even sanctioned is a different, and always alive, source of controversial concern—of which more below. But whatever one's conclusions on that question, our jurists have long demonstrated that they are eminently capable of keeping the constitutional "spirit alive by their judgments and their words."[2] Rare is the visitor to the Supreme Court of the United States, whether he came to praise or scold, who does not stand in awe of its institution and its members—who does not willingly conclude that it is in-deed, in Lewis's prose, "entitled, as an institution, to our faith."[3]

THE JUDICIARY

The Judicial branch is not, of course, free from either pragmatic or philosophical operational problems. Two among these most vital to enhanced effectiveness are, first, that eternal question of finding a viable line between "judging" and "legislating" (or, as it might be put more descriptively, "judicial self-restraint" and "judicial activism") and, second, the ever-alive issue of what may be broadly subsumed under the concept of "court reform." Let us examine the latter first.

Any judicial system or structure in democratic society with a constitutional base must essentially meet two basic requirements of public policy: namely, to protect society and to be fair to those accused of infractions of its legal structure. These two are naturally not incompatible, but they do demand the kind of line-drawing and/or balancing of which philosophical as well as pragmatic concepts of government and politics are made.

Whatever one's views of the particular success or failure of specific judicial systems to draw these vital and so often vexatious lines may be, in the eyes of knowledgeable students of courts and judges there is always room for improvement. Suggestions abound. In general, they fall into three broad, interrelated categories: (1) those dealing with the institution and modus operandis of the courts themselves; (2) those concerned with the human beings who staff the courts; and (3) those dealing with the legal framework mandated by a society's lawmakers

1. Anthony Lewis, "A Day in Court," *The New York Times*, 16 October 1975, p. 39c.
2. Ibid.
3. Ibid.

and its constitutional constellation. All three categories presumably are dedicated to the fundamental goals of any free, democratic, judicial system, which are those of:

1. peaceful resolution of "private" civil conflicts;
2. enforcement of criminal laws;
3. safety valve for the amelioration of "repressive laws";
4. efficient operation;
5. restraint of governmental intrusions—both in the realm of individual rights and that of the separation of powers.

Couching the following analysis chiefly in the form of questions that are sometimes, but not always, followed by suggested answers, we turn first to the institution of the Judiciary and its modus operandus under our particular branch of the common law system.

At the trial and pre-trial level, these questions arise: (1) How effective is the adversary process, the "sporting game," in the quest for truth and justice? The late Judge Jerome Frank, in his still indispensable critique of that process and its substructure, *Courts on Trial*,[4] could think of none less effective for and in that quest! Between the "lawyer game" and the "jury game" in a system "that treats a law-suit as a battle of wits and wiles,"[5] he could thus visualize none less likely to bring out the truth than our adversary process. Indeed, it is a system geared crucially to the discovery of facts in a hostile, an adversary, setting in a court of law, in which a body of jurors—who are usually, at best, but marginally

qualified to judge the issues and are increasingly chosen from panels of noncontroversial individuals whose regular activities society apparently does not value, with ample time on their hands and opinions, let alone training, on preferably nothing— pronounces a verdict more often than not on the basis of its views as to which of the two sides had the better (more colorful?, more attractive?, more vocal?, more charismatic?) lawyer. It may well be doubted that juries are in fact capable accurately to answer the general question of guilt or lack thereof; at best, they can probably respond to specific questions.[6] This is not the place to discuss the ethics of lawyers in an adversary system, but as an increasing body of literature[7] has begun to reemphasize, the average attorney's quest is more often than not victory for his client (and thus concurrently for himself) and not for principled justice. The Canons of Ethics, the Code of Professional Responsibility, seem to offer no serious competition, no particular barrier, in the pursuit of that victory, which is commonly attained—if not without hard work and careful planning—as a direct result of what Judge Frank pungently termed the successful invocation of the "Fight" v. "Truth" theory cum game.[8] It is one, as he concluded acidly—in words written 27 years ago and still decidedly apposite—in which

the lawyer aims at victory, at winning in the fight, not at aiding the court to

6. For a less than complimentary, extensive, analysis of juries, see Henry J. Abraham, *The Judicial Process*, 3rd ed. (New York: Oxford University Press, 1975), pp. 110–33.

7. For example, Monroe H. Freedman (Dean of the Hofstra Law School), *Lawyers' Ethics in an Adversary System* (Indianapolis and New York: The Bobbs-Merrill Co., 1975).

8. Frank, *Courts on Trial*, ch. 6—a brilliant, devastating analysis.

4. Jerome Frank, *Courts on Trial: Myth and Reality in American Justice* (New York: Atheneum, 1963).

5. Ibid., p. 85.

discover the facts. He does not want the trial court to reach a sound educated guess, if it is likely to be contrary to his client's interests. Our present trial method is thus the equivalent of throwing pepper in the eyes of a surgeon when he is performing an operation.[9]

It may thus well be asked whether the Continental inquisitory system (the French enquête, featuring the institution of the juge/d'instruction) might not be considered as a viable alternative to our accusatory one? How long can our society continue to practice a criminal trial system in which, in the words of attorney Jerry Paul, who successfully defended Joan Little in August 1975 in a widely-publicized and dramatized murder case, "the question of innocence or guilt is almost irrelevant."[10] In an interview following the trial, Mr. Paul said he "bought" Miss Little's acquittal and that it cost $325,000. "I can win any case in this country," he cockily-proudly contended, "given enough money. I'm going to tell you the truth. You must destroy the charade, the illusion of justice." Mr. Paul continued that, by admitting that the acquittal was "bought"—the money was there to hire the best counsel, to mount an extensive jury selection process, to hire investigators, to fly in expert witnesses, to spend thousands on "counseling" for Miss Little to prepare her for her testimony—he was pointing up the defects of the system.[11] The presiding jurist in the case, North Carolina Superior Court Judge Hamilton Hobgood, observed that he thought Mr. Paul was quite wrong—that the American legal system, not money, should be credited with the acquittal of the accused.[12]

Yet the haunting doubts are not readily stilled. There is a crying need for dramatic change in the adversary system and its protagonists; and as Frank put it, "a considerable diminution of the martial spirit in litigation."[13] Neither minor nor major changes, however, can be effected absent active cooperation, and some genuine largesse, by and of the legal profession—whose members, after all, comprise fully two-thirds of the nation's legislators.

What of the efficacy and adequacy of the sundry tribunals that presently exist at the trial and the appellate levels of the Judiciary? Actually, our federal system of constitutional, special, and legislative tribunals is well-organized, relatively simple in design, and would conceivably be quite capable of handling the enormous load of litigation—were it not for the increasingly overly-easy access (especially to the appellate level); excessive jurisdiction (on both trial and appellate levels); chronic understaffing of lower and intermediate courts; and the almost axiomatic resultant delays (notwithstanding some noble statutory efforts to speed trials—noble in theory, irresponsible in design, for, as the chief justice of the United States has consistently complained publicly, the laudable statutory demand for speeding up of trials was not accompanied by the obviously vital statutory authorization for the concomitantly essential increases in court staffing). There is no dearth of advocacy[14] for reform to alleviate the fundamental problems

9. Ibid., p. 85.

10. "Justice," The New York Times, 26 October 1975, sec 4, p. 16e.

11. Ibid.

12. Ibid.

13. Frank, Courts on Trial, p. 102.

14. For example, the 16-member "Commission on Revision of the Federal Court Appellate System" (known as the "Hruska Commission") and the Report of the Study Group on the Case Load of the Supreme Court (known as the "Freund Report"). See also the Chief Justice's "Annual Report

alluded to, yet changes in the judicial structure have chronically been even more difficult to sell to the public and its representatives in legislative halls than have other measures and matters.

De minimis, the following changes ought to be effected in the federal realm: (a) Three-judge courts should be abolished forthwith; their work has tripled in the past 10 years, their jurisdiction and relative promise of Supreme Court review being tailor-made for stimulated as well as genuine litigation. Their functions should be submerged in the general orbit of the district courts. (b) Congress might be well-advised to consider some tightening of the rather generous appellate as well as trial pathways for habeas corpus and in forma pauperis cases, which presently constitute half of the Supreme Court's work load. Legislative tampering with the former is admittedly fraught with danger, yet it should be possible to continue to provide access for bona fide habeas corpus claims without entertaining "court games" (Justice Douglas's words!) and uncalled for duplicate filings and transfers. The latter have gotten out of hand and need jurisdictional as well as statutory remedial consideration. (c) There is simply no excuse for the continuation of the federal jurisdictional luxury of diversity of citizenship suits. These suits, which, of course, ought to be handled at the level of the states—especially since the federal courts have since 1938 been obliged to apply state law[15]—now constitute the single most numerous category of cases filed as civil suits. Chiefly

comprising insurance claims, automobile accident, and personal injury suits, they should preferably be removed totally from judicial tribunals and placed at the bar of administrative, ideally arbitration, panels. Some states, such as Pennsylvania for its first-class cities,[16] have mandated resort to arbitration panels, requiring resort to such panels in all civil cases up to $3,000 in value, and permitting them up to $10,000. Found administratively at the county court level, Pennsylvania's arbitration panels handle an average of 10,000 cases annually—inexpensively, speedily, effectively.[17] (d) Notwithstanding Justice Douglas's often-voiced denial—and indeed his insistence, even during the months immediately prior to his health-dictated retirement from the Court after more than 36 and a half years of service thereon, that the highest tribunal was not overworked but underworked!—and, as the chief justice once again pleaded in his Year End Report 1975,[18] help is needed. The Supreme Court's case load is staggering. Whether the much-debated, widely suggested and almost equally widely condemned, proposal of the creation of a new appellate tribunal between the courts of appeals and the Supreme Court, to be known as "The National Court of Appeals," is the appropriate answer to the very real problem, is contentious. In any event, the current debate in the legal profession and in Congress is healthy.[19] My own preference would be for a reduction of jurisdiction

16. See the description in Abraham, *The Judicial Process*, p. 142, fn. 10.
17. Ibid.
18. See *The New York Times*, 4 January 1976, p. 1.
19. See the special issue of *Judicature*, "Bail Out the Supreme Court?," vol. 59, no. 4 (November 1975).

on the State of the Judiciary" (A.B.A. Mid-Winter Meeting, 23 February 1975).
15. *Erie* v. *Thompson*, 304 U.S. 64 (1938).

along the lines of some of the above-suggested remedial steps rather than for the establishment of the new tribunal.[20] (e) To increase judicial effectiveness in terms of time utilization at the level of the Supreme Court, it has been suggested that it abandon oral argument; yet the latter's drama, its visibility, and its undoubted educational facets, both internal and external, are born of the kind of commendable values that underlie the democratic process under law. (f) Periodically, Congress—as it, fortunately unsuccessfully, endeavored in the draconian Jenner-Butler Bill in the mid and late 1950s—toys with the notion of depriving the federal courts of significant areas of jurisdiction in favor of state courts. While there may well be considerable merit in some modest proposals along these lines of what is a periodic love affair with the federal system—some have been suggested immediately above —there must be no tampering with fundamental constitutional appellate prerogatives (as distinguished from trivial and frivolous ones). The presence of a multiple judicial structure of 51 separate systems is a fascinating dichotomy of blessing and bane. As long as our federal system endures—and Professor Tugwell makes an intriguing case for what to all intents and purposes is its abandonment—both the problem and promise inherent in such a structure in terms of the judicial process represents a genuine opportunity for the enhancement of governmental efficiency. But the baby must not be thrown out with the bathwater.

Second, what of the status of court personnel, court staffing? There is neither space nor need in this forum to embark upon a detailed examination of the "who," "why," and "how" of court staffing—it has very recently been done in two extensive book-length studies for the federal Judiciary,[21] but a few basic observations[22] antecedent to analyzing the profile of that personnel and possible reforms is warranted.

The question of the principles that govern the selection of the men and women who sit on our judicial tribunals is both a moral and a political one of the greatest magnitude. Their tasks and functions are awe-inspiring indeed, but it is as human beings and as participants in the political as well as the legal and governmental process that jurists render their decisions. Their position in the government framework must assure them of independence, dignity, and security of tenure. The two basic methods of selecting jurists under our system are still appointment and election, although today a system combining the two is becoming increasingly prevalent. Yet the process of selection is assuredly more complex than that suggested by W. Curtis Bok's fictional Judge Ulan in *Backbone of the Herring*, who quips: "A judge is a member of the bar who once knew a Governor."[23]

Most of the roughly 12,000 judges on our state and local courts continue to be elected, although the gubernatorial appointive method,

20. Some colleagues have suggested that, conceivably, my position is influenced by the vista of having to revise four books were the proposed court to be established!

21. Harold W. Chase, *Federal Judges: The Appointing Process* (Minneapolis: University of Minnesota Press, 1972), for lower federal judges, and Abraham, *Justices and Presidents: A Political History of Appointments to the Supreme Court* (New York: Oxford University Press, 1974, and Penguin Press, Inc., 1975), for Supreme Court judges.

22. They are taken largely from chs. 2 and 3 of Abraham, *Justices and Presidents*.

23. W. Curtis Bok, *Backbone of the Herring* (New York: Alfred A. Knopf, 1941), p. 3.

often with legislative or bar advice and consent, is being resorted to increasingly—generally a development to be welcomed. On the other hand, the number of states adopting versions of the California and Missouri plans, which combine the elective and appointive methods,[24] is growing rapidly.

The founders of the Constitution struggled at length over the selection of the federal Judiciary. Under the Randolph Plan of Union, selection as well as confirmation by the "National legislature" was proposed; an inevitable counter-suggestion would have vested that power in the chief magistrate alone. Representatives from the small states were unhappy with the notion of exclusive executive appointment, fearing favoritism toward the large states, which they suspected might "gratify" the president to a greater extent. Madison recommended appointment by the Senate alone, but after second thoughts disassociated himself from this proposal. Ultimately, Ben Franklin's efforts and a spirit of compromise between large and small interests resulted in the adoption of a system modeled after one then being used in Massachusetts. It is still used today, and on balance it has proved to be workable professionally as well as politically.

It is not universally understood that no legal or constitutional requirements for a federal judgeship exist—an especially surprising fact since each state in the Union has at least some statutory and/or constitutional requirements for at least some judicial posts. There does exist, however, an unwritten prerequisite for a post on the federal bench—a bachelor of laws degree.

No one can become a member of the Supreme Court without that degree. Although it is not necessarily mandatory either to have practiced law or to have been a member of the bar, the American Bar Association Standing Committee on Federal Judiciary not only demands trial experience of a candidate for the Judiciary, it also requires some 15 years of legal practice to qualify the candidate for a passing rating. As a matter of historical record, no non-lawyer has ever served on the Supreme Court of the United States. Yet since most of the important questions to come before the Supreme Court, for one, today raise social and political issues, one might well ask why does an appellate jurist, especially at the highest level, have to be a lawyer? In one of his last public statements prior to his retirement and death, Justice Black formally urged the appointment of "at least one non-lawyer" on the Court. The chances of affirmative action on that proposal are nil—but it raises intriguing questions about the role of the Court, one so frequently criticized as "legislating" rather than "judging."

In a learned essay calling for selection of Supreme Court justices "wholly on the basis of functional fitness," Justice Frankfurter keenly argued that judicial experience, political affiliation, and geographic, racial, and religious considerations —characteristics that have loomed large, indeed, in presidential selections to date—should *not* play a significant role in the selection of jurists.[25] He contended that, instead,

24. See Abraham, *Justices and Presidents*, pp. 13–15.

25. His one-time colleague on the Court, Sherman Minton, in a letter to "FF," fully seconded the latter's view: "A copy of your letter should be sent to every member of Congress. Your statement explodes entirely the myth of prior judicial experience. I am

Supreme Court jurists should be at once *philosopher, historian, and prophet*—to which Justice Brennan, in a conversation with this writer, proposed to add "and a person of inordinate patience." Justice Frank-furter viewed their task as requiring "poetic sensibilities" and "the gift of imagination," as exhorting them to

pierce the curtain of the future . . . give shape and visage to mysteries still in the womb of time. . . . [the job thus demands] antennae registering feeling and judgment beyond logical, let alone quantitative proof. . . . One is entitled to say without qualification that the correlation between prior judicial ex-perience and fitness for the Supreme Court is zero. The significance of the greatest among the Justices who had such experience, Holmes and Cardozo, derived not from that judicial experience but from the fact that they were Holmes and Cardozo. They were thinkers, and more particularly, legal philosophers.[26]

Felix Frankfurter was quite right on the "functional fitness" issue. Objective merit, competence—and, why not, qualities of "philosopher, historian, and prophet"—should be the sole criteria. Their presence need by no means vitiate considera-tions of political and ideological compatibility—there is nothing whatsoever wrong with so-called "court packing," provided the se-lectee is indeed meritorious and competent—but "personal friend-ship," unless quite secondary to the basic qualifications, and "equitable" considerations of geography, race, sex, and religion should have no

place in choice motivations. Even, indeed infinitely, more so than judi-cial experience, they are rank non-sequiturs qualitatively and should be shunned resolutely. The Judicial branch was neither intended to be, nor should it be, a representative body! For representation, let the body politic turn to the Legislative and Executive branches. The Judi-ciary's role is a dramatically different one—and ought to remain so.

If the nominating authorities on both the federal and state levels will overridingly base their actions on considerations of merit and com-petence, there seems little need for any drastic overhaul in present selection methodologies—provided they are either of the appointive or combination appointive/elective (Missouri-California model) variety. The practice of election, however—still so widely present in most of the 50 states—be it partisan or what is often euphemistically called "non-partisan," should be shunned re-solutely. Neither pragmatically nor philosophically is election compati-ble with judicial service. With re-gard to the appointive mode, pro-posals abound for alterations in present practices, above and beyond the adoption of Missouri-California plans. Although, as suggested, there appears to be no pressing need for changes in the typical appointive practice, assuming the presence of the appointees' qualifications, a good many thoughtful observers, troubled by the continuing practices of senatorial courtesy, executive political cronyism, and the political role of the Department of Justice, have advanced the possibility of moving toward some type of judicial selection commissions. Variously conceived, a typical one on the fed-eral level would be composed of in-dividuals designated by the presi-

---

a living example that judicial experience doesn't make one prescient." (Frankfurter's Papers, Library of Congress, S.M. to F.F., 18 April 1957. Minton had served eight years on lower courts.)

26. "The Supreme Court in the Mirror of Justices," *University of Pennsylvania Law Review*, 105 (1957), p. 781.

dent upon recommendation of the chief justice, drawn from both the organized bar and citizens' groups—confirmed by the Senate or not, depending on the plan's authorship. In either instance, however, the commission would recommend circa five candidates for each vacancy, with the president required to select one within 30 days (or advance a viable reason to the Senate why none of the five is acceptable to him and thus request a new group of names). Other plans for alteration of the existing method of selection would vest the appointive function in upper level sitting jurists.[27]

A matter of infinitely more pressing concern, and of a far more vexatious and subtle nature, is the already severally alluded-to central question in the judicial process of the basic role of the judge or justice, namely, how to confine him or her to judging rather than legislating. A truly fascinating problem, it has defied line-drawing, and will assuredly continue to defy it—with apologies to Professor Wechsler's "neutral principles." Viewing this matter at the highest judicial level, does the Supreme Court, do its justices, merely judge each case on its intrinsic merit or do they also legislate? In textbook theory—and virtually in the eyes of the average observer—all the members of any judicial tribunal do is to judge the

controversies over which they have jurisdiction and arrive at a decision in accordance with the legal aspects of the particular situation at issue. Yet the nine justices of the United States Supreme Court especially are often charged with legislating rather than judging in handing down their decisions. This charge usually admits, and indeed grants, that the Court must, of course, possess the power to interpret legislation, and, if "absolutely justified" by the particular issue at hand, even strike down legislation that is unconstitutional beyond "rational question." The charge against the high tribunal insists, however, that a line must be drawn between the imposition of judicial judgment and the exercise of judicial will. The latter is described as legislating, presumably the function of the legislature, and hence reserved to it. But, no matter how desirable one may be in the eyes of a good many observers, is it possible to draw such a line?

It is, of course, impossible. As with every line, questions arise at once as to how, where, when, and by whom it shall be drawn. But it is obvious that the judges do legislate. They do make law. One of the most consistent advocates of judicial self-restraint, Justice Holmes, recognized without hesitation that judges do and must legislate. But, he added significantly that they "can do so only interstitially; they are confined from molar to molecular motions."[28] Judges are human, as indeed all of us are human—but also they are judges, which most of us are not. Being human, they have human reactions. "Judges are men, not disembodied spirits; as men they respond to human situations," in Justice

27. Ex-Senator Ervin would thus like to see all federal judges selected by a panel of sitting senior jurists, followed by Senate confirmation. Professor Chase, *Federal Judges*, favors the selection of all lower federal judges by the U.S. Supreme Court alone. Professor Peter Graham Fish of Duke University, also disdaining any senatorial role, suggests the vesting of the appointive power of all judges in the chief justice of the United States alone, acting under the "Heads of Department" provision of Article II-2-1 of the Constitution.

28. *Southern Pacific Co.* v. *Jensen*, 224 U.S. 205 (1916), at 221.

Frankfurter's words. Justice McReynolds insisted that a judge neither can, nor should, be "an amorphous dummy, unspotted by human emotions." (He certainly sported many such spots!) And Justice Cardozo spoke of the cardiac promptings of the moment, musing in his lively prose that "the great tides and currents which engulf the rest of men do not turn aside in their course and pass the judges by."[29]

But, being human, as indicated, does not stand alone in the judicial decision-making process. A jurist is also presumably a qualified and conscientious member of the tribunal; he or she is in no sense of the term a free agent—free to render a decision willy-nilly. There is a deplorable tendency on the part of many observers to over-simplify the judicial decision-making process. Judges are "rigidly bound within walls that are unseen" by the average layman. These walls are built of the heritage of the law; the spirit of the Anglo-Saxon law; the impact of the cases as these have come down through the years; the regard for stare decisis (although there are, conveniently, often several precedents from which to choose), for a genuine sense of historical continuity with the past, as Holmes put it, "is not a duty, it is only a necessity";[30] the crucial practice of judicial self-restraint[31]—in brief, *the taught tradition of the law.*

Moreover, to reiterate an earlier point, the judges are very well aware of at least two other cardinal facts of judicial life: that they have no power to enforce their decisions, depending, as they do, upon the Executive for such enforcement; and that they may be reversed by the Legislature, albeit with varying degrees of effectiveness and if not without some toil and trouble—as the Crime Bill of 1968, for one, with its three-pronged attack on the Court, demonstrates. But not only do we often expect too much from the Court, we consciously or subconsciously encourage it to endeavor to settle matters that ought to be, yet for a variety of reasons are not, tackled by the other branches—witness such contentious issues as desegregation, reapportionment, redistricting, criminal justice, and separation of church and state.

How to draw the lines? Anthony Lewis has observed perceptively—but hardly definitively—that "judicial intervention on fundamental issues is most clearly justified when there is no other remedy for a situation that threatens the national fabric —when the path of political change is blocked."[32] This was the case with the areas of endemic racial desegregation and persistent legislative mal-, mis-, and non-apportionment. But it was not the case with such contentious criminal justice decisions as *Miranda* v. *Arizona.*[33] There, by reading a particular code of police procedure into the general language of the Constitution, the Court may well have overreached itself (although the police were hardly hobbled by the decision). Nor was it the case with the Court's recent involvement with a host of nonjudicial and perhaps nonjudicious aspects of the vexatious realm

29. Benjamin N. Cardozo, *The Nature of the Judicial Process* (New Haven: Yale University Press, 1921), p. 169.

30. As quoted by Alpheus T. Mason and William M. Beaney in *American Constitutional Law*, 5th ed. (Englewood Cliffs, N.J.: Prentice-Hall, Inc., 1972), p. xxvi.

31. For a list of 16 "maxims" of this self-restraint, see Abraham, *The Judicial Process*, ch. 9.

32. *The New York Times*, 15 November 1971, p. 41.

33. 384 U.S. 433 (1966).

of abortion[34] (though I happen to agree with the results it reached). Nor, to point to another realm, is it true of the Court's increasing involvement—some have styled it meddling—with discipline in the public schools.[35] Even its extended forays into the realm of morals are of dubious wisdom, given profound and widespread popular opposition. Our courts should not be viewed as wastebaskets of social problems, which does not mean, of course, that law does not play an efficacious role in social reform. It does, however, point to the inescapable fact that the other branches must do their jobs.

Of course, the Supreme Court of the United States is engaged in the political process. But, in Justice Frankfurter's admonitory prose, it is "the Nation's ultimate judicial tribunal, not a super-legal-aid bureau."[36] Neither is the Court, in the second Justice Harlan's words, "a panacea for every blot upon the public welfare, nor should this Court ordained as a judicial body, be thought of as a general haven for reform movements."[37] It may, thus, be questioned on grounds of both wisdom and justifiability—and ultimately governability—whether the Court should be involved, as it has become increasingly, in such realms as economic as distinct from political and legal, equality, and private as distinct from public morality.

Moreover, the type of judicial activism evinced by the highest tribunal in the land is hardly confined to it. Indeed, whether it be because of cue-taking from above, or because of indigenous oat-feeling, the lower federal courts, particularly the United States district courts, have ventured forth in policy-making of the most obvious kind, policy-making that should be left to the legislative function by the people's representatives. Thus, to question just two or three recent federal trial court actions that veritably smack of legislation—no matter how noble their intent and how desirous their consummation at the bar of public policy—is it really a judicial function to decree-prescribe:

the F degree of temperature of thermostatically-controlled hot water for state mental patients or residential use (110 F at the fixture) and for mechanical dishwashing and laundry use (180 F at the equipment);[38]

or

that dieticians *and* recreational officers in state penal institutions possess college degrees;[39]

or

that the percentage of women that receive job offers from a certain law firm in the next three years must be at least 20 per cent higher than the percentage of women in the graduating classes of the law schools from which the firm recruits new lawyers?[40]

Decisions such as the above, and a host of others, give pause for thought and raise fundamental role-questions, not only in the minds of professionals[41] and students of government, but also in those of the general public.[42] Caveat Judiciary!

34. *Roe* v. *Wade*, 410 U.S. 113 and *Doe* v. *Bolton*, 410 U.S. 179 (1973).

35. *Goss* v. *Lopez*, 419 U.S. 565 (1975) and *Baker* v. *Owen*, 44 LW 3235 (1975).

36. *Uveges* v. *Pennsylvania*, 335 U.S. 437 (1948), at 437.

37. *Reynolds* v. *Sims*, 377 M.S. 533 (1964), at 624.

38. *Wyatt* v. *Stickney*, 344 F. Supp. 373, 382 (M.D. Ala. 1972).

39. *N.Y.T.*, 14 January 1976, p. 1.

40. Ibid. 7 February 1976, p. 1.

41. See Louis Lusky's searching new book, *By What Right?*, "A Comment on the Supreme Court's Power to Reverse the Constitution" (Charlottesville, Va.: The Michie Company, 1975).

42. See the special issue of *U.S. News and World Report*, 19 January 1976, pp. 29–34.

Withal, that public has continued to turn its face toward the Judicial branch for the resolution of issues that had better be settled elsewhere. It has done so because courts in general, and the Supreme Court in particular, seem to provide responses to issues where the other branches, especially the Legislature, fear to tread.

When all is said and done, the Court, at the head of the United States Judiciary, is viewed—and quite properly so—as not only the most fascinating, the most influential, and the most powerful judicial body in the world, it is also the "living voice of [the] Constitution," as Lord Bryce once phrased it. As such, it is both arbiter and educator, and, in essence, represents the sole solution short of anarchy under the American system of government as we know it. It must act, in the words of one commentator, "as the instrument of national moral values that have not been able to find other governmental expression"[43]—assuming, of course, that it functions within its authorized sphere of constitutional adjudication. In that role, it operates as the "collective conscience of a sovereign people."[44] And no other institution "is more deeply decisive in its effect upon our understanding of ourselves and our government."[45] In other words, through its actions the Court defines values and proclaims principles.

Beyond that, moreover, the Supreme Court of the United States is the chief protector of the Constitution, of its great system of checks and balances, and of the people's liberties; it is the greatest institutional safeguard Americans possess. The Court may have retreated, even yielded to pressures now and then, but without its vigilance America's liberties would scarcely have survived. Within the limits of procedure and deference to the presumption of the constitutionality of legislation,[46] the Court—our "sober second thought"[47]—is the natural forum in American society for the individual and for the small group. It must, thus, be prepared to say "no" to the government—a role which Madison, the father of the Bill of Rights, fervently hoped it would always exercise. There are many citizens— indeed most, once they have given the problem the careful thought it merits—who will feel more secure in the knowledge of that guardianship, one generally characterized by common sense, than if it were exercised primarily by the far more easily pressured, more impulsive, and more emotion-charged Legislative or Executive branches. All too readily do these two yield to the politically expedient and the popular, for they are close, indeed, to what Judge Learned Hand once called "the pressure of public hysteria, public panic, and public greed." The Court, which thus often

43. Anthony Lewis, *The New York Times Magazine*, 17 June 1962, p. 38.

44. U.S. Court of Appeals' Judge J. Skelly Wright, "The Role of the Courts: Conscience of a Sovereign People," 29 *The Reporter* 5 (26 September 1963).

45. Alexander Meiklejohn, *Free Speech and Its Relations to Self-Government* (New York: Harper & Row, 1948), p. 32.

46. Justice Holmes once stated this (his own) constitutional philosophy to the then 61-year-old Stone: "Young man, about 75 years ago I learned that I was not God. And so, when the people . . . want to do something I can't find anything in the Constitution expressly forbidding them to do, I say, whether I like it or not, 'Goddammit, let 'em do it!' " (As quoted in Charles P. Curtis, Jr., *Lions under the Throne* (Boston: Houghton-Mifflin Co., 1947), p. 281).

47. Charles L. Black, Jr., *The People and the Court* (New York: The MacMillan Co., 1960), p. 12.

has had to act as a "moral goad" to the latter two, is neither engaged in, nor interested in, a popularity contest—its function is emphatically not one of counting constituents! Should that time ever arrive, the supreme judicial tribunal, as we now know it, will have lost its meaning.

Even if a transfer of that guardianship to other institutions of government were theoretically desirable, which few thoughtful citizens believe, it would be politically impossible. "Do we desire Constitutional questions," asked Charles Evans Hughes, then not on the bench, in his fine book on the Court, "to be determined by political assemblies and partisan divisions?"[48] The response must be a ringing "No!" In the 1955 Godkin Lectures which he was to deliver at Harvard University when death intervened, Justice Robert H. Jackson had expressed his conviction eloquently and ably: "The people have seemed to feel that the Supreme Court, whatever its defects, is still the most detached, dispassionate, and trustworthy custodian that our system affords for the translation of abstract into constitutional commands."[49] And we may well agree with Thomas Reed Powell that the logic of constitutional law is the common sense of the Supreme Court of the United States—which continues valiantly and admirably to strive to maintain that blend of continuity and change which is so vital to the stability of our basic democratic governmental processes.

48. *The Supreme Court of the United States* (New York: Columbia University Press, 1928), p. 236.

49. Robert H. Jackson, *The Supreme Court in the American System of Government* (Cambridge: Harvard University Press, 1955), p. 23.

FEDERAL SYSTEM

Our federal system is the structure that underlies a generous number of both the disappointments and the accomplishments of the American government "of, by, and for the people," as we know it. Federalism is either a failure or a success, depending upon the point of view of the protagonist, both extremes being represented at the Academy's Bicentennial Conference on the United States Constitution in the persons of two leading experts on the subject: Rexford Guy Tugwell and Daniel J. Elazar, respectively. The latter, while duly acknowledging the obvious need for constant reexamination and amelioration, is basically committed to its overall viability;[50] the former, more than twice as old in years and the holder of sundry responsible high government posts in the past, has long been convinced that only radical surgery, perhaps even extinction, will do.[51] A host of views hues to intermediate shadings. Neither the controversy nor the difference in perception is astonishing. For, as a team of contemporary commentators puts it well, the "genius of the Constitution is also its vulnerability. A document that gives powers to different political institutions is sooner or later going to be caught in a squeeze when the interests of those are in sharp conflict."[52] The answer to the ques-

50. Daniel J. Elazar, *American Federalism: A View from the States*, 2d ed. (New York: Thomas Y. Crowell, 1972).

51. Rexford G. Tugwell, *The Emerging Constitution* (New York: Harper's Magazine Press, 1974).

52. Kenneth Prewitt and Sidney Verba, *An Introduction to American Government* (New York: Harper & Row, 1974), p. 303. See their excellent ch. 10, "White House, State House, and City Hall: Federalism in America," pp. 312ff.

tions—at which level, national or state, (1) was power supposed to lie?; (2) where does it lie?; and (3) where should it lie?—are basic to both the argument(s) and to any proposed solution(s).

But there is no argument, whatever, on the patently obvious fact of federal life that, notwithstanding lip-service to the contrary, and notwithstanding such questionably honest decentralizing concepts or measures as revenue sharing, the long apparent trend toward centralization of federal power at the seat and in the hands of the national government is, at once, an axiom of modern American federalism and irreversible—absent drastic and dramatic constitutional changes, which simply will not take place. New York City's 1975 financial Waterloo, its own and its parent state of New York's desperate turn to Washington for the sole practical source of tangible succor, and the New Year's Day 1976 urgent appeal by four leading governors to have the national government take over the entire welfare aid program because "it is out of control . . . a patchwork . . . and not working"[53] are merely the latest and most visible indices of that conclusion's proof positive. This does not, of course, mean that one needs to embrace the off-with-his-head solution of Professor Tugwell; but it does mean listening to his reasoned critique.[54] It may well be that there is really no effective reversal of the trend toward centralization of power—assuming we could agree that reversal were in the system's best interest—and that we ought to adapt the subterfuge so

charmingly suggested severally by ex-Senator George Aiken (R.–Vt.) during the agonizing years of the Vietnam War, when he repeatedly, and quite seriously, importuned presidents to proclaim victory and withdraw all forces forthwith!

As I have had occasion to suggest elsewhere,[55] federalism is a point on a continuum reaching from complete isolation to complete absorption, neither of which is really ever found in the actual life of actual states. As Aristotle might have said, there is no such thing as federalism; there are only federal states—states reflecting the federal principle. Hence, the federal idea, defined by the then Governor Nelson A. Rockefeller in Harvard's Godkin Lectures[56] as a "concept of government by which a sovereign people, for their greater protection and progress, yield a portion of their sovereignty to a political system that has more than one center of sovereign power, energy and creativity," features dramatic differences.

These differences point to a salient underlying aspect of federalism: its pragmatism. Thus it was for entirely pragmatic reasons that the Constitutional Convention on 5th and Chestnut Streets in Philadelphia almost 190 years ago determined upon a federal structure, then as now appropriately known as a dual form of government, calculated to reconcile unity with diversity: the pressing common interests and purposes shared by the uniting colonies, which were desirous of securing themselves

53. See *The New York Times*, 4 January 1976, p. 1.

54. See ch. 3, "Parts and the Whole," pp. 89ff., of Tugwell, *The Emerging Constitution*.

55. J. A. Corry and Henry J. Abraham, *Elements of Democratic Government*, 4th ed. (New York: Oxford University Press, 1964), ch. 6, "Federalism" *passim* (from which much of this section is adapted).

56. "The Future of Federalism," February 1962.

against any European imperialism, and the desire of each of the uniting communities to maintain their identity and a large measure of independence—a desire that, in part, springs from the same mysterious sources as national pride and national exclusiveness. In those days, the framers' main concern was whether the fledgling nation, about to be created, would and could endure. Today, as has been true for some time, the question must be stood on its head: will the states, that is, the component parts of the nation, endure? Three major developments have occurred that have prompted that role-reversal. In chronological order, they are: (1) the predisposition of the Supreme Court of the United States, and notably its chief justice for 34 and a half years (1801–1834), John Marshall, to resolve all doubts in favor of the nation via a broad and decisive interpretation of Article 6, the "Supremacy Clause"; (2) the military triumph of nationalism under Abraham Lincoln in the Civil War; and (3) the still accelerating growth of economic and social welfare service demands by the electorate that have inexorably commanded national action for their solution.

The naked facts today, as they have been for several decades, are that it is the federal government that has to deliver the goods. No matter how well-intentioned the component parts may be, they are more often than not incapable of the kind of service performance for which a seemingly steadily increasing popular demand clamors—even while concurrently mouthing platitudes about "returning power to the local levels of government." On the other hand, since the excessive rigidity of centralization is a serious weakness, regional, state, and local governments, with control over matters of unique concern to their own areas, should retain a substantial sphere of independence. And they do—which proves that federalism is not obsolete, although particular aspects may badly need revision. Moreover, as the Canadian as well as the American federal system have proved amply, it is doubtful, indeed, that democratic government could survive except through the device, or at least the trappings, of federalism.

Democracy, which essentially is government by consent, needs mechanisms through which to construct electoral majorities that can agree on what the government should do. The states and localities, by providing such mechanisms under our federal systems, are often able to settle political squabbles in their decentralized realms without forcing them into the national forum where they might cause the sharpest of conflicts. Federalism, at its best, hence enables many regional interests and idiosyncrasies to have their own way in their own areas without ever facing the necessity of reconciliation with other regional interests. Individuals can thus identify themselves with particular regional interests and find in them a satisfying expression of many facets of their personalities. When thus viewed, federalism approaches the textbook ideal: a device for combining unity and diversity in accordance with the requirements of liberal democratic ideals.

The problem with the aforegone analysis of federalism is that, while undoubtedly true in democratic theory, and devoutly to be wished as a manifestation of the liberal democratic ideal, it but scarcely has practical application to the pressing issues of the day. The overriding key contemporary issues are simply beyond local, state, and even regional solution. Witness such as the cascading plight of the great cities of the nation; the incessant augmentation of demands for economic and social security; affirmative egalitarianism; and yes, even the once sacred bastion of local control, education. It is visionary to exhort the states to be innovative: their financial plight—with but rare exceptions, such as Texas—renders innovation a luxury; day-to-day survival is the contemporary preoccupation, inexorably bringing with it longing, albeit not necessarily fond, glances toward Washington. No wonder, then, that the Advisory Commission on Governmental Relations wondered officially as long ago as 1968–69 whether contemporary crucial questions, such as those of the urban centers, were still solvable by the American federal system "or if only a centralized and unitary governmental system will be equal to the task."[57] Or can our leadership somehow devise, and sell, reforms that will adapt the venerable federal structure to "the needs of a technological, urban society in an age of onrushing change?"[58] It is excrutiatingly difficult to still the haunting doubts.

And yet, federalism is at least one answer to the vexatious problem of how to conduct effectively the affairs of a nation-state as large, diverse, and complex as ours; provided

we do not become the slaves of political theory or terminology; provided that we are not afraid to experiment; provided that we are willing to share/distribute economic bounty (and bane); and further provided that we allow an umpire—that is the federal Judiciary, with the Supreme Court at its apex—to decide winners and losers in governmental-societal combat. Many a crime has been, and undoubtedly is being, committed on the altar of federalism, commonly referred to as "states rights," particularly when the issue at hand deals with the realm of civil rights and liberties. Yet, considerable advantages have also accrued, and will continue to accrue, from the federal system, not the least of which is that it allows more voices to be heard, more governmental experiments to be rendered—in short, more direct and more personalized political participation at a grass-roots level.

Given the inexorable centripetal force of governmental power during the past four decades, however—led by the power of the purse—it may well be asked whether the United States is still properly classifiable as a federal state at all? That the period indicated has witnessed a drastic modification in the role of the constituent states is beyond dispute. Yet they are hardly in total eclipse, and assuredly not in terms of their identity. Their individualized administrative, basic internal governmental structures continue to exist, antiquated as many of them are; they are usually faithfully, probably too faithfully, represented—at least in terms of state and local interests—by their generally parochial congressional delegations; their often provincial and obstructive veto power is omnipresent (and occasionally omnipotent) vis-à-vis

57. *Urban America and the Federal System: Commission Findings and Proposals* (Washington, D.C.: U.S. Government Printing Office, 1969), p. 1.

58. Milton C. Cummings, Jr., and David Wise, *Democracy under Pressure: An Introduction to the American Political System*, 2d. ed. (New York: Harcourt Brace Jovanovich, Inc., 1974), p. 89; ch. 3, "The Federal System," pp. 65ff., is a pithy, succinct evaluation and exposition of essentials.

general national programs; grants-in-aid continue to abound; revenue-sharing programs, while probably visionary and at least partially self-deceptive in their long-range implications, have provided a proverbial shot-in-the-arm; multitudinous social service and welfare programs of a host of stripes are increasingly financed by the national government, underscoring contemporary facets and notions of cooperative federalism, and, on many a delicate matter involving civil rights and liberties, the states have been taken off the hook by one or more of the three branches of the central government in Washington. The national psyche could probably not accept a departure from the federal arrangement: the knowledge of its existence, far more than its fact, represents a veritable security blanket to the average citizen! Perhaps that knowledge, so dear to our heterogenous society, vitiates basically more crucial questions of its effectiveness in the governmental modus operandus—and, indeed, its future role.

ANNALS, AAPSS, **426**, July 1976

Report on Committee II

By JAMES O. FREEDMAN

ABSTRACT: Professor Abraham's paper presents considerable evidence that the American people consider the Judiciary the most effective of the major government institutions. One of the committee's questions was why this was so. Two possible reasons are: the Supreme Court has shown a capacity to resolve issues the nation felt should be resolved; the Court has often met people's expectations better than other government institutions. The committee gave considerable attention to the selection of judges, particularly the criteria for their selection. It devoted some time, also, to issues relating to the organization of judicial resources: whether diversity jurisdiction and 3-judge courts should be abolished, and whether federal judicial salaries should be raised. Surprisingly little time was spent on questions of the proper role of the Supreme Court in American society. Four major themes were the focus of the discussion of federalism: what are the implications of federalism for governmental efficiency; would a system placing more authority at the local level result in greater citizen participation; how much is known about how federalism operates; and should governmental units be designed which are appropriate in scale to the tasks expected of them?

James O. Freedman has been a Professor of Law at the University of Pennsylvania since 1964 and University Ombudsman from 1973–76. He was a Law Associate with Paul, Weiss, Rifkind, Wharton and Garrison in New York from 1963–64. He served as Law Clerk to U.S. Appeals Court Judge Thurgood Marshall from 1962–63. His publications include "Crisis and Legitimacy in the Administrative Process," in the Stanford Law Review, *and "Summary Action by Administrative Agencies," in the* University of Chicago Law Review.

IT IS my responsibility to report on the work of committee II in two areas: the area of the Judiciary and the area of federalism. Although I cannot report to you that we achieved consensus on any issue, I suspect that it was the secret observation of a great many committee members that the lawyers tended rather vigorously to dominate the discussion on the Judiciary and that the political scientists tended rather vigorously to dominate the discussion on federalism! As a consequence we were treated, as it were, to seminars of very different pedagogical styles.

THE JUDICIARY

We were fortunate in discussing the questions of the Judiciary to have an issues paper written by Professor Henry Abraham, who is, of course, one of the nation's leading scholars on the work of the Supreme Court. As a consequence we had a great many important issues raised for us in a concise and direct fashion.

Professor Abraham's paper presents a considerable amount of evidence to suggest that the American people are of the view that, of the nation's major governmental institutions, the Judiciary is the most effective; that if one asks people, in all kinds of contexts, by all kinds of means, how effective are the governmental institutions of this nation, the Judiciary always comes out first.

One of the committee's questions was why this was so. The feeling of the meeting, I think, was that in at least two respects the Supreme Court, by the quality of its performance, had contributed to this rather high public estimate.

One of those respects, of course, has been the capacity that the Supreme Court has shown, particu-larly in the last generation, to resolve issues of a kind that the nation felt should be resolved and that the political process had been unable to resolve. When the political process has been in stalemate, when it has been paralyzed on significant public issues requiring resolution, the Supreme Court of the United States has been the forum in which these issues for the national good have in fact been resolved.

If examples are to be given, two of the most important surely would be *Brown* v. *the Board of Education*, which resolved the historic dilemma of segregation, and *Reynolds* v. *Sims*, which resolved the historic problem of malapportioned legislative representation—both issues as to which the political process was peculiarly unable to reform the nation in ways that, in retrospect, most people now quite clearly understand reform was needed.

In addition, many members of the committee expressed the sense that the Supreme Court has often met people's expectations in a better way than other institutions of government. There was considerable discussion of the Supreme Court's decision in *United States* v. *Nixon*, enforcing the Special Prosecutor's subpoena for certain presidential tapes, and of the sense that the American people expected no different result and indeed would have been quite surprised and chagrined had the result in fact been different.

The Supreme Court's effectiveness as an institution of government, then, is perhaps measurable by or responsive to concerns of these two basic kinds: its preparedness to resolve significant national issues that the political processes cannot resolve and its preparedness to meet the American people's expectations in rendering decisions of a kind that people expect some branch of the government to make. These considerations led many members of the committee to the view that one ought to move slowly in recommending changes of a constitutional dimension respecting the nature or the role of the Supreme Court.

The committee did, however, give a considerable amount of attention, perhaps the major amount, to the selection of judges and particularly to the criteria by which judges should be selected. There seemed a general agreement on the quite mild truism that judges should be selected by merit. The more difficult question, of course, is how to measure or define merit.

Despite the efforts of one of our colleagues to suggest that this was essentially an existential question, not capable of quantification in any clear way, the committee forged ahead and began to talk about whether criteria beyond technical or professional competence were appropriate to take into account in appointing individuals, for example, to the United States Supreme Court.

There are many people—Justice Frankfurter, I suppose, foremost among them—who have taken the view that the relationship between prior judicial experience and effective service on the Supreme Court is exactly zero. Other qualities, however, and particularly qualities of diversity in representation, were the qualities that the committee focused upon.

Is it appropriate to take ethnic considerations into account? Is it appropriate to take into account the race, the sex, the national origin, the geographical roots of individuals being considered for appointment to the Court? These were questions which, as perhaps one can imagine, exercised a great many people in a great many directions. The concern was focused primarily upon issues of the acceptability and legitimacy of the Supreme Court's decisions.

Was one able to say, committee members asked, that the Supreme Court's decisions had a greater measure of acceptability, a greater measure of legitimacy in the country at large because they were reached by a group which reflected among its members a broader cross-section of the population than might be achieved if a narrower range of qualities—for example, professional, technical competence alone—were the only considerations in appointing people to the Court?

One member of the committee suggested that a second prescription of Justice Frankfurter was the one that should be primarily followed: that a Supreme Court justice should be (I don't recall if it's necessarily in this order) a lawyer, a historian, a philosopher, a prophet, and a person of inordinate patience.

Other members of the committee thought that one must add to that list a concern for geographic distribution and perhaps a concern for group representation. Indeed, the suggestion was made by at least one person that the decision in *Brown* v. *the Board of Education* may have gained some marginally greater acceptance in the South because of the fact that Justice Black, an Alabaman, sat upon the Court. The question that intrigued the committee was whether, over a whole range of substantive issues, the participation of those who have a firsthand knowledge of the matter at hand is an important factor in enhancing the acceptability and the legitimacy of the decisions that are reached.

There was also some concern expressed that a further reason a president should look for a diversity of background as well as a diversity of geography in appointing people to the Supreme Court was that public officials who live in Washington, D.C., for long periods of time, as Supreme Court justices do, tend to absorb (or be absorbed by) what was described as an Eastern United States worldview, and that that Eastern United States worldview can be seen as working itself out in decisions of the Court, particularly in areas where societal standards are changing, such as civil liberties and morals.

Mention was made in this connection, for example, of the abortion decision, the school prayer decision, and the series of criminal procedure decisions that have enlarged the rights of persons suspected or accused of crimes. There are surely exceptions to this hypothesis, as the Supreme Court's recent decision sustaining Virginia's criminal prohibition against adult homosexual activity, even when consensual and done in private, suggests.

But the basic argument was that diversity of background among Supreme Court justices was particularly important as a possible counterforce to the ideological impact of living for a great many years in Washington, D.C., where views regarded by many parts of the country as peculiarly "Eastern" are thought to prevail.

There was some nostalgic reference to the fact that in the days when Supreme Court justices were circuit riders there was at least some opportunity—indeed, some obligation—for a judge to get out of Washington and gain exposure to a new and presumably wider range of views

in a way that judges do not necessarily do today.

A rather different concern with respect to the appointment process was also expressed: that presidents of the United States in recent years have played less of a role in the appointment of inferior federal judges than used to be the case; that they have essentially delegated that task to the dominant political party's senators from the state in which the appointment is to be made; and that as a consequence the constitutional scheme which calls for a judgment by the president as well as by the Senate in the appointment of federal judges has been greatly diluted. In point of fact, the Senate rarely gives the kind of concern, the kind of inquiry, the kind of scrutiny to appointees to the lower federal courts that it does to Supreme Court appointees—a consequence that makes the practice of recent presidents even more alarming.

At the suggestion of Professor Abraham, the committee focused, although only briefly, upon the utility of the adversary system, upon questions of whether the adversary system is the best method not only to attain justice in mine-run lawsuits but also to try issues of constitutional moment. Professor Abraham's issues paper had urged that the United States should consider adoption of the inquisitorial system, a system used in many European countries. But other committee members suggested that the chief virtues of an inquisitorial system were the maintenance of order and the enforcement of discipline, rather than the refined attainment of individualized justice. They added that inquisitorial systems of justice have worked well in military regimes and in such contexts as courts-martial, but would work much less well if there were an attempt to transplant them into a nation with traditions of the kind we have.

The committee also devoted some time (none of it sustained) to issues relating to what might be called the organization of judicial resources. At the federal level, those issues go, for example, to the lawyers' time-honored quarrel over whether diversity jurisdiction should be abolished, whether three-judge courts should be abolished, and whether federal judicial salaries should be raised.

At least some members of the committee thought that any argument that federal judges' salaries should be raised was inappropriate or unseemly when others on the committee were asserting that the crisis of the cities was attributable in part to the excessive demands of public employees—who don't call themselves judge, but call themselves postal worker or fireman or sanitation man.

The committee spent relatively little time, perhaps surprisingly, on questions of the proper role of the Supreme Court in American society: on questions that Professor Abraham described as line-drawing questions —questions involving the separation of the judicial function from the legislative function, the separation of the process of adjudicating winners and losers in lawsuits on the one hand from that of making large policy determinations on the other.

There was some brief discussion of whether the Supreme Court should play a larger role in the area of national security. One member of the committee argued quite vigorously that the Supreme Court should undertake to assert jurisdiction and to decide cases on the merits involv-

ing claims of national security and the control of what he called the police bureaucracy—the FBI, the CIA, and other paramilitary operations.

Other members suggested that not only would Article III's case-and-controversy requirement stand in the way of many such proposed judicial interventions, but also the absence of a State Department adjunct to the United States Supreme Court would make it very difficult for the Court to feel comfortable or be adequately informed in deciding such cases.

FEDERALISM

The committee turned then to questions of federalism. Those questions focused around four major themes. The first theme—I suppose most intimately tied to our mission as a committee—was the question of what are the implications of federalism for governmental efficiency. It was suggested that once upon a time, in a quainter age, the question of federalism was seen primarily as one of eliminating duplication of excessive services, of eliminating services already being provided by another level of government. Under this conception, one looked to federalism for a rule or guideline that would suggest how the duplication of the provision of governmental services could be eliminated.

That conception, it was suggested, has now given way to a far more sophisticated understanding of federalism, to a conception which suggests that questions of localism and questions of national centralization are primarily questions of politics. Indeed, it was suggested that what we now see going on in Great Britain—the question of independence for Ireland, the question of independence for Scotland— perhaps supplies proof of the fact that questions of local control as against national control, questions of the division of governmental authority, are primarily questions, so it was said, of politics.

For the committee, the central question became whether the trend toward centralization of authority in the federal government either can be reversed or in principle ought to be reversed.

There was considerable discussion of the so-called "new federalism" of the Nixon administration. On the basis of the committee's discussion, one might have been led to conclude that the words "new federalism" were perhaps more Orwellian than precise, at least if one believes those who reported that the consequence of the new federalism was to greatly centralize authority in Washington with respect to the programs included within it. The assertions were that what the new federalism essentially did was to centralize in the Office of Management and Budget authority which was not centralized there before, thereby permitting the president to cut across cabinet, bureaucratic, and departmental lines with respect to programs that formerly were fragmented or segmented among those divisions of government. Thus, a program that was decreed as a new federalism was, in fact, a new centralization.

A number of committee members expressed the view that the revenue-sharing programs of the last decade had been too modest in dimension to be regarded as significant experiments in federalism. Yet there was also a sense among many committee members that these programs had, in small ways, at least brought a new public focus to federalism and given some kind of support, if only moral or largely symbolic, to the belief that local communities are important units in decision-making that affect people directly.

Paradoxically perhaps, many committee members thought that any significant attempt to enlarge the dimensions of revenue-sharing programs would inevitably be accompanied by efforts to impose greater federal control, because one could hardly believe that the federal government, in giving substantial amounts of money to the states and to local governments, would not ultimately be led to impose conditions upon its use—an action that would reverse the political consequences of delegating power to local units of government in the first place.

Other committee members were concerned that, with respect to the issue of centralization, there was really no alternative to centralizing increasing amounts of power in the national government. Reference was made, for example, to the environmental crisis. One committee member suggested that, to the degree to which power is not centralized in the federal government, each individual state or locality would have an incentive to set pollution standards that might well lure industry to it, as well, of course, as having a deleterious impact on the environment of neighboring states—a situation that the federal government could not long permit to persist.

The questions were asked: Can one really believe that state governments like those of New York and New Jersey will finally be able to prevent the Concorde from landing there when the federal government has made the decision to permit supersonic flights? Can one really believe that the large corporations and multinational corporations which have come into such prominence in the American and world economy in the last decade can truly be regulated, except at the national level?

New York City, as you may well imagine, dominated a good part of this discussion. Many thought that the conclusion to be drawn from the New York experience is that local control cannot be effective given the size of many of our urban problems, and that centralization of power in the national government is inevitable if government is to be an effective problem-solver.

Beyond the theme of the implications of federalism for governmental efficiency was a second theme, that of citizen participation in government decision-making. Is it the fact that a system of federalism which placed more authority at the local level would result in greater citizen participation in the decision-making processes of government?

One suggestion for achieving that goal, if one thought that goal worth achieving, was to redefine—in order to reinvigorate—the Ninth Amendment. The argument was that the Ninth Amendment should be redefined from being concerned primarily with protecting individual privacy to being concerned with strengthening local control and local power. I dare say that we were the only committee that concerned itself with the Ninth Amendment during this whole week!

There was considerable challenge, however, to whether our experience as a people demonstrates empirically that local participation is an effective force in controlling governmental decision-making. Repeated reference was made to the War on Poverty, from which many drew a general conclusion of failure with respect to local participation in decision-making. The melancholy experience of ineffective local participation in the War on Poverty led several committee members to express a sense that the problem of structuring effective citizen representation and participation at the local level is far more complicated than was formerly understood, and that it cannot be met merely by making reference, as some did, to juries and suggesting that because juries are conscientious groups, serious of aspiration, one has a model for small-group decision-making which one ought to try to transfer to other parts of government.

Indeed, some committee members expressed the sense that the federal government, perhaps paradoxically, remained the most open of the various levels of government to citizen participation, and that it also probably remained the most responsive of the three levels of government to citizen concerns. There was considerable discussion of the question of whether citizen participation in government decision-making can be increased in scope and enhanced in quality by structuring that participation in the federal system to enter at the local level rather than at the federal level.

The third theme that the committee discussed, quite akin to the one I've just reported on, has to do with how much we know or don't know about the way federalism operates in fact. A number of political scientists on the committee suggested that we know very little about the actual operation of federal programs at the state, county, and local levels. We know a great deal about how lawyers think a theory of federalism should be framed. We know a great deal about what lawyers believe the public law of federalism ought to be. But we have very little empirical understanding of how the 3,500 counties in this nation work when they administer a program that filters through the federal government, that filters through the state government, and that may filter through to a governmental unit smaller, for example, than a county.

What, we were asked, do we know, for example, about how the thousands of community mental health centers of the nation work? Do we know whether they are dominated in fact by the professionals who staff them, despite formal opportunities for citizen boards to participate? Do we even know where decision-making power ought to be with respect to community mental health programs? And one can, of course, multiply that homely example by any number of other programs that now operate through the interdependence of the federal, the state, the county, and perhaps an even smaller local level of government.

Indeed, if there is a paradox in all of this, it is that we know so little about why it is that citizen participation at the local level has so disappointed those who have created programs designed to achieve a greater degree of such participation. If one were to draw any moral from this, it might be that we need to know empirically a great deal more about how the federal system operates in the administration of programs that cut across governmental lines than we know now.

The final topic that the committee discussed as part of its inquiry into federalism related to considerations of design and scale. The theme of that discussion was the desideratum in the federal system of designing governmental units which are appropriate in scale to the tasks they are expected to perform.

One member of the committee suggested that if the recent economic difficulties of New York City demonstrated anything, it was that New York violated the basic canon of federalism that governmental units should be of an appropriate scale; that any government of 8 million people was not a local government—it was something, but it could not be considered an effective local government.

But how does one decide what is an appropriate scale for government units at any level in a federal system? A number of criteria were suggested: criteria relating, for example, to the desire to optimize citizen participation, to optimize efficiency, to optimize the productive base, to optimize the tax base.

What became clear to many members of the committee from this discussion was that we now have a nation in which the individual governments—local, county, state, and federal—with respect to some functions may well be of appropriate scale, but with respect to other functions may not be of appropriate scale.

If we are to talk about federalism at all, it seemed to many members of the committee very hard to talk about it in the large or at wholesale, as it were, and that rather, one had to talk first about finding measures and criteria of efficiency that were responsive to concerns of the appropriate scale for government. I suspect that what this suggested was one of the morals that the framers of the Constitution must have had in mind: that the heterogeneity of this nation is so great that across-the-board revision of concepts like federalism is hardly a wise move.

Report on Committee II

By FRANK GOODMAN

ABSTRACT: In the committee's discussion, 3 criteria were suggested for measuring government effectiveness: (*a*) the degree of public approval it has; (*b*) the extent to which it has provided solutions to important problems of society; and (*c*) the extent to which it has given the public what it wants. In assessing the effectiveness of the presidency, the main theme was that the office has grown too great, is insufficiently accountable to Congress or the public, and should be cut down to size. One suggestion that met with no opposition was that Congress should spell out the concept of high crimes and misdemeanors and set up an ongoing institutional mechanism for impeachment. In evaluating the Legislative branch, there was general agreement that Congress was not as bad as its reputation. There was discussion and some disagreement as to the utility of procedural and structural reform.

Frank Goodman is currently Professor of Law at the University of Pennsylvania. He served as Research Director of the U.S. Administrative Conference from 1972–73 and as Law Clerk to U.S. Appeals Court Judge William H. Hastie from 1959–62. He was Professor of Law at the University of California, Berkeley, prior to coming to the University of Pennsylvania. Among his publications are: "De Facto School Segregation: A Constitutional and Empirical Analysis," California Law Review; *co-author, "Judicial Review of Federal Administrative Action: Quest for the Optimum Forum,"* Columbia Law Review.

THE committee began by examining the key concept of governmental effectiveness and by considering possible yardsticks for its measurement. In the course of discussion, three criteria were put forward as appropriate measures of the effectiveness of government in general or of any particular organ of government: (a) the degree of public approval it enjoys; (b) the extent to which it has been able to provide solutions to important societal problems; and (c) the extent to which it has given the public what the public wants—that is, adopted specific programs and policies demanded or favored by a clear majority of the electorate.

Judged by either of the first two standards, our national government (the Judiciary excepted) would be found seriously wanting. Congress and (in lesser degree) the presidency receive consistently low approval-ratings in public opinion surveys; and even the Judiciary, the least disfavored branch, falls short of majority approval. Similarly, the existence of unremedied social problems—urban blight, the energy crisis, crime in the streets, and others—would indeed be strong evidence of governmental default if government could fairly be held accountable for all in society that is wrong.

Many members of the committee, however, disputed the appropriateness of these criteria. Public disapproval of government, they argued, may simply reflect an unrealistic level of expectation and demand, a tendency to look to Washington for solutions to problems that are beyond the capacity of any government to solve. By the same token, the persistence of important social evils—poverty, injustice, crime, and the like—may be seen to reflect a failure, not of government, but of other institutions or of society itself. Government, as one member of the committee put it, is no more to be blamed for crime in the streets than to be credited for the gross national product.

There was also disagreement about the third criterion of governmental effectiveness—responsiveness to the clear wishes of the electorate. It was pointed out not only that government has obligations to the minority as well as to the majority but also that, when Congress fails to enact legislative measures (such as gun control) clearly favored by the majority, the reason may be that the minority cares about the issue more intensely, a factor which, in democratic theory as well as in political practice, is entitled to no small weight.

In sum, the committee was unable to agree, at least without substantial reservations, upon any single criterion, or combination of criteria, as the operative test of governmental effectiveness. In the ensuing discussions, that concept remained largely undefined.

ASSESSMENT OF THREE BRANCHES OF GOVERNMENT

Presidency

The committee then turned to an assessment, one by one, of the three branches of our national government. With respect to the presidency, the pervasive theme was that the office, and in particular the White House staff by which the president appears to be increasingly surrounded and insulated, has grown too great, is insufficiently accountable either to Congress or to the public, and by one means or another should be cut down to size.

Three specific proposals to that end were put forward for discussion: (a) that appointment of the principal members of the White House staff should be made subject to senatorial confirmation; (b) that the concepts of national security and executive privilege should be clearly defined and narrowly circumscribed either by statute, by judicial decision, or, if necessary, by constitutional revision; and (c) that the Constitution should be amended to make easier the removal of a president who has either abused his office or can no longer govern effectively.

It is fair to say that none of these proposals found a great deal of support among the committee members. Senatorial confirmation of chief White House aides was viewed as a futile gesture, since the power to confirm is not necessarily the power to control and, even if it were, the power to confirm those who nominally hold high-ranking White House titles is not necessarily the power to confirm those to whom the president actually listens and assigns responsibilities. Congressional scrutiny of top White House appointments would not, in short, prevent the president from relying, in whatever way he wished, upon nominally inferior aides of his own sole choosing. The larger point was that the White House is essentially a political institution; its formal structure is unimportant, while its true operating structure cannot be imposed from the outside. "The structure of the White House," as one member of the committee observed, "is, inevitably, the structure of a bowl of jello."

The second proposal—that national security and executive privilege be clearly defined—stirred neither opposition nor enthusiasm. Some members took the view that,

in the long run, these concepts will mean as much or as little as the president can persuade the country to accept; and, in any case, even if executive privilege were defined more narrowly and governmental secrecy considerably relaxed, it is unlikely that Congress or the public would be any better informed. Pressed for information, the president might simply send to Congress a paper haystack without disclosing where the critical needles of information were to be found.

One proposal relating to executive privilege did, however, appeal to the committee members: that the privilege should be available only when invoked by the president himself, on a case-by-case basis, in writing and with accompanying reasons. These procedural requirements, it was hoped, might reduce the number of occasions on which executive privilege is claimed and, even more important, might be the most effective means of scaling down the White House staff: a president might be more reluctant to surround himself with a legion of assistants if he knew that each could be called before congressional committees without the shield of executive privilege.

With respect to the third proposal —relating to presidential removal— several specifics were discussed. One was to institute at the federal level the recall device so widely adopted in the states. Another was that Congress, by a suitably large majority, should be permitted to cast a vote of no confidence in the president and, thereby, secure his removal. Still another suggestion was to relax the present standard for impeachment—"high crimes and misdemeanors"—so as to permit removal for "conduct unbecoming the presidency."

None of these ideas got much support. The prevailing view seemed to be that both the recall and no-confidence devices would seriously destabilize the office and that loosening the constitutional standard for impeachment would introduce too large a measure of subjectivity and discretion. The one suggestion along these lines that met no opposition was that Congress, by statute, should spell out the concept of high crimes and misdemeanors and set up an ongoing institutional mechanism for impeachment, perhaps in the form of a standard impeachment committee with jurisdiction to investigate charges against executive officers.

Legislative

The committee turned next to the Legislative branch. There was fairly general agreement that Congress is not as bad as its reputation. It was the view of several committee members that those who condemn Congress for its inadequacies as a planning and policy-making institution misapprehend the nature and proper function of the body. Congress, like the White House, is, above all, a political institution; it cannot fairly be judged by the criteria of rationality, foresight, efficiency, and purposefulness that are rightly applied to the administrative and bureaucratic sectors of government. It is the arena in which conflicts of interest, philosophy, and values within the body politic are thrashed out and, when possible, crystallized, clarified, and resolved. In terms of this model, it is not surprising that Congress typically adopts only those legislative measures which are supported by a broad popular consensus and is moved to action only after sufficient pressures have

built up to overcome the inherent inertia of the legislative process. The difficulty of developing a measure of consensus sufficient to move Congress is compounded by the absence in this country of a disciplined party system on the British or continental model. Here it is not enough for a group seeking legislation to bring persuasion or pressure to bear on a few party leaders; they must disperse their efforts among nearly 500 individual congressmen, many of whom are more sensitive to currents of opinion in their own local districts than to the prevailing views of the national parties. This bias in favor of inaction is reinforced by a further consideration: the average congressman sees it as more important politically to avoid making enemies than to make new friends, and the risk of making enemies is greater when he supports controversial legislation than when he finds reasons for withholding that support.

Surprisingly, this perception of Congress as a vessel floating more or less passively on shifting political currents was not seriously challenged. Nor was there any real attempt to evaluate the effectiveness of Congress in terms of this model. There was, however, some discussion, and a measure of disagreement, as to the possible utility of procedural and structural reform.

As in the discussion of the presidency, some committee members felt that no amount of tinkering with the machinery of Congress would significantly affect its work product. According to this view, the presence or absence of the seniority system, the number of committees, the degree of power exercised by committee chairmen, the existence or nonexistence of a rules committee or a seniority system make little difference; Congress will behave in much the same way regardless. Not all members of the group, however, shared this view. It was noted, for example, that the effectiveness of the individual congressman is unnecessarily impaired by lack of information about fiscal matters, about the internal workings of the Executive branch agencies subject to congressional oversight and, less importantly, about conditions in society at large. A suggested remedy was the establishment by Congress of a special Legislative branch agency responsible for gathering, digesting, and transmitting in usable form such information as Congress may need for purposes of legislation and effective oversight. Other committee members, however, were doubtful that this service would do much good and noted that agencies charged with informing members of Congress already exist.

In addition to these procedural matters, the committee gave some attention to structural changes of a more basic nature. One proposal called for the enlargement of congressional districts and corresponding reduction in the membership of the House of Representatives—a measure, it was thought, that might promote the development of a more disciplined party structure. This proposal was received with skepticism. Committee members observed that larger congressional districts would mean less effective representation, would make congressmen less aware of and responsive to the felt needs of their constituents, and would reduce the number of minority group members in Congress; and all this would be lost, it was argued, without compensating gain in party discipline—witness the Senate, where, despite statewide constituencies, party discipline is notably weak.

*   *   *   *

QUESTIONS AND ANSWERS

Q: My name is Anthony Wermuth. I am a political scientist at the U.S. Army War College. There is one problem that seemed very urgent to me that I am very surprised didn't arise, that is how to change the system by which power was transferred from Nixon to Ford and Rockefeller.

A (Abraham): I think a short response to you would be, we have the Twenty-Fifth Amendment, under which it is possible for an outgoing president, or for that matter it would be possible for a president, to appoint a successor.

When President Ford speaks, as he does on occasion, of being the elected head, he doesn't really mean it. He was not elected, he was appointed, and he in turn appointed someone else. Whether that is wise or not is, of course, another matter. The transition is now enshrined, for better or worse, in the Twenty-Fifth Amendment. There was a long time when we had nothing whatever, as you know, which dealt with such problems as disability. In theory, at least, we now have that. When I say in theory, I mean it's in the amendment.

I would hate to put that to a test, but if we wish to put it to a test, if the time arises, we have a procedure for it, and what President Nixon did was, in effect, entirely constitutional. We discussed the issue, and, I might say, if we had taken a vote in the committee the amendment would not have found universal approbation—quite to the contrary. But it is in the book.

Q: I'm Kenneth Abel from Huntsville, Alabama. I was hopeful that I would hear some real progress toward the solution of our manifest problems. I must say, however, that I have listened attentively and heard nothing but a lack of consensus which is worthy of Congress itself.

One issue lacking consensus was whether our government is ineffective or not, apparently because it was not possible to decide which of three reasons would really be the most persuasive for determining that the government is ineffective. It appears to me that common sense would indicate that, if our problems are continuing to grow more outrageous, it is obvious there is a considerable measure of ineffectiveness in the operation of our government.

With regard to the Congress, for example, to which we alluded a moment ago, I was surprised to hear the view that perhaps we should be realists and content ourselves with the concept of Congress that would relieve them of any serious burden of arriving at national goals or national policies. This apparently emerged from the same group that moderately agreed that we have an imperial presidency and that this is bad. I would submit the question, if the Congress is not to be the creator of influence in establishing national policies and national goals, where should the imperium reside, in an appointed Judiciary or in the presidency which, at least in some

measure, is responsible to the people of the entire nation?

We have reason to be less than delighted with the manner in which the president is selected, but nevertheless this is the only office in our national government that even constructively reflects the public will as a whole.

A (Goodman): Well, I would agree wholeheartedly with the last part of your statement, though I'm perhaps not the appropriate person to respond to it. I was, myself, very much disappointed that there wasn't sufficient or greater recognition on the part of the committee of the implications of saying that we can't look for creative leadership from Congress. I agree with you entirely that, if we can expect creative leadership at all from the federal government, it must come from the presidency, and that aspect of the presidency was wholly neglected in a discussion which, I think, owed much too much of its impetus to the recent Nixon events.

Also, let me say I was a little bit disappointed that the committee didn't spend a greater amount of time and attention than it did on some rather more fundamental and more forward looking questions, such as the viability of the separation of powers as it now stands and whether or not the present basic relationships between the two branches of government are acceptable. With respect to your first point, however, obviously the committee did disagree with you that the existence of unsolved problems in society is a measure of governmental ineffectiveness. I think for my own part, I would tend to agree with the committee on this. It doesn't seem to me that just because there is crime in the streets, and perhaps increasing crime, that this is necessarily to be laid to government any more than to the church, the home, or any number of other institutions in society.

One member of the committee asked the question of whether, if we are going to blame crime in the streets on the government, should we also credit the federal government with the gross national product? It does seem to me that it isn't necessarily an attitude of complacency about these problems which says that we may be misplacing our search for a solution if we look to the federal government as the only source of salvation.

Q: I'm Peter Fish at the Department of Political Science at Duke University. I'd like to address one question to Professor Abraham. He mentioned, as among the possible reforms of the federal Judiciary, reducing the role or eliminating the role of the juries and further undermining the adversary system which has already been weakened to some extent by pretrial procedures. He proposes to move toward an inquisitorial system.

In other words, with the jury system we're reducing the influence of popularism in the judicial system. With the reduction of the role of the adversary system, we're reducing the function of the non-judges in the system, and at the same time intermediate appellate courts are making use of more and more permanent career law clerk type staff in the state system. It seems to me this is going to further enthrone either the judges or the judicial bureaucracy, further insulate it from the populous at large.

Professor Abraham has proposed

a type of parliamentary address vis-à-vis the president—recall of the president by a special majority of Congress. I wonder if the solution to this trend of orthodox judicial reform and further insulation of, say, the federal judges might not be some form of congressional recall of judges who hold office on good behavior, whatever that means. It apparently means removal only for high crimes and misdemeanors by the impeachment process.

Professor Freedman mentioned that the people do not seem to be participating at the local level to the extent that they should. This ties in very nicely with the meeting we had this morning, I think. I wonder if, as a hypothesis, one could say that perhaps the people are not participating at the local level because the sense of community has been or is being shattered.

What is the end result of the progress toward individual liberty and individual equality? Is it going to be a fair redistribution of economic resources as Dean Harris postulated this morning, or is it going to put the whole country under psychoanalysis 100 years from now?

A (Abraham): You're obviously concerned about the jury problem, as I am too. I think you like juries more than I do, but the point is, I don't think, for example, that depriving juries of a general verdict power and clothing them with a special verdict or authority such as exists in a good many European countries and many states would necessarily make the jury less of a popular institution. I realize that is a danger, but it doesn't necessarily follow.

Many of these are devices with which we are comfortable because they've always existed, and I do think that one ought to give it a try.

We indeed have given it a try. Now my suggestion to move to the inquisitorial from the adversary process is fraught with dangers. I realize that, and anyway neither of these will be accepted, although we have been limiting juries more and more.

We could, of course, do away with a lot of these artificial, time-consuming, court-clogging jurisdiction requirements by going to the kind of system which works very well in civil cases above $5,000 and/or $10,000 in Philadelphia. We've saved 10,000 cases of a small civil nature every year, because arbitration panels, consisting of three voluntary lawyers, handle approximately 10,000 cases a year.

In other words, I think that a lot that we now do in court could be decided at the level of the administrative process. Someone, of course, has got to do it. Diversity jurisdiction in the states means the federal courts have less to do, but the states will have more to do.

A (Freedman): I can't equal that. I think the puzzlement that you speak to, of why there has not been more effective participation on the local level in governmental programs, was one that the committee spent some time with. I think there were some on the committee who think we know very little about this, that very few studies have been done. There were some who thought perhaps we haven't tried opportunities for local participation enough. And some may have thought that the War on Poverty, which was the example that the committee tended to focus on, wasn't a useful or typical example.

You suggested some reasons of your own which may help to explain it. I think if there was any view that more members would have sub-scribed to than any other, it may have been that we have yet to find someone who will try to describe to us why this has happened.

Q: My name is Robert Lockwood. I'm from the Social Scientist Department at West Point. I question Professor Freedman's indictment of the American political processes as a generator of greater respect for the judicial system, because it seems to me the political processes respond differently to different types of political issues. I'm thinking specifically of Vietnam which generated a rather widespread, yet spontaneous, political response to an issue, whereas the domestic political issues which tend to be considerably more complex in nature defy political consensus. Doesn't the distinction between the types of issues generating different types of political responses tend to narrow somewhat your indictment of the political process? In fact, doesn't it tend to qualify further the respect that we may think exists for the judicial system?

A (Freedman): I surely indicted no one. I was trying to report on what I thought the committee's consensus was, which was that, of the processes of American government, the judicial process was the one that seemed consistently to earn more respect from the American people than the Executive or the Legislative.

Q: I'm Dorothy Robbins, with the United States Information Agency. I was rather startled to hear some of the comments in relation to this whole matter of the balance of strength between the national and the local levels in a revenue area. I know this has just recently been spoken to, but in recent conversations, our feeling has been that many people have come down very strongly on the creativity of the local groups compared to what has been produced on the national level. I wonder that, if you look at something besides the welfare program, you would be coming up with rather different answers?

A (Freedman): I think I can tell you no more than that the group might have benefitted by having someone with your perspective in the room. That perspective was not discussed or expressed, I think, at any great length in the group.

A (Abraham): I might add that there was a feeling that if one were pressed, in a rather limited and perhaps childish dichotomy, to choose between having or not having the revenue sharing system with control at the local level, one would opt for the former. In other words, it's better to have it than not to have it, but there was a general feeling that it wasn't working as it should be, which doesn't mean that one cannot work on it. It hasn't really had enough of a chance. Many people are suspicious of it.

———————

Q: I'm from New York and I am a professional social worker. At this point, I just wish to reaffirm my deep belief in citizen participation, having spent a great deal of my life in helping it happen and knowing what it does. I really feel a bit offended that we had to make the conclusion from your committee out of the one experience in the Office of Economic

Opportunity. I don't think it is complete and fair.

A (Abraham): Thank you very much. I do think you would agree that the thrust of our comment has displayed a very profound concern with citizen participation. The kind of experience which the last two speakers have had is, of course, not only helpful, it also helps to give us some hope which we must nurture and nourish.

———————

Q: We are speaking of effectiveness of governmental operations and not mentioning the quality of government operations. It is not the same thing. The way I see effectiveness of operations, I think I would, instead of staying with the two-year congressman for election, propose a constitutional amendment and recommend a four-year period, simply for reasons of efficiency, as it takes at least half a year or a year for a congressman to learn what is going on, and then maybe another year to be accepted, and by the time he is ready to act he has to go out and either campaign again or lose it all. Then another man comes in and starts from scratch.

I agree with your proposal to increase the length of presidency from four to six years and also that a president could be voted out if the Congress no longer feels he is acting in the interest of the nation, but at the same time Congress should also vote itself out. I think that's an excellent suggestion and proposal.

Another idea is that the justices of the United States Supreme Court could be elected too, but that they could be elected for eight years. This would overlap the presidency time and would depend less on the presidential whims or political views or party affiliations. Then they could be reelected for another eight-year period.

A (Abraham): Thank you very much. I might say that all of these ideas were given consideration except the last one. I think the last one is rather thoroughly rejected by implication. However, as I'm sure you know, there are always numerous bills in the legislative hopper that would require reconfirmation of Supreme Court appointees. I hope that never occurs. That doesn't mean that there may not be some merit to it, I would certainly vote against it, especially given the performance of the Court as I view it, and I view it as a healthy one by and large.

On the former proposals, both were given very cautious and careful consideration. In fact, Professor Goodman reported on the two-year term and the attitudes of the committee, and the question of a single presidential term was debated at some length. There was a feeling that the lame duck implications of a one-term presidency were fraught with danger. I might say that this proposal is before Congress.

In Professor Tugwell's model Constitution, there is a proposal for a nine-year single-term president who could be recalled by two-thirds of the voters after three years, but your suggestions are very helpful.

The Shaping of Public Policy

By CHARLES E. GILBERT

ABSTRACT: "The Shaping of Public Policy" might be construed as the public shaping of policy—reflecting concern about the republican or democratic or popular aspects of constitutional government in the U.S. One must ask what tendencies may shape fundamentally the shaping of policy in the nation's third century. Ten such tendencies are: environmental constraint, the modern mixed economy, the changing international order, postindustrial society, changing political values and ideologies, modern mass communications, urban society, the growing density and changing balance of federalism, the modern administrative state, and the changing character of public policy. Popular soverneignty, the people's ability to control government, is a useful rubric under which to consider democratic conditions for shaping public policy. The party system is critical in effectuating popular sovereignty. Other concerns are the role of interest groups, political and civic participation, and elections. Requirements of popular sovereignty culminate constitutionally in policy shaping by responsible officials: Congress and the president. Our ways of shaping policy are as subject to constructive change through public understanding as through legislative actions or constitutional amendments.

Charles E. Gilbert is Professor of Political Science at Swarthmore College, where he served as Provost from 1969–74. He is currently Senior Fellow at Brookings Institution and was formerly a Fellow in the Rockefeller Foundation. His publications include "Welfare Policy" in the Handbook of Political Science *and* Governing the Suburbs.

THIS is a drastically abbreviated version of the paper written as background for the Bicentennial Conference on the Constitution. I thought the original paper stringently selective and even summarily obscure, so its distillation presents a problem. In this version I shall omit some topics of the original entirely and truncate discussion of others severely.

The four topics of the Bicentennial Conference overlap constructively. In particular, issues about "The Shaping of Public Policy" and "The Effectiveness of Governmental Operations" seem reciprocal. "The Shaping of Public Policy" might equally be construed as the public shaping of policy—as reflecting concern about the republican or democratic or popular aspects of constitutional government in the United States. That is how I have construed it, with a weather eye on revolutionary values, governmental effectiveness, and foreign affairs.

In this interpretation, which relates the constitutional order to liberal democratic values primarily, the topic remains immense. Still, if we can refer without hubris to the proceedings at Philadelphia in 1776 and 1787, we can see that the popular dimension of government was, for the participants in those proceedings, just that—a dimension of government presumptively critical for most and pervasive for many, but not the entirety of government for anyone. Liberty, equality, justice, and the effectiveness of government in behalf of security and welfare were all concerns potentially limiting the popular dimensions of government as well as dependent on popular sovereignty in degree. But these issues of limitation and dependence—of the scope and structure of popular sovereignty

—are, I suppose, more difficult today institutionally than they were in the founding period; and there is probably no more theoretical agreement about them today.

In my definition of the topic and appraisal of the issues it presents, formal revision of the Constitution turns out to be of marginal concern. For the most part, this paper deals with extraconstitutional institutions; and I conclude that constitutional amendment is unlikely to contribute substantially to their improvement.

This seems to me so despite vast changes in American life since the founding period—changes accompanied, however, by operative changes in the Constitution as well—and despite the changes in our immediate experiencing and in prospect today. But neither my constitutional conclusion nor the changing conditions of American public life should be taken for granted. So this exercise begins with an attempt to identify trends and prospects in American society that seem most likely to be troublesome for the shaping of public policy.

TRENDS AND PROSPECTS

Nearly two centuries ago, the movement toward the American Constitution was grounded consequentially in analysis of American society and of its relation to the world abroad. Now American society sustains professions for planning and futurism, and our literature of grand analysis and extrapolation is enormous. But there is no avoiding the controversial task of selection from this literature, as well as from one's own observations and speculations; one must ask what tendencies may shape fundamentally the shaping of policy in the nation's third century. I shall identify 10 elliptically, prescinding, I hope, from the most obviously topical, attempting to steer between apocalypse and complacency, pursuing no particular order of urgency or priority, and foregoing elaboration.

1. *Environmental constraint.* This might be termed the Heilbroner prospect, consisting in resource shortages and growing pressure on the human habitat, posing limits to economic growth and prompting prodigies of public regulation or even allocation.[1] If this is ultimately a controversial prospect, scenarios short of the ultimate—nevertheless entailing altered growth and more collective allocation—are less so; and in almost any version of this prospect public regulation appears more pervasive and the "people of plenty" hypothesis about American democratic politics is qualified.

2. *The modern mixed economy.* This economy may be more susceptible to inflation than its pre-Keynsian precursor—not just politically, but endemically. If so, it poses hard decisions both technically and politically in pressures for regulation and redistribution, complicating social justice; and the destructive effects of inflation on modern democracies have been considerable. This economy is also more characteristically a service economy whose "new property" and "new income" tend to enlarge dependence on public institutions and collective decisions.[2] The govern-

mental sector bulks larger in its national-income accounts, enlarging the scope of public policy; but it also exhibits a growing "third sector" largely dependent on public policy and raising difficult issues of subsidy and accountability.[3] This economy is further characterized by large organizations in all sectors, raising political issues of elephantine pluralism difficult to compass for individual actors and for democratic theory, allegedly generating a bureaucratic symbiosis of public and private organizations and pressure for planning in and from the private sector.[4]

3. *The changing international order.* Certainly international considerations, political and economic, played a large role in the constitutional movement and in the evolution of early American political alignments. Arguably, our international conditions today are more like those of the late eighteenth century than like those of the late nineteenth century; but the critical question for the shaping of public policy now is how they may be historically and categorically unique—a question considered more extensively in Professor Oliver's paper. Some aspects of that question stem from topics already mentioned: for example, environmental and resource controls and the multinational corporation, along with inchoate issues of global income distribution. In the shaping of American public policy, national security bulks conspicuously in the federal budget; and foreign affairs

---

1. Robert Heilbroner, *An Inquiry into the Human Prospect* (New York: W. W. Norton and Company, 1974).

2. Charles Reich, "The New Property," *Yale Law Journal*, 73 (1964), p. 733; S. M. Miller and Frank Reissman, *Social Class and Social Policy* (New York: Basic Books, 1968).

3. Theodore Lowi, *The End of Liberalism* (New York: W. W. Norton and Company, 1969).

4. C. W. Mills, *The Power Elite* (New York: Oxford University Press, 1956); J. K. Galbraith, *The New Industrial State* (New York: Signet Books, 1967).

nearly preoccupy the president. The capacities of political organization and of Congress to relate the national interest to the rest of the world are taxed; and they are strained by the close interpenetration of foreign and domestic policy. The issue of political and governmental capacity is perhaps most cogent in foreign affairs, where the case for constitutional reform is perhaps most apparent; but one may also ask whether the reality of bureaucratic politics is ineluctable in both foreign and domestic policy, regardless of constitutional framework.

4. *Postindustrial society.* This complex, problematical tendency is a nest of implications. As Daniel Bell and others have adumbrated the trend, its educational and professional base poses a prospect of more stringent social stratification or of meritocratic tensions and the white-collar unionism they tend to engender.[5] The large, labor-intensive service sector of this society may generate implicit tensions between social sectors apparently and independently productive in markets and those dependent on public subsidy of the functions they perform.[6] The technological and educational bases of such a society may produce demands for more explicit policy-making—for systemic approaches to policy beyond our political, administrative, or intellec-

tual capacity; for more attention to quality of life not only in the environment but also in side effects of social transactions on life-styles as well as on life chances and in social as well as economic development. Arguably, these emphases tend toward a more importunate, moralistic politics in which interests construed as values are difficult to aggregate or integrate. Historically, economic issues are commonly said to have been easier to compromise than social or cultural issues; but these types may be more closely combined in postindustrial society.[7] In such a society, public policies may seem more arbitrary as they are more general; claims for consultation and participation may be more urgent; and sensitivities to power may circumscribe public authority. Governmental devolution is apt to seem a logical response to such problems; but it may also exacerbate them while complicating accountability and neglecting general issues of regulation and redistribution.

5. *Changing political values and ideologies.* Postindustrial society may or may not materialize as an aggregate; its emergence may or may not rival that of the Industrial Revolution in profundity of effects on politics and policy. But some putative postindustrial attributes are already affecting American political organization and alignments; and some scholars think they are altering American revolutionary values toward a more ideological and divisive politics.[8]

5. Daniel Bell, *The Coming of Postindustrial Society* (New York: Basic Books, 1973). See also Samuel P. Huntington, "Post-Industrial Politics: How Benign Will It Be?," *Comparative Politics* (January 1974), pp. 163–91.

6. On the sectors, see Talcott Parsons, *Structure and Process in Modern Societies* (Glencoe, Illinois: The Free Press, 1960). On wage inflation in the service sector, see William J. Baumol, "The Macroeconomics of Unbalanced Growth," *American Economic Review*, 57 (1967), p. 415.

7. An interesting statement on this point is that of Peter Drucker, "On the Economic Basis of American Politics," *The Public Interest*, 10 (Winter 1968), p. 30.

8. The speculations I offer here derive primarily from Huntington, "Post-Industrial Politics"; Nicholas Rescher, *Welfare* (Pitts-

Most speculations I have read suggest growing strains on governmental authority and political capacity resulting from something like elite or middle-class populism. Among the values and attitudes expected to contribute to these problems are: an assumption that public solutions to problems can and should be handled technologically instead of politically; a kindred expectation of continuous technological change or progress and of institutional lag, thus challenging institutional legitimacy; a heightened emphasis on active participation, especially in the professional classes, as a moral imperative or mode of self-realization instead of a contingent protection of discrete interests and traditional rights; a resulting inflation of liberty toward the negation of power construed as arbitrary decision or interference with self-development or failure of consultation and opportunity for participation; a growing stress on equality in the de Tocqueville sense of envious leveling down as well as the charitable sense of leveling up— not necessarily with centralizing tendencies, but with chronic meritocratic tensions; more particularistic interests in communities defined by attributes of culture or life-style; increasing attention to quality of life through public provision of amenities and environmental regulation; and rejection of political bargaining and compromise, as opposed to participation and integration.

Such tendencies may be adduced pejoratively, as threats to political legitimacy and stability, or they

may be approved as natural extensions of American revolutionary values. They might be both; they may not develop any way. The likeliest trend in revolutionary values, I think, is the progressive assimilation of liberty to equality. There is probably also some tension between revolutionary values (including humanistic, altruistic values) and the conditions of large-scale, programmatic, and pluralistic government. Apparent disjunctions between overt and covert policies— between the rhetoric of electoral politics, the terms of interest-group negotiations, and the mechanics of political coalition—can stimulate the issue of trust, so much discussed today.[9]

While political tolerance and understanding might as plausibly wax in the technological and educational circumstances of postindustrial society, this seems likeliest to occur in diffusions of authority and devolutions of function at odds with systemic conceptions of policy. In any case, there are outstanding claims for racial equality and social welfare left over from agrarian and industrial stages that can hardly be settled equitably in a generation.

6. *Modern mass communications*. Social science seems to be agnostic on the effects of electronic mass communications for individual development and social organization. I think common sense suggests they are pervasive. And I suppose the effects of television for political organization and opinion formation have been profound—taken in tandem with other tendencies mentioned here and together with electronic data processing. The most general effects, I believe, have been

burgh: University of Pittsburgh Press, 1972), ch. 9; and M. Donald Hancock and Gideon Sjoberg, eds., *Politics in the Post-Welfare State* (New York: Columbia University Press, 1972), esp. pp. 1–113.

9. On overt and covert policies, see Robert A. Dahl, *Who Governs?* (New Haven: Yale University Press, 1961).

the nationalization of issues and organizational erosion of political parties, especially in presidential politics. A combination of communications technology, market organization, and professional ethos has probably produced a pattern of journalistic homogeneity in the mainstream media that has high influence contingently. More pertinent may be the allegation that during the last decade the major media adopted a doctrine of active opposition to governmental policy, especially at the presidential level, and emphasized shaping, not merely informing, of public opinion.[10] On this view the fourth estate now plays a more deliberate and partisan role in shaping policy, competing more directly with political and governmental institutions. I don't profess to know whether such allegations are well founded; but I suspect the problem stems inherently from the scale and visibility of our principal journalistic enterprises and is perhaps reciprocally enhanced by the decline of political organization and by less tractable issues of governmental secrecy and publicity, including the opportunistic use of the press by pluralistic public bureaucracies. Allegations of journalistic partisanship are not new in American politics with respect to either substantial accuracy or systematic bias: remember Thomas Jefferson! Still, the corporate status and professional conventions of the principal journalistic enterprises are more strictly important, if largely implicit, issues of public policy today; and as public policy becomes more technical and recondite, so do the problems of informative reporting and media marketing.

7. *An urban society.* Preceding postindustrialism logically and chronologically, urbanization changed American political organization and challenged its Jeffersonian doctrines. This has long been an urban nation; but the problem of the "spread city" is more recent in its demands on politics and policy. These include disparities between territorial community and large-scale industrial organization or association.[11] They probably also include the public-service diseconomies of large agglomerations—not only economic and environmental, but also in the problems of bureaucratic capacity and responsiveness in dealing with people directly where they live. Such urbanization has raised potentially serious jurisdictional issues in relating the functional logic of public management to political organization and civic participation based on residential patterns within governmental boundaries, while the urban regions and their jurisdictional divisions are the loci of basic cleavages—racial, class, and cultural—in American politics. They long have been. But these tendencies are more apparent in national policy now and prospectively; and, as remarked below, national policies reach more deeply into local governance today.

8. *The growing density and changing balance of federalism.* Probably the majority view among scholars is that American federalism has always been a system more of shared than of compartmentalized functions as well as of close public-private collaboration, though inter-

10. The bases of this allegation are discussed in Huntington, "Post-Industrial Politics," pp. 182–86. The allegation antedates Watergate, and is perhaps most persuasive with respect to the war in Vietnam.

11. This is a prominent theme of Scott Greer, *The Emerging City* (New York: The Free Press, 1962).

pretations differ in degree.[12] But in the last 15 years particularly, there has been a quantum increase of density, complexity, and (less certainly) centralization in American federalism. In that period, federal grants to state and local governments have risen from 16.4 to about 28 percent of national domestic expenditures and from 11.6 to about 21 percent of state and local revenues. Direct federalism (grants to localities, bypassing states), private federalism (grants to nongovernmental institutions), and regional federalism (grants to regional planning or functional agencies) are, frequently in combination, responses to problems or importunities in urban and postindustrial society. They strengthen new program constituencies and establish new professions; they are sometimes attempts to target on national objectives through new jurisdictions or quasi-governments; and their clientele-participation requirements seem an equalizing sequel to earlier civil service requirements.

Scholars disagree about whether the balance of centralization and decentralization has really altered much in recent years (prescinding here from the role of the federal courts).[13] But the national policy

role in such fields as education, child and youth development, and health care has probably grown by comparison with state and local roles since 1960, and federal regulatory measures for environmental control and resource conservation have developed the putative national police power through state and local governments and sanctioned state and local policies through grants.[14]

Anent the shaping of public policy, the new patterns of federalism exemplify tendencies remarked in the preceding topics. They also pose political complexities of their own through new functional or professional constituencies and some further erosion of general-purpose local government. Thus, they raise issues of public accountability at all governmental levels, as well as through devolution to private institutions, even as they create new channels of participation and marginal redistribution.

9. *The modern administrative state.* The problems of this topic are familiar enough, although the basic change in scale of the federal bureaucracy has occurred in less than the last half century.[15] In the shaping of public policy, this has been a change of constitutional importance, although the federal bureaucracy hardly holds the implicit constitutional status of adminis-

12. Morton Grodzins, *The American System* (Chicago: Rand-McNally, 1966). For the minority view, see Harry N. Scheiber, *The Condition of American Federalism: An Historian's View* (Washington: U.S. Senate Committee on Government Operations (Committee Print), 1966).

13. Numbers in civilian public employment at the several governmental levels are not, I think, at issue here (compare fn. 15). Since World War II, state and local public employment (excluding education) has risen much more rapidly than federal government employment—at the state level most rapidly of all, and especially in the 1960s; and the state-local increase is still larger comparatively if educational employment is included.

14. The automobile figures in two random examples: EPA's mandated standards for state and local air-pollution control programs, currently under litigation (the Clean Air Act of 1970), and the grant condition that state laws permit right-hand turns at red lights (Energy Conservation Act of 1975).

15. Federal civilian employment increased by 70 percent, 1930–40; by 97 percent, 1940–50; by 17 percent, 1950–60; and by 20 percent, 1960–70. Per 1,000 population, it increased by some two-thirds in the 1930s and by some three-fourths in the 1940s, leveling off thereafter in this ratio.

tration in Britain or in some European nations: it raises issues of accountability to elected officials, of internal conceptions of responsibility and technical rationality, of appropriate responsiveness to clients, and of cost-productivity. The inertial properties of bureaucratic pluralism raise obvious problems for popular sovereignty. What effects public-employee organization and collective bargaining may have at the federal level remains to be seen; but this uncertain prospect assumes a constitutional importance similar to that of the decline of the legal doctrine of privilege. Both tendencies depart potentially from traditional democratic understandings of administrative responsibility, as do modern developmental doctrines of organization and management or, in another direction, conceptions of efficiency adapted from conglomerate management. Clearly, the organization, staffing, public relations, and managerial premises of public administration are central in the shaping of public policy.

10. *The changing character of public policy.* The more public policy there is, the more it is shaping—cumulative and reflexive—as well as shaped. Moreover, in a systems conception of politics, policies are not only outputs in response to demands; they also generate new expectations, demands, and (perhaps) political overloads. Such obvious considerations as these seem likely to become more consequential than they already are with the growing density and complexity of policy.

One classical democratic challenge lies in the technicality of much of modern policy. The problem of relating layman and expert in governance goes back to Plato; but science, technology, and economics

have complicated it in ways still classically identified by Don K. Price.[16] Then there is the challenge of connection and comprehensiveness in large-scale government—how everything potentially relates to everything else—which administrative organization can only mitigate. The problem of clustering policies under systemic priorities and administrative rubrics is an organizational classic, if increasingly acute. In one formulation, it is the problem of planning, which has figured ambiguously in the language of economic policy since the Depression and the Employment Act of 1946, reemerging now in the Humphrey-Javits Bill and, with proposals for deregulation, challenging our capacities for more selective, less generally crescive policy-making.[17] One harbinger of postindustrial society may have been the advent of federal planning for professional manpower together with abundant subsidies of research and development in higher education after mid-century. Such policies create personal equities and fiscal entailments that tend to endure: they are hard to plan intelligently and hard to alter politically. In the same period, the objectives of social policy have become more explicitly developmental and redevelopmental—by which I mean to suggest the promotion of individual and community improvement or rehabilitation through public services and subsidies. Such poli-

16. See, for example, Don K. Price, *The Scientific Estate* (Cambridge, Mass.: Harvard University Press, 1965).
17. On this argument, see Galbraith, *The New Industrial State*; and Robert L. Heilbroner, "The American Plan," *The New York Times Magazine*, 25 January 1976. And consider the preference of business leadership for statutory and administrative regulation over effluent and emission charges as a form of environmental policy.

cies commonly depend on the motivation of individual subjects and the mobilization of particular communities for their results, so they are hard to implement effectively on a large scale. The range and penetration of public regulations have been extended impressively through national policy: civil rights and equal opportunity legislation (and adjudication) are examples, as are the intensification of professional regulation and extension of measures for environmental protection and energy conservation already remarked.

A well-known analysis of public policies classifies them as distributive (most subsidies), redistributive, regulatory, and constituent (alterations of rules, structures, and opportunities for shaping policy).[18] One point of this analysis is that the characteristics of policies tend to determine the modes and loci of shaping policies. Conceding that these distinctions frequently apply more to perceptions than to effects (and that the classification seems incomplete), one may still suggest a general tendency to try not only to reach but also to mitigate redistributive objectives through other types of policy. But it seems likely that redistributive perceptions in policy are becoming more general as policy is more extensive and as the quest for equality quickens. And regulatory measures, as they become more pervasive, may also appear more invidious and redistributive. So the emollient tendency toward distributive and constituent policies is understandable, though it may be running out of room and (as I'll suggest below) may not be unequivocally good for democratic institutions.

Finally, this may be the place to note the growing role of the federal trial judiciary in shaping public policy. Environmental and civil rights regulation are leading examples, wherein district courts function roughly as regulatory commissions pursuant to generous statutory delegations under relaxed rules of standing and of extended discovery, finding legislative facts and fashioning comprehensive remedies prospectively in analogs to equity for grievances based in public-policy claims. This extension of civil proceedings to public law has been paralleled by the expansion of statutory interests open to judicial review of administrative action at all levels through congressional objectives, including federal-grant standards, and perhaps through taxpayer standing to press certain constitutional interests against federal policy.[19] In short, more national policy is being made by courts (as much local policy long has been) —not through judicial review of legislation, but by judicial participation in administration, and increasingly by trial instead of appeal.

Some of the trends and prospects just suggested are undeniably real; others—their projections especially —are problematical. That goes for their institutional implications as well. Only one general implication need be remarked now. In the terms of the Bicentennial Conference, tensions among governmental effec-

18. Theodore Lowi, "Four Systems of Policy, Politics, and Choice," *Public Administration Review*, 32 (1972), p. 298.

19. See, for example, *Flast* v. *Cohen*, 392 U.S. 83; the discussions in *Barlow* v. *Collins*, 397 U.S. 159; and *U.S.* v. *Students Challenging Regulatory Agency Procedure (SCRAP)*, 412 U.S. 669.

tiveness, the popular role in the shaping of policy, and the evolution of revolutionary values may continue to intensify. Some trends discussed above—for example, the administrative state, the modern mixed economy, and the more pervasive regulatory role of the national government—are at odds with aspects of the doctrinal revolutionary heritage. The popular and righteous aspects of that heritage are at odds not only with the large-scale elite pluralism of major American institutions, but also with certain republican versions of the constitutional heritage that tend to reinforce the bargaining mode in policy-making. These tensions will be evident in the balance of this paper.

THE THEORY OF POPULAR SOVEREIGNTY

I take this section title with some reservations from the conference agenda. Technically, I take popular sovereignty to mean the grounding of government—both its Constitution and its continuing rule—in the population at large as a legal or contractual understanding; or, practically speaking, "the people's ability to control their government."[20] It is an ancient notion, historically fundamental in democratic development, though fraught with ambiguities and hardly the whole of democratic thought. In modern usage it is apt to convey a populistic emphasis on absolute majority rule at the same time that, in modern political analysis, the formal conception of popular sovereignty is increasingly problema-

tical.[21] In this form, popular sovereignty conflicts potentially with conceptions of constitutionalism or limited government.[22] Still, the conception has figured prominently in American revolutionary values, and in a limiting sense it is a useful rubric under which to consider democratic conditions for the shaping of public policy. Such conditions are considered most summarily here.

As to the dominant issues of twentieth-century constitutional criticism, I suppose the founding compromise was anti-populist but not anti-popular or anti-democratic. It provided a system of republican, or representative, government, but with emphasis on arrangements for balancing responsiveness by responsibility. These arrangements— primarily the federal bargain and the separation of powers—reflected serious concerns for liberty, security, tranquility, and official effectiveness; and I believe they reflected also the framers' preponderant view of their society as one in which serious inequalities of

20. Charles S. Hyneman, *Popular Government in America* (New York: Atherton, 1968), p. 8.

21. On the connection with majoritarianism, see Austin Ranney and Willmoore Kendall, *Democracy and the American Party System* (New York: Harcourt, Brace, 1956). For some criticisms of the conception from different perspectives, see Robert A. Dahl, *A Preface to Democratic Theory* (Chicago: University of Chicago Press, 1957); and Giovanni Sartori, *Democratic Theory* (New York: Praeger, 1963).

22. S. M. Lipset, in *The First New Nation* (New York: Basic Books, 1963), argues that, through the heritage of constitutionalism, American politics was able to maintain a distinction between the source of authority (or sovereignty) and the agents of authority, avoiding populistic excesses, or what Samuel P. Huntington terms "praetorian politics": *Political Order in Changing Societies* (New Haven: Yale University Press, 1968).

condition (as distinct from sharp political competition or animosity) were unlikely to develop within the constitutional provisions for liberty and a national economy.[23]

According to some closely related lines of constitutional criticism, the framework of federalism and imperfectly separated powers is at once redundant in distraint of tyranny and overabundant in restraint of majority rule. In the most general version of this view, the "large republic" originally created through federalism is the sufficient condition of liberty through its natural pluralism, while the reinforcement of localism and fragmentation of majorities through formal constitutional arrangements are otiose or perverse or both with respect to liberty, equality, and public capacity. But I suspect that this view ignores the founding concern about how factional designs within government might encourage the mobilization of passionate or intolerant publics; and I suppose that this view identifies liberty with equality and responsibility with responsiveness in greater degree than did the preponderant republican opinion of the founders.[24]

These issues of assimilation or distinction of liberty and equality, and of responsibility and responsiveness, are a continuing heritage in American democratic theory, I

think, though I have to neglect their various implications here.[25] Perhaps it will suffice to say that majority-rule and minority-rights conceptions of American politics, and pragmatic and formalistic conceptions of American politics, remain pertinent tensions in American democracy today in arrangements for the shaping of policy.[26]

Finally, I hope it will also suffice here merely to point to the pertinence of certain modern perspectives on American democracy. I'll identify these as elitist, pluralist, popular (or electoral), and participatory. The labels alone may suggest enough for present purposes to readers of contemporary American political science. In certain versions, as I observed in the original paper, each of these perspectives stands for critical attributes of American democratic politics. Within limits, these pertinent versions include elite pluralism and elite electoral democracy, participatory pluralism and participatory electoral democracy; but I suppose the tension between pluralist and popular conceptions of American politics is central, even though such conceptions overlap in their attention to popular consultation and electoral competition. They also contend at least marginally with regard to conceptions of liberty and equality, majority rule and minority rights, responsiveness and responsibility. Thus summarily observed, these

23. A fine analysis of the framers' views on representation is contained in David G. Smith, *The Convention and the Constitution: The Political Ideas of the Founding Fathers* (New York: St. Martin's Press, 1965).

24. Dahl, *A Preface to Democratic Theory*; and M.J.C. Vile, *Constitutionalism and the Separation of Powers* (Oxford: Oxford University Press, 1967). See also William Riker, *Democracy in the United States* (New York: MacMillan, rev. ed., 1964), and *Federalism* (Boston: Little, Brown, 1964).

25. J. Roland Pennock, "Responsiveness, Responsibility, and Majority Rule," *American Political Science Review*, 56 (1952), p. 791. For an opposing view, advocating constructive accountability to electoral majorities, see Riker, *Democracy in the United States*.

26. David G. Smith, "Pragmatism and the Group Theory of Politics," *American Political Science Review*, 58 (1964), p. 600; Lowi, *The End of Liberalism*, pt. 1.

four perspectives may nevertheless provide some useful orientations in the following material.

The Practice of Popular Sovereignty

The popular dimensions of the American Constitution are constitutional emanations historically in the basic organization of the party system deriving from federalism and the separation of powers and in the constitutional protections of political activity. But they are more largely conditioned today by factors of culture and technology outside the constitutional framework. While constitutional in an Aristotelian sense, and while deeply implicated in the shaping of policy, they are subject to shaping themselves more through the understandings of citizens and practitioners than by deliberate measures of policy— critical as the latter may be on the margins.

From the comments of the organization committee for the Bicentennial Conference, I take the practice of popular sovereignty to be the central concern of committee III. And, in its extragovernmental dimensions, I'll consider the party system together with the institutional conditions of political pluralism and participation and the role of elections, omitting from the original paper material on the formation of public opinion (including mass communications) as well as elaboration on the functions and future of the party system.

1. The party system. It is a commonplace of modern political analysis that parties are strictly critical in effectuating popular sovereignty— that institutional variations in party structure and functions tend cen-

trally (but no doubt not ultimately) to determine theoretical issues discussed in the preceding section. They do this, presumably, by regularizing and legitimating opposition, organizing government (perhaps especially American government, with respect to the separation of powers), consolidating policy options for popular choice while aggregating public opinion, providing labels and at least rudimentary organizational interests to the end of electoral accountability, mitigating oligarchy and "mobilization of bias" through electoral competition, and (perhaps) encouraging participation through electoral organization. There is less analytic emphasis on the centrality of party in democratic systems today then there used to be; it is hard to say how much this disposition reflects modern reality on the one hand or historical reanalysis on the other hand. In any case, there has always been a strong strain of anti-party thought in American politics and society, beginning with the founders' animadversions on faction and continuing with concern about partisanship and the public interest.[27]

Naturally, some of this thinking has reflected official and factional dislike of opposition, but much of it appeals to views of liberty and justice discussed above. One result of this strain of thought has probably been the weakening of parties as agents of political equality; and, as I'll suggest presently, this strain of

27. See, for example, Richard Hofstadter, *The Idea of a Party System* (Berkeley: University of California Press, 1969). See also Charles S. Hyneman and George W. Carey, *A Second Federalist* (New York: Appleton-Century-Crofts, 1967), pt. 4, for selections from early congressional debates on the role of faction or party.

thought is strongly recrudescent to-day. Still, there are ample other reasons for the weakness of party in American politics.

One way to explore the role of party is through analysis of several putative party functions in the polity. Such analysis appears in the original paper anent the structuring of public opinion, social integration and the aggregation of policy interests, political mobilization and the encouragement of participation, the regularization of opposition and competition, nomination of candidates for office, organization of government, and formulation of policy. It must suffice to say here that the American party system holds a monopoly position today in none of these putative functions, liberally but (I think) realistically understood, and approximates monopoly only in nominations—where the direct primary has much mitigated party's original role. As in nominations so in other functions also the organizational role of party has been diminished considerably in the twentieth century; and this seems provisionally true of the ideological role of party in public and governmental alignments. Institutional reforms, educational and cultural change, and the progressive complexity of public policy all probably figure in this historical decline of party.

The contextual trends can be described as a progress from the conditions of a traditional to those of a modern party system, less traditionally organized and (perhaps) more rationally aligned. Arguably, such a modern party system will at last realize the designs of majoritarians for a more highly coherent, presumptively responsible two-party system; but my own argument in the original paper suggests, rather, that neither the organizational nor the ideological conditions of such a party system are cogent today.[28] Instead, the trend has been toward atrophy of party roles in communication, nomination, and organization of government across the separation of powers. Among many secular elements of this trend, recent developments in the presidential primary—abetted as I suppose by development of the electronic media—have perhaps been most influential, pulling presidency away from party in the large and apart from Congress in organization across the separation of powers.

So the condition of integral organized leadership by presidents in the responsible-party formula may be deteriorating. The conditions of party consolidation in Congress might improve a little with party realignment; but party reorganization in Congress has hardly enhanced this prospect. Presidential independence through personal coalitions and preoccupation with the media and bureaucracy may be no less a problem for party responsibility than congressional fragmentation or intractability. The shaping of public policy follows coalitions of interests, including party. These may be increasingly discrete from one sector of policy to another. The more policy there is, the more interests it engages. This

28. On the responsible party government doctrine, see Ranney and Kendall, *Democracy and the American Party System*, esp. chs. 6, 17, 20–22. On the argument for a larger party role in congressional organization, see Samuel P. Huntington, "Congressional Responses to the Twentieth Century," in David B. Truman, ed., *The Congress and America's Future* (Englewood Cliffs, N.J.: Prentice-Hall, 1965).

might strengthen party against large interest groups; but it may also make it harder for party to hold together homogeneously.

The reality of coalitions suggests a similarity in all modern democratic systems, whether two-party or multi-party. Some people infer from this similarity that which kind of party system a nation has matters little for the prospects of governmental responsibility, responsiveness, and effectiveness. Some remark a convergence of party systems in much of Western Europe, the United States, and the British Dominions from either direction toward a highly qualified two-partyism, or hybrid arrangement, functioning in any case through executive-bureaucratic interest-group coalition.[29] Some think the multi-party variant preferable for the United States— more responsive to the tendencies of postindustrial society, and in any case a logical continuation of institutional developments in the present party system and of the role of minor parties in the past.

I won't conceal my own unreconstructed dislike of this idea. One needn't be an unrestricted majoritarian to conclude that responsibility in some balance of accountability, responsiveness, and rationality is best served by a two-party system with sufficient discipline to play a considerable role in most of the functions just discussed. And coalition as an abstract noun too easily obscures, I think, the traditional distinction between coalitions formed prior to elections and those formed afterward, with its implications for governmental capacity and for

29. See, for example, Gordon Smith, *Politics in Western Europe* (New York: Holmes & Meier, 1973).

moderating or obviating conflict. I mention this issue because of its bearing on issues for consideration in the final section.

I suppose that certain formal, effectively constitutional changes would much promote multi-partyism in modern America. Scholars disagree strongly on this point; but I believe the evidence compelling that the roots of the American two-party tendency are primarily institutional, having to do with the prevalence of single-member-district plurality elections, with the Electoral College (which, with the exception of its aggregate majority requirement, is such an electoral system), and with the separation of powers. Given the qualification "primarily institutional"—in recognition of the fact that institutions are not mechanical in effect but rather condition human aspirations and efforts— I think it problematical that any one of these institutions would suffice to preserve the two-party tendency in both branches under so-called postindustrial conditions. All of them together are not strictly sufficient for unalloyed two-partyism; and this, I think, has been a good thing in our history.

Another, related prospect for the American party system is much discussed today: that is its progressive degeneration or decomposition.[30]

30. For divergent views on this prospect, see, for example, David Broder, *The Party's Over* (New York: Harper & Row, 1972); W. Dean Burnham, *Critical Elections and the Mainsprings of American Politics* (New York: W. W. Norton and Company, 1970); Everett Carll Ladd, Jr., *Transformations of the American Party System* (New York: W. W. Norton and Company, 1975); Samuel Lubell, *The Hidden Crisis in American Politics* (New York: W. W. Norton and Company, 1971); Kevin Phillips, *Mediacracy* (Garden City, New York: Doubleday, 1975); Gerald

This forecast starts with the growing independence of voters; the declining institutional and communicative role of party with the access of education and the changing popular impact and institutional position of mass media; and the culture of postindustrial society with respect to technology, authority, commitment, accommodation, and community. In one systemic version of this prognosis, the progressive regional liquidation of party competition after 1876 and 1896, sustained by the Progressive reforms that followed, served the interests of industrial capitalism by suppressing relevant economic issues, and so eroded the party system organizationally and psychologically that its recovery in the Depression and New Deal realignment was incomplete. This version doesn't logically rule out party restoration through a further, fundamental realignment; but it suggests that the vestiges of party in American practice and opinion are unlikely to sustain such a realignment. In another view, many of the presumptive functions of party in the past are redundant or performed by other institutions today: modern party structures and functions reflect the perceptions and values of postindustrial culture. The substantial atrophy of party is less ineluctable in this perspective, but at any rate probable.

In none of these prognoses is the elimination of some kind (perhaps the present kind) of party labels in elections implied; but the label would cover a low-proof, if nonetheless volatile, blend: realignments would occur with high frequency, or electoral (especially presidential) coalitions would be continuously labile and unstable. The present popular distrust of politics and low turnout in elections would presumably continue, possibly punctuated by populistic movements.[31] Government would likely lack effective composite majorities based on prescriptive popular alignments. More minor-party presidential (and perhaps congressional) campaigns would occur, abetted by recent campaign-finance legislation and imaginably by new election laws. Some minor-party continuities might develop, although many campaigns would be personal and episodic: absent effective institutionalization, the American demand for autonomous leadership would intensify. Conceivably some minor parties would, in combination, forestall Electoral College majorities, forcing coalition politics to a new stage and enlarging the role of unpopular political bargaining. A likelier scenario, I suppose, relates the modern presidential primary process to the Electoral College: in this prospect, a popular candidate counted out in the convention pursues his campaign through the Electoral College to Congress and to the point of a corrupt bargain.

None of the prognoses has, so far as I know, gone on to speculate in detail about which so-called functions or contributions of the sometime American two-party system would be most seriously diminished or missed in this scenario. The distributive implications of such a new populist mode in the

Pomper, *Voters' Choice* (New York: Dodd, Mead, 1975); James Sundquist, *Dynamics of the Party System* (Washington: The Brookings Institution, 1973).

31. Such current tendencies in the electorate are discussed in Arthur H. Miller et al., "A Majority Party in Disarray: Policy Polarization in the 1972 Election" (The Center for Political Studies of the University of Michigan, mimeo).

educational and occupational class pattern of postindustrial society are, I think, disturbing. Competition for equalization of political influence would probably be destabilizing and perversely effective in the absence of secular conservative majorities. The popular accountability of public bureaucracy and thus of much public policy would probably be diminished. So would the integrative effects of the two-party system if realignment were more substantially perpetual; politics would be much less emollient. Governmental capacity for decision, and the apparent responsibility of policy, would presumably be reduced. So, then, would authority and the prospects of liberal democracy.

I believe the foregoing prognoses should be taken seriously. But we are now in a period of some academic and popular skepticism about the contributions of party in the past (and especially in modern democracy), so not everyone will share this concern. Moreover, many scholars believe the prospect I have outlined uncertainly is likely to be avoided, indefinitely deferred, or even reversed by emergence of a modern, responsible party system. James Sundquist presents a strong case for the likelihood that the party alignment of about 1960, appropriately modified, will be restored in the aftermath of issues of the 1960s orthogonal to the alignment.[32] Others think that alignment already much changed in its regional and class composition, if perhaps insufficiently so for party stability and capacity.[33] Still others think basic party realignment on regional,

occupational, educational, religious, and maybe racial grounds possible or likely or perhaps necessary for restoration of the role of parties. Just now, the imponderable claims of the young demographic bulge in the electorate are probably of critical significance for long-run consolidation of the party system. And there are others who perceive a trend toward more rational, issue-oriented voting in recent presidential elections suggesting that, with appropriate realignment (and perhaps the reorganization of Congress), a more consolidated, responsible two-party system will result.[34] In this prospect, party degeneration and voter alienation are far from inevitable; they are potentially signs of realignment and of demand for party reorganization.

If the future of party is in the balance, then we have a critical issue of how to provide for a system of institutionalized national leadership and opposition that is electorally responsible. That includes the issue of whether a more consolidated, tightly aligned, and highly programmatic party system is either feasible or preferable to the party system of the recent past. In any case, no satisfactory substitute for party is in sight, or, I think, imaginable. We cannot count on necessity to reconstitute party. So we should consider the conditions of party restoration.

Foremost among those conditions today, I suggest, is some retreat from the current presidential-primary system. One useful modification along this line might be Senator Walter Mondale's proposal for the regional scheduling of primaries. But I'll observe in the concluding section that a large role

32. Sundquist, *Dynamics of the Party System*.

33. Phillips, *Mediacracy*.

34. Pomper, *Voters' Choice*.

for the party convention and for congressional delegates in it seems to be desirable. And, lest the scenario mentioned above mislead, I'll also plead for continuation of the Electoral College as a likely institutional support of two-partyism in the United States.

2. *The role of interest groups and associations.* The issues bearing on group and associational roles in shaping policy derive from issues of democratic theory mentioned in the second section. They have to do with elite, pluralist, electoral, and participatory perspectives on national politics; with the articulation of liberty (or autonomy) with equality; and (ambiguously) with responsible versus responsive views of the public interest. In particular, two concerns mark current discussions of pluralism in the shaping of American public policy. One is whether the group-competition system is too considerably elitist and exclusive. The other concern is whether the shaping of policy is insufficiently public—that is, whether the terms of group interaction with government, combined with conceivably excessive devolution of policy to participating or autonomous private organizations, impairs governmental responsibility.

There is no satisfactory way of settling these issues empirically. The participation of groups and private institutions in policy shaping is simply too diverse and profuse; and there is no agreed upon methodology for analyzing the interaction of group influence and governmental authority, or even its results in, say, the federal budget. I don't mean that patterns of group importunity in government, or specific decision-making procedures, can't be analyzed; and they have been analyzed extensively and inten-

sively. I do mean that ultimately one consults one's general experience of American politics and one's normative conceptions of American democracy to evaluate the contribution of pluralist arrangements to the shaping of policy.

I think American intellectual perspectives on pluralism have been changing recently and that the system of organized and corporate pluralism is increasingly seen as unduly elitist and exclusive. Popular and participatory concerns are more urgent today. So the perception of undue pluralism can create a kind of political malaise. At the same time, attempts to counter this in public policy through distributive and constituent policies (see the first section)—that is, by extending the pluralist subsystem—may ultimately seem a hair-of-the-dog cure, warping and mortgaging the substance of policy through arrangements for the shaping of policy.[35] In any case, the problem of organized pluralism in popular and participatory perceptions is, I think, one of both appearance and reality; and, as I've suggested, the reality is hard to evaluate.

Pluralist interpretations of American politics usually have to do with cultural tendencies and potential groups and with circles or institu-

35. A couple of such participatory arrangements may be provocative illustrations: the Community Action Program and Comprehensive Health Planning (based on legislation of 1964 and 1966). There were cogent reasons for both in the targeting of policy—in one case largely on neighborhoods; in the other on regions. And there were persuasive constituent reasons in the countering of state and municipal bureaucracies or of hospitals and medical societies. But in each case there was also much diffusion of policy instead of more focused redistribution of income in the Poverty Program or effective regulation of medical facilities to reach a major source of escalating health care costs.

tions of leadership, as well as with the direct access of organized interests to government. Pluralist interpretations make claims for the political functions of the pluralist system much like those made for political parties; indeed, a crucial issue in pluralism concerns the balance of pluralist with popular (electoral) elements, as well as with elite and participatory elements. For the group-competition system to serve its purported functions of informing policy, adjusting equality with equity, modulating conflict through organization and overlapping membership, and mediating mass society, several conditions have been stipulated by both pluralists and their critics.[36] Group membership should be prevalent, overlapping, and voluntary; group interests should be largely homogeneous and group organization basically ubiquitous; group leadership should be responsive or accountable; opportunity for governmental access should be general, equitable, and applicable to all sectors of policy; and group competition or countervailing power should therefore be effective.

I think political scientists with no particular ideological axe to grind have increasingly challenged the foregoing assumptions empirically and in degree; and others contest them more categorically. For example, with respect to national politics, organizational membership is considerably less ubiquitous, more perfunctory, and less unprejudicially distributed than the assumptions require in any stringent sense. The extent to which overlapping group memberships tend to obviate or mitigate conflict is also uncertain,

especially for the population at large, though the theory of cross-cutting cleavages with respect to more contingent cultural and economic alignments in relation to political party identification, finds more empirical support. Such general consensus on liberal-democratic rules of the game as might prompt emergent organizational resistance to their violation by group arrangements with government is empirically problematical; so, on close inspection and consideration of potential issues and concerns, are the essential homogeneity of many group interests and the responsiveness or accountability of many group leaders. The voluntary nature of interest-group membership is frequently qualified by sanctions or incentives designed to internalize the benefits of membership—for example, the union shop or professional accreditation. So the organization and political negotiation of groups appear to reflect the entrepreneurialism of leaders more than the demands of members—from which follows a proclivity toward collusive or protective bargaining and the mutual recognition of spheres of influence.[37]

Such findings and inferences (some of them partial or primarily theoretical) tend to qualify the pluralist assumptions. But they are eclectic, as pluralism is disparate.

36. For example, David B. Truman, *The Governmental Process* (New York: Knopf, 1951).

37. The vast literature on this subject is reviewed in J. David Greenstone, "Group Theories," in Fred I. Greenstein and Nelson W. Polsby, eds., *Handbook of Political Science*, vol. 2 (Reading, Mass.: Addison-Wesley Pub., 1975); and Robert Salisbury, "Interest Groups," vol. 4, ibid. Two remarkable recent analytic treatments are: Mancur Olson, *The Logic of Collective Action* (Cambridge, Mass.: Harvard University Press, 1965), and James Q. Wilson, *Political Organizations* (Cambridge: Harvard University Press, 1973).

Critics have tended to focus on economic policies—on subsidy, regulation (especially), or protection of certain large economic sectors and factors. Corporations, trade associations, labor unions, and farm organizations come prominently to mind. (Such issues as licensure, franchising, and contracting in state and local politics have seemed troublesome but less portentous.) There has been less concern about the trend of public devolution and subvention in the nonmarket sector that I have termed "private federalism" in the first section.[38] No doubt, whose ox is gored or whose axe is ground affects one's critical perspective.

Four major, intermingled concerns about the place of organized pluralism in the shaping of policy may be identified. One is the problem of vested, preemptive privilege in the reciprocal pervasion of governmental and private purposes.[39] A second is the problem of internal group organization—of bureaucratic management and entrepreneurial autonomy.[40] A third is the mobilization of bias that group strategic position and elite symbolic leadership may contribute to public opinion and electoral politics.[41] And a fourth is the implica-

tions of interest-group liberalism and group bargaining for administrative responsibility in discretion and administrative rationality in decision.[42] Scholars tend to argue now that congressional lobbying is more protective than aggressive— that constituent pressures and legislators' electoral independence together are, with the promptings of party loyalty and professional staff, effective counterweights.[43]

No doubt this depends on the nature of the legislative issue. But scholars tend to worry more today about administrative action—about regulatory capture, agency cooptation, bureaucratic decorum, and Executive-branch coordination— where institutional public-interest norms are appropriately more stringent than in Congress, but also subject to more rigorous public expectations. Such tendencies and concerns suggest an establishmentarian style of policy shaping to populist critics.

In response to such concerns, populist critics turn first to other topics of this section—to party organization for responsible leadership and popular influence through elections and to distributed participation. The latter approach, as was observed in the second section, has lately been a trend of national policy in numerous functional fields.

38. Not that officials of the federal government have been unconcerned about problems of accountability in this trend. See, for example, the looseleaf *Grants Administration Handbook* of DHEW.

39. Grant McConnell, *Private Power and American Democracy* (New York: Knopf, 1966); Lowi, *The End of Liberalism*.

40. McConnell, *Private Power*, Galbraith, *The New Industrial State*.

41. E. E. Schnattschneider, *The Semisovereign People* (New York: Holt, Rinehart, & Winston, 1960); Peter Bachrach, *The Theory of Democratic Elitism* (Boston: Little, Brown, 1967); Murray Edelman, *The Symbolic Uses of Politics* (Urbana, Ill.: University of Illinois Press, 1964).

42. Lowi, *The End of Liberalism*; Robert A. Dahl and Charles E. Lindblom, *Politics, Economics, and Welfare* (New York: Harper & Row, 1953), ch. 12. See also David G. Smith, "Pragmatism and the Group Theory of Politics."

43. See, for example, Heinz Eulau, "Lobbyists: The Wasted Profession," *Public Opinion Quarterly*, 28 (1964), p. 27; Raymond Bauer et al., *American Business and Public Policy* (New York: Atherton, 1964). Compare E. P. Herring, *Group Representation before Congress* (Baltimore: Johns Hopkins University Press, 1929).

As a subject of public policy, it provides, I think, some evidence that pluralism flourishes innovatively as well as conservatively.

Another option, subject to constitutional limitations, is the promotion, protection, and regulation of opportunities for participation in associations and functional constituencies as an object of public policy. Constitutional law has increasingly sustained legislative regulations of group organization and participation.[44] Here (determinations of socially harmful association aside) the problem is to balance organizational capacity with accountability, and collective purpose with individual rights. American public policy is less pervasive in this field than is the case in democratic nations with more Hobbesian or Rousseauian residues; and it is more normally a state than a national concern. Most commonly in national policy it accompanies group or constituent privilege, as in agricultural or labor organization, and more recently in the social services sector. Few policy issues entail more delicate calibrations of autonomy with equality. And the effective reach of statutory or judicial regulation has its limits, whatever the scope of affectation with a public interest or of formal participatory rights. But this recondite field of policy should not be ignored in contemplation of the shaping of policy.

Besides political organization and such regulation of interest-group organization as is politically and constitutionally feasible, two elements of the constitutional order should be considered seriously in concerns about imbalance or im-

mobility in the pluralist demand-response system. These are the Executive branch and the federal system. Anent the Executive branch, four perennial issues might be considered. One is closer congressional and/or judicial control of legislative delegation. Another is reconsideration of the independent-commission form of regulatory administration, together with selective deregulation. A third is further judicialization of (primary regulatory) administration through internal procedures, special appellate jurisdictions in the Executive branch, or expansion of judicial review. And a fourth is personnel reform toward administrative consolidation and general management through something like the senior-civil-service proposal of 20 years ago.[45] These issues are more appropriately discussed in the fourth section. Here I'll merely observe that, together with proposals to reconstitute the party system toward enhancement of the popular demand-response system, they raise subtle issues of the meaning of responsibility in government and politics—issues adumbrated in the second section.

Finally, one should consider the larger role for public planning projected tentatively in section 2, whatever planning may mean. Inter alia, I suppose it means at least an expansion of regulation of particular market practices under general legislative standards to the selective direction and control of investment and development pursuant to changing national objectives. Then the question is how national objectives are to be determined; that is, in what balance of governmental and industrial, legislative and executive

44. There is some discussion of these issues in Hans A. Linde and George Bunn, *Legislative and Administrative Processes* (New York: The Foundation Press, 1976).

45. Readers may recognize in these suggestions—the first and fourth especially—the program of Lowi, *The End of Liberalism*.

determination.[46] If "the prerequisites of more rational collective choice begin with the prerequisites of improving hierarchy and polyarchy"—that is, public bureaucracy and organized electoral responsibility—then more than marginal alteration of regulatory administration (and probably of legislative delegation as well) is implied.[47] The common criticism that regulation might gain in planning capacity through more integral location in the Executive branch might become more cogent; and high-level civil service consolidation might become more pertinent in determining the balance of governmental and corporate or associational roles in planning. But ultimately, I suppose, this balance would depend on political organization toward legislative-executive responsibility, including such patterns of political leadership and public opinion as would tend to preclude domination of the parties by economic organizations and radical instability of national objectives. And that, I think, means something less than the thoroughgoing responsible-party-government program, which seems infeasible anyway.

I'll return to these issues briefly in the next section. And I'll notice some issues of federalism in the following subsection.

3. *Political and civic participation.* The access of large-scale organization and the perceived practice of elite pluralism have produced an interesting doctrinal reaction. In this reaction, the state-society distinction of liberal and classical popular-control democracy has been challenged both in substantive policy and popular sovereignty—largely on the ground that it is no longer consistent with political reality. Participatory and popular theorists urge that the scope of policy be extended more broadly into industrial and professional organization so as to broaden participation (and vice versa), both functionally and electorally.[48] In its functional thrust, such theory is a partial reformulation of pluralism (with antecedents in early twentieth-century British and European thinking).

This approach may argue for functional supplementation of electoral participation, or it may go further toward displacement of majoritarian electoral control through proportional representation and functional participation. In the latter vein, it tends to redefine traditional notions of political equality. In any case, it looks primarily to local government, functional quasi-governments, and regulated industrial self-government in some degree as the arenas of participation. While the first and third of these arenas have been the traditional foci of proposals for participation, the second has figured more prominently in federal public policy: here I have in mind such disparate instrumentalities as soil-conservation districts, community-action agencies, health service agencies. To these random examples, one might add the recent consultative and advisory requirements in block-grant programs, or in child-development and compensa-

46. For some tendentious but provocative views of the former balance today and tomorrow, see Galbraith, *The New Industrial State*; and Robert L. Heilbroner, *Business Civilization in Decline* (New York: W. W. Norton and Company, 1976).

47. Dahl and Lindblom, *Politics, Economics, and Welfare*, p. 436.

48. For example, Peter Bachrach, *The Theory of Democratic Elitism*.

tory-education grants. One might also add the modern proposals for community control, neighborhood government, and the territorial dismemberment of large cities.[49] Conceivably these are straws in the wind, listing toward an extended conception of federalism as distributed self-government.[50]

I mentioned above that issues of federalism figure in concerns about pluralism; and this seems an appropriate place at which to notice them. They have loosely to do with perspectives I have termed formalist and pragmatist. One issue concerns the erosion of general-purpose, broadly responsible local government under modern conditions. If there is a classical democratic theory, then one of its antipathies in early utilitarianism was toward separate functional jurisdictions, noncomparable and thus electorally unaccountable in politics.[51] Special-purpose public authorities and subsidized nonprofit corporations as governmental surrogates for certain public functions, as well as "marble-cake" federalism with its functional bureaucratic articulation, are modern analogs of those concerns about oligarchies and electoral accountability. Such tendencies are ancient and basically irreversible in American politics.[52] Pure jurisdictional homogeneity isn't feasible;

and federal-grant requirements are designed about as frequently to contain local oligarchies (including political organizations) as to sustain them.

Nevertheless, I shall suggest three considerations as critical for distributed self-government in the federal system. The first is the potentiality of general-purpose local government for political responsibility and participation; its functional dilution or gratuitous territorial enlargement is unlikely, I think, to serve popular sovereignty. The second consideration is that strengthening of the states in our federal machinery can contribute to both local and national capacities respectively through constitutional responsibility for local action and prudent decentralization of national policy.[53] This is to suggest, finally, that federalism is functional for modern constitutional democracy as a system of public devolutions and appeals—for relieving national overload and controlling local improbity or prejudice.

It will not be appropriate to pursue these considerations further. I mention them because issues of centralization and decentralization in the shaping and implementation of policy are apt to concern us in discussion. In this connection, it seems to me that, whatever the prospects for individual participation and vocational association, civic participation necessarily depends on definitions of locality and community or of functional responsibility. The problem is to organize local government to balance community and diversity, formality and responsiveness, functional generality and political scale, administrative capacity

49. Alan Altschuler, *Community Control* (New York: Pegasus, 1970); Milton Kotler, *Neighborhood Government* (Indianapolis: Bobbs-Merrill, 1969); Robert A. Dahl, "The City in the Future of Democracy," *American Political Science Review*, 61 (1967), p. 953.

50. On distributed self-government, see Charles S. Hyneman, *Popular Government in America* (New York: Atherton, 1968).

51. See, for example, Elie Halevy, *The Growth of Philosophic Radicalism* (London: Faber & Faber, 1928), pt. 2, ch. 1; pt. 3, ch. 2.

52. Grodzins, *The American System*.

53. For an interesting discussion of this point, see Daniel J. Elazar, "The New Federalism: Can the States Be Trusted?," *The Public Interest*, 35 (Spring 1974), p. 89.

and accountability, fiscal responsibility and distributive equity—so as to encourage participation while protecting rights and promoting managerial capacities. These balances will seem banalities; but I think they support suggestions for attention to federalism in the preceding paragraph. That is, from the standpoint of participation, they imply local governments subject to responsible participation by ordinary residents, not simply by cosmopolitan professionals; and they imply state arrangements for protecting rights against local oligarchies or majoritarian aggrandizements.

While the foregoing conception of the federal system is no doubt utopian, accessible local government seems critical for civic participation. And civic participation seems prospectively—in the traditional, liberal view—more consequential than vocational forms of participation for individual development of political skills and for the shaping of public policy. But neither approach to participation is as relevant to national policy—or to the demands of management and challenges of large-scale pluralism —as participation relating to elections, especially voting by ordinary citizens.

This seems the more so in the light of recent research suggestions that, in the context of American political organization and ideology, participation tends to work perversely from the standpoint of equalization of influence, reinforcing socioeconomic inequalities through its association with social status.[54] This

54. Sidney Verba and Norman H. Nie, *Participation in America* (New York: Harper & Row, 1972).

inference, coupled with the well-documented effects of higher-level education in promoting civic competence and participation, and with the speculative tendencies toward a social-class system rather sharply demarcated by college education, and with the problems of large-scale organization in American pluralism, seems reason for concern about how to reduce disparities of influence in American politics and policy. Professional, public-interest participation hardly serves this concern, I suppose, in comparison with more general engagement of the population through partisan and electoral organization in ways to be considered now.

4. *The place of elections in shaping policy.* Accepting the centrality of elections for popular sovereignty, and of party for electoral effectiveness, I'll raise summarily now some complicating issues.

Whatever the claims of incumbents, elections are rarely mandates. While majoritarian convention might conceivably lend elections this character, the ambiguities of party alignment and of political communications (noticed below) leave large margins of official discretion in reality. Voting is probably more often retrospective than prospective. There is no doubt a certain rationality in this perspective: voters need not invest in comprehensive, high-level ideologies to evaluate policy in the light of their own condition; governmental incumbents nevertheless are circumscribed anticipatorily.

Still, there is persuasive evidence that the general, programmatic commitments of parties in presidential elections are intelligible and are characteristically honored by incumbents—at least in legislative effort, if not effectively.[55] Through secular alignments primarily, and in some respects more immediately, elections tend to settle basic issues —to remove them from controversy and to establish their resolutions as premises of policy. Subject to these premises, or a moving consensus, many presidential elections are contested primarily over what have been termed "valence issues"— which candidate or party or program will better serve an emergent concern; not which party's conception of distributive justice should prevail.[56] There is also evidence of congruence between majority opinion in constituencies and the behavior of legislators, though it is reasonably clear that legislative discretion varies with the characteristics of issues and that there is commonly room for maneuver or for assertion of leadership.[57] Yet off-year congressional elections have been plausibly interpreted as referenda on the conduct of national administrations.[58]

To these degrees, American national elections tend to be meaningful and effective, though our ability to characterize their influence (or their effects on the distribution of influence) more specifically is limited. For example, it appears that tight electoral competition frequently leverages organized groups —that, regarding equalization of influence, popular (electoral) democracy augments pluralist democracy, though it probably tends to redress political effects of large-scale organizations. But these permutations have yet to be worked through in democratic theory. Moreover, the logic of electoral coalitions suggests that even in less secular and consensual, more majoritarian systems than the American there are limits to the electoral pursuit of distributive justice: the claims of small or (in particular) unpopular minorities are still likely to be discounted. Their electoral inclusion is likely to depend on legal protections or direct action within "a scheme of ordered liberty" and on popular allegiance to constitutional values.

Within modern democratic ideologies, both totalitarian and liberal, popular elections are alleged to foster regime allegiance and stability through civic participation and responsibility.[59] However that may be, the evidence suggests that popular sovereignty in elections is more a matter of influence in government than of direct power over government—a matter of anticipatory circumscription: elections are contextual for the shaping of policy.[60] But this role seems more considerable today than it was in early constitutional expectation: the balance of electoral demand and electoral protection has altered with

55. Gerald M. Pomper, *Elections in America* (New York: Dodd, Mead, 1968).

56. Angus Campbell et al., *Elections and the Political Order* (New York: Wiley, 1968), ch. 9; V. O. Key, *Political Parties and Pressure Groups* (New York: Crowell, 5th ed., 1964), ch. 8.

57. Warren E. Miller and Donald E. Stokes, "Constituency Influence in Congress," *American Political Science Review*, 57 (1963), p. 45. As to the expressed policy positions of candidates interviewed, this survey found generally greater congruence with majority constituent opinion among winning candidates than among the losers.

58. Edward R. Tufte, "Determinants of the Outcomes of Midterm Congressional Elections," *The American Political Science Review*, 69 (1975), p. 812.

59. Richard Rose and Harve Mossawir, "Voting and Elections: A Functional Analysis," *Political Studies*, 15 (1967), p. 173.

60. Pomper, *Elections in America*, p. 253.

institutional evolution, especially in presidential elections. This is a way of saying that traditional party organization and alignments no longer control the electoral process so effectively and also that electoral demand may tend to outrun electoral support.

One issue in proposals for party modernization today is whether more specific (and presumptively effective) party commitments and more thoroughgoing electoral ideology would be desirable (if feasible) regarding the density, extensity, complexity, and technicality of policy today. On this score I'm skeptical; but I must omit the speculations of the discussion paper on the logic of party alignments in the future.

THE SHAPING OF POLICY BY PUBLIC OFFICIALS

Whatever the requirements of popular sovereignty on extragovernmental public behavior, I suppose they culminate constitutionally in the ultimate shaping of policy by responsible officials. However that may stand as a matter of liberal democratic theory, I'll review most selectively and summarily some issues in official policy shaping; but, owing to constraints of space, I'll pass over consideration of constitutional revision.

1. *Congress.* In this century the decline of legislatures has become a familiar lament. In the Western world, party, lobby, executive authority, bureaucracy, and the complexity or exigency of policy have all been blamed for legislative decline. And decline implies alteration not only of constitutional balance, but of both responsibility and responsiveness in the shaping of policy. Congress has not been

thought exempt from these tendencies: yet Congress has remained —if in a dispersive rather than a parliamentary sense—the strongest Western legislature.

Two considerations in academic literature are central, I think, to assessment of Congress. One is suggested by Theodore Lowi's distinction (see section 1) between distributive, redistributive, regulatory, and constituent policies. It turns out, on historical examination, that Congress has probably been more effective (compared with other forces, governmental and nongovernmental) in some types of policy than in others, and moreover that Congress tends to function collectively or parliamentarily in some types and fragmentarily in other types.[61] Thus, legislatively, Congress probably cannot devise an energy policy, but it can take the initiative in environmental regulation; it probably cannot function independently in global fiscal or monetary management, but it can write tax legislation in detail.

The other consideration is the multifunctionality of Congress as compared with many legislatures.[62] The functions of Congress have been endlessly and variously listed, but I shall identify four: legislation; control of administration; inquiry— that is, fact finding and consciousness raising; and constituency service, including intervention with administration. These functions are frequently indistinguishable in

61. Lowi, "Four Systems of Public Policy." The nature of redistributive and regulatory policies will seem clear enough. Distributive policies confer benefits without apparent costs to other parties; constituent policies alter institutional opportunities for access and influence.

62. On this point, see Nelson W. Polsby, "Legislatures," in Greenstein and Polsby, *Handbook of Political Science*, vol. 5.

practice. They are fused in the representative role of Congress as the republican, nonplebiscitary element of the Constitution.

Short of thoroughgoing constitutional reforms, four issues in congressional structure seem most critical today: leadership, committees, staffing, and representation. Scholars have disagreed over the extent to which Congress (especially the House of Representatives) might feasibly and effectively function legislatively through a caucus style of party leadership instead of the network style based on negotiation, log rolling, and stability through seniority and prerogative that has developed in this century.[63] I think most scholars have supposed that strong party leadership of Congress would necessarily rest on a responsible-party model in which presidents would dominate and the congressional role would be rendered less autonomous—that Congress as a legislative engine would tend to displace Congress as agency of representative integration and protection.[64] We are witnessing now an attempt to test this supposition. I'm willing to bet that more immediately caucus-based leadership will not provide higher coherence in policy than did the old leadership mode, though I would not give long odds. The result depends, I suppose, on opinion distributions and party alignments outside Congress.

In any case, the strength of Congress's standing-committee structure will, comparatively speaking, remain remarkable. Recent reforms of this structure with respect to authority and prerogative seem likely to reduce the extent to which committee behavior has varied as a function of corporate congressional interests and, especially, of the political implications of policy.[65] Some committees that have functioned effectively (if not always responsively) as more or less autonomous centers of policy may become less ultimately influential arenas for policy conflict.[66]Then the question is whether Congress collectively can take up the slack through party leadership based primarily in like-mindedness and electoral alignments and whether, as I hope, institutional necessity will mother institutional invention.

As I see it, institutional necessity rests on some imperatives of policy—on the need, to which budgetary reform is as yet a problematical response, to redefine policy in conception and jurisdiction. The price paid for strong committee responsibility has grown in terms of specialization and segmentation. Congress probably needs a committee structure somewhat more accommodative to continuously changing categories of policy, while, for

63. The discussions in Truman, ed., *The Congress and America's Future* (Englewood Cliffs, N.J.: Prentice-Hall, 1965).

64. Representative discussions include, James M. Burns, *The Deadlock of Democracy* (Englewood Cliffs: Prentice-Hall, 1963); John Saloma, *Congress and the New Politics* (Boston: Little, Brown, 1966). On congressional reform, see, for example, Stephen K. Bailey, *The New Congress* (New York: St. Martin's, 1966); Richard Bolling, *House out of Order* (New York: Dutton, 1966); Joseph S. Clark, *Congress: The Sapless Branch* (New York: Harper & Row, 1964), and *Congressional Reform* (New York: Crowell, 1965); and Roger H. Davidson et al., *Congress in Crisis* (Belmont, Calif.: Wadsworth, 1966).

65. See Richard F. Fenno, Jr., *Congressmen in Committees* (Boston: Little, Brown, 1973).

66. The House Ways and Means Committee seems a case in point. See John Manley, *The Politics of Finance* (Boston: Little, Brown, 1970).

general legislative effectiveness, it still needs a standing committee structure reasonably (*not* identically) consistent with Executive branch organization. Congress has tended to sustain more comprehensive purviews most effectively, I think, in non-legislative and in financial committees. Some morselization in the shaping of legislation seems essential to congressional effectiveness. Thus, one question regarding the altered balance of plenary and committee leadership in the House of Representatives is whether it can lead to a better (and stable) balance of specialization and integration.[67]

A prominent trend in congressional reform—geared to both individual and committee effectiveness and to the full range of congressional functions—has been staff enlargement. The doctrine of salvation through staff now applies to political direction and control of government in both branches. So do its practical problems in the theology of popular sovereignty and responsible government: *delegata potestas non potest delegari*; and too many cooks spoil the broth. The issue here is whether proliferation of staff is reaching a point where the question arises seriously, with respect to legislative multifunctionality: is Congress endeavoring to do too much? This question pertains less seriously so far to the shaping of policy in the large, where congressional responsibility functions necessarily through negotiation and voting by principals in the end, than it does to detailed intervention with the administrative implementation of policy, where staffers can

navigate independently.[68] The danger is that congressional institutionalization is accentuating the dispersive tendencies of Congress while diluting its representative tendencies.

The foregoing issues—leadership, fragmentation, morselization, and political responsibility—come to a focus in Congress's representative functions. The evolution of somewhat more consolidated, more plenary leadership and committee structures would presumably turn the staff professionalization of Congress more clearly toward shaping of policy. Both the political conditions and results of such change would tend to alter—perhaps marginally, perhaps more drastically—the institutionalized pattern of legislative representation that has developed in this century. That pattern has emphasized multifunctionality. In legislative and electoral organization, it has emphasized insulating properties (seniority, protection of incumbency, distributed leadership sanctions and incentives) to balance the necessities of direct responsiveness.[69] This pattern has given Congress a dilatory and particularistic cast; but I think it has

67. This question pertains to the House more consequentially than to the Senate, where institutionalized specialization affects the shaping of policy much less.

68. As to the shaping of policy, the rise of some senatorial professional empires, reflecting the financial means of individual senators as well as more liberal staffing provisions, may well be unbalancing influence in the shaping of policy. And some professional enterprises—for example, technology assessment—seem problematical for Congress, however well intentioned.

69. See, for example, Nelson W. Polsby, "The Institutionalization of the U.S. House of Representatives," *American Political Science Review*, 62 (1968), p. 144; H. Douglas Price, "The Congressional Career: Risks and Rewards," in Polsby, ed., *Congressional Behavior* (New York: Random House, 1971); and Lewis Mayhew, *Congress: The Electoral Connection* (New Haven: Yale University Press, 1974).

generally fostered congressional response to aggregate national opinion when it emerges through congressional constituencies. Such opinion is frequently inconsistent with opinion in the presidential constituency. But the equilibration of the constituencies and substantial autonomy of Congress are important questions in proposals for fundamental reorganization of Congress to cope with the modern imperatives of policy and administration.

Short of such proposals, the long-standing reform ideal of a Congress more frequently capable of plenary action and of both general and perspicuous legislation (no less liberally, if less pluralistically, delegated) depends for its effect on the party system. I have suggested that, in the comparative perspective of parliamentary government, Congress is peculiarly productive as a legislature. This is to suggest (not to document) that serious erosion of the separation of powers, as the presumptive condition or accompaniment of stringent party discipline, might be counterproductive. Within the separation of powers, one logically looks for more marginal changes in congressional organization—changes not likely, I think, to challenge seriously the concerns of the preceding paragraph.

2. *The presidency.* I cannot avoid the standard observation that the presidential role, like that of Congress, is multifarious—though I shall neglect its specification here. The question arises whether the several presidential roles are also integral, mutually enhancing roles. If they are, then they are also apt to be reciprocally deleterious from time to time. There is strength in the combination of formal headship and political leadership; but there is also a danger to legitimacy, since,

save for generalized allegiance to constitutional values, so much combined responsibility rides on the president personally. Proposals for alteration of the separation of powers can hardly ignore the American problem of fusion of dignified and efficient functions.[70]

This problem becomes the more considerable as the presidency cuts loose from party organization progressively through the reciprocal effects of mass communications, popular nominating procedures, and deterioration of party structure. In any case, the presidential constituency tends to be virtual and vague; with respect to issues more nearly susceptible to direct accountability, it is highly heterogeneous. Presidential representation thus has plebiscitarian elements and (depending on election-finance laws) plutocratic elements as well. Popular support of presidential performance can be mercurial—subject to precipitous decline and hard to recoup, save through election campaigns or spectacular events. The dynamics of opinion formation figure in this vulnerability, but so do the functional problems of the presidency.

With respect to the Executive branch, the putative tools of the presidency for shaping and implementing policy have had increasingly to reckon with intractability. Budgetary discretion and control, reorganizational authority, and personnel management are circumscribed by the economy, the Congress, and the conventions of civil service. The presidency is confined to selective initiatives in legislation and selective interventions in administration. The president as

70. Walter Bagehot, *The English Constitution* (London: Oxford University Press, 1928, originally 1867).

energetic general manager of the Executive branch is not, I think, a workable conception.[71]

Within the ambiguity of presidential strength and weakness, the question naturally arises whether the office can be institutionalized to the end of responsibility in its several significations. Short of constitutional amendment (to be considered below), the chief possibilities, I think, are three. One is progressive reorganization of the party system toward the responsible model in which presidential leadership would be more subject to partisan loyalties, collaboration, inhibition, and opposition. But party responsibility implies party organization—more than mere ideological agreement. In particular, the machinery of presidential nomination and campaigning would need reinstitutionalization, extending perhaps to congressional politics as well, and reversing current developments.

A second possibility, long advocated, looks to several objectives: stabilizing of executive-legislative relations, consolidation of legislative leadership, and collegial supplementation of the presidency. It takes the form of a legislative-executive council engaging the effective leadership of both branches in the shaping of policy.[72] The congressional membership might be bipartisan, or it might not be; the council might de facto expand the cabinet to congressional positions without portfolio, or legislative and managerial functions might (insofar as feasible) be distinguished. In one version or another, this proposal emphasizes the stabilization, depersonalization, and containment of the presidency, or the integration and augmentation of general policy leadership in both branches.

A final possibility is movement toward a better balance of consolidation and devolution in the Executive branch. This implies some retrenchment of presidential attempts at comprehensive direction and control. The managerial and collegial responsibilities of cabinet officers would be emphasized; the machinery of central administration (for example, OMB) would be further institutionalized; perhaps a senior civil service would be established. The limits of presidential ability to manage the Executive branch would be acknowledged; regularization of management would be emphasized within these limits.

These three lines of development are logically compatible, I think. I also think the dispersive tendencies of American politics and administration are unlikely to favor the first and third developments alone or in combination; some governmental fulcrum or nexus is probably essential to either or both. Then the question is whether the second proposal would, in effect, supply enough institutional leadership and conventional leverage to serve the purpose. I suppose the best way to find out is to try it. The trouble is that presidential necessities seem to run the other way, and presidential incentives almost certainly do. The

71. I think a useful recent treatment of these matters is Erwin C. Hargrove, *The Power of the Modern Presidency* (Philadelphia: Temple University Press, 1974). See also George E. Reedy, *The Twilight of the Presidency* (New York: World Publishing, 1970).

72. For different versions of this proposal, see Edward S. Corwin, *The President: Office and Powers* (New York: New York University Press, 3rd ed., 1948); and Charles S. Hyneman, *Bureaucracy in a Democracy* (New York: Harper & Row, 1950).

modern presidency seems mort-
gaged to personal ambitions, popular expectations, and functional contradictions beyond those operable in
large-scale organizations generally,
so its institutionalization is peculiarly difficult.

3. *The problems of administrative responsibility* are, as already
indicated, increasingly central considerations in popular sovereignty.
Indeed, modern issues of bureaucratic rule, discretion, accountability, rationality, responsiveness,
efficiency, and effectiveness are
among the central issues of modern
democratic theory in any practical
sense.[73] Here the concerns of committee III merge most integrally
with those of committee II.

I'll identify these issues in national administration under three
heads: constitutional, internal, and
external. The constitutional avenues
of responsibility are those per-
taining to president, Congress, and
the courts, distinctly and relatively
in direction and control of administration.

As to the presidency, can the chief
executive either lead or manage effectively the shaping and implementation of policy? Could he do so
even if Congress were not so prominently in the picture? Has the trend
toward White House centralization
impaired departmental management? With the enlargement of the
presidency, has staff passion for
anonymity been coupled unduly

with autonomy and authority? Are
superdepartments or czars really
superior to a larger number of more
manageable departments? To raise
these questions is to indicate concerns and at least a qualified perspective on the answers. If the presidential role in shaping policy is
necessarily other than immediately
and comprehensively managerial,
then this implies more reliance on
Executive office, cabinet, and departmental management assisted by
restoration of presidential reorganization authority (subject to congressional veto), some consolidation of the higher civil service, and
selective applications of managerial
technique. As to the last of these,
"the triumph of technique over purpose"[74] is a constant danger in personnel administration, budgeting,
and policy analysis; and, in this regard, the present trend of "MBO"
seems more politically responsible
and administratively adaptable to
presidential purposes than its an-
cestor, "PPB," because less arcane
and procrustean.

The role of Congress in direction
and control of administration has
been a staple problem in the American separation of powers. But its
principal aspects—collective or
parliamentary versus dispersive
or fragmentary congressional oversight of administration, and the desire of presidential protagonists or
bureaucratic rationalists that Congress retreat from its pervasive administrative intervention in many
sectors—are basically intractable.
Congress relates to administration
as it does largely because Congress
is organized and electorally condi-

73. A general discussion of some of these
issues may be found in Mark V. Nadel
and Francis E. Rourke, "Bureaucracies," in
Greenstein and Polsby, *Handbook of Political Science*, vol. 5, esp. pp. 411–29, with
references to the large literature of the subject. I sought to identify some of the issues
in the meanings and modes of responsibility
in "The Framework of Administrative Responsibility," *Journal of Politics*, 21 (1959),
p. 373.

74. The quoted phrase is that of the late
Wallace S. Sayre, who applied it to personnel administration in "The Triumph of
Technique over Purpose," *Public Administration Review*, 8 (1948), p. 134.

tioned as it is. Congressional priorities may change with imperatives of policy the new budget procedures; general standard-setting legislation and more use of the legislative veto (in spite of constitutional purists) are consolidating possibilities. But Congress will typically relate to administration through its committees, where its strength resides; and the more critical issue has to do with institutionalization of assistance in legislative oversight through, for example, the General Accounting Office and Congressional Research Service.

While the judicial role in administrative responsibility is too technical for consideration here, it relates to a couple of large issues worth mentioning: the scope of legislative delegation and the organization of regulatory administration. As to the latter, all three branches might make progress with the regulatory fourth branch together (short of its dismembership and merger) through provision for presidential directives on general policy, investigation, or jurisdiction subject to judicial review and legislative veto.[75] And as to delegation, congressional provision for more extensive agency rule making and policy formulation might help tighten judicial review for consistency of decision, besides which the time may be ripe for more judicial pressure on legislative delegations independently through some sophisticated revival of the dormant nondelegation doctrine.

The internal modes of administrative responsibility pose issues in civil service organization and regulation. The American public service is much less a guardian class or autonomous elite, much more a system of social and functional representation, than are most modern national bureaucracies.[76] These attributes are "in the wood"; they cannot be altered more than marginally with regard to the shaping of policy. Within these traditional limits, two alternatives are worth considering anent the higher public service: one is its consolidation as a more corporate career service; the other is extension of presidential appointments to lower levels.[77] Of these, I favor the former; but in either case, the practical intractability arising from programmatic pluralism and the molecular tenacity of American bureaus, along with resistance from civil service unions, will be fundamentally troublesome.

Among the external dimensions of administrative responsibility, I'll identify contracting, publicity, clientele participation, and intergovernmental relations for brief discussion. In contracting, especially for research, development, advice, and evaluation, the problem of administrative responsibility is to retain it unimpaired—that is, to maintain public capacities for definition, evaluation, and decision. This is no

75. See Lloyd N. Cutler and David R. Johnson, "Regulation and the Political Process," *Yale Law Journal*, 84 (1975), p. 1395; and James O. Freedman, "Crisis and Legitimacy in the Administrative Process," *Stanford Law Review*, 27 (1975), p. 1041.

76. Kenneth J. Meier, "Representative Bureaucracy," *American Political Science Review*, 69 (1975), p. 526; V. Subramaniam, "Representative Bureaucracy," *American Political Science Review*, 61 (1967), p. 1010; Frederick C. Mosher, *Democracy and the Public Service* (New York: Oxford University Press, 1968); John Armstrong, *The European Administrative Elite* (Princeton: Princeton University Press, 1973).

77. See esp. Mosher, *Democracy and the Public Service*, and Paul Van Riper, *History of the United States Civil Service* (Evanston, Ill.: Row Peterson, 1958).

trivial problem today, but I need not review it here.[78]

Administrative publicity (and secrecy) pose similarly well-documented issues—publicity as a form of institutional or programmatic advertising and constituency cultivation, or as damaging persons or properties through adverse publicity attending regulation; secrecy in the competing requirements of "sunshine," journalism, public information, and equalization of interest-group access, or of national security, personal and corporate confidentiality, the encouragement of candor in administrative judgments, and of prudential autonomy in administrative decisions.[79] Such considerations figure ambiguously in the statutes on publicity and disclosure.[80] Insofar as publicity is

influence and knowledge is power, the regulation of secrecy and publicity will always be critical in the shaping of policy.

By clientele participation, I mean arrangements more integral to policy shaping than ordinary negotiation with interest groups. These may range from advice to devolution; from formal to informal. They may be justified by the shortcomings of ultimate accountability and the need for something more immediate; by pragmatic or indigenous contributions to administrative information or to client motivation through participation; by the necessity of winning consent; as programmatic targeting and constituency building; as appropriately modulating bureaucratic uniformity; or as civic development through popular involvement. The problems of public purpose and governmental responsibility arise over the whole range from advice to devolution, and especially as arrangements depart from formality. In the shaping of policy and in democratic theory, functional and electoral responsibility (or participation) are potentially at odds in distribution of the new property and regulation of the old. How shall we balance the claims of decentralization and participation with administrative responsibility?[81]

Finally, I'll recur to federalism as an external dimension of administrative responsibility, limiting its

78. See, for example, *Report of the Commission on Government Procurement* (Washington: Government Printing Office, 1972), 4 vols.; Clarence Danhoff, *Government Contracting and Technological Change* (Washington: The Brookings Institution, 1968).

79. Useful discussions include Francis Rourke, *Secrecy and Publicity* (Baltimore: Johns Hopkins University Press, 1961); Rourke, ed., "Symposium on Administrative Secrecy," *Public Administration Review*, 35 (1975), p. 1; Joseph Bishop, "The Executive's Right of Privacy," *Yale Law Journal*, 66 (1957), p. 477; Douglass Cater, *The Fourth Branch of Government* (Boston: Houghton, Mifflin, 1959); Norman Dorsen and Stephen Gillers, *None of Your Business* (Baltimore: Penguin Books, 1975); James O. Freedman, "Summary Action by Administrative Agencies," *University of Chicago Law Review*, 40 (1972), p. 1; Ernest Gellhorn, "Adverse Publicity," *Harvard Law Review*, 86 (1973), p. 1380; Edward Newman, "Government and Ignorance," *Harvard Law Review*, 63 (1950), p. 929; Archibald Cox, "Executive Privilege," *University of Pennsylvania Law Review*, 122 (1974), p. 1383.

80. On the Freedom of Information Act see, for example, Note, "The Freedom of Information Act," *Harvard Law Review*, 86 (1973), p. 1047; U.S. Senate, Judiciary Committee, *Freedom of Information Act Source Book* (1974).

81. For conflicting views on just two such participative programs, see John D. Lewis, "Democratic Planning in Agriculture," *American Political Science Review*, 35 (1951), p. 232, and R. Frieschknecht, "The Democratization of Administration: The Farmer Committee System," *American Political Science Review*, 47 (1963), p. 705, on the farm committee system; and Peter Bachrach and Morton Baratz, *Power and Poverty* (New York: Oxford Uni-

consideration to a couple of aspects of federal grants in aid. One has to do with their regulative effects (incidental or deliberate) on the structure and functions of distributed self-government. I have in mind not so much the implicit conditioning of priorities through matching provisions as the more thoroughgoing constituent policies of restructuring state and local government through professionalization, regionalization, functional particularization, clientele targeting, and participative or consultative requirements. This is simply to suggest again that there is an issue of the future of general-purpose, electorally responsible jurisdictions in the federal system implicit in the programmatic and interest-group pluralism of national policy.

A second issue concerns the organization and balance of fiscal federalism. The organizational possibilities range from narrow grant categories through functional or general block grants to true revenue sharing. We can probably expect this pattern to oscillate more or less as it has in the past. Programmatic categories have tended to reflect congressional concern for accountability as well as congressional response to group importunity. Project grants have favored federal administrative initiatives as well as private federalism. They have also favored functional, territorial, and redistributive targeting. Both categorical and project grants build constituencies. Functional block grants (with or without matching provisions or

copious regulations) are a means of broadening national priorities and, especially, the federal position of the states. So-called general revenue sharing is likely, I think, to facilitate inflationary response to public-employee unions, though it is also a method of redressing fiscal disparities in the nation and its metropolitan areas while favoring general-purpose government.[82] The question is whether the constituent politics of federalism can be squared with a realignment of functions more rational financially and administratively. In the long run, such a federal realignment might contribute marginally at least to resolution of problems of political alignment suggested in section 3.

PUBLIC POLICIES FOR SHAPING THE SHAPING OF PUBLIC POLICY

It was suggested at the beginning of this paper that our ways of shaping policy are as subject to constructive change through public understandings as through legislative actions—though I should add that more explicit attention to the reflexive effects of substantive policies through their effects on public institutions is probably in order today. This paper concludes with a list of issues for committee consideration in the Bicentennial Confer-

---

versity Press, 1970), and Daniel P. Moynihan, *Maximum Feasible Misunderstanding* (New York: The Free Press, 1969), on the Community Action Program of the War on Poverty.

82. See, for example, Wallace Oates, *Fiscal Federalism* (New York: Harcourt-Brace-Jovanovich, 1972); Charles E. McLure, Jr., "Revenue Sharing: Alternatives to Rational Fiscal Federalism?," *Public Policy*, 19 (1971), p. 457; and Richard A. Musgrave and A. Mitchell Polinsky, "Revenue Sharing: A Critical View," *Harvard Journal on Legislation*, 8 (1971), p. 196. For a politically sophisticated discussion, see Daniel J. Elazar, "Fiscal Questions and Political Answers in Intergovernmental Finance," *Public Administration Review*, 32 (1972), p. 471.

ence—though not all of them have figured in the present version of the paper. The measures most worth considering can be classified as constitutional, pragmatic, and prudential for want of better terms: that is, as entailing constitutional reform or its functional equivalent, as subject to statutory action, or as depending on opinion leadership and civic endeavor. In my view, the constitutional revisions (not canvassed in this version of the paper) are, for the most part, least important.

Among the difficulties, present and prospective, identified in section 1, I tend to take most seriously the balance of competition and interpenetration among market, governmental, and subsidized public-service sectors in so-called post-industrial society along with that system's probable propensities toward inflation and cumulative educational class cleavages; the ambivalent trends toward centralization and private devolution in modern American government; the complexity of public organization and management resulting from the density and extensity of public policy and the trend toward public-sector trade unionism; the regulatory and allocative problems posed by endemic inflation, materials scarcity, and environmental stringency; the ideological assimilation of liberty to equality along with pressures toward public-service entitlements; and the likely challenges of planning in a society characterized by large-scale pluralism. Together with garrison-state tendencies, this constellation of difficulties seems likely to render the shaping of policy less subject to popular sovereignty as well as less susceptible to political leadership. This is the more so as it contributes—with the secu-

lar and reciprocal effects of congressional delegation, presidential aggrandizement, and electronic mass communications—to the erosion of party as a structure of leadership and participation as well as a buffer of responsibility.

Certain concerns will probably have been apparent in section 2. These include the growing tension between government by institutionalized, electorally responsible elites and the populistic strain in American politics now fortified by highly educated aspirants to participation and respondents to electronic communication. I suppose a productive balance of responsibility and responsiveness in government implies some institutional insulation of decision and an ideological regard for liberty or autonomy consistent with, but not simply assimilated to, political equality. Still, the condition of political inclusion is critical. It implies, I think, not only continuing electoral organization and competition, but also the improvement of local governing institutions subject to civic and electoral participation. Other avenues of participation surely contribute to the social conditions of popular sovereignty; but insofar as they tend to adulterate electoral organization and distributed self-government, they may also be deleterious. In general, therefore, I suspect that liberal pragmatism and private federalism will tend to generate privilege, to dissipate legislative and administrative responsibility, and to frustrate political inclusion despite the recent reliance on delegation and devolution in national policy to redress imbalance in participation.

Several concerns dominate sections 3 and 4. For the shaping of policy through the concert and control of leadership and the diffusion of influence, there seems no suitable substitute for the two-party structure. It is difficult today to take an oracular stand between the responsible-party-government optimists and the Cassandras on this score, or between the pluralist complacency of a decade ago and those who favor a corporate politics of programs without reference to party. I'm persuaded that the Cassandras have rightly identified some worrisome prospects for party organization and alignment; and I think the restoration of more than a modicum of party responsibility is a cause of high priority if public policy, leadership, and participation are to be institutionalized effectively. I guess it will be evident that my aspirations for the party system fall well short of high majoritarianism.

It may also be evident that I think the federal system needs attention. Indeed, I'm perverse enough to believe that the improvement of state governments as policy shapers and structures of sovereignty in relation to local government is conceivable and (for reasons adduced in sections 3 and 4) desirable. Inter alia, this implies some sorting out of functions and grant patterns at the national level, with early emphasis on public-welfare policy and long-run attention to its containment.

I suspect Congress will find it increasingly difficult to function adequately in its multiple roles, and especially in the deliberate shaping of policy. The technicality and schematic requirements of modern policy are less at issue here, I suppose, than decline of the conditions of legislative leadership and deterioration of the presidential connection. The materials of legislative leadership, like those of party restoration, are not apparent now, though the importance of preserving the several functions of Congress in its quintessential representative role is more apparent than ever.

Finally, whatever the inevitable dispersive effects of a strong Congress, together with those of liberal-pragmatic doctrines of administrative responsibility, I think we need to work toward more administrative consolidation. I don't mean by this larger departments or more immediate presidential supervision or even the bureaucratic merger of appropriately independent agencies. I do mean more managerial integration toward the top and through the line departments. I suppose the conditions of modest progress on this score lie in more collective, consultative presidential leadership and liaison with Congress; in greater organizational integration of the higher civil service; and in managerial doctrine and practice that are both technically sophisticated and politically sensitive. These are also conditions of response to the challenge of planning, not as desirably global and comprehensive, but as sufficiently purposive and articulate to render planning selective and politically responsible.

Even modest progress toward administrative consolidation in this sense is a tall order. Its proximate condition is probably the repair of checks and balances toward a system sustaining more collective leadership in both Legislative and Executive branches and more consultation between them. Some visible party organization and viable party alignments would help a lot in these connections. Here the problem is to reconnect presidency and party, and to that end some retrogression in presidential nominating arrangements might be helpful. That would mean party conventions without too many pledged delegates and with ample representation of congressional membership; and if such proceedings don't justify prime television time, then perhaps they could be reported in the newspapers. Toward the connection of president and Congress, I think the cabinet expansion toward a legislative council discussed in section 4 is worth trying; and if that's insufficient, then a constitutional amendment to provide for a vote of confidence might be considered.[83] This could discipline the consultation, while also encouraging factional challenges in Congress.

Save possibly (with reservations) for adoption of four-year terms in the House of Representatives, concurrent with presidential terms, I don't look toward formal constitutional alteration for help.[84] That is partly because, with reference to issues suggested in section 2, I suspect the separation of powers

makes a practical, beneficial difference for liberal-democratic values in American society, on balance. (Among its institutional benefits, a strong Congress and reinforcement of the two-party system merit mention.) In my reading, the founding compromise has served effectively and flexibly, for the most part, to balance responsibility and responsiveness in national leadership, and I doubt the interpretation that it induced civil war in the last century. In the course of this century, it seems to me, the balance of responsibility has gradually tilted too far on the presidential side, exceeding reasonable limits of executive capacity and accountability. Now the system's insulating and plebiscitarian properties there need more institutionalization and, especially, congressional participation in an age of massive administration and mass communication. Measured progress toward a modern party system seems paradoxically in order now, when the popular conditions of it seem problematical; but I'll suggest that we might best begin at the top, with presidential and congressional leadership, responding to a sense of necessity through more conciliar responsibility.

83. See, for example, James L. Sundquist, "Needed: A Workable Check on the Presidency," *The Brookings Bulletin* (Fall 1973) (Washington: The Brookings Institution), p. 7.

84. On practical difficulties in the four-year term, see Charles O. Jones, *Every Second Year* (Washington: The Brookings Institution, 1967).

ANNALS, AAPSS, 426, July 1976

Report on Committee III

By GERALD FRUG

ABSTRACT: Political parties have been the traditional means by which the various groups in our society are able to articulate their views and goals; however, there has been a significant decline in the role of political parties in our society. One basic cause has been the primary system. Problems created by reliance on primaries are that this process encourages more extreme candidates and reliance on style rather than program. It is argued in favor of primaries that conflict between Congress and the president is not a bad thing and the primary system is more democratic than the party system. A possible resolution to this debate is the idea of the regional primary. Concerning the separation of powers, there is an increasing tendency of Congress to delegate unchecked authority to the Executive branch. Possible solutions to the problem are congressional oversight, unconstitutional delegation of powers, congressional veto, and the power of impeachment. Finally, there is the problem of Legislative effectiveness and the Executive function of planning. Congress must work as a whole on plans to deal with the country's problems, but this is a difficult change for Congress to make.

Gerald Frug has been Associate Professor of Law at the University of Pennsylvania since 1974. He was Deputy Administrator of Health Services Administration of the City of New York from 1970–73 and Administrator from 1973–74. From 1969–70 he practiced law with Cravath, Swaine and Moore. He served as Special Assistant to the Chairman of the United States Equal Employment Opportunity Commission from 1966–69.

THERE are three topics that I will be covering: "Political Parties," "Separation of Powers," and what the chairman called "The Effectiveness of the Legislative Branch," or you might as well call it, "The Effectiveness of the Executive Branch." Then my colleague, Professor Honnold, will deal with the last two topics: "Federalism" and "Citizen Participation."

POLITICAL PARTIES

The committee started with the role of political parties because they have been the traditional means by which the various groups in our society, which together we call as an aggregate "the public," are able to articulate their views and goals toward creating a government program. Having stated this traditional role, we noted that there has been a significant decline in the role of political parties in our society, a decline evidenced by the increase in ticket-splitting in the American electorate and the increasing number of our citizens calling themselves "Independents."

One of the basic causes of this decline is the primary system for the selection of presidential nominees. We, therefore, focused on the primary system to determine whether its benefits outweigh the detriments that have come from the decline of the political party system.

When we turned to the primary system, we started out with the ideals of the progressive movement which, at the turn of the century, created the direct primary. These ideals, which were rearticulated by a number of the members of our committee as still vivid and fresh today, boil down, if I can over-simplify, into two basic categories.

First, there is a strongly felt opinion in our country that there is something good about voting for the man and not the party. There is the idea that a political party simply muddies the waters and doesn't, itself, add to the selection process. We would, therefore, get better candidates if we relied not on the party, but on the voters themselves.

Secondly, even if one doesn't accept the proposition that the direct presidential primaries produce better candidates than the party system, there is a certain value to having a presidential primary in itself—the value of having a democratic way of choosing our candidates; of taking political parties out of the selection process and connecting the public and the nomination process more directly. A number of people on our committee rearticulated the desirability of direct democracy as a reason for the presidential primary.

Once these ideas were put forward, a number of people found problems with them. The first concern was that there is a need in the country for cohesiveness, and one of the functions the political parties have served is to draw together a variety of groups into a coalition for a presidential campaign. If we relied solely on a presidential primary, particularly because presidential primaries have a low turnout and a very high ideology component in that turnout, we are more likely to get candidates of one extreme or another winning the selection process than we would if we had a convention system, which allows the kind of negotiation necessary to form a broad base of support.

Another concern expressed was that the role of the media, particularly television and radio, encouraged reliance on style and not program. Since the rewards of publicity are so high in campaigning for president, people would run solely for those rewards, and some of the reasons that people vote in elections in the first place—for example, the need to express some sort of meaningful choice—would be lost. However loose and ill-defined some of the political parties' programs may be, a number of people identify with their programmatic approaches; and to the extent that we exchange that type of position for style, the interest of the electorate in the election system would decline.

In this connection, it was interesting for us to talk about the primary system this week, because we had here in the United States several presidential primaries to look at, and we also had in Britain the process that they were going through to choose their Prime Minister. The ability of the governing party in Great Britain to sit down and decide which one among the candidates, many of whom they had known for 20 or 30 years, would best govern the country—the British ability to screen candidates—had an advantage, some felt, over our emphasis on the values which a television or a radio program might bring out.

The final advantage political parties serve is as a bridge between the president and the Congress. To the extent that they are of the same party (which, of course, is not always true), the party connection enables them to build together a sort of program which would be less likely to occur as the parties begin to disappear. Some saw this as further erosion of the powers of government, an undesirable result.

But the people who argued for the direct presidential primary didn't accept all of these arguments. First, they responded that this concept of a conflict between the presidential and congressional parts of the government was a good thing—not a bad thing. To the extent that we are trying to build a kind of cohesiveness based on party, they argued, that may turn out to be undesirable. Also, a number of people noted an antidemocratic flavor in the argument against the direct primary, noting that it runs simply along the lines that, "We don't trust a free and open majority decision." This was troubling to a number of people. Finally, they saw the fact that when we talk about the decline of the party, we are talking more about the decline of the party as an organization, the concept of the party boss, than we are talking about the party as an ideology or as a way of looking at the world. If we look at the people who called themselves Independents and ask them, "Do you lean toward the Democratic or the Republican party even though you call yourself an Independent?" we find people have a lot of identification with one or the other party. Thus, even in the direct primary system, some felt there would be enough programmatic content left in the election process.

The debate had no final resolution, except for one middle position which seemed to attract people from both points of view—the regional primary idea. A "regional primary" would envision each region of the country agreeing that all of the states in that region, if they wanted to hold a presidential primary, would hold it on the same day, and that the regions would be staggered over a several-week period. We would, then, have a chance to take a second look as campaigns moved around the country, and we could thus form cohesive alliances to moderate the primary process. A number of people saw another advantage to this type of regional primary over, for example, a direct national primary. It would allow for people to run uncommitted delegations, as we do now; people could run for the popular candidate, "no preference," and also for favorite sons, and these delegates would bring a force of moderation, bridging various ideologies, to the convention. They would provide a healthy balance between the direct-democracy concept, on the one hand, and the need for a party ideology on the other hand.

SEPARATION OF POWERS

The concept of bridging the gap between the president and the Congress, of bridging it on the basis of political party, led us in our second session to the talk about separation of powers. We focused, however, not so much on the role of party in bridging the separation of powers, but on the concept of delegation of legislative powers to the Executive. We found an increasing tendency in Congress to delegate authority in a very unchecked way to the Executive branch for two different reasons. On the one hand, we found that Congress, having decided on what its policy was, left the details of administration to the Executive branch by delegation. We also found another type of delegation—when Congress can't decide what the policy is, it delegates to the Executive branch a very broad level of authority that might simply be described as, "Here's a problem; let's do something about it."

The first question was whether this kind of delegation from a popularly elected, diverse body to the Executive was inevitable and whether there was anything we could do about it. If one accepts

the proposition that the Executive and Legislature can't administer a program together because of the fundamental provision of the Constitution, which no one proposed to change, that congressmen can't serve as members of the Executive cabinet, it is going to be very hard for Congress to help formulate any program. What then, some asked, can we do about trying to control this amount of delegation, shifting power back to Congress from the Executive branch?

One idea that interested a number of people was an emphasis on the ability of Congress to oversee the administration of programs. Once the programs were underway, once the regulations were issued, once the Executive began to formulate exactly what it was trying to do, then Congress, through an oversight process, could work in a very informal but nevertheless effective way to evaluate and revise policy.

A number of the members felt that this oversight power was simply not an adequate check on Executive power. For one thing, it could not work in those situations in which Congress itself had not formulated a policy, but had simply delegated to the Executive both the formulation of policy and the power to carry it out. When the Executive showed up at the committee session, in such a case, either the committee would try to make up what the policy was and the Executive would defend its own policy, with no way to resolve this conflict without congressional action, or what seems to be increasingly true, the end result of this conflict would be a lawsuit, bringing into the federal courts the kinds of questions which Congress was unable to decide. The tendency to get the federal Judiciary to make the types of basic policy decisions which Congress avoided by passing the buck to the Executive branch was widely criticized. The Employment Act of 1946 was mentioned by some as an example of a congressional delegation to the Executive that gave Congress no ability to continue to control policy, because there was no firm standard on which to base that control.

Another problem that people found with oversight was that it came too late. Even if you could have a congressional hearing by a committee, much of what the Executive had done would already have happened. Some felt that in a number of situations a congressional committee could build change into future actions and, therefore, could have some effective control on presidential policy. But others said, with examples in the foreign affairs field, that all the important action may well be over by the time Congress can hold a hearing.

Another problem found with the oversight power was simply that it is not a very glamorous job. There was a fear that many members of Congress would not opt for this kind of day-to-day oversight function, but would delegate it to staff. You would then have the somewhat unsettling concept of congressional staff members, not directly elected, and administrative staff members, not directly elected, negotiating over what American policy should be.

Those who felt the oversight process was not an acceptable answer to the excessive delegation of congressional power to the Legislature came up with a variety of possible alternatives—and there was by no means unanimous agreement to any of them. One was simply a revival of the Supreme Court doctrine of unconstitutional delegation of powers —that it is unconstitutional in certain cases for the Legislature to delegate to the Executive certain authority without specifying what the policies would be. Another was the creation of a built-in time frame for legislation; so that the program would end automatically at a given date. This would force Congress to look at what has happened, to force a periodic reevaluation, before it recreated the program.

Finally, people noted the tendency to build into the legislation in modern times the concept of the one-house veto: one house of Congress can veto Executive action or, sometimes, even one committee of Congress could veto the act of the Executive. A number of constitutional problems with that scheme were raised.

At least one member of our committee felt that none of these ideas went far enough. The real problem of the legislative delegation by Congress came from the fact that, as we saw recently in 1974, we can have a situation in which the Executive is simply unable to function. He feared a situation, for example, in which an economic policy was working very badly, or a war was being run very badly, and Congress would have no real power to deal with the president who is inadequately performing his job. Incompetence is not an impeachable offense; and the president may not be mentally or physically disabled so as to bring into effect the disability clause of the Constitution. He simply may be doing such a bad job that it would be intolerable for the country to wait two or three, or maybe even four, years before we could have a new election and a new direction. The committee member proposed, as a way of handling this problem, that the Congress ought to be given the power to vote no confidence in the president. This, of course, requires a constitutional amendment. Since this would be a very powerful weapon, there was a lot of concern that it not be used too often. One method suggested to prevent its being used too often would be to provide that, if Congress voted no confidence in the president, not only would the president have to seek reelection, but the whole Congress, House, and Senate, would also have to seek reelection at the same time. This would give members of Congress some reluctance to use the vote of no confidence lightly; but in some cases, perhaps one in recent memory, they may feel strong enough in their views that they would be willing to do so.

THE EFFECTIVENESS OF THE LEGISLATIVE BRANCH

The concept of the separation of powers led us to the third topic that I will discuss, which concerns the responsibility of the Executive branch to formulate and execute the policy that is given to it. We found that many states had begun to rely on the federal government to formulate policy, much as the Legislature has relied on the federal government to formulate policy; then the question is, "Who in the Executive branch formulates our policy?"

We found, of course, at least two different parts of the federal Executive branch. One was the political leadership—the people, assistant secretaries of a cabinet department for example, who come in for perhaps 18 months, and who, a number of members felt, didn't learn enough to know what the problem was by the time they left, let alone have the time to solve it. Even more important, if you want to find someone who is an expert in the problem and bring him into government from the outside, you would bring in, together with his expertise, a built-in conflict of interest. If someone comes from the private sector—from the industries which are regulated—and in 18 months or three years returns there, the result is an unsatisfactory and unreliable political leadership. Particularly in the case of administrative agencies, where the oversight of appointments is lax, the danger of capture by the regulated industries is very high, causing some to suggest that moving a number of the functions from the administrative agencies back to the president under a cabinet official would be a desirable step.

Under this unstable and constantly changing political leadership in the Executive branch, there is the civil service system. A number of people expressed concern about the stability and permanence of the civil service system, although we never did discuss it at any great length. Suffice it to say that, while we could take some comfort in the fact that even though the political leadership of the country was unable to govern the country in 1974 the bureaucracy ran on its own, we could also have some discomfort that it reflected the fact that neither the president nor the Congress has the power to control the bureaucracy, which in many ways has a life of its own.

The particular Executive function that we concentrated on was planning, because there was agreement by the members of the committee that government should be able to plan, given the complex energy, environmental, and economic problems facing the country. This is not to say that government needs to intervene more in the economy, because, as a number of people point out, planning and intervention in the private sector are two very different things. Indeed, some of the most dangerous intervention in the private sector comes, not when there has been planning, but when there has been no planning, so that we don't know why the government is intervening. What people felt was a need for a plan—not a plan in the sense of a crystal-ball idea of what is going to happen in the future, but a plan in the sense of a statement of our goals and a formulation of alternatives. Once we have alternatives to consider, the electorate, the Congress, and the public at large can evaluate them. Any talk about the need for planning assumes that there is some data from which we can plan. This is an assumption which a number of the members of the committee felt was a very healthy one. But the principal questions about government planning are: Given the separation of powers, can the government plan? And given that separation of powers, can the government implement a plan, even if it could plan in the first place?

As to the first questions—can the government plan—there was at least some confidence that in some measures now being considered by Congress, such as the Humphrey-Hawkins Bill, a mechanism is being devised for planning. Congress would set some goals and direct the president to articulate policies within those goals so that Congress can evaluate them. There is some hope that Congress can set goals and then discipline itself, as it has in the Budget Act, to respond to some sort of Executive planning. Whether that plan could ever be implemented, however, is more difficult to say, since, if the president sends a complex series of legislative proposals to Congress, they might go to 40 different subcommittees for consideration. Congress must work as a whole on a plan for an economic or energy solution, and this is a very difficult change for Congress to make.

But I don't want to suggest that we ended on a pessimistic note, because a number of the members of the committee continued to remind us that we are the oldest democracy in the world, and they reminded us of the fact that a democracy at any age is a very rare commodity today. This gave us some sense of confidence that we could overcome our new problem as well.

Report on Committee III

By John Honnold

ABSTRACT: One committee session was devoted to problems resulting from division of power between the nation and the states and cities. The committee dealt with the dilemma of the need for the taxing power and capacity to deliver funds to the points of greatest need on the part of the national government, on one hand, and the greater responsiveness of local programs to local conditions, on the other. It was also noted that many problems are regional, and consideration was given to the question of whether the Constitution permitted the creation of regional governments. The final committee session dealt with vehicles for citizen impact on government, which has been enhanced by the growth of public interest groups. The view was expressed that most problems were too complex for citizens to play a large role in government operations. Citizen impact is greatest at election time, and ways to enhance citizen participation in elections were considered.

John Honnold is the Schnader Professor of Law at the University of Pennsylvania. He served as Chief of the International Trade Law Branch of the U.N. from 1969–74 and practiced law with the New York firm now called Cahill, Gordon and Reindel prior to that. He was also associated with the Securities and Exchange Commission and was the Chief of Court Review of the Office of Price Administration. His publications include The Life of the Law: Readings on the Growth of Legal Institutions and Cases on Constitutional Law (co-author).

IT IS my task to report to you on the discussions at two sessions of the committee.

NATION-STATES-CITIES

One session was devoted to problems resulting from the division of powers between the nation and the states (including, most insistently, the cities and metropolitan regions).

The committee took note of the striking increases in national influence, particularly through grants of funds. It was noted that such programs had created new specialized constituencies interested in the receipt of funds, but had failed to provide appropriate constituencies for review and control.

The committee's discussion dealt with a basic dilemma. On the one hand, there is need for the strong taxing power of the national government and also for its capacity to deliver funds to the points of greatest need. On the other hand, state and local programs are more responsive to local conditions and provide more opportunity for participation in the process of government. Local programs also provide the opportunity for low-risk experiments to test the practicality of attractive-sounding projects.

The committee noted that some of the most urgent problems are regional and need to be dealt with by governmental units that reach across state lines. It was agreed that providing structures to deal adequately with regional problems presented urgent issues of political and constitutional dimensions. For example, federal grants to regional units often lacked a system for responsible control by a local constituency. Furthermore, in metropolitan areas, the necessity to levy increased taxes to provide funds for education, health, welfare, and other social services encouraged business units and residents to relocate in lower-tax areas.

Was it possible to create governmental units of a size that fit these problems? Attention was given to the use of interstate compacts to create governmental units to deal with regional, multi-state problems. It was noted that in some settings structures created by interstate compacts had been effective, but experience in negotiating compacts has shown that it was difficult to secure unanimous agreement for the relinquishment of substantial governmental power. It has been impossible, so far, to establish new regional constituencies with power by the ballot to control programs and to raise taxes.

Consideration was given to the question of whether the Constitution permitted the creation of regional governments with such powers. Most members thought there should be no serious difficulty under the federal Constitution. Much greater difficulty was presented by restrictions in some state constitutions and by the reluctance of state governments to relinquish powers to new governmental units. The committee was generally of the view that finding a way out of this impasse presented an urgent—and unsolved—problem.

CITIZEN PARTICIPATION AND LEGISLATIVE STRUCTURES

The final session of the committee considered vehicles for citizen impact on government. Citizen influence has been enhanced by the growth of public interest groups— that is, groups not tied to a political party and not serving a narrow interest. Attention was given to procedures set forth in a few laws (such as revenue sharing) requiring that there be a public hearing before programs are finalized. It was noted that the effect of such procedures has been disappointing. Suggestions were made for strengthening public participation—by requiring more effective notice of hearings and by requiring officials to set forth their responses to the material supplied by the public.

One view was that most problems were so complex that one could not expect citizens to play a large role in the detailed operations of government; the impact of citizens could best be felt at election time. However, in this regard, the committee recalled the problems presented by programs based on federal grants where there is no local, responsible constituency.

The committee also considered ways to enhance citizen participation in elections. It was noted that in some countries there was automatic, universal registration of voters through door-to-door canvassing. This approach received widespread support in the committee.

Consideration was also given to

proposals to modify the structure and organization of Congress. Among various proposals, interest was expressed in requiring candidates to make public disclosure at least of the sources of their income.

Finally, the committee considered procedures for selection of the vice-president. It was noted that current procedures can result in hasty and unrepresentative action, with untoward consequences when the vice-president must assume to the office of president. Attention was given to a proposal that only a president be elected; the president would then nominate a vice-president who would be subject to confirmation by both houses of Congress, as under the Twenty-Fifth Amendment.

In view of the limited time for consideration, no final position was taken. The committee, however, concluded that it was important that further attention be given to the procedures for selection of the vice-president, and also to his role in government, and that the need to improve the present procedures might well justify amendment of the Constitution.

*　　*　　*

QUESTIONS AND ANSWERS

Q: I'm Dr. Nesvitus, a citizen and a member. I want to ask Professor Gilbert how many regions have been planned and when can we expect the implementation of this program for primary elections.

A (Gilbert): Plans to regionalize the country would be a matter presumably of a fundamental revision. There are two approaches to that. I suppose there are more, but let's consider two. One would be a fundamental revision of federalism

in which we would simply consolidate the present number of states and reduce their number into regions that made more sense, and the intriguing thing about that is, which regions make sense? The federal government has not been strikingly successful in agreeing on how many regions they should have, simply for their own enterprises. But that would be one approach, and it's obviously the hard approach, since states are, constitutionally, very hard to abolish.

The other approach is some high degree of regionalization of federal government activities with the decentralization to the regions of much of the grant-monitoring and, indeed, grant-giving activities, so that a federal region becomes a kind of a superstructure, essentially an administrative region over state and local governments. But that's a region with no electoral constituency; it's simply an administrative region.

I suppose a third approach is an authority approach—Tennessee Valley Authority or something of that sort.

Q: I'm Philip Smith. I'm from Bucks County. I would like to have your explanation of why our government has carried out so many unwise policies instead of wise ones.

A: Well, I'll undertake to respond to your question in these terms. This is the question our committee was really addressing: how do you improve the processes by which the citizenry of this country can obtain the policies, through government, that they would like to see in this country? And I believe that all of these five areas that we addressed ourselves to are relevant to the question of how to accomplish that. But, foremost, I would say would be the first and the fifth areas, the first being the exercise of the franchise —how do you impose the process by which that franchise is more effective in expressing the viewpoint of all of us—and the fifth being how does a citizen, through various groups, the media, his local organizations, and national organizations, express himself on these questions.

I don't believe there's anyone to answer your question except in terms of improving both of those processes.

Q: I'm Ray Martin from Riverdale, Maryland. There was some suggestion about a one-house veto of executive actions. Before I get to the point, I'd like to make a report that a one-house veto of administration action will probably get its first test under the Energy Policy and Conservation Act of 1975. Now to my question. Was there any consideration given to the fact that professional staffs rather than the elected representatives and senators determine policy from the legislative point of view and that it is indeed rare to have other than professional lobbyists appear at hearings. I would also like to know whether the committee gave any consideration to one of the more spectacular parts of the revolution that put the present United States government apart from the rest of the world's governments, in that it does not own the mineral resources.

A (Frug): I'll undertake to comment on part of this and then ask Professor Gilbert if he will add to it. With respect to the role of congressional staffs, we did give some consideration to that in recognizing that the size of congressional staffs has increased very sharply in recent years, adding to some 12,000 professional staff members who serve either members or committees.

We recognize this as a matter of concern, if it reaches the point where a member himself cannot be personally involved in the legislative process for which as a committee member he has a reponsibility.

A (Gilbert): Mineral rights have not been talked about, so the simple answer to the last part of your question is, no, we didn't talk about them. I guess we talked about professional lobbyists as we talked about the whole problem of participation and of the so-called public interest groups and their work. I guess you have to say they're professional lobbyists also. And not all of us were ready to agree that there's a sound distinction between public interest representatives and special interest representatives.

Beyond that, I don't think we did talk about the problem of the professional lobbyist. I would say, just in my own experience, that on issues of general public import and interest, it's common for a considerable number of nonprofessional witnesses to appear before congressional committees. They're usually professional people, but they are not professional lobbyists: for example, the people in my own trade, from the Academy.

A (Frug): I might simply add here that we did talk about the question of the implications of the growth of public interest groups. These are groups that have sprung up in the last 10 years. Certainly, they've made themselves felt—the civil rights issue resulted in that. But the more fundamental question that was raised was why this has happened. It either means that the organized interest groups—labor, business, education, so forth—have not performed the function or that the political parties, perhaps, have not performed a function fully. But this is a new phenomenon and we're not quite sure what it represents as yet.

———

Q: My name is Gersten Eisenberg. I'm from Baltimore and my academic background has been in economics and public finance. The problem of city finances has been mentioned tonight, but I think it's such a serious one, not only at the city level, but at all levels of government, that I want to reemphasize it or would appreciate additional comment.

I recall an issue of *Time* magazine, as far back as 1972, which had a cover story, headlined "Is the U.S. Going Broke?" and even at that time they talked about the financial difficulties of cities, the cutback in services of all types, the reluctance of citizens to vote for bond issues for fear of increasing their taxes, the flight of wealthy taxpayers to the suburbs. And, I think, at other levels of government things aren't very much better.

There has been talk that the states should take over educational costs and the federal government should take over welfare costs; but I think the federal government has been running a deficit under both Democratic and Republican administrations since World War II in every year, except possibly three or four, and Mr. Ford is talking about holding the budget to $400 billion and the defense appropriations to $100 billion and cutting back on social services. And Mr. Reagan has been talking about cutting on governmental costs while, at the same time, he wants to increase military costs so that the United States is number one in the world, as far as military power goes.

I also read statistics that the cost of government, overall—federal, state, and local—is increasing proportionately faster than that of the Gross National Product. Where is this all going to end and are we going broke?

A (Staats): Well, I'll undertake to respond to that. I really wouldn't want to attribute any of this to our committee, but, on an individual basis I think your real test here is whether the economy is growing as fast as the public service sector of the budget, and we've already answered the question in part. The public service sector of our total economy is growing faster than our total economy, proportionately, which means that it's inevitable that the burden on the taxpayer has increased, particularly in the last 10 years.

Whether the economy can be strengthened so that the revenues will go up and the cost of public services will go down is what the issue is all about, and this is, of course, the main issue that's before the electorate in the coming presidential election. One thing I would add to that is, as far as the cities are concerned, the problem here, then, is the growing burden of public services, particularly in the area of health and welfare.

New York City is, of course, a dramatic case in point, but it is not alone. New York City has been in the headlines and its situation is probably the most acute, but Detroit, St. Louis, and Cleveland are other examples. However, as far as the total situation is concerned, part of it is a matter of distribution of the tax burden, and New York City cannot deal by itself with this problem, nor can New York State deal by itself with New York City's problem.

It's got to be dealt with on a more regional basis or we're going to have more serious trouble than we have today. That's my opinion.

Q: I'm John Snavely from Philadelphia, attorney and social scientist by discipline, lately retired from six years of trying to make the Federal Crime Control Act work, which it didn't. Your attention is directed to the dilemma of this growing fiscal responsibility to, or growing jurisdictional responsibility to, deliver services efficiently versus the probably vanishing fiscal ability of government at all levels to do so.

I was surprised that I did not hear some concern with why the Joint Funding Simplification Act has not been implemented in its fullest spirit, theory, and concept. The thing, as an administrator both at city and state level, that has been very predominant in my observation has been the tremendous duplication in spending: duplication in management responsibility, duplication in federal grant funding, redundancy in agency administration, and fragmentation in agency administration. All of which causes a great deal of expenditure, duplication of effort, and reduction in effective service delivery, and all of which was the target for the Joint Funding Simplification Act. And yet I've seen, after years of development of that act, almost no implementation of it.

A (Staats): Well, our office has been, of course, critical on this same point, and we think more emphasis should have been given, not only to that, but to the whole area of grouping categories of grants into block grants or what the administration has called special revenue sharing. The administration, as you may know, has recently submitted a program in community development and one in the area of health.

I personally think this is a good move and it's a good step forward, but it needs a lot more emphasis. But this gets back to some of the matters that our committee discussed: one of the reasons that we have not done more by way of consolidating these programs into more useful programs at the local level is that there are special constituencies who have wanted to preserve a particular category of grant, whether it's for mental health or any one of literally a thousand different categories of grants.

Until those people are willing to recognize the seriousness of these problems of the people who are on the receiving end at the local level, we're going to have trouble, but I think that the real need here is to consolidate those grants.

Q: I'm Kenneth Abel, from Huntsville, Alabama, an economist by profession. I listened with great interest and fascination to Professor Gilbert's discourse, particularly on the conceptions regarding the environment in which our government finds itself. But I was left rather disappointed at the end when it seemed that the environmental factors were to be taken as given and there is really no need for constitutional reform.

It would seem to me that the problem of the mass media, which has become a virtual branch of the government, but is responsible to no one and its control is relegated to a few individuals, is perhaps the most classic example of monopoly you can find in the country today. Another problem is public employee unionism, in which unions are permitted to extort at their pleasure what they want from government, particularly at the local level of government. The practice of strikes which is bringing the cities to their knees, presently an accepted mode of

life, is contrary to a tradition which we once had in this country that public employees were not permitted to strike against the government and withhold necessary services in order to enforce their demands.

My question is, has this group really done its job? I'm sorry to say that I think the earlier two groups did not do their job, and as I listened to Professor Gilbert, I had hopes that this committee had. But I wonder what constructive contribution this whole session is making to finding and proposing honest-to-God solutions to the problems that we face.

A (Staats): I feel compelled to make a reply to that. First, you're getting the summation of a considerable amount of opinion and commentary that I hope may be available to you in written form later, so that you will not be so disappointed. Secondly, there have been in this evening alone, along with the two prior sessions, very specific, honest-to-God, as you called them, suggestions that have appeared in the committee sessions and that were reported in the excellent distilled reports of our reporters—suggestions that did not always have consensus. As a matter of fact, we were not looking for consensus or resolutions or majority voting. That was not the purpose of this constitutional conference, and some of these suggestions would indeed require constitutional amendments. These are not something that one does by majority vote or by total consensus in a matter of four days.

The purpose of this conference, I think, has been admirably filled by the very detailed, in many cases, and, I think, brilliant reflections on the document that we call the American Constitution.

The United States and the World

By COVEY T. OLIVER

ABSTRACT: Most experts on America's dealings with other nations would agree that we have a unique, complicated, energy-depleting system of law for allocating authority to govern our official conduct offshore. The U.S. state and federal constitutions incorporate some version of separation of powers with checks and balances, requiring the inter-related independence of 3 branches of government. At the constitutional level, this system allocates action and commitment ability related to foreign affairs between the Executive and Legislative branches, but so far the courts have not ventured far into resolution of conflicts between them. The Constitution says the president has executive power and Congress does not have express, general power to legislate or manage in foreign affairs. It does not resolve the question of who is master in foreign policy. A number of problem cases influencing the shaping of our external relations are military policy, control of expenditures, and arms control and disarmament. The possibility of a transnational government, citizen participation in policy decisions, America's good faith in international agreements, and the constitutional revision for foreign affairs are also important questions concerning America and the world. And in this complex it may be that for the first time in the nation's history the people have to live with unrelieved separation of powers, while Congress increasingly asserts a will to participate in foreign affairs.

Covey T. Oliver is now Ferdinand Wakeman Hubbell Professor of International Law at the University of Pennsylvania, and previously taught at the Universities of Texas and California, Berkeley. He served as U.S. Ambassador to Colombia from 1964–66, Assistant Secretary of State for Inter-American Affairs and U.S. Coordinator for the Alliance for Progress from 1967–69, a member of the U.S. delegation to the Paris Peace Conference in 1946, U.S. Executive Director of the World Bank Group in 1969, and Lecturer at the Hague Academy of International Law in 1955 and 1974. He co-authored Restatement of the Foreign Relations Law of the United States *and* The International Legal System.

IT WOULD be interesting to know whether the American people believe there is a crisis today in the management of American foreign relations under the Constitution of 1789. Most expert American observers of, or participants in, the conduct of the nation's official dealings with the rest of the world would agree that we have a unique, complicated, energy-depleting system of public law for the allocation of authority for the governance of our official conduct offshore. And they would find the present situation of this system at least somewhat controversial, both at home and abroad.

But these same American experts would divide as to whether anything can or should be done structurally. A considerable majority, probably, agree with the general thrust of Appendix L[1] to the Report of the Commission for the Study of the Organization of the Government for Foreign Affairs,[2] that by mutuality, patience, and other attitu-

1. This report, "Organizing the Government to Conduct Foreign Policy: The Constitutional Questions," was distributed along with this issues paper to participants in the work of committee IV through the courtesy of the *University of Virginia Law Review*, 747 (1975), p. 61.

2. Widely referred to as the "Murphy Commission" in honor of its chairman, the Honorable Robert D. Murphy, a distinguished senior American diplomatist, this commission was required by Section 603 (a) of the Foreign Relations Authorization Act of 1972, Pub. L. No. 92–352, 86 Stat. 489. The singularity of the requirement for reauthorization, as distinguished from fiscal appropriation, of the Department of State among the established departments of the Executive branch is discussed herein. A livelier account of the origins of the commission than that of its General Counsel in his *Introduction* to the law review printing cited above is to be found in B. Welles, "The Genesis of the Murphy Commission— Congress, Commissions, and Cookie-Pushing," 53 *Foreign Service Journal* 11 (January 1976).

dinal acts of moderation, the qualified players of the "Foreign Relations Game" for the American side can improve the "game plan" result for the United States. So far as the evidence from writings goes, it seems that the preponderant opinion of experts, with some exceptions (as always among experts), is that it is unnecessary, unthinkable, or illusory to contemplate changing significantly the structure of American government for any reason linked to "The United States and the World." Nonetheless, some believe that it might be useful now to go through the exercise of reviewing the basic law controlling America's relationships with the rest of the planet.

Basic issues of governmental structure for foreign relations should not always be examined, as they usually are, only from the standpoint of our internal concerns and expectations about the Constitution and our associations with the rest of the world. The rest of the world is also vitally concerned with, is affected by, and hence reacts to, how America does things internationally.

Let us begin by seeing ourselves as others see us. We are a country that in its first 200 years has been phenomenally successful in every way in which the achievements of nations are measured; but usually the world does not credit our institutions and our way of life for this, as we tend to do, but rather believes that the good fortune of natural riches explains our success. Major resources, however, are seriously depleted now; and substitutes have not yet been assured. Some foreigners, following Adam Smith's view as to the fundamental wealth of nations, are willing to credit the American people also for the nation's success. But even this limited perception of us, the people, as the true wealth of the nation is in decline now.

The United States is a federal, participatory democracy, whose state and federal constitutions all incorporate some version of separation of powers with checks and balances—thus requiring the inter-related independence of three branches of government. This makes us unique—*truly solitary*—in the world community. As Ambassador Moynihan did not tire of saying, democracy itself is no longer the form of government that a majority of states provide for or practice. Within participatory democracies, only a very few (not more than a dozen) states are federal in form, and of these options federalism is a serious legal factor in the foreign relations of only five![3] Finally, no other federalistic democracy has an operational separation of powers/checks and balances constitutional system. Nor, for that matter, do unitary (non-federal) states often practice separation of powers. In Iberic-America, for example, where the American Constitution was the model, of the few remaining democracies, only in Colombia and Costa Rica have separation of powers problems occasionally arisen in regard to relations with other states.

Although in the world community the American system of governance for foreign relations is thus exotic, our national tendency, exhibited even in the evaluation of our Constitution, is to disregard this basic fact and to treat the problem of foreign affairs and the Constitution largely as a matter of internal values and preferences. We ascribe an almost incontestable value to the constitutional status quo and expect the rest of the world to adjust to it; or, at most, we assume that the domestic gains outweigh the possible foreign affairs losses, now and possibly for all time to come.

But there is a rising tide of evidence that the rest of the world—especially the shrinking world of our friends—is finding our blandness in this particular increasingly irritating and destabilizing. We should not accept such evidence as conclusive, but we should not disregard it either. Thus, consider two recent illustrations:

1. Alfonso Lopez Michelsen, elected President of Colombia, observed, in regard to an unannounced shift in United States policy (from supporting a Colombian cut-flower export industry as relevant to Colombia's development to a Congress-pressured Treasury investigation of Colombian cut-flower imports as being subject to extraordinary [dumping] duties) that the episode brought sharply to attention questions of the reliability and authoritativeness of United States foreign policy declarations and assurances.

2. The Prime Minister of Singapore at a White House dinner in his honor remarked in his toast that the friends of the United States are becoming increasingly uncertain and concerned as to who effectively speaks for the United States.[4]

Hence, as we proceed in accordance with the wishes and interests of the participants to examine issues of (or close to) constitutional dimensions arising from America's contemporary and projected roles in the world community, let us consider the perspectives of that community, as well as our attachment to our present system. "Interdependence" requires no less.

3. Covey T. Oliver, *The Enforcement of Treaties by a Federal State*, ch. 3, I-1974 Recueil des Cours 346, 348, Hague Academy of International Law.

4. Remarks of the Prime Minister of Singapore at the White House (12 May 1975), 11 Pres. Doc. 501, 502.

As we go forward, I remind you that the official report cited previously, and whose Appendix L was sent to the conference participants for prior study, is the eighty-third[5] officially-commissioned study of United States foreign relations arrangements since World War II![6] These studies are not famed for focus on the types of questions that the conference should focus on here.[7] It has been 200 years, after all, since our government under the articles began, and the soon-perceived inadequacy of this original system for the conduct of the nation's foreign relations was one of the major inducements to the Constitutional Convention of 1787. That conclave did result in a new system. It seems fitting now to move ahead with re-evaluation, freed from the limitations of realism, practicality, and ethnocentricity that seemingly always bind official commissions. Perhaps if the framers had been practical—or realistic—they would merely have adjusted the Articles of Confederation a bit. We know to our advantage that they let their minds be bold.[8] Let us be bold enough to inquire.

5. The tally is that of B. Welles, "The Genesis of the Murphy Commission."
6. Even by 1949 in the writer's recollection, "reorganizing the Department of State" had become rather repetitive in Washington.
7. The reasons for modest scope in official reports on the reorganization of the government, especially as to its basic structure, are quite understandable. They are, perhaps, the same reasons the Congress of the United States, under the Articles of confederation, did not undertake directly the revisory tasks that came to be performed by the Federal Convention of 1787. See, generally, Max Farrand, *The Framing of the Constitution* (New Haven: Yale University Press, 1913), ch. 1.
8. J. Brandeis, dissenting in *New State Ice Co.* v. *Liebmann*, 285 U.S. 262 (1932), from the then-reigning notion that substantive due process required invalidation of state

FOREIGN POLICY AND THE SEPARATION OF POWERS

The internal situation today

The American system of separation of powers with checks and balances is a system that, at the constitutional level, allocates action and commitment authority related to foreign affairs functions between the two political branches of government. The nonpolitical (Judicial) branch, generally speaking, has shown almost "unjudicial" awareness of the practical needs of untroubled foreign relations where issues have arisen as between people and the Executive,[9] but so far the courts have not ventured far into Constitution-level resolution of conflicts of jurisdiction between the Executive and the Legislative branches.

Those who have read Appendix L, who have studied Professor Louis Henkin's elegant small treatise,[10] or have otherwise absorbed our constitutional fundamentals know that the Constitution of 1789 creates an executive who (although this is not said in so many words) internationally is the American chief of state (not merely head of government). The powers of this executive are not elaborately enumerated, as are those of the Congress. The Constitution says the president has the executive power. It is clear that under the Constitution the president

legislation limiting entry into a business denominated in that legislation as one affected with the public interest.
9. In the matter of the determination of the immunity of defendants from suit under the claim of "sovereign" immunity, settlement of nationalization claims, and so on. See, generally, *Restatement of the Law Second: The Foreign Relations Law of the United States*, sec. 69, R.N. 1; 71; 212; 213; 214.
10. Louis Henkin, *Foreign Affairs and the Constitution* (Mineola, N.Y.: Foundation Press, 1972).

personally or through his delegates is the sole organ of official communication with other states. Broadly speaking, the Constitution as written does not give to Congress a general power to legislate as to foreign affairs,[11] although some of the specified powers, such as over foreign commerce, have high degrees of foreign affairs relevancy.

The Constitution gives one-third plus one of the senators present and voting both a veto and a delaying power over "treaties." And in America even the traditional "envoys extraordinary and ministers plenipotentiary" of age-old ambassadorial communications patterns between chiefs of state cannot be appointed by the American chief of state alone, although after Senate approval (by simple majority), office is held at the pleasure of the president. The Constitution makes the president the commander-in-chief of

11. Why it did not is often said to be one of the several enigmas of silence in the Constitution as to arrangements for foreign relations operations. However, Farrand, *The Framing of the Constitution*, by his time-sequence rearrangement of what went on at Philadelphia, tends to show that no mysteries were involved but, rather, that the framers had far more delicate and difficult internal issues of union than foreign affairs ones to face and settle and, having done so, engrossed their document and adjourned, leaving us with ". . . the 'bundle of compromises' known as the constitution of the United States . . . a practical piece of work for very practical purposes . . ." (p. 201). "[The framers] were dependent upon their experience under the state constitutions and the articles of confederation. John Dickinson expressed this very succinctly in the course of the debates when he said: 'Experience must be our only guide. Reason may mislead us' " (p. 204).

Nowadays, thanks to the Supreme Court's accretive creation of an unwritten constitution, the "foreign affairs legislative power of Congress" has become a commonplace. Compare Henkin, *Foreign Affairs and the Constitution*, ch. 3, pp. 74-6.

the armed forces of the United States, without specific distinction as to where he may command these forces to be. But only Congress may declare war.

This brief recitation of constitutional fundamentals, amply buttressed and elaborated elsewhere, suffices to support these descriptive observations:

1. The constitutional architecture of separation of powers with checks and balances requires executive and legislative cooperation and compromise as to most major or enduring aspects of American foreign relations. A president cannot for very long do very much that is highly significant in foreign relations on his own; and Congress on its own is not legally authorized to deal with other states and international organizations. The result is a dualism. Viewed from abroad, it has happened with some frequency in our history that deficiencies in American reliability that really result from the inherent nature of the system are seen elsewhere as excuses for American manipulation, evasion, and breach of commitment.

2. At best, the Constitution and its gestation are enigmatic as to a question that, had it ever been answered clearly and definitely, would have mitigated the problems sketched in 1, above. The question: between Congress and the president, who is to be master in the realm of international affairs?

The Constitution is generally silent—some say secretive—as to the foreign affairs roles of the three branches. There is also reason to doubt the conflicts-resolution utility—if not the authoritativeness —of some rather fanciful Supreme Court "doctrines of obiter" about the direct descent of the foreign affairs executive power from the British Crown to the "executive in Congress" of the articles and on to the president under the Constitution of 1789.[12]

In providing a scheme of government "for ages to come," did the founding fathers consciously decide to avoid coming to grips with the issue of who is ultimately to be master? If so, why? Or did they assume that Congress remained paramount, as it had perforce been under the articles? Contrariwise, did they choose to leave it to the two political branches to grapple and contend and eventually to adjust as circumstances would make necessary, from epoch to epoch and from one president and Congress to another?

Perhaps, though, the silences of the Constitution simply reflect a now-obsolete perception of the foreign relations process. In this regard, it bears noting that one thread running through several of the viewpoints expressed in Appendix L of the Murphy Commission Report[13] is that things really have not changed as to the process, because in our formative years under this Constitution our foreparents in office had to contend with the infinite complexities of America's relations with the convoluted "European System" of the eighteenth century. Do the writers really mean this? Do *you* agree that picking America's way between revolutionary France and the pre-Concert of Europe presents the

policy choices and the operations difficulties that face this country today, on a planet of 150 states, rich-poor, socialist-nonsocialist, old-new, with nuclear proliferation, runaway arms races, a population explosion, and environmental exhaustion blended in? I personally differ, and furthermore I suspect that the framers did not, in 1787, see foreign relations for what it has become, particularly the rather threatening reality that, in terms of survival—of values as well as of the nation—there is no longer any sharp line between internal and external affairs.

Nor should we lose sight of the political fact that the separation of powers system has been bridged almost from the beginning of our history under the present Constitution by party politics, a term and concept as to which the Constitution is entirely silent. A fundamental question cutting through all of the topics of this conference is whether the American people may not have come, after nearly 200 years, to have to try to live for the first time with unrelieved separation of powers.

In orthodox American governmental theory, the Congress and the Executive were once thought to be coordinated through the president's political leadership of the dominant party in Congress. Woodrow Wilson, early in this century, shifted coordination theory to the concept of the president (if to be "strong," that is, "effective") as the articulate voice, vis-à-vis Congress, of the ideals, values, and wishes of the American people in his time. From time to time, particularly in the aftermath of World War II, foreign policy has been characterized as outside political contention—as "bipartisan."

Now, however, looking back we

12. The reference is to an interpretation of the wide-ranging obiter dictum of Justice Sutherland, as the opinion-writer in *United States* v. *Curtiss-Wright Export Corp.*, 299 U.S. 304 (1936), *post*, p. 57.
13. Note, particularly, the comments of Professor G. Casper, "Organizing the Government," p. 777.

note that since World War II, Truman, Eisenhower, Nixon, and Ford have been part- or full-time "minority" presidents and that Kennedy never had and ultimately Johnson lost the support of majorities of their own parties in Congress.

The Wilsonian version of the strong president putting the fear of God into the Congress in the name of the people did not, tragically, work for him, or for any president after him except for Roosevelt—and even he failed in efforts to purge senatorial recalcitrants.

Bipartisanship in foreign affairs began to die when Eisenhower campaigned on "I will go to Korea. . . ," despite occasional efforts since to revive it.

Strangely—eerily almost—today there may even be a kind of reverse bipartisanship at work, in that the foreign affairs issues that divide the president and the Congress are not so much based upon political differences as on different senses of mission between the two sets of institutions involved. Certainly today the issue "Who shall be master?" is not a party issue but an issue of congressional power versus presidential power, as the Democratic Majority Leader in the Senate never hides.[14]

14. Consult the dissent of Senator Mike Mansfield to the Report of the Murphy Commission. Welles, "The Genesis of the Murphy Commission," selects these phrases from this nonconcurrence of a commissioner: ". . . even a cursory reading of the Commission's report reveals a . . . timidity and paucity of substance . . . obvious lack of any consensus among the Commissioners . . . *almost total absence of any consideration of the role of Congress* . . ." (emphasis added). The same source quotes Senator Mansfield on interview as characterizing the Murphy Commission Report as ". . . thin gruel . . . served in a very thick bowl. . . ."

Major issues of foreign policy and the separation of powers

The basic, externally-oriented issues of constitutional limitation are herewith stated and explained. The panel may wish to disregard, debate, restate, or accept them as a backdrop to the evaluation of other issues. As already indicated, I consider these factors to be neglected or undervalued in conventional American appraisals of the Constitution and foreign policy. The issues are mainly ones of separation of powers and of checks and balances, although possible constitutional restrictions upon the types of official actions that representatives of the United States may take are also involved.

Issue: What is the capacity of the United States to act in ways and along lines that other states in the world community use?

Discussion of Issue: Customary international law and international relations modalities still reflect their origins in Western state systems between 1300 and 1500, when the people and their representatives had no legal power or authorized role in any aspect of foreign statecraft. Even in Great Britain, where Parliament developed to the level of virtual omnipotence in domestic affairs behind elaborate fictions as to the continuation of monarchial prerogatives, the Crown has kept control of foreign relations, including the making of international agreements. Thus, in Britain to this day Parliament is not called upon to approve a treaty as a condition of its coming into existence.[15] Her Majesty's

15. See Oliver, *The Enforcement of Treaties*, ch. 4, pp. 363–65, for a short explanation of the classic British discon-

Principal Secretary of State for Foreign Affairs, although a member of the cabinet and sitting in Parliament, is usually not effectively questioned[16]—or his party turned out—where issues of controverted foreign choice are present in the political atmosphere. Recently, even, the Court of Appeals has held that, despite the doctrine that no Parliament may bind another, the national legislation required to enable Britain to perform its obligations under the European Community treaties is impervious to fundamental variance by another Parliament thereafter.[17]

The American president, acting personally or through the Department of State or other executive agencies, is treated on the world scene as being authorized to act for the United States as if an absolute monarch. He and his subordinates may commit the country, notwithstanding the Constitution, internationally. Lack of capacity domestically is no legal defense internationally to an undertaking made by a chief of state.[18] When presi-

dents, secretaries of state, ambassadors, and other authorized Americans meet with their peers from other countries, the inheritance from what for modern democracies is an outmoded but still living system tends to influence the way things go, especially where the issues involved relate to the intensity with which policy objectives of the chiefs of state are pursued.

Despite all this, however, the American chief of state increasingly finds himself cut down well below his peers in the world system as to powers related to foreign affairs operations that even in other modern democratic societies are exclusive to the foreign affairs executive there.

And, of course, absolute power-wielding chiefs of state have increased in numbers in modern times as participatory democracy has been displaced or is not practiced in fact. I know of no other government in the world in which the legislative branch claims, as Congress seems to be claiming today, that the executive departments are not privileged to keep internal operations communications to themselves (executive privilege) and that state secrets must be revealed to legislative assemblies. In most other democratic states, the foreign affairs executive is able to maintain executive privacy and state security, because the constitution places the control of parliament in a group of officials who occupy dual roles, those of executives and legislators.

Anyone who, knowing of congressional inquisitions in Washington, has observed question time at Westminster and has seen the foreign affairs executive blandly answer, "No, Sir" (which means "No comment"), to a pointed Parliamentary question related to foreign

---

tinuity between treaty-making and internal treaty performance needing legislation and of the "Ponsonby Rule," whereby HMG usually provides Parliament with informational scrutiny of treaties by laying them on the table for a time.

16. This generalization is based upon personal observations and the reality that if the foreign minister's party has the votes, the opposition cannot make much of a not untypical "No, Sir" refusal to respond at question time.

17. *Blackburn* v. *Attorney-General* [1971] Common Market L. Reps. 784 [1971] 1 W. L. R. 1037 (Ct. of App.).

18. Compare Articles 27 and 46 of the United Nations (Vienna) Convention on the Law of Treaties; *Restatement Second: Foreign Relations Law of the United States* (1965), sec. 123, 132, 163; Oliver, *The Enforcement of Treaties*, pp. 354–60.

affairs operations understands the difference between the systems. Which is not to say, of course, that one of them is, in the nature of things, preferable to the other. It is only to say that the American executive, charged with giving course and direction to American foreign affairs, is not, in law, as invulnerable to destabilizing internal counterpressures as are his opposite numbers in other countries, including democratic allies as well as dictatorships.

In this analytical summary, it is also worthy of brief reference that in the United States, unlike most other states, there are constitutional limitations upon the subject matter of international agreements. The pointed dicta of Holmes in *Missouri* v. *Holland*[19] and of Black in *Reid* v. *Covert*[20] establish that it is beyond the capacity of the United States to comply with an international agreement obligation to give internal legal effect to an exercise of authority that the Constitution prohibits, such as a treaty, for example, under which the gist of the agreement is that the contracting states each agree to suppress defamatory utterances about the government, leaders, or people of the other.

The Supreme Court, moreover, in *Youngstown Sheet and Tube Co.* v. *Sawyer*,[21] and in other decisions, has shrunk to negligibility notions that the president has "inherent executive power," linked to foreign policy considerations, under which he may ensure to other states the internal legal effectiveness of mutually agreed foreign policy lines of action that depend upon parallel internal application.

19. 252 U.S. 416 (1920).
20. 354 U.S. 1, 16–17 (1957).
21. 343 U.S. 579 (1952).

Finally, as to constitutional limitations upon the legal capacity or the immunity of American officials from liability when they act abroad, instead of at home, there may be emerging an extension of the old "When does the Constitution follow the flag?" problem. Mr. Dooley, with the Insular Cases[22] of our Spanish-American War period of imperialism in mind, used to say that the Constitution followed the flag on certain days of the week only. But the basic issue in those cases was whether United States governmental action on American-conquered and -acquired territory offshore was controlled by the Constitution as to process, other fundamental rights, and the like.

Today, problems in this regard seem to be much more complicated. Consider the situation in *United States* v. *Jordan*,[23] recently before the United States Court of Military Appeals: is evidence obtained by search and seizure to be excluded at a court-martial of an American airman charged with off-base burglary in the United Kingdom, because American airbase police accompanied but did not participate in an on-base search of the accused's quarters by the British police?

The military appeals court held that the Supreme Court decision in *Mapp* v. *Ohio*, a domestic case,[24] had shifted the invalid search rule from an evidentiary base to a "positive command of the Constitution," thus compelling the abandon-

22. Contrast *Downes* v. *Bidwell*, 182 U.S. 244 (1901) with *Hawaii* v. *Mankichi*, 190 U.S. 197 (1903); *Dorr* v. *U.S.*, 195 U.S. 138 (1904); *Balzac* v. *Puerto Rico*, 258 U.S. 298 (1922). See, generally, Henkin, *Foreign Affairs and the Constitution*, ch. x.
23. No. 29, 592, ACM 21707, 22 August 1975. Modified on reconsideration, 44 LW 2466 (1976).
24. 367 U.S. 643 (1961).

ment of all precedents in prior military justice that made inadmissibility of search and seizure evidence in foreign base cases turn upon the participation, *vel non*, of the American military police in the search. The court concluded:

In sum, then, we hold that evidence obtained by search and seizure in a foreign country must meet Fourth Amendment standards in order to be admitted in evidence in a trial by court-martial, *regardless of whether it is obtained by foreign police acting on their own or in conjunction with American authorities.* . . . (Emphasis added)

Readers who know something about the workings of our *Status of Forces Agreements* are in a good position to conjecture as to what the consequences of such a decision are apt to be when, in the next case of an off-base, off-duty offense by an American soldier, the United States base authorities wish the host state to yield primary jurisdiction to try the defendant in the American military courts. Yet, could such a reader agree as a matter of constitutional analysis with the dissenting judge? He began:

To say that our armed forces carry with them the Constitution as well as the flag is one thing. To say that the Constitution operates against a foreign government in its own country is quite another. . . .

And who among us could give with complete assurance a categorical negative answer to this question: could an American official be held liable, assuming statutory specification, for the violation in another country of the "constitutional rights" of an alien under the Bill of Rights?

Another type of restriction on United States power to act in the foreign affairs field exists de facto only, but it exists nonetheless. It is

the actual reluctance of the Executive to negotiate arrangements with other states, especially self-executing ones, that under the Constitution lie within the range of the treaty power but are believed to be apt to cause objections within the states of the Union—or among congressional groups. This reluctance is not entirely new, but it has certainly become a negative factor of wider ambit since the Bricker Amendment controversy of the 1950s.

One embarrassing aspect of this reluctance is that from time to time the United States seeks special exceptions to its obligations under a treaty, to which other states are unconditionally bound, on the ground that "considering its Constitutional structure" the United States is obligated only to use its good offices to persuade the states of the Union to perform.[25] The hypocrisy—and known as such in international circles—is that the constitutional structure of the United States does not impose limitations upon the power of the federal government to override "states' rights" by a treaty.

As bearing on this Issue very specially (although relevant to some others also), consideration should be given to contemporary courses of conduct of the Congress (mainly through key committees and subcommittees thereof) that trench directly upon the traditional powers of chiefs of state as to the conduct of international relations:

1. *Secrets of state*: Until contemporary times the general assumption, certainly so within the

25. Loper, "Federal State" Clauses in Multilateral Instruments, 1960, *University of Illinois L. For.* 375 (a reprinting in monographic compendium); Oliver, *The Enforcement of Treaties*, ch. 6, pp. 404–7.

foreign affairs component of the American Executive branch, has been that Congress and its committee staffs have no legal right to share in the knowledge of, and certainly not to publicize without the consent of, the Executive "secrets of state," leaving open for the moment the content of this phrase. Until recently, indeed, it was the assumption of perhaps most interested legislators that the classified information collected by the foreign affairs apparatus of the American chief of state could not be demanded under claim of right, but could only be used by the Legislative branch at the discretion of the Executive. Now, as the activities of the House Select Committee on Intelligence and various proposals for legislation to provide for prior clearance by the Congress of clandestine intelligence operations inform us, different winds are blowing from the Hill. Compare, further, the discussion below of a proposal, that building upon legislation now existent (requiring that *all* international agreements made by the Executive, even those under inherent executive authority, be reported to the Congress) would further provide for legislative rescission of some types of such executive agreements without presidential veto. The trend noted cannot but have inhibiting effects (even before final determinations of validity, if such are possible) over a very wide field of normal conduct for the chief of state of any state, including, for example, political, intelligence cooperation, international organizations voting plans, and other informal operating understandings.

2. *What remains of executive privilege*? Also very much under attack from congressional quarters today is the claim of executive privilege (or bureaucratic right of privacy) as to the internal workings of the Executive branch with regard to foreign operations. Foreign affairs operations decisions are often "made" by the human affairs equivalent of resultants of forces in traditional physics. And it has been the contention recently of both the president and Secretary Kissinger that required revelation to the Congress (which they imply means virtually always revelation to the media as well) consigns the process just described to unworkability. The issue joined goes out beyond where the legal trail ended in *United States v. Nixon*,[26] for it is to be recalled that the Supreme Court was careful, when balancing public interests in that case, to note that sensitive issues of foreign affairs operations would not be exposed by denying executive privilege under the facts before the Court.

3. *Legislative trends toward denying the president the veto*: In "Hoover Commission" days, few difficulties were seen with arrangements under which the Congress delegated to the president authority to reorganize the government in accordance with congressional guidelines and subject to congressional invalidation of any particular executive plan by *concurrent resolution* voted within stated (fairly short) time periods. In modern times, however, Congress has drawn upon the concept that a concurrent resolution, unlike a *joint resolution*, is not legislation (and hence is not subject to the veto over laws given to the president by the Constitution) to claim for itself a capacity to rescind, as to internal legal effect, international undertakings made by the chief of state.

Useful illustrations of the process

26. 418 U.S. 683 (1974).

and of some problems it creates can be found in the Trade Reform Act of 1974.[27] Until renewal of legislative authorizations that ended at midnight, June 30, 1967 (the expiration date of the Trade Expansion Act of 1962), it was not worthwhile for there to be further tariff and nontariff barrier reduction negotiations (through the General Agreement on Tariffs and Trade or otherwise) in the world community, because the American Executive had no authority to put negotiated reductions into effect in the tariff laws of the United States.

The executive departments, naturally, bore the brunt of concern about the situation, seeing as imperative the enactment of new trade legislation. Eventually it came, in 1975, burdened with a number of nontrade preconditions required by Congress. (Some of these, such as the Jackson-Vanik Amendment on emigration, were foreign affairs innovations, for hitherto it had not been international practice to attach nontrade conditions to trade concessions.) An important economic need in the new trade legislation was for more effective reduction of nontariff barriers to international trade, such as quantitative restrictions (quotas), the valuation of certain imports at "American Selling Price," and the like.

For trade reasons, it was necessary for the present executive to accept an extension of the concept of congressional post hoc review and possible invalidation by concurrent resolution of presidential negotiations under the powers delegated to him. (A rather exquisite question here is whether the president's nonveto of the trade bill—he could not

afford to—has barred him and his successors, by some sort of constitutional-level estoppel, from attacking the circumvention of his normal power through the veto to require Congress to muster two-third votes in both houses to override his rejection of congressional action that has legal effects.)

Internationally, the apparent power of the Congress to undo a trade negotiation to which the United States is a party is already seen as both inhibiting the chief of state and creating an unsettling degree of uncertainty in regard to the next or "Tokyo" round of multilateral trade negotiations.

The augmentation of earlier usage of the concurrent resolution seems still to be of some interest to groups in Congress. There is now before Congress what may possibly be a high-water mark among legislative efforts to insulate from the veto the will of Congress that certain executive agreements not come into effect if disapproved by concurrent resolution. This proposal is not here discussed in detail, because it is still pending.[28]

4. *Selective use of traditional powers by Congress*: The Issue above directs attention to the actual capacities of the United States as a state among states and of the American chief of state among chiefs of state. The view is from the pit of the world arena. It is submitted that the situation of the United States, unique from the beginning, seems to

27. PL 93–618, 3 January 1975, sec. 102 (e), 125, 151, 152, 161.

28. Readers may wish to consider H.R. 4438, 94th Cong., 1st Sess. A high-water mark among legislative efforts to insulate the will of Congress as to the effectiveness of foreign affairs undertakings of the United States from presidential veto is a proposed "Executive Agreements Review Act of 1975," which deserves wider, scientific attention than so far it appears to have received.

be moving toward even more unusualness.

In this subanalysis, the obvious powers of Congress as to appropriations and investigative post-audit have not been discussed, because as to the first of these powers, history shows that even absolute monarchs have been vulnerable to it and, as to the second, even dictators are reviewed by those who overthrow them.

It does not follow, however, that the use of certain entirely classic and traditional powers of Congress is always directed truly toward the powers used. Subcommittees of regular committees, such as on Government Oversight, Armed Services, and, of course, Appropriations, can be and are used by the legislators who dominate them to seek to force the executive to move along foreign policy lines that reflect the foreign policy preferences, not of the Congress as an entity, but of particular legislators and sometimes those of committee staffers, who, no more than the executive bureaucracy, were ever elected by anybody.

A newly-created discrimination against the Department of State that is linked to particularized interests in explicit influence on foreign affairs operations should now be noted: it has come to pass that the first ministry to be established under the Constitution of 1789, is now, alone among the established departments of government, required to be reauthorized as an agency periodically by Congress.

Watchers of the United States government, here and abroad, have over time become familiar with the fact that a major difference between the permanent executive agencies (the ministries) and temporary agencies, such as, say, the United States Agency for International Development and its many-titled predecessors since the Economic Cooperation Administration of Marshall Plan days, is that the latter die if not periodically reauthorized by Congress.

But now, as a result of the "advise and consent" drive of the Senate Foreign Relations Committee from roughly 1964 on, the Department of State carries on under a second-class agency requirement of having to answer on money matters, not only to the appropriations committees, but to the Senate and House committees for foreign affairs at an "authorization" stage. In contrast, the Treasury Department—the second oldest of the established ministries and one of immense consequence in international relations—need not answer in Congress other than as to its actual appropriations. Of course, if Treasury were to support a particular piece of legislation, such as the replenishment of the American share of the soft-loan capital of international development banks, it would have to go on the merits to the relevant committees, one of which[29] is not charged in Congress with general responsibility for foreign affairs matters.

Issue: How will the reaction of other entities in the world community affect United States interests if present constitutional structure and practice thereunder are continued into the next century?

29. The key committee in the Congress as to this vital aspect of foreign affairs policy is the House Banking and Currency Committee, not the House Committee on International Relations. In the Senate, consideration is by the Committee on Foreign Relations.

Discussion of Issue: To ensure discussion of issues not very often examined in appraisals of the United States Constitution in relationship to international relations, we referred earlier to the evidence of rising foreign impatience with what, in world terms, is a peculiar American system for the conduct of foreign relations. The legal and structural aspects of our present situation in foreign affairs policy-making and performance have also been sketched. Additionally, as to the Issue, there are these questions:

1. Is there buried in a national attitude toward our way of life, including the inertia of normalcy, an assumption that for reasons of virtue, power, or democratic institutional values the United States is entitled to expect to continue to enjoy special toleration for its foreign affairs system?

2. If the answer to (1) is "yes," does world response to rapidly changing world environment (as to international law, forms of government, ideology, resource allocations, population, ecology, neonationalism, irrationality in the conduct of foreign relations, and the like) justify a continued expectation of no-cost toleration?

These questions are intended simply to call attention to the undesirability of letting events take us by surprise, as they have the former colonial powers in one particular and the United States in another. The former did not see early enough the end of a cycle and we did not anticipate the present chaos in the national state system that the end of colonialism has brought.

It may be offensive to some even to suggest considering that our highly-valued constitutional sys-

tem may be a product of times that, for the world as a whole, have passed or are passing.[30]

Realistically, nonetheless, for the near future at least, America is not getting the general deference it once could take for granted. No matter how we may paper it over to ourselves at home, the world knows that America has been defeated—in a professional, Von Clausewitzian sense—in a war; that, although our institutions worked to turn a power-abusing president out of office, they did not earlier reveal his defects to the electorate that voted him into office; and that for the first time in the country's history the chief of state cannot match the authority that members of Congress derive from having been elected.

As we turn again, in the next section, to the more familiar home ground viewpoint, let us ask ourselves whether the sense of mission as to integrity and effectiveness in foreign relations operations that comes to characterize virtually all who are involved in the process as acting parties in the Executive branch can really be shared by the Congress as a whole or the people as a whole.

In all democracies—usually in nondemocracies too—there is a suspicion of those fellow citizens, the "foreign office chaps," who deal with foreigners and become sensitive to their expectations of rights, comity, reciprocity, respect, and even justice. If this reserve becomes rejection, how will the United States

30. This is intended as a serious reflection on what may be the typical political organization of most of the world in a time of resource depletion and population increase, assuming for this purpose that mankind's seeming problems are not dissipated by benign development not now foreseeable.

ever be able to attempt to explain itself abroad?

PROBLEM CASES THAT TODAY INFLUENCE THE SHAPING OF EXTERNAL RELATIONS

Linkages

We are aware that constitutional issues were not considered in a vacuum at Philadelphia in 1787.[31] As to foreign affairs, real problems of national concern about international relations and of the national interest under the articles existed. Today, many pressing questions of value-choice, rather than of structure, also link to our governance for foreign affairs.

I shall attempt to raise the appraisal of these in a governmental context, but without foreclosing others that members of the panel may propose to the chairman and their colleagues. One problem, "Disarmament and Arms Control," I have added to the outline, out of

31. Farrand, *The Framing of the Constitution*, repeatedly brings his readers back to the fundamental fact that the opposite was true in the beginning and in his time. He summarizes pertinently in his conclusion: "Neither a work of divine origin, nor 'the greatest work that ever was struck off at a given time by the brain and purpose of man,' but a practical, workable document is this Constitution of the United States. Planned to meet certain immediate needs and modified to suit the exigencies of the situation, . . . it has been adapted by an ingenious political people to meet the changing requirements of a century and a quarter." (The year was 1913.)

But compare Henkin, *Foreign Affairs and the Constitution*, who ends his book with an approving requotation of what some others have considered "the sneer implicit" in Gladstone's peroration on the American Constitution, quoted and rejected above by Farrand, and the Liberal Prime Minister's contrasting reference to the British constitution as ". . . the most subtile [sic] organism which has proceeded from the womb, and the long gestation of progressive history. . . ."

an affectionate respect for the person and profound admiration for the conscience, wisdom, and vision of a Philadelphian so great as to have assuredly been among the founding fathers had he lived in 1787, Senator Joseph S. Clark.

Military policy

Korea, Vietnam, unbelievable budgets, and a general sense that President Eisenhower was saying something of great importance in his farewell warning as to a military-industrial complex have brought about a situation in which many representatives of the people—we do not know as much about the people themselves—feel that Congress must "Do something," because the Executive will not or cannot control a runaway military state within the state.

In contrast, military affairs professionals, not all of whom are in the armed services by any means, look dubiously at détente, appraise what they consider to be an unchanged (and probably unchangeable) threat situation, and align themselves with certain seniority-entrenched elements in the Congress to resist legal and financial restraints upon American military power-in-being.

So far, the results of this contention have been rather erratic. To illustrate: a few years ago, there arose within the anti-armaments group in Congress a strong determination to force United States development assistance recipients in Latin America to eschew even a modicum of modernization in their military equipment, such as replacing 35-year-old piston-engined military aircraft with the only kind now manufactured, jets.

What then-Assistant Secretary of

State Lincoln Gordon called an "arms crawl" in Latin America, dominant congressmen called, in support of riders to the Foreign Assistance Act, "a run-away arms race." Actually, Latin America then, as now, spent less of its gross national product on arms and the military than any other sector of the planet.[32] And at that time of amendments to the annual Foreign Assistance Authorization Act enforcing the above views, Southeast Asia, the Middle East—even Ethiopia— were freed by waivers from these congressional controls.[33] Result: more and more, the military took over governments in Latin America and the countries turned elsewhere for modern materiel. Also, the Latin countries saw the United States action as not only interventionist, but what is worse, ridiculous or hypocritical.

Structurally viewed, the most significant result of the pulls and hauls partially illustrated here is the War Powers (Joint) Resolution, passed in 1973 over presidential veto.[34] In constitutional terms, the issue presented is between the president's power as commander-in-chief to deploy forces and the power of Congress to protect its power to declare war from situational preemption by such deployment. Although at the time of its con-

sideration, enactment, veto, and passage over the veto, issues of constitutionality figured in debate, President Ford has so far bowed to its mandate.

While it may be that (standing to sue aside) the decision of the Supreme Court as to the *Federal Elections Board*[35] January 30, 1976, will spark a revival of separation of powers adjudications and that the federal courts will not reject the present issue as a political question, the basic issue for us here seems to be whether there should be resolution by constitutional respecification of congressional power to curb the president's volition on deployment of forces.

On a somewhat broader front, the landmark decision referred to above may presage a judicial endeavor to set limits beyond which Congress may not go in acting authoritatively under the Constitution with intent to administer, rather than to legislate or investigate.

Expenditure levels

There are two possible questions for us here:

---

32. Giandoni, "Latin Americans spend little on the military," Copley News Service, *Dallas Morning News*, 10 March 1976, p. 70.

33. The president, who had been given the power to waive these but not all conditions precedent to American development assistance if, in his determination, the foreign affairs interests of the United States should so warrant (but with a burden of reporting and explaining), knew that the congressional groups involved would tolerate waivers as to countries in other areas for a variety of reasons but not as to the recipients of development assistance in the Western hemisphere.

34. P.L. 93–148 (1973).

35. *Buckley, et al.* v. *Valeo, Secretary of the U.S. Senate, et al*, 44 LW 4127, 4159 (Nos. 75-436 and 437, 30 January 1976); 96 S. Ct. 612. In holding that the Federal Elections Commission created by the Federal Elections Campaign Act of 1971 could not continue to function in a rule-making and executive management way for more than 30 days after mandate, the Court relied upon the separation-of-powers system of the Constitution and, following *Springer* v. *Philippine Islands*, 277 U.S. 189 (1922), held that legislative appointees to governmental bodies cannot perform executive functions. Compare Watson, "Congress Steps Out: A Look at Congressional Control of the Executive," 63 *California Law Review* 983, 1029–1048 (1975). The holding in part 4 of the lengthy opinion was unanimous in the per curiam decision.

1. The control of Congress over expenditure levels and disposition of government property being plenary under the Constitution, should there be some mechanism, other than waiting until the next election, to correct asserted-to-be serious congressional damage to foreign policy goals of the United States stemming from reductions or cutoffs of programs, such as military cooperation, foreign intelligence operations, and support for bilateral and multipartite development assistance?

As to expenditures, I join those who say, "We just have to live with what we have." I do so, because even major constitutional change, such as going to ministerial responsibility, would surely leave the money power squarely with the legislative body. Perhaps there could be experimentation with bicamerally-approved foreign assistance international agreements under which the House of Representatives would be committed, along with the Senate, to fund, for periods of years, certain types of foreign assistance programs.

Or, perhaps, the House might initiate a "foreign development tax" to provide for our general welfare through reducing the turbulence of a world otherwise irreversibly divided between rich and poor nations.

It is important to ponder, in passing, why it has been that Congress has been so very reluctant to use its most unquestioned and most powerful control over external operations, the money power. American foreign policy is today—and for some time has been—based upon large expenditures of money. Ergo, even foreign policy is controllable under the money power. Answers seem to lie along one or the other of these lines: (1) internal factors that congressmen cannot ignore are also in play; (2) Congress does not want to wreck, but only influence, major aspects of foreign policy, as to the substance of which it does not disagree with the Executive; (3) using the money power to enable Congress to shape foreign policy throws the control within Congress to inappropriate committees; (4) Congress is aware that it should not use the money power to distort the Constitution.

2. The question of the constitutionality of executive impoundment of foreign affairs appropriations has not moved in practice beyond President Truman's rejection of a congressional directive to spend on Spain funds that he did not wish to spend on Spain, even though executive domestic impoundment seems controllable by congressional specification in law.[36] The separation of powers issue as to executive impoundment related to international operations is an issue seemingly left unresolved by the present Constitution. Perhaps it will appeal to some of our participants for further —or divergent—analysis or as a topic for revisionary attention. Again, perhaps, the *Election Law Case* speaks to the separation of powers issue here, although I doubt that it does.

36. I am indebted to William Bailey Lockhart, Yale Kamisar, and Jesse H. Choper, *Constitutional Law-Cases, Comments, Questions* (St. Paul: West Pub. Co., 1975), pp. 277–88 for very useful notes on impoundment and for reassurances as to the position taken in the text as to impoundment and foreign affairs. A disclaimer provision (Section 1001 (1)) declares that nothing in the Congressional Budget and Impoundment Control Act of 1974 ". . . shall be construed as asserting or conceding the constitutional powers or limitations of either the Congress or the President. . . ."

Arms control and disarmament

The first of Professor Louis Henkin's useful books[37] on the Constitution and America's public affairs projected an international agreement on arms control and disarmament and proceeded to analyze, solidly and imaginatively, the constitutional issues that might be raised.

Unhappily for us and for the world, Professor Henkin's projections have never had an opportunity to guide events. Today, arms control and disarmament seem far from presenting us with constitutional problems.

As with regard to military policy and levels of military expenditure, the heart of the difficulty seems to be that polarizations of viewpoints cut across separation of powers and involve *pro* and *anti* alignments in both the Executive and Legislative branches. The state of readiness/threat situation professionals in the Executive departments find counterparts in the Legislative branch, especially among the authoritative chairmen of some key committees. It is very difficult for any responsible person to be detached about the situation, because deeply-held moral feelings are so strongly involved, the risks so awful, and the unknowns so enigmatic. Some say the area is one in which nothing much will be accomplished until the world has a severe but survivable nuclear experience or, short of that and in the case of the United States, until the country shall have—if ever it does—an executive chief who is both a fully effective national leader and a person assuredly knowledgeable on nuclear arms and threat matters.

It is almost impossible, in my opinion, for steadfast leadership of the required level of effectiveness to develop in Congress, even though substantial numbers of individual legislators be committed to sound principles as to the fundamentals of arms control and disarmament.

This observation on the probable exclusive effectiveness of executive leadership on arms control and disarmament derives from personal experience with leadership as to levels and continuity of American contributions to development—to the international war on poverty. Congress has never taken leadership initiatives on foreign aid, and the spiraling-down of our development assistance effort largely reflects presidential disinclinations or perceived inabilities to lead affirmatively in this field. And these two deficiences in leadership may become tragically linked—in a rich-poor world of nuclear proliferation.

THE CONSTITUTION AND UNITED STATES PARTICIPATION IN TRANSNATIONAL GOVERNMENTAL PROCESSES

Evolution beyond the national state system—something to consider?

Nine democratic, free, developed countries, all allies of the United States, have found it necessary to create by treaty regional institutions that have authority to act directly upon persons, including governmental agencies, within the member states, much as the federal government acts directly within the federal sphere in this country. These countries, too, have a community Court of Justice, which is the final legal

37. Louis Henkin, *Arms Control and Inspection in American Law* (New York: Columbia University Press, 1958).

authority over national courts on matters of interpretation of the organic treaties creating the European Economic Communities. Several of the European Community countries had to alter their constitutions to permit this result.

No one is suggesting that the United States—at this time, at least—seek to join the European Communities or to become a member of a Western hemisphere common market with our Latin American neighbors. The latter would be impossible for the neighbors to live with economically, considering the overwhelming cost-effectiveness of American industrial production in comparison to theirs.

But there is Canada, with which we already have a free trade area in motor vehicles and parts, and which could probably hold its own if all tariff walls should come down between us. More importantly, there is the century ahead to think about. The logical result of the "interdependency" that present leaders in the Executive and in the Congress support is evolution beyond the present national state system and the present types of international organizations that are not directly organs of human governance.

Would supra-nationality be constitutional?

Could the United States under its present Constitution enter into a regionalistic or planetary federalism of limited powers? I fear that, without standing the Constitution, written and unwritten, on its head, we could not.

Item: to provide by treaty for an external agency to make and enforce law in the United States would involve the use of the treaty power to do what the Constitution prohibits as to due process, delegation of Legislative power, and the exercise of Executive and Judicial powers; and the Court has said, twice at least, that the treaty power cannot be used to do by treaty that which the Constitution prohibits.

Item: American legal opinion, including that of secretaries of state and attorneys-general, has consistently held that the Constitution does not permit appellate review by international tribunals of process in domestic tribunals.

Item: beyond the issue of federalism settled by Missouri v. Holland lies the question of whether the treaty power may validly be used to displace states' rights in favor of some rule-making and authority-wielding entity other than the federal government.

Item: a national plebiscite of the sort that eventually settled—for now, at least—the troubled question of British entry into the European Communities is difficult indeed to fit into our present constitutional system.

Are not these matters that are worth thinking about as we peer ahead as best we can into a murky future, from a present in which we are constantly being told that multinational enterprise has already seen the future of society on this small planet better than governments have?

THE STATES OF THE UNION AND FOREIGN AFFAIRS

Other than the problem of "federal reluctance" to use the treaty power, where doing so invades legal domains that fall to the states in the absence of treaties, and legalistic odds and ends of federalism, such as the recently restored power of the states to impose nondiscriminatory property taxes on imports not yet in the stream of commerce, formal federalistic issues are not of present or of foreseeable future difficulty as to the conduct of foreign relations under the present Constitution. To overstate a bit, whatever remained of "states' rights" in foreign affairs after *Missouri* v. *Holland* probably was swept away by the Supreme Court's self-made version of a "non-treaty supremacy clause" in *Zschernig* v. *Miller*.[38]

Even the theoretical question of secession in a new guise, self-determination of peoples, seems quite remote in a nation increasingly homogenized as to values, tastes, outlooks, and life-styles. The main question about the states of the Union and foreign affairs under

the Constitution is whether states "as we know them" (that is, in present numbers and distributions of population) are any longer utile. This is a matter that has been addressed in a stimulating and provocative study by Dr. Rexford Tugwell and others.

This is not to say, of course, that the states do not have certain bearings on foreign affairs, as when the state police insist on escorting speeding but immune Soviet diplomats off the New Jersey Turnpike, which the Department of State tells the Russians they must not deviate from in motoring between New York and Washington.

And it is not to say, either, that the very existence of a federal structure does not impose some restraints upon national foreign policy. It is a reality that the states—and the cities—tend not to become affirmatively involved in foreign relations matters and hence do not give much weight to what is desirable in foreign policy, especially when a transnational perspective threatens an expectation that federal financial assistance to them might be affected.

THE PEOPLE AND FOREIGN AFFAIRS

The discourse just concluded leads to a very significant matter, one that justifies being stated as a third Issue:

Issue: Do present constitutional arrangements adequately provide for the participation of the citizenry in value choices related to foreign policy?

Discussion of Issue: Statistical realism requires us to admit that a very large proportion of our population does not even understand basic aspects of our Constitution, such as the Bill of Rights, to say nothing

---

38. 389 U.S. 429 (1968). Henkin, *Foreign Affairs and the Constitution*, ch. 9, is more moderate and restrained in his evaluation of this case. In it the Supreme Court, even with a disavowal of foreign affairs concern filed by the federal executive, held invalid an Oregon escheat statute denying inheritances to persons behind the Iron Curtain, unless the Oregon probate courts should be satisfied that these persons would actually be able to receive and enjoy the inheritances. Professor Henkin notes that the Court declared this to be an unconstitutional ". . . intrusion by the State into the field of foreign affairs which the Constitution entrusts to the President and the Congress. . . ." He adds:

"This is new constitutional doctrine. No doubt, an act of Congress or a treaty, probably an executive agreement, perhaps an official executive declaration, possibly even a rule made by the federal courts, could have forbidden what Oregon purported to do. Here there was no relevant exercise of federal power and no basis for deriving any prohibition by "interpretation" of the silence of Congress and the President. . . .

"[The case] then, imposes additional limitations on the States but what they are and how far they reach remains to be determined. . . ."

of its convoluted arrangements as to foreign relations and its even more complicated unwritten growth in this sector. Nonetheless, modern mass media, TV especially, have brought the world and America's stance therein very close to a concerned minority of the citizenry; and, if an international relations issue is a very big (and therefore a starkly simple) one, even the populace as a whole may involve itself.

Assuming a significant degree of popular involvement, particularly in election years, in foreign policy, let us consider constitutional theory and practice in regard to the people's role. In constitutional theory, the president is not chosen by the people; but in practice, and making allowance for the "winner-take-all" effect of our state-linked electoral voting pattern, the people now select the president by popular majority. In doing so, the people elect a chief of state who is not legally or politically explicitly committed for his four-year term to follow any course of action, but only to use his best judgment in giving course and direction to American foreign policy.

The House membership is also elected on a theory that the people of a congressional district choose, not "mouthpieces," but wise and good people to go to Washington and make wise and good decisions. Originally the Senate may have had a different function,[39] but since the

Seventeenth Amendment, providing for the statewide popular election of senators, there has been a shift from the senator as delegate of his state to the Washington government to the senator as a "super-congressman" (having a bigger district and a longer term, but no higher pay).

In practice, over the whole range of political values, the picture is much less clear. The prevailing popular belief is probably that all members of Congress jerk into motion when predominant interests (of the left or right, capital-labor-farmer, ethnic) in their electoral constituencies pull the strings. Yet, it is observable fact that some senators and some representatives usually vote as to international issues in accordance with their own judgments, although there are usually also some distortions, for which some otherwise independent solons become well known. Discounting personality factors, what is the line of cleavage? It is the safety of the member's seat; and even with longer Senate terms, there is notable correlation between a senator's independence of mind and his confidence in being reelected.

It seems reasonable to conclude that, generally speaking, members of the House and Senate are in practice more independent-minded in foreign relations than in domestic matters, mainly because their constituencies do not have definite views on foreign relations issues, unless the issue be as basic as staying in or getting out of Vietnam

---

39. The widely-accepted notion that the framers assumed from the beginning that the Senate should represent the states (almost as if official delegations from the States to the seat of the federal government) may be another of the numerous post hoc myths about the creation; see Farrand, *The Framing of the Constitution*, ch. 7. The Virginia Plan provided for the lower house to elect the Senate from nominees made by each state. The small states resisted a sys-tem of representation proportional to population in both houses; the "Great Compromise" was to give them an assured two seats in the Senate, not necessarily to provide for the selection of these two by state legislatures.

or of electoral district concern. A plausible hypothesis is that the theory of delegation of popular sovereignty to elected representatives works in foreign relations most of the time as the founders assumed and that it does so because the people of the constituencies are not massively attracted to personal involvement in foreign affairs activism.

If this analysis is correct, then the people have delegated their popular sovereignty as to foreign affairs to both the president (on a national basis) and their representatives and senators on voting district bases. The result is that the people do not, in practice, decide who wins when there are controversies between the president and the Congress, but only watch the fray.

It may well be that our panel should speculate about what the people ought to be doing in foreign relations, how they could be induced to do it, and how they should be prepared informationally to discharge their responsibilities if they should become active. This is to ask: For the future on a rapidly changing planet, should the American people more closely couple themselves to the making of basic choices, such as the shaping of external relations, peace or war, negotiated arms reductions or unilateral disarmament, military policy, contributions to development, doing or not doing "dirty tricks" abroad, and many others? Or should the present system continue, with the people leaving these questions to those they select by vote to make choices? Is our present system too reflective of a bygone age at a time when "Yea-Nay" buttons on the family cable television set could give a national viewpoint on an issue within milliseconds? Or is it still wise and desirable for the people to let others decide values for them, subject to post hoc correction at the polls? If so, why? avoidance of having to decide? specialization of knowledge? an assumption that the representatives chosen are superior to the people in ability to make these decisions?

At this point, it is appropriate to make a cross-reference to a later discussion of the question of whether there is utility in considering on the merits a shift in our form of government to a system of "legislative domination with cabinet responsibility." The linkage relevant here was well-expressed by a British laborer who, when asked why it was useful to have a general election at a particular time, responded: "So's we can throw the buggers out!" This is another way—an older and pre-TV button way—of bringing the people closer to the actual processes of decision-making. But, as noted earlier, it is not often in the political practices of "ministerial-responsibility" democracies that the "buggers" get turned out on foreign affairs issues.

Finally, in regard to this Issue, we should evaluate the roles and the power of modern mass media in foreign affairs choice-making. The American people are not fully informed by their government. (No people anywhere are.) We are just beginning, under the Freedom of Information Act, to use a statutory people's right to know (with security limitations) what has been done in the past. So far, there is no recognition of a citizen's constitutional right to be kept informed as to ongoing operations. The question might be asked, in the light of a present separation-of-powers controversy between the president and two congressional committees, "If the Congress has a right to know, what about the people?" Note that if only Congress but not the people shall have the right to know, the people—to the extent interested at all—remain ineluctably relegated by informational disadvantage to the secondary and passive role ascribed to them by the eighteenth-century theory of representative government, unless, of course, they decide to intervene on the basis of what the "TV tube masters" and other media "authorities" tell them they should know—and do.

THE INTERNATIONAL AGREEMENTS POWERS AND GOOD FAITH PERFORMANCE OF THE INTERNATIONAL OBLIGATIONS OF THE UNITED STATES

Congressional disregard of international agreements

By judicial decisions and in governmental practice,[40] Congress is recognized as having the capacity to rescind the legal effect of a treaty as internal law, even though to do so puts the United States into breach of the treaty internationally.

Today, as we have seen, Congress practices veto-proof invalidation of executive agreements based upon congressional authorization, and it may claim the power to review and similarly invalidate executive agreements made under the inherent powers of the president as chief of state and commander-in-chief.

In his commentary upon Professor Henkin's presentation in Appendix L to the Murphy Commission Report, Professor Falk calls for greater respect in practice for international law by the United States. This appeal includes a preference for constitutional stipulations

40. *Restatement of the Law Second*, sec. 145.

under which an international agreement, having internal effect as law, cannot be undone by a later inconsistent act of the legislature.

The question of whether the Constitution should be amended to conform in this fashion to the constitutions of some other countries is a matter for consideration. This concern is voiced, of course, against the background that, increasingly, an objective of treaties and other international agreements is to provide for parallel internal legal treatment of matters that touch and concern the interests of all the parties—and often of the planet as a whole.

Additionally, Americans should consider seriously whether their assumption that the United States almost always performs its international obligations is correct. There is reason to believe that, largely for structural reasons, there is sometimes ineffectual government agency policing of the requirements of international agreements. Private parties may assert treaty rights affirmatively or defensively in legal proceedings brought in federal and state courts; but, unless a treaty setting performance standards has been implemented by domestic criminal or regulatory law, there is no governmental agency but the Department of State, motivated by diplomatic considerations, to push for observance. And some other former officers of the Department of State might recall, as I do, a tendency within the department to leave worries about seeing to it that an international agreement is "lived up to" to the persons and/or office that negotiated it. This tends to make *uberrima fides* respect for treaties vulnerable to the passage of time and shifts in the attention and interest spans of the higher echelons.

Consider in this regard this question: Assume that the Third United Nations Law of the Sea Conference does produce a full-range law of the sea convention, one that, as to nine or ten major areas of normation, involves the spheres and interests of almost every one of our executive departments and a number of independent agencies and commissions as well. What agency will be responsible for the overall coordination of United States application of the convention? If there is no localization of sense of mission as to United States official performance, United States compliance cannot but be disjointed and episodic. The problem is highly important for the future, as it is foreseeable that more and more matters of planet-wide concern will come to be regulated by treaty in the same way for all nations.

Should "treaties" be approved only by simple majorities in both Houses?

One of the conference participants, Professor Myres McDougal, with a co-author,[41] demonstrated some years ago to the satisfaction of most students of the subject that "executive-legislative" agreements that come into effect by bills voted in both houses are entirely interchangeable with treaties ratified and promulgated by the president after he has received the advice and consent of two-thirds of the senators present and voting.

The fine question, whether international agreements coming into effect in this bicameral way are "treaties" within the Supremacy Clause, may be debated here, but the issue approaches mootness as judicial restrictions on the legislative powers of Congress have been relaxed.[42]

The more important question now is whether the time has come to "democratize" the treaty process by deleting from the Constitution the old bias in favor of the Senate (the two-thirds principle), which has both made the Senate "the graveyard of treaties" and fed senatorial pretensions that they, but not members of the House of Representatives, are entitled by the Constitution to advise and give consent to presidential foreign policy lines of action that are not sent to the Senate for approval as treaties.

In this connection, it is perhaps useful to keep in mind both the well-known account of President Washington's formal consultation with the Senate,[43] never repeated by him or by any other president since, and the uniqueness of the unicameral, weighted majority, upper chamber treaty-approval provision of our Constitution among the constitutions of other modern, developed, democratic states. In most other democratic states, indeed, the upper house is vestigial and can only delay,

41. Myres McDougal and Lans, "Treaties and Congressional-Executive or Presidential Agreements: Interchangeable Instruments of National Policy," 54 *Yale Law Journal* 818, 534 (1945). Consult, generally, Henkin, *Foreign Affairs and the Constitution*, ch. 6.

42. The point is often made that at any time since roughly 1938—at the latest—it would not have required a treaty with Canada to provide internal legal effect for preemptive federal legislation on migratory game birds because of judicial relaxation of old judicial limitations upon the subject-matter reach of ordinary legislation under the Article I enumerated powers—or even the evolved legislative powers, such as the "foreign affairs legislative power." Compare *Missouri v. Holland*.

43. Bernard Schwartz, *A Commentary on the Constitution of the United States: The Powers of Government* (New York: Macmillan, 1963), pp. 101, 150.

but not eventually prevail over, the legislative will of the more populous branch.

Self-executing treaties

On most matters, the president and two-thirds of the senators may legislate (give internal effect as positive law) by treaty. Self-executing treaties are possible in a few other democratic systems, but not in most. They are impossible in Great Britain, where there is complete disjunction between the Crown's sole power to bind the realm internationally and Parliament's essential role in making the law of the land. In the constitution of the German Federal Republic, international agreements may only be ratified by legislation that first comes into effect as national law.

In the United States, self-executing treaties have given some problems. These are problems of (1) determining which treaties are self-executing and which are not, usually a matter for judicial determination; (2) whether the president and the Senate may, by treaty, preempt the rights of the House to initiate (and a fortiori to vote on) revenue measures and to participate in laws for the disposition of the property of the United States. The last-stated problem may become crucial in the proposed new treaty with Panama as to the Canal and Zone.[44]

44. In some congressional and public opinion quarters, opposition to modification in Panama's favor of the 1903 treaty has taken to a "high ground" defense that, regardless of the constitutional power of the president and two-thirds of the Senate to alter our "as if sovereign" status in the Canal Zone, the land area is owned (in fee simple) by the United States by purchase and hence cannot be disposed of without the consent of both houses. (Compare Article IV, Sec-

Should self-executing treaties continue to be permitted? There is a link between this question and the one posed in the previous section. However, it should be noted that in executive practice—apparently acquiesced in by the Senate—treaties intended to have internal effect as law are no longer put into effect by use of the self-execution principle, because the Department of State no longer forwards treaties to the Senate for advice and consent until any needed implementing legislation is certain of approval by regular majorities in both houses. This practice, of course, tends to slow materially the completion of the treaty-approval process itself; and such delays are inherently contrary to the normal expectations of other nations that ratifications be speedily sought by any party signing a treaty *ad referendum* to such action.

CONSTITUTIONAL REVISION FOR FOREIGN AFFAIRS REASONS: STRUCTURAL ISSUES AND THE RANGE OF CHOICE

We have now reviewed, mainly from the standpoint of substantive policy preferences, the making and management of foreign policy under the Constitution of 1789. Attention should now shift to some very significant Issues of structure and function and to a sketch of possible constitutional revision, in a range from major change to no change. The Issues set out and discussed immediately following are seen as preliminary or conditioning

tion 3 and Article I, Section 8). However, at the present time, the degree of opposition in the Senate itself suggests that even a new treaty arrangement would not receive the requisite extraordinary vote in the upper chamber.

factors in regard to revision, *vel non*, the last Issue posed herein.

Four conditioning Issues

Issue: Under the present Constitution, is there a reliable and definitive process for deciding the respective foreign affairs authorities of the two political branches of the government?

Discussion of Issue: Attention here very rapidly comes to adjudication and impeachment-and-removal-from-office. However, the latter is almost as impracticable an alternative as two others that are only mentioned for analytical completeness, due to their entire inappropriateness to situations of international crisis, where speed as well as sharpness of resolution are of the essence. The two possibilities rejected out-of-hand are: (1) the president or his congressional opposition goes to the country, à la Woodrow Wilson; (2) waiting for a series of "eyeball-to-eyeball" confrontations to cause one side or the other to blink—but not necessarily with all blinks in the series coming from a single side.[45]

The only additional comment that occurs as to impeachment-removal-from-office is that it settles nothing in a normative, authoritative manner, being always a highly political process as well as one that causes discontinuity in government, as distinguished from shifts in the law by which governors are to be governed. The question of whether the judicial process should expand to deal with areas clearly within the power of Congress to indict and remove from office, but not yet clearly declared by the Supreme Court also to be within judicial jurisdiction and willingness to adjudicate, is not, analytically, essential to this evaluation.

Turning, then, to the fundamentals given to us so far by the Supreme Court, we find one line of judicial utterances ("holdings" is too strong a word here)—the *Curtiss-Wright Export Company*[46] line—that tends to discourage resort to litigation to resolve separation-of-powers issues in the foreign relations field, precisely because the Court appears to give constitutional carte blanche to the claimants of power. If, as Justice Sutherland's pre-appointment viewpoint that he later wrote into his *Curtiss-Wright* opinion asserts, the foreign affairs sovereignty of the nation is not limited by the Constitution, there seems very little more that the courts can do to resolve power struggles between the president and the Congress. However, the famous dictum probably lives today mainly in *U.S. California*[47] and its progeny, denying to the states of the Union the benefits of any independent juristic existence in the international legal order; and this is a matter of federalism that is off the mark for us here.

A relevant speculation as to the predictable limits of judicial resolution of the respective foreign affairs authorities of the president and the Congress must project from *Baker* v. *Carr*[48] through *Powell* v. *McCormick*[49] to the *Federal Elections Act Decision*[50] of this past

---

45. Sometimes, as January 1976 news items remind us, the Congress blinks, as when the House refused to uphold the sweeping claims of its Select Committee on Intelligence.

46. *United States* v. *Curtiss-Wright Export Company.*
47. 332 U.S. 19 (1947).
48. 369 U.S. 186 (1962).
49. 395 U.S. 486 (1969).
50. Sup. n. 33.

January. In the first of these cases, known to our political history for "one man-one vote," the Supreme Court (in dealing with the argument that the application of the guarantee of a republican form of government to the states had been held a non-justiciable "political question" in *Luther* v. *Borden*[51]) reviewed the concept of "political question" as a limitation on justiciability. In a discourse designed to show the relativism of "political question," the majority said:

Foreign relations: There are sweeping statements to the effect that all questions touching foreign relations are political questions. Not only does resolution of such issues frequently turn on standards that defy judicial application, or involve the exercise of a discretion demonstrably committed to the executive or legislature; but many such questions uniquely demand single-voiced statement of the Government's views. Yet it is error to suppose that every case or controversy which touches foreign relations lies beyond judicial cognizance. Our cases in this field seem invariably to show a discriminating analysis of the particular question posed, in terms of the history of its management by the political branches, of its susceptibility to judicial handling in the light of its nature and posture in the specific case, and of the possible consequences of judicial action. For example, though a court will not ordinarily inquire whether a treaty has been terminated, since on that question "governmental action . . . must be regarded as of controlling importance," if there has been no conclusive "governmental action" then a court can construe a treaty and may find it provides the answer. . . .

Consider whether there is, in the above, any promise of a workable rule for resolution of the problem of this Issue, or in this, from the opinion in Representative Powell's successful suit against not having been allowed by the House to take his seat:

Respondent's alternate contention is that the case presents a political question because judicial resolution of petitioner's claim would produce a "potentially embarrassing confrontation between coordinate branches" of the Federal government. But [our interpretation of Art. I, Section 5] falls within the traditional role accorded courts to interpret the law, and does not involve a "lack of respect due (*a*) coordinate branch of government," nor does it involve an "initial policy determination of a kind clearly for nonjudicial discretion." *Baker* v. *Carr*. Our system of government requires that federal courts on occasion interpret the Constitution in a manner at variance with the construction given the document by another branch. . . .

Nor are any of the other formulations of a political question "inextricable from the case at bar." *Baker*. Petitioners seek a determination . . . for which clearly there are *"judicially manageable standards*. . . ." (emphasis added)

U.S. v. *Nixon*,[52] of course, distinguishes, from what the Court decided in that contention was within its power to say "what the law is," an executive-legislative-jurisdictional dispute about foreign affairs powers. And Holtzman's effort[53] against Secretary of Defense Schlesinger to have the Judiciary rule on the constitutionality of American combat presence in Southeast Asia attracted only two justices. As Cox has put it: "The task of formulating a workable principle for delimiting the President's power to engage in

---

51. 7 How. 1 (U.S. 1849)—guarantee of a republican form of government; not a foreign relations "political question" case.

52. 418 U.S. 683 (1974).

53. 484 F.2d 1307 (2d Cir. 1973), cert. den. with opinions by Marshall and Douglas, JJ, 414 U.S. 1304 (1973).

military activities overseas is far from easy. . . ."[54] True enough for courts, but seemingly not for Congress under the War Powers Joint Resolution, unless the courts should be willing (and a movant have standing) to review the Congress!

The *Federal Elections Law Case*[55] seems to track the *"Marbury* v. *Madison* revived" line of cases just outlined, that is, while it is indeed the courts' business to say what the law is, they do so largely on the Supreme Court's terms. And these terms seem not sharp enough or predictable enough for reliable resolution of power contention between the two political branches as to their respective foreign affairs authorizations.

Hence, the answer to this Issue, it would seem, is "No." So the question becomes, should the Constitution be changed so as to fix authority to resolve these contentions speedily, effectively, and normatively? This can be a question of the evolutionary structural adequacy of what we have. Consideration of this question need not necessarily lead to a proposal for amendment. Institutional determination by the Judiciary might suffice, assuming there are not too many doubts about a "Book of Judges" approach to America's future governance.

Issue: Under present constitutional arrangements and congressional traditions, can Congress act effectively to discharge the new foreign affairs authorities that are being claimed in its name?

Discussion of Issue: This conditioning Issue as to future structure is well known to any person who has had acquaintance with Congress at work. There are two basic problems: (1) *the conditions under which the Executive branch must attempt to cooperate with the Congress*; (2) *the committee structure and traditional practices of the Congress*.

Even in the best of times there are conditions of endemic civil war between the two political branches. On the Hill, Executive spokesmen are suspect because, at the least, they are wary. Often they are deceivers. Sometimes they are perjurers. Congress tends to conceive of itself as "un-engaged," as not being a part of the government in the sense of sharing responsibility, even for the continuation of foreign affairs lines of action that would not have been possible without its concurrence at an earlier time, as Dean Rostow's contribution to Appendix L of the Murphy Commission Report demonstrates.

The committee structure of Congress is notorious for its multifariousness and for the undemocratic seniority system. As bearing upon operations across the separation-of-powers chasm, it is well known that the multiplicity of congressional committees and empire-building chairmen and subchairmen depresses the quality of government in a range from undue demands upon the time of ministers and subministers of the Executive to legislation-distorting conflicts of jurisdiction between committees and even subcommittees.

Also, the committee staffs are growing phenomenally, rapidly tending toward becoming a second bureaucracy. And this second bureaucracy, unlike the bedeviled first (of the Executive branch), is

---

54. The citation is available thanks to the richness of the notes in Lockhart, Kamisar and Choper, *Constitutional Law Cases*; Cox, "The Role of Congress in Constitutional Determinations," 40 *U. Cinc. L. Rev.* 199, 204 (1971).

55. *Buckley et al.* v. *Valeo et al.*

not compelled by congressional intervention to be alert to or answerable to public interest. Doubters may resort to a simple test: as a citizen, try to get an answer from (a) the Executive bureaucracy and (b) the Hill bureaucracy. You will not get it from (b) unless you are important to an important legislator on that committee or subcommittee. You can almost always command it from (a), if other means fail, by getting your legislator to write to the agency where the Executive bureaucrat works.

Perhaps the situation just described is merely transitory. In the beginnings of Executive bureaucracy under the Constitution of 1789, it may have been that Mr. Jefferson's several clerks at the "Department of Foreign Relations" were as remote from the demands of the citizenry as congressional staffers tend to be now—the mores of primitive bureaucracies being that the clerks answer to their masters, not to the public.

And so, an old question repeats itself: *Quis custodiet ipsos custodes* —not at the next election, but during the first three or four years, say, of a "safe" Senate term?

There are, here, other questions pertinent to the governance of foreign affairs. I limit myself to posing only those of particular relevance, assuming the continuation without substantial modification of the present separation-of-powers system:

1. Why continue the special foreign affairs powers of the Senate? For that matter, why a Senate any longer—at least beyond an upper house that, representing establishmentarian interests, may delay but not prevent legislation? Perhaps our senatorial tradition, amply buttressed by the attitudes of certain members of that "club," is a bit more Roman than is safe if we are to ensure a non-Roman future.

2. If we were to consider essential unicameralism for the future, is the House too large? Are the terms of representatives too short?

3. What of congressional committee structures, functional non-parallelism with the executive departments, overlapping jurisdiction, seniority?

The main problem the American people have to face, though, as to the future role of Congress in relationship to foreign affairs, is this Issue:

Issue: Does Congress accurately represent the outlooks and attitudes of the American people from time to time as to America's relationship to the rest of the world? Or does it distort both the people's outlooks and their attitudes?

Discussion of Issue: Serious appraisers should at least think about the above Issue. Does Congress— always, usually, sometimes, or at this point in time—reflect better the foreign affairs goals and outlooks of the American people than does the president? If the answer is "always" or "usually," and if what have been normal congressional attitudes continue, we may have to resign ourselves to a maverick and isolated role in the world community, unless we are willing—and if willing, know where and how—to change our constitutional structure. Alternatively, what of the possibility that Congress might develop a continuous sense of responsibility to the country's relationships with the rest of the planet? As Justice Brandeis used to argue in another context, perhaps it is also true here that only from having real responsibility will true congressional effectiveness evolve.

Issue: How much do contemporary problems being experienced by the United States in foreign policy formulation and execution arise from temporary conditions of American politics? and how much from the early stages of structural defects that will eventually require correction?

Discussion of Issue: The pattern of increasing discontinuity between the political alignments of presidents and of congressional majorities has been referred to previously, and the singularity of the Ford presidency is too well known to require comment.

The question seems to come to be whether the present situation is too unusual to last, but to others it seems to be whether the present situation is or is not a mere variation of a fairly stable new pattern.

It is hard for us to imagine unorthodox change under stress in this country. But 10 years ago, unilateral, unannounced internationally unauthorized devaluation of the dollar was also unthinkable, and America's shift toward what other nations do in financial trouble was at first indirect and inadequate. But, before long we engaged in a straight-out writedown, as if we had been France, Germany, Great Britain, or numbers of other countries "less of the law" than these or we. And a president has been driven from office by his vulnerability to legislative trial. Unorthodoxies do happen!

It is a simple fact of international life, amply recognized in customary international law, that states are more enduring than their forms of government. Stresses incompatible with governmental structure will change it to preserve the state itself. Is it only our good fortune that so far has immunized us from this reality. Or is our Constitution less vulnerable than others have been? If so, why?

The range of structural change in the Constitution

Issue: Shall there be constitutional revision for foreign affairs reasons, and, if so, what should be its dimensions?

Discussion of Issue: It is beyond the function of this issues paper to propose an answer to this Issue or, if it should be answered "Yes," to submit a plan for change. The function of this writer ends with the following sketch of attitudinal alternatives and of schematic variables that are to be taken as merely suggestive, not as exclusionary or definitive.

A synopsis of constitutional revision for foreign affairs reasons

I. "Practicality" aside, is constitutional change worth considering? Why or why not?

II. Alternatives to revision—the range of: (*a*) institutional and individual self-restraint as between the "political branches" and the actors therein; (*b*) institutional rearrangments not requiring legislation or constitutional change: the institutionalization of Executive-Legislative cooperation; limits of, under the *Federal Election Law Case*, if any; (*c*) legislative changes not involving constitutional revision—as against the backdrop of the preceding Issue and the *Federal Election Law Decision*.

III. Changing the Constitution—the range of possibilities: (*a*) major change:[56] abandon separation of

56. There are very few proposals for general change on a major scale. See, generally, Rexford G. Tugwell, *The Emerging Constitution* (New York: Harper's Magazine Press, 1974), issued under the imprimatur of the Fund for the Republic and based

powers and put the executive for foreign affairs in the legislature (a cabinet form of government for foreign affairs); (*b*) constitutional adjustments not negating separation of powers (some possibly by "judicial amendment").

---

upon studies prepared for the Center for the Study of Democratic Institutions. This plan for major revision is not, on the whole, oriented particularly toward the crisis of separation of powers in foreign relations; but there is a perspective in the introduction (p. xv) that is highly pertinent to the perspective of this issues paper:

"A serious difficulty with any agreement embodied in a document and widely accepted, as the Constitution of 1787 eventually came to be, is that its provisions eventually tend to become scriptural. . . . Because this charter is thus massively founded it may easily . . . become obsolete as economic and social changes occur.

"The American instance of obsolescense is a serious one, strangely ignored in constitutional commentaries even by students of public law. . . ."

Yarmolinsky, "Organizing for Interdependence: The Role of Government," Interdependence Series No. 5/Aspen Institute for Humanistic Studies, Program in International Affairs (1976), proposes elaborate reorganization of the Executive branch and slight changes in congressional structure as necessary for the United States in a future of planetary "interdependence." The study also notes the existence now of a congressional bureaucracy, adding that as of the beginning of fiscal year 1976 there were 11,500 members of congressional staffs. The major thrust of the reorganization plan is that there be recognition in law of a diminished role for the Department of State, provision for the redistribution of powers in the Executive branch to reflect the senses of mission and of capabilities for coping of a number of other executive units, and congressional-legislative cooperation based upon the concept that no valid line exists any longer between "domestic" and "foreign" lines of action. The current crisis at the constitutional level and the *erga omnes* problem are not featured in this study of "interdependence," which is, of course, not necessarily an idealized ingredient of the future, but a likely necessity.

1. State the territorial reach of the Constitution, function-by-function, if need be.

2. Eliminate the exclusive role of the Senate in approving treaties and provide that international agreements (all but very minor or technical ones) come into internal legal effect only by simple majority approval in both houses.

3. Create a treaty-performance agency to ensure that in day-to-day operations the international treaty obligations of the United States are, in fact, lived up to throughout the federal government and by the states. (This could probably be done without amendment of the Constitution.)

4. Permit certain types of regional or international entities which the United States may enter to act directly (*erga omnes*) upon persons and interests in the United States.

5. Fix the limits of validity, if any, of executive privilege and of official secrecy in a foreign affairs context.

6. Clarify the authority of the Judiciary in contentions between the Congress and the Executive as to their respective authorities ("political questions").

7. Make structural changes in the Congress (not that Congress could not make these without amendment, but because it does not do so).

8. State clearly whether the president's power as commander-in-chief includes sole or controlled authority (other than the congressional money power) to deploy military force outside the United States.

9. Modernize the concept of declaration of war.

10. Settle by positive constitutional determination the question whether Congress may participate in foreign affairs operations especially in regard to: (*i*) negation free of

presidential veto of executive agreements made under previously delegated authority and under the president's chief of state (inherent) powers; (ii) mandatory executive application or not of appropriations to fund congressionally-chosen foreign affairs goals; (iii) Senate "advise and consent" beyond its treaty-approval function; (iv) constitutional principles of separation of powers unsettled (if unsettlement there was) by the Supreme Court's decision in the *Federal Elections Law Case* as to the inability of congressional appointees to engage in other than legislative and investigative functions.

11. Weigh the desirability of giving the people plebiscite, initiative, and referendum powers, possibly by electronic voting.

12. Abolish or curtail the foreign relations powers of the Senate now denied to the House.

13. Provide longer terms and fewer numbers for members of the House of Representatives.

14. Expand congressmen's standing to sue and to object administratively to governmental foreign policy lines of action.

15. Provide that subsequent inconsistent legislation may not contradict the internal legal effect of a treaty until it is legally no longer in effect.

16. State clearly whether the power to end international agreements, including those with internal legal effects, is solely executive; or, alternatively, provide for legislative participation in the treaty-termination power.

17. Decide whether the Executive shall have (as presently the Judiciary claims to have, not in decisions but in approaches to Congress) a right to funds adequate to maintain basic effectiveness as to its foreign affairs responsibilities.

18. Clarify the inquiry power of Congress as to the president's non-departmental assistants and advisers.

19. Readjust federal-state relationships in the foreign affairs area if any such readjustment seems necessary in the overall interests of the nation.

20. Evaluate a plural presidency or some redistribution at the constitutional level of the present vast range of presidential responsibility.

21. Reexamine the amendment process under the Constitution of 1789 to determine whether it is too rigid and too difficult to achieve.

22. Reappraise, if relevant, the extent to which the Supreme Court has expanded the concept of judicial review and the use of contingent and conditional mandates and decide whether the powers of the courts in these particulars should be moderated or denied.

23. Shall the president be authorized to veto items in appropriations bills relating to the conduct of foreign affairs?

ANNALS, AAPSS, **426**, July 1976

Report of Committee IV

By STEPHEN J. SCHULHOFER

ABSTRACT. The committee took the view that bridges are needed to permit more effective cooperation between the two branches of government in foreign affairs. Three areas for change were considered. The first involves decisions to use military force. Concern was expressed that the War Powers Resolution does not go far enough. The committee also saw a need for legal restraints upon the use of nuclear weapons. Members of the committee endorsed exploration of mechanisms to involve Congress in decision-making on this particularly momentous problem. The second area of change concerns, specifically, state secrets and the problem of executive privilege. It was felt that confidentiality and secrecy are invoked too often by the Executive branch, though some confidentiality is necessary. The third area concerns legislative oversight after the event. The committee would endorse constitutional amendment, if necessary, to permit sharing of authority in foreign affairs.

Stephen J. Schulhofer is Assistant Professor of Law at the University of Pennsylvania. He practiced law at Coudert Frères, Paris, from 1969–72. He also served as Law Clerk to Supreme Court Justice Hugo L. Black. His publications include "Harm and Punishment: A Critique of Emphasis on the Results of Conduct in the Criminal Law," University of Pennsylvania Law Review, and "Due Process: Civil and Criminal," Harvard Law Review.

M Y COLLEAGUE, Professor Leech, covers very thoroughly the general attitudes that were expressed in the committee with regard to the distribution of authority between the president and Congress in the foreign relations field. He also focuses specifically on the process of making and breaking international agreements. My job is to pull together some of the remaining areas of foreign relations in which the allocation of power or the separation of powers may be of consequence.

The loose ends that I have on my agenda are the formation of our overall policy toward foreign countries, the day-to-day conduct of our relationships with the rest of the world, control of the military establishment, spending for defense and foreign aid, decisions regarding the use of military force, and, finally, decisions with particular regard to the use of nuclear force.

To cover these adequately will take me, or at least my chairman has instructed that it will take me, not more than 15 minutes.

In order to simplify the problem a little bit, I am going to avoid, where possible, getting into the substance of these matters, and rather focus on the question of whether we have organized ourselves in such a way as to make sound decision-making on these questions even possible in our third century.

We should also note, as Senator Clark quite properly reminded us, that these are the issues that determine whether there will be a third century at all. At the beginning of the week, our conference keynoter, Dean Pollak, very pointedly drew our attention to the fact that, as we close our second century, we do so under the cloud of the tragedy of Vietnam. As we end our

deliberations now, we feel strongly the responsibility to examine in some detail the arrangements that condition whether catastrophes of that magnitude or of even greater magnitude will be among the events that we should anticipate or must anticipate during the 100 years to come.

The committee did not find the kind of tendency observed by committee III, a tendency on the part of Congress to delegate more and more authority to the Executive branch of the government. On the contrary, our committee found in the field of foreign affairs a growing congressional will to participate actively in the conduct of the government's business. The view taken in the committee was that this should be encouraged, but not encouraged by giving Congress new powers or new weapons to use against the Executive. Rather, it was the general view that we should seek ways to build bridges that will permit more effective cooperation between the two branches of government.

CHANGES IN EXECUTIVE-LEGISLATIVE BALANCE

Now, how can this noble aspiration be fulfilled? The committee considered first the possibility of changes at the constitutional level and then studied a variety of sub-constitutional changes. The constitutional changes that were discussed included such things as modernizing the provisions for the declaration of war, granting explicitly to Congress the executive power to manage certain types of foreign relations activities, and defining the scope of official secrecy and executive privilege in the foreign relations area.

The general view, although not a

unanimous one, was that constitutional change was not necessary or even desirable at the present time. The present Constitution provides an adequate framework for the evolution of the kind of creative efforts at cooperation between the Executive and Legislative branches that the committee considered necessary.

When we descended to the subconstitutional level, the committee became just a little bit less conservative. The general perception was that a wide range of changes would be necessary to enable Congress to play the kind of active and constructive role that I have described.

Now, what are these changes? As I start to depart from the generalities that I have given you so far, I may begin to get into trouble. Some members of our committee may disagree or contradict me. If they do not, I am sure many of you will be happy to do so for them. None of the proposals that I am about to describe was favored by everyone. Some of them clearly were not favored by a majority of the committee. Nevertheless, it will be useful and necessary to go down this list in order to give you an idea of how very seriously the committee took the need for basic, structural changes.

Use of military force

The first problem concerns the use of military force. The War Powers Resolution, which Professor Oliver has outlined for you, provides the beginnings of congressional control over the deployment of American forces. There has been a great deal of public discussion concerning the constitutionality of the War Powers Resolution. The committee did not view this measure as an unconstitutional interference with the president's authority as commander-in-chief.

On the contrary, the concern that was expressed, and very forcefully expressed by some members of the committee, was that the War Powers Resolution simply does not go far enough. In the War Powers Resolution and in congressional action generally, there has been great insensitivity to evolving restrictions under international law upon the use of force as an instrument of national policy. The committee felt the need for much greater attention to these evolving limits, not only in day-to-day practice, but also in the applicable domestic legislation.

Beyond this, the committee saw a need for special attention to the use of nuclear force. We discussed in some detail the procedures that could permit congressional consultation prior to the use of nuclear weapons. These procedures are not nearly so impractical as they might at first blush appear, and those members of the committee who spoke to the matter very strongly endorsed further exploration of mechanisms to involve Congress in this very momentous type of decision.

The committee also considered the possibility of substantive limits as a matter of domestic law on the use of nuclear force. The kind of thing that would be possible here would, for example, be a rule prohibiting first use by the United States. Many members of the committee favored the exploration of a limitation of this type.

The committee's view, it is fair to summarize, was that expansion of congressional control over war making, in the ways I have described, would be constitutional. The attitude was somewhat less widespread that all the proposals I have mentioned would be desirable, but the committee nevertheless endorsed as a general matter the notion of exploring these possibilities very seriously.

In spite of these reservations, the committee was clearly unanimous in feeling that changes of the kind I have described, whether desirable or not, cannot by themselves accomplish very much.

Regardless of the statutory principles in force, the effectiveness of congressional control in the final analysis depends upon Congress's ability to evaluate particular fact situations, usually at a time of crisis. In this, Congress has not been particularly successful, as most of you know. Prior to the War Powers Resolution, the experience with Tonkin Gulf makes it quite clear that, even if that resolution had been in effect, the outcome would have been exactly the same. Subsequent to the War Powers Resolution, we had the congressional response to Mayaquez, and this points in exactly the same direction. So the committee concluded that there was need for changes of a very different type.

State secrets and executive privilege

This second group of changes concerns getting information to Congress and improving its ability to use that information. Here, I have in mind particularly state secrets and the problem of executive privilege.

The committee expressed very strongly the view that secrecy and confidentiality are invoked far too often by the Executive branch of the government. On the other hand, there was a recognition that some confidentiality and indeed a good deal of confidentiality is necessary not only to protect American inter-ests but also to ensure full debate at the lower levels of government.

In this area, the committee saw a need for much greater restraint by the Executive in invoking privileges of confidentiality and in addition a need for a total overhaul of our classification system for official secrets.

Now, the other branch of this process is the need to strengthen congressional capacity to use effectively the information that, hopefully, it will be able to obtain. In this area, Congress already has three very important arms for research and analysis. These are the Office of Technology Assessment, the Library of Congress, and the General Accounting Office. To date, however, these tools have not been used as frequently in the foreign relations area as they could be. The committee found a definite need to strengthen these three arms of Congress and, in particular, to involve them actively in the problems of defense and foreign relations. In addition, there has recently been put into operation a new committee structure for evaluating the budget. This was considered a most promising development, and the committee took the view that this new device should be put to more active use in evaluating military and foreign relations questions.

Legislative oversight

Now, that brings us to a third area that poses considerable difficulty. Even if the two groups of recommendations that I have thus far described can be fully implemented, the committee unfortunately was not particularly optimistic about their ability to produce a vast change in the quality and nature of decision-making. Congressional participation in advance of decisions on major issues is seldom likely to be effective in influencing the result. Therefore, the need that was perceived by many was for a much more active use of the technique of legislative oversight after the event.

Our committee did not share the reservations that were expressed with regard to this technique by committee III. The predominant view taken in committee IV was that Congress should be the Monday morning quarterback and should play that role not rarely and reluctantly but willingly and often, not only when Executive actions are unpopular or would appear to be unsuccessful from the military standpoint, but whenever foreign policy or military initiatives of major significance are instituted.

SEPARATION OF POWERS

The three groups of changes that I have described are very basic changes, but they are not barred by constitutional concepts of the separation of powers. The recent Federal Election Commission decision does raise some question about whether the Supreme Court may be taking a stricter view of the required division of functions among the branches of government. The committee did not view this decision as posing an impediment to the kind of cooperation that I have outlined. If, however, judicial decisions should evolve in such a way as to cast doubt upon the validity of such measures, then the committee would endorse constitutional amendment to permit the kind of sharing of authority in the foreign relations field that most panel members regarded as appropriate.

Now I have not mentioned one device that is somewhat familiar to most lawyers and especially constitutional lawyers, who were not, by the way, unrepresented on our committee, and that device is the courts. Professor Leech touches on the possibility of using the courts to help resolve questions concerning statutes in derogation of treaty obligations. The same possibility arises in connection with questions regarding the scope of claims of executive privilege, the validity of deployments of troops under the War Powers Resolution, and other issues of law that might arise under the type of legislation that I have described.

The view has been expressed, I think most notably and most forcefully by Dean Pollak in his President's Lectures last year at the University of Pennsylvania, that Congress should be given standing to sue, in its own name, to obtain a judicial declaration of what the law is on questions of this kind.

In the committee, a number expressed reluctance to take that step. I think that reluctance was based primarily on two factors. First was a hope that restraint will prevail. Several members of the committee expressed the view that, in the field of foreign relations, separation of powers will work best if each branch of government refrains from pushing its power to the limit.

Now, if a clash should come, a number of members of the committee concluded that present doctrines of justiciability, such as standing, ripeness, the political question doctrine, and so on, provide the appropriate tools for judges to determine for themselves whether they ought to become involved in questions of this delicate nature. The concern expressed by these members, though it was not by any means the unanimous view, was that a more active judicial role in matters of this kind might put a strain upon the courts and, in particular, upon their ability to play a role in a variety of other important tasks for which they will be vitally needed. All agreed, however, that the very sensitive questions concerning the role of the courts should remain in the forefront of those under examination.

It is well to stress that there was no unanimity with respect to the various issues that I have covered. There was, however, a very pervasive attitude in the committee that a more active role by Congress is desirable and that a number of institutional changes, some of as yet uncertain shape, need to be pursued to make this role possible. These changes, all of them sub-constitutional, many of them even sub-statutory, will nevertheless yield what we have to recognize is a quantum change in the level of congressional involvement in the foreign relations field and hopefully a quantum change in the quality of that involvement.

Now with that, the committee permitted itself what was perhaps the luxury of hoping that changes of this nature would yield a somewhat sounder basis for making the decisions on which our future will depend in our third century.

Report on Committee IV

By NOYES LEECH

ABSTRACT: Professor Oliver observed that the current expression of Congress' will to participate in foreign policy and the unrelieved separation of powers impose serious impediments on the ability of the Executive branch to enter into reliable, immediate foreign commitments. The committee appeared to recognize that the crisis in the exercise of our foreign relations power existed and was in some measure created by congressional will to participate and complicated by our separation of powers; but it did not agree that the U.S. was unduly hampered in its power to carry on foreign relations effectively. The committee dealt with the relationship between the Executive and Congress as one of continuing political balance that could be accommodated within our present Constitution. It considered how certain problems of congressional-Executive branch organization related to international agreements might be approached. In looking to the future, the committee projected that the U.S. would want to join international organizations of an increasingly sophisticated type. The view was expressed that constitutional problems arising from joining such organizations, if the matter were approached without amendments, could be quite complex.

Noyes Leech has been a Professor of Law at the University of Pennsylvania since 1950. He practiced law with Dechert, Price & Rhoads from 1948–49 and 1951–53. He is a member of the American Society of International Law. He is co-author of The International Legal System.

THIS paper only reports on the varying responses of a diverse group of individuals to Professor Oliver's paper. It does not report my own point of view and my own reaction to his paper. The committee did not consider the issues paper as an adversary document, but rather, as, in fact, what it purported to be: a statement of issues that ought to be considered by the committee.

FOREIGN RELATIONS POWERS

However, there was a thematic point of view that did run through the paper and to which the committee did respond. In his statement of several of the issues, Professor Oliver observed that the current expression of Congress' will to participate in the making of foreign policy and the unrelieved separation of powers impose serious impediments on the ability of the Executive branch, and therefore of the United States, to enter into reliable and immediate commitments with foreign states. The committee appeared ready to recognize that the phenomenon described by Professor Oliver, namely, the crisis in the exercise of our foreign relations power, did exist in some measure and that this was created by the congressional will to participate, complicated in part by our system of separation of powers. However, the committee did not share his view that the United States was in such a peculiar position internationally that it was unduly hampered in its power to carry on foreign relations effectively. Although it was recognized that the requirement either of Senate advice and consent to treaties or of congressional approval of international agreements did impede the making of commitments by the Executive that could be immediately and confidently relied upon by foreign states, it was observed by the committee that other countries are frequently impeded by parliamentary rules with like effect, although of a different structure.

In any, event, the committee was almost completely of the view that no need presently exists for amendments to the foreign affairs provisions of our Constitution. And in reporting that, I do not mean to imply that the committee was responding negatively to an urging by Professor Oliver that there were a number of amendments that needed to be made. He did not urge that upon us. Although the committee was reminded that its charge enjoined it to look off into the distance of our third century, no one was able confidently to predict that there were developments that would inevitably require constitutional amendment. However, as I will discuss later, there was recognition of some remote contingencies that might signal the need for some specific amendment.

EXECUTIVE AND CONGRESS

In the main, the disposition of the committee was to deal with the relationship between the Executive and the Congress as one of continuing political balance that could be comfortably (and by that term I don't mean to say "serenely") accommodated within the confines of our present constitutional structure. The tension that exists between the two branches was recognized as a more or less permanent feature of our governmental structure, with the ultimate balance of power the product of a process variously described as a "tug of war," "push come to shove," and "ebb and flow." It was emphasized that many of the evils that are seen flowing from the so-called "imperial presidency" resulted not from Congress' lack of constitutional authority but from its non-use of its admitted powers. The cure for these evils was perceived as attainable through what the committee came to call "subconstitutional means": new practices, new institutions, new legislation—in short, through ordinary political and legislative processes.

One particular point of view about Congress' alleged inability to act with efficiency should be mentioned. It was not shared wholly by all members of the committee, but it does represent a distinct and different attitude that should be described. It was asserted that if, indeed, the present organizational arrangement of our government impedes efficient action in the foreign affairs field, this may be desirable. The argument proceeds somewhat as follows. There is not a popular consensus favoring national action in many matters, for example, our involvement in Angola. The Executive branch should not act without a widespread consensus. Congress is now the better institution to record the existence of such consensus as may develop. The Executive should not act until Congress supports national action on the basis of whatever consensus it observes, reports, or represents. If, as a consequence of congressional participation in the process, the Executive cannot take immediate action of its own choosing, that is simply an inevitable consequence of a process that promotes desirable political values. This, as I say, was one attitude expressed in the committee.

It was observed by one member of our committee that there are a number of serious substantive problems that will have to be solved through our government if we are to survive very far into or through the third century. Included among these problems are the following, as they relate to foreign relations: the need for a new world order, planning for use of global resources, determination of limits to national sovereignty, keeping the peace, uses of the oceans, international trade reform, and expanding the scope of international law. The committee recognized the imposing and impending nature of these problems. Members of the committee nevertheless asserted that it was highly appropriate for the committee to focus its own study on the question of the way in which the United States could organize itself to deal rationally with those problems. Therefore, it identified the constitutional and subconstitutional issues to which it was addressing itself at this conference as useful questions to be considered in the process of creating the necessary organization of the resources of the United States government and of its people for the solution of those vital substantive problems.

INTERNATIONAL AGREEMENTS

The challenges posed by Congress' assertion of its will to participate in the making of foreign policy raised a number of discrete constitutional problems, some of which have been reviewed by Professor Oliver. The committee considered how certain problems of congressional-Executive branch organization relating to international agreements might be approached. These problems are: the making of international agreements, the termination of the internal legal effect of international agreements, and joining and participating in the work of international organizations. My colleague, Mr. Schulhofer, addresses a number of diverse questions that have arisen in the area of separation of powers; I would like to speak about these three matters relating to international agreements.

The committee expressed a preference for entering into international agreements through the device of the agreement made by the Executive branch, under authorization by both houses of Congress, including, in some cases, broad policy authorization. Authorization might be given prior to the making of the agreement or by ratification after the agreement has been made. In any event, such authorization would be given through the normal legislative process, as described by Professor Oliver: a simple majority vote by the House and the Senate, followed by the signing of the authorizing bill by the president. This mode, of course, should be contrasted with the treaty-making process, requiring a two-thirds vote by the Senate. The committee gave consideration to proposing an amendment to remove from the Constitution the requirement of two-thirds Senate advice and consent. Such an amendment would leave, as the main agreement-making device, authorization or ratification by the two houses in the normal legislative process. There was a widespread feeling in the committee that, in principle, the two-thirds vote was not desirable or, indeed, supportable rationally under today's conditions, and that the ability of one-third of the Senate plus one senator to block international agreements should not be imbedded in the Constitution. Most members of the committee were reluctant, and at least one member was unwilling, to assume what they saw as serious political costs in trying to procure

that amendment at this time. One other member, however, was of the opinion that these costs might well be paid at some time not too far in the future.

The committee addressed the further question of Congress' regulation of the executive agreement by devices other than normal legislative authorization or ratification. Consideration was given to a possible procedure that could operate as a congressional veto but that would itself be free of the presidential veto. Under this procedure, all executive agreements would be reported to Congress, but Congress could veto the effectiveness of the agreement if, within 90 days, it should vote by concurrent resolution of both houses not to allow the agreement to stand. Since the concurrent resolution does not require presidential signature, the device would operate both to give Congress a veto and, in any event, to contribute to delay in the international agreement-making process. The committee did not favor this device as a general proposition; in any case, it was particularly certain that to the extent that the concurrent resolution was used to veto an agreement made on the president's own constitutional authority, for example as commander-in-chief, it would be unconstitutional and thus was not a desirable process to adopt.

The committee came to the question of terminating the effectiveness of international agreements as internal law. As described by Professor Oliver, it is currently understood to be the law that, although a treaty made under the authority of the United States is the supreme law of the land, if Congress enacts a statute inconsistent with the prior treaty, the statute (which is also the supreme law of the land) supplants the treaty as internal law. The committee deplored the casual use of such a practice by the Congress, since it would leave the country in violation of its international duties under the treaty. However, there was no disposition to alter the Constitution to change Congress' power to do this. There was a strong disposition on the other hand to devise procedures, if possible, to make Congress aware of the seriousness of breaching international obligations in this fashion. Suggestions were made—and appeared well received by the committee—that our treaties might well be drafted to include sanctions to be suffered by the United States in the event of treaty breach (which would include breach resulting from congressional enactment of inconsistent legislation).

It should be pointed out, as it was in the committee, and I think there was agreement on this matter within the committee, that to make these sanctions effective internationally, there would be need to make it possible for an aggrieved state to resort to some form of international adjudication to redress the breach. As is well known, the so-called Connally reservation to our general submission to the compulsory jurisdiction of the International Court of Justice contains a provision allowing the United States to be the judge of whether it will submit to that jurisdiction in the particular case (that is the clause allowing the United States to decide whether or not a matter falls essentially within our domestic jurisdiction). I think there was sentiment in the committee that there was good reason to repeal that reservation, so as to make effective our willingness to subject ourselves to sanctions in the event of breach of an international agreement.

Further on the subject of the internal effect of legislation, there was inconclusive discussion in the committee about amendment of the Constitution to enlist the Judiciary in processes that would prevent Congress from enacting treaty-breaking legislation over a presidential veto. The disposition of the committee was to give that matter further study.

INTERNATIONAL ORGANIZATIONS

The question of joining and participating in international organizations resulted from the committee's looking down the years into the next century. The committee projected that there would be a desire on the part of the United States to join international organizations of an increasingly sophisticated type. Such highly developed organizations, possibly regional in character and dealing with technical concerns such as trade, might follow the pattern of some European organizations that provide for dealing directly with persons and entities within the territory of the member states. Organizations of this type do not act simply on the state alone. As Professor Oliver indicated, he posed to us the question of whether under our constitutional structure (on such matters as the judicial power of the United States and the guarantees of the Bill of Rights) the United States could lawfully join such organizations without violating constitutional provisions. It was the view of some of the committee members that the cases (such as *Reid* v. *Covert*) that appeared to nullify international agreements that conflicted with the Constitution may not in fact do so in this instance. Indeed, no one argued that the charters of international organizations, a form of treaty in themselves, are not subject to the Constitution, but it was urged by some that judicial development might well accommodate the United States' joining such organizations without the necessity of constitutional amendment.

This is not to suggest that the courts would not be alert to protect our citizens against deprivation of liberties. Presumably the courts will insist upon fair procedures in any international organization we join, even though the procedures do not follow the same patterns as those in our own country. Some members of the committee expressed the view that the constitutional problems arising upon our joining some kinds of international organizations, if the matter were approached without amendment of the Constitution, could be quite complex. I think that the committee agreed with one member who asserted that this was an area in which the necessity of constitutional amendment ought to be reserved on what he called a contingency basis. If, at some time in the possibly distant future, our courts are not sufficiently sensitive to our national needs, and do not interpret the Constitution so as to permit United States membership in highly-developed international organizations essential to our interests (and possibly to our survival), it would then, as he asserted, be necessary to make membership possible in those organizations through whatever amendments of the Constitution were required.

* * *

QUESTIONS AND ANSWERS

Q: I'm Dr. Fred Greenwald of the United States Probation Office in Philadelphia. My question relates to the world order and peace-keeping problems. I feel that both are affected by the operations of international criminal cartels and by terrorist activists. The United States participates in the World Court and there is precedent for special criminal justice action in the Nuremburg trial, to which one of the speakers has already referred. Should there not be a criminal division to the World Court? Is there a move in this direction and is this nation a participant in it?

A (Dr. Fisher): A statute was drafted, back in 1951 or 1952, by George Maurice Myers. It was primarily directed toward the problems of international crime of the sort dealt with in the Nuremburg trials.

But our concern was primarily with the constitutional problem. Is there anything in the Constitution that would prohibit an international criminal court? Well, our panel, and I will ask anyone else who cares to, to comment on this, felt that in the matter of an international criminal court, we would have to be satisfied that the basic provisions of our Bill of Rights were met, but, subject to that, we didn't foresee any serious problems. We had a pretty good set of precedents in the extradition treaties and in some of the treaties by which we turned over American soldiers to be tried by Japan.

We did not feel there was any ban on this as long as the procedures were basically satisfactory to our Bill of Rights.

———

Q: Mr. Chairman, my name is John Ward. I believe I'm one of the few delegates, if not the only one, on the roster representing a private enterprise at this convention. I'd like to ask my friend and fellow Texan, Mr. Covey Oliver, in view of his lengthy and extensive experience in the State Department, whether this committee may not have made a grievous omission in one respect. Have you considered the so-called Act of State Doctrine, which has been invoked by the Supreme Court in numerous instances, refusing to hear complaints and criticisms and pleas for relief by not only United States citizens, but also foreign citizens?

I strongly urge that the committee consider this matter, and I will very briefly read one paragraph in file by the United States government, a pending case before the Supreme Court, which to my knowledge has not yet been decided.

This case is the Alfred Dunhill case. The State Department has taken a position, which I believe is a drastic change from their prior position, "in general, this department provides little support for the presumption that adjudication of acts of foreign states in accordance with relevant principles of international law, would embarrass the conduct for foreign policy. Thus, it is our view that the court should decide to overrule the holding in *Sabatino* so that acts of state would then have to be subject to adjudication in American courts under international law."

I respectfully submit that this issue appears to be overlooked and I urge the committee to take it under consideration.

A (Dr. Fisher): The committee considered this in the particular context of how does the United States get around it. We can break international law if we want to, and we were not helped in that by the decision of Justice Harlan, not exactly a radical justice, in the Sabatino case in which he indicated that there wasn't much international law there anyhow.

We then thought that under the circumstances, particularly in view of the Supreme Court's requesting that the Sabatino case be directly considered in the case, that the thing wasn't large enough for us. It may well be that that will be subsumed under the general area when the papers are written of the various ways in which the United States enforces international law, rather than saying we are free to break it. But we didn't think the case was ripe yet and there are going to be other papers written soon, and by the time they're written I hope the Dunhill case will be decided and we'll know what to say on this.

A (Mr. Oliver): I simply wanted to say that I did not raise the Act of State—*Banca Nationale Cuba* v. *Sabatino* decision—in the issues paper, and the reason was two-fold. One, the case is sub judica in the Dunhill case, as Dean Fisher has mentioned. The other reason was that I had already raised the general question in the paper of how international law comes into our system.

I think the Act of State doctrine is, as long as it stands, a manifestation of a judicial disinclination to get involved in foreign affairs matters, and I think, even if *Sabatino* should be reversed, we have to weigh the question as to how far we can expect the courts to be a kind of second foreign office for the United States.

I think that's a very difficult problem and I personally do not think that the courts are going to go very far in arbitrating foreign affairs issues. I think if they don't protect themselves by acts of state, it will be a political question, it will be rightness, it will be standing to sue. The courts are just not very happy about getting into this act.

Q: My name is Richard Clark from Widener College, and I just have a very short question here for you. In this problem of changes in the administration and conducting long-term policy, particularly in regard to disarmament negotiations which may spread over several administrations, with changes in negotiators, perhaps some concept of permanent negotiators might be helpful. Particularly, I was thinking of James A. Wadsworth and Arthur Dean changing in the midst of the administration negotiations, and I believe that still goes on in different types of negotiations where you have a complete change.

A (Dr. Fisher): Well, it very often varies. You could have permanent experts. I don't see how you can bind a subsequent administration to the political decision-making process of the prior administration. Now, to the extent that you have a turnover in the experts, that is bad. The worst turnover, strangely enough, came in 1973. I speak with a certain knowledge of this because this was my line of endeavor for some years.

But usually the turnover has been

confined to the man at the top, the politically responsible official, and I see no way you can prevent that. Even if we followed the British practice of having a permanent civil service delegation, they send in a minister of state about once every two weeks. But I think we ought to keep the continuity up to the top levels as much as possible. I greatly regret that there were so many turnovers, in all places, in 1973, though not very many in 1969.

A (Oliver): In the issues paper, I addressed what I considered to be a very serious problem, and that was the effect of time on the intensity with which the United States as a government supervises the performance of our international obligations. It pains me to say, and I say it as a former official in foreign affairs, that the record of the United States as a full faith performer of treaties is not nearly as good as we Americans think; and, in large part, this is not because Congress passes inconsistent legislation but because even in the bureaucracy there is a tendency to leave the enforcement of treaties, within the government, to the unfortunate people who negotiated them. And in time, they die or retire and then there is no one around who remembers.

I want to add just one point here. I happen to be an advisor to the U.S. delegation on the law of the sea conference now going on. If we get a treaty of that sort, it's going to be wider than I am by quite a bit, in terms of coverage. I calculate that 35 agencies of the U.S. government will be directly involved in one way or another in the provisions in that treaty. And what agency of government is going to ride herd on the other agencies of government with respect to the good faith attention within the bureaucracy to the treaty itself? It's a serious problem.

———————

Q: I'm Sister Alice Gerline, a Professor of History at the College of New Rochelle, and I'm here as a delegate of the National Catholic Conference of Bishops. I would like to commend the committee for the analysis of our foreign policy in terms of constitutional problems and cases, but I'm a little disappointed that in celebrating this conference as part of the Bicentennial, not much difference in attitude seems to be reflected here from a traditional United States foreign policy attitude.

By that I mean that last night we were told that in our Constitution the liberty-equality balance is shifting a little more toward emphasis on equality, and it seems we've heard that in celebrating the Bicentennial we celebrate the independence that we declared 200 years ago and the interdependence that is the need today. I simply don't hear very much of the profession focusing on that shift to a world of interdependence, where our approach to the rest of the world is not so much national interest and legal concerns, but one of world vision and global hopes.

A (Dr. Fisher): We accept the impeachment. However, in defense of the committee, we should point out that part of our concern was whether our constitutional structure would make such interdependence possible. We felt that it would and recommended that, if it turned out that it wouldn't, the Constitution ought to be amended.

———————

Q: I'm a delegate for the Embassy of Cyprus in Washington. I'd like to pose a question concerning this problem of the tug of war between the Congress and the Executive branch in the execution of foreign policy. I'd also like to ask, what powers does Congress have in the lack of action or the action of the Executive branch in the face of a violation that has been committed with respect to a U.S. treaty by a foreign power? A case that might make it clear is the violation in the use of arms that have been supplied for, let's say, defensive purposes and used for aggression.

A: Well, normally what you have to do is to bring that to the attention of the relevant agency in government, the Department of State. Normally you bring it to the legal adviser's office, although if the treaty has a certain functional area, you bring it to the people that negotiated the treaty. Usually a private citizen doesn't have standing. He can supply them the information, but they have to supply the will to make something out of it. The best way to supply that will is to go to congressional sources. That's a rather primitive way of doing it, but that's the way it works.

Annals, AAPSS, **426**, July 1976

Luncheon Speech

By Herbert Wechsler

I may say that, when I was asked to take the chair at the conference, I deemed it a great honor. I did not realize, however, how small the function was that I would be called upon to perform, so that I, for the first time in my life, have been the incumbent of a position that I can only describe as a sinecure.

That was due, of course, to the genius that went into the organization of this conference, both on the part of the Academy committee and the superb staff headed by Mrs. Truscott, the Coordinator. I run many conferences myself, and I have never encountered one where the participants were so unanimously grateful for the arrangements made, the solicitude of their host, and the pleasure of the meeting. It is perfectly true that the target was not thought by most of the conferees to be to produce an agenda for reform, and I make no apology for the fact that many of them had as a very serious purpose merely the improvement of their own minds.

In this age of activism and activity, such simple, personal desires as the desire for understanding and information are often lost sight of, but it surely was appropriate, from the point of view of the Academy, that that purpose be given the priority that it received in the conference. The format was such that the advantages that we perceived in the interchange over the days that we were together will, through careful editing and significant publication plans, be made available in the future to all our colleagues in this field.

I should say a word about the people who were present, because I don't think you have had any information on that score. As far as I can see, aided by Mrs. Truscott, we had between 75 and 80 participants, not all of whom were present all the time, but most of whom were with us most of the time.

As you would suppose, it was a fairly heavily academic group. We had 12 law professors, 10 professors of political science, 4 professors of history, 2 professors of sociology. The significant point about these academics was, however, a point that I think is important in our culture—that though they are academics now, they haven't been all their lives. They illustrated the mobility that our culture provides among government, educational activities, pedagogy, business, and other forms of participation in the life of our time. In any event, the present academics were not alone in the group. There were three sitting congressmen, an ex-United

States senator; there were government officials, both federal and state, labor union people, people in business, management of corporations, practicing lawyers—and again that illustrates the point. One of the practicing lawyers was the former solicitor general of the United States, Erwin N. Griswold, one of the best solicitors, I think, in many years. He is now in private practice but was, as you know, for so many years dean of the Harvard Law School; so—government official, teacher, lawyer, all in the person of the same man.

Then we had 10 active judges, sitting judges, five drawn from the United States Courts of Appeals, all of great ability and distinction in my profession. Mr. Justice Tom C. Clark, a retired justice of the Supreme Court, after 18 years on the bench, was also present. He is still sitting, as a retired justice may, in the lower federal courts.

There were also two journalists, and so it went. While I suffered from the inexorable limitation of not being able to be in more than one place at once, I did make an effort to move around from group to group, and I never encountered a moment where the interchange was not hot and heavy. I thought some pretty stupid things were said and some very wise things were said, and it was, perhaps, the pace and quality of that dialogue that even our superb reporters were not quite able to put before you in their summaries, because the nature of their task was, of course, to impose order upon chaos, which they did superbly. The chaos was, however, both instructive and interesting. I hope that the final publication will draw more heavily on the actual text of the dialogue in these proceedings, which were stenotyped, taped, video taped—I don't suppose anything in the history of the world has ever been as fully recorded as these discourses. For that, we are indebted to the Sun Oil Company, as we are for the other aspects of the great hospitality that we enjoyed.

At the opening of the conference, I took the occasion to speak very briefly, and one of the things that I mentioned—because of some of the mail I had been getting—was that the idea seems still to be abroad that it is impious or worse to undertake to criticize our basic charter. I asked the conferees to repudiate that point of view, and to feel as free to criticize as to extol. This was a bit of advice that I'm glad to say they followed. I must confess, however, that I felt a little supererogatory in making that point to a group of people who didn't need it made to them. But I felt quite vindicated the next day when there appeared out front a band of pickets who were denouncing us as traitors and conspirators. When I saw them, I thought I had done very well as an inadvertent prophet. They provided a formal demonstration of what I was talking about in referring to that sentiment in the land.

I wish those pickets knew, however, how little basis there was for their suspicions in the actual deliberations of the conference. Indeed, on Thursday, Senator Clark, as you may know, attacked us bitterly as a bunch of mossbacks and conservatives because we didn't really take on the problems of nuclear war and the threatened destruction of the world. In Senator Clark's view, there is grave doubt whether there will be a third century, and he thought we should somehow deal with that doubt. Well, maybe we would have had something to contribute on that score, but I doubt it; and having heard his speech often enough, I haven't yet discovered that he has very much to contribute on it either.

The other incident that was amusing to me—because in my professional career, I represented newspapers in cases involving First Amendment problems, including the *New York Times*—was that we were roundly castigated for not admitting the press to these committee discussions. Indeed, here in Philadelphia, I think you've seen enough of that in the papers.

I must say that this was not an unforeseen problem. We had been pressed in the preliminary planning to open the entire conference to the press, and I want to express my admiration for the Academy committee, your committee, in standing firm for the proposition that admitting the press to these committee discussions would simply have destroyed the spontaneity and usefulness of the proceeding. But that response did not satisfy the reporters who wanted to get in, because they knew something about the First Amendment and it was put to us that they had a First Amendment right to sit in our proceedings. When President Wolfgang pointed out to them that the Constitutional Convention had been closed and that the Fathers had pretty well agreed that, if it hadn't been closed, there wouldn't have ever been a Constitution, my old friend, Mr. Israel Shenker of the *New York Times*, made the insightful lawyer's observation that that was before the First Amendment.

Well, having represented the *New York Times* and knowing the publisher and many of the editorial staff, I thought to myself that it would be amusing, when I get back to New York, if I wrote a letter to Mr. Sulzburger demanding the right all the next week to attend the editorial conferences of the *New York Times*, placing my demand, of course, on First Amendment grounds and invoking Mr. Shenker in support.

I must say, as I read what has been published, I think it provides a visual demonstration of how useful it was to close the committee sessions. For what has the press found interesting about our conference? The only things that the reporters have been disposed to give attention are the few inflammatory and critical remarks that were made in the course of the plenary session on Thursday. And that, of course, is exactly what would have happened if they had been sitting around during the committee deliberations. I wonder if the time may not some time arrive when we will have a press that is able to take ideas seriously and not feel the need to ferret out inflammatory headlines on which to hang a story. But I'm still prepared to fight and die for their right to make fools of themselves, as they do.

I am sure you were intimidated, if you looked at the program, to see that I am scheduled to make a speech on major themes of the Bicentennial Conference. Of course, the thing that you need at this point is a summary of the summaries you have been listening to for the last couple of days! I can assure you that I have no such intention, and ought to be forcibly removed if I did.

But, I do wish to say a few things that simply embody some reflections of mine on what might be called the thrust or the conclusions of the conference. I'm reminded of a story told about Gertrude Stein. On her deathbed, her biographer and great friend, Alice Toklas was leaning over her and heard her whispering something. What she heard was: "What is the answer? What is the answer?" When no one responded, she said: "Well, then, what is the question?" And at that point, she died.

I think this has a certain application to the work of our conference. I would be far from saying that the days produced answers, but I think you'll find—have already found from the reporters' and keynoters' participation here, but will find it more clearly when you study the record—that we did produce a marvelous canvass of the questions. And I mean by that, the questions that people who are serious about our government and our culture and our future ought to focus on as they participate in our political and governmental processes and ruminate about our prospects.

At the start of the conference, I had attempted to stimulate the conferees to take a precise focus on constitutional issues, that is to say, on issues that could be resolved either by agreeing to, supporting, or rejecting specific proposed changes in the fundamental law. That little speech of mine was like the chaplain's prayer before a political meeting, of which it has been said, that it is always unexceptionable in itself, but never determinative of the subsequent proceedings.

My suggestion certainly was not determinative of the subsequent proceedings, because the committees ranged very broadly over problems of government in general. But as I wandered around, I concluded that this was a virtue rather than the contrary. That is to say, how could you tell whether the fundamental law was in need of change, unless you assessed the problems that government faces and may be expected to face in the future and the means that are available for the solution of those problems?

And so it was, I think, enormously significant that it was the general view of these conferees and the four groups in which they talked for so long, that we could not perceive major problems of our government, culture, and social order that we could say were insoluble within the framework of our present charter. That is a negative conclusion, if you like, and yet, it seems to me, a conclusion of enormous importance.

Even here, I must say, I had made an effort at the beginning to stimulate attention to what I thought might be taken to be a problem, namely, the enormous obstacle that the Constitution as it stands poses to amendment. That is, the provisions of Article Five, the amending clause, require a two-thirds vote in each house in support of a resolution of amendment and then ratification in three-quarters of the states, either by their legislatures or by conventions, as Congress may determine when the amendment is proposed.

Whether a country of over 200 million people can live with a fundamental law born in the eighteenth century and supplemented, as Dr. Wolfgang said, only really significantly by the Civil War Amendments, with change possible only by a consensus of that magnitude, seemed to me, in itself, a constitutional problem of major significance. Well, again, the chaplain's prayer. You will be interested to know that no one on the four committees even considered this an issue worthy of consideration. So, I must read the record to mean that our conferees, at least, are satisfied with the amending process as it stands. Again, I think this is an enormously significant conclusion. I don't say that it's wrong, I say that it's significant. Now, how could this be the case? Well, obviously only because the framers were perspicacious enough to establish a governmental structure with sufficient flexibility in the joints so that adaptations can be made as needed, to a very considerable degree at least, without the necessity of amendment.

I thought this general satisfaction with the amending clause particularly surprising, I may say, in relation to the role of the Supreme Court of the United States as the final interpretative voice of the Constitution, since I put it to you that the impact of the amending clause, as it stands, really falls most heavily there, in the magnitude of the political support required to overcome a decision that is restrictive of the legislative power. That is, in the structural part of the Constitution, the establishment of the organs of authority—bicameral legislature, and so on—even today, one would be hard put to persuade that a different structure would produce a better result. It's simply too incalculable. It's too hard to prove, to envisage what different consequences might be. The difficulty of amendment does not weigh heavily upon that area of our polity.

But as to the Bill of Rights and its Fourteenth Amendment, we know that, to a very considerable degree, the moral standards of our culture have been transformed by decisions of the Court in our own lifetime and that that Court continues to exert a major role in the unfolding of safeguards for individuals, the autonomy of individuals, that no other government in the history of the world has ever achieved or, indeed, is every likely to achieve. And for the most part, the sole escape from such determinations of the Court is by amendment!

Well, this problem was discussed in committee I, but as the report of that committee indicated, that committee viewed the ravages wrought by decisions of the Supreme Court not as a problem, but, indeed, as one of our principal glories as a people, a nation, and a government. I was struck by this consensus, I must say. I've been a politician too long not to remember when it wasn't so. Indeed, did any of you attend the meeting of this Academy 40 years ago, at which Thomas Reed Powell, speaking of a very different Supreme Court, imposing very different kinds of restraints, produced a cheering audience by his denunciation of that august body and the substance and reasoning of its decisions?

I wondered, I must say, how representative the view of committee I was in its complete and total acceptance of the role that the Court has performed in recent years. We had no one who apparently objected to the decision on school prayers, for example, or to the decision on abortion. We had no exponent of the current Boston view on busing and, indeed, it wasn't even there, but in another committee, that there was extended discussion on problems of crime and the call for greater security in the streets.

I should like to think that the acquiescence and acceptance and approval of committee I and, indeed, its incitement toward an even greater judicial drive toward the realization of equality of opportunity, which you heard in the report, does represent an American consensus. I have my doubts about it, however, and was impressed by what was said in committee II by George Reedy, a man of considerable wisdom and experience, who you remember was press secretary to President Johnson. He said he liked what the Court was doing but could not avoid the apprehension that it was taking an awful lot of money out of the bank and would do well to put a little money back from time to time.

I thought that was a rather nice way of expressing a concern that, I think, the conference might have examined in greater detail than it did, but please don't construe this as an attack on the Supreme Court or on any particular decisions. I do not mean it that way. I do mean to say that any serious consideration of the Constitution must reflect on the fact that the Supreme Court is called upon to apply to the varying demands of humanity over time such brooding phrases as privilege and immunities of citizens of the United States, due process of law, equal protection of the law, and so on. I'm reminded, in this connection, of a passage in Professor Fairman's current volume of the Supreme Court history, quoting a comment by Congressman Boutwell of Massachusetts about Congressman Bingham of Ohio, the draftsman of Section One of the Fourteenth Amendment, particularly concerning the privileges and immunities clause: "Its euphony and indefiniteness of meaning were a charm to him." Well, its euphony and indefiniteness of meaning have given the Supreme Court the enormous role that it performs in our lives, and this is neither politically, governmentally, nor socially a matter to be passed over lightly.

I had the pleasure only the other day of reading the lectures given by Archibald Cox at All Souls College in Oxford, the Chichele lectures of 1975, just published by Oxford Press under the title, *The Role of the Supreme Court in the American System of Government*. Professor Cox, who is in general, as I am, a supporter of the Court, develops in an enormously perceptive way in these five lectures the concerns to which I have briefly alluded.

I had another real surprise in the conference. Both committee II and committee III devoted an enormous part of their time, particularly committee III, to talking about presidential primaries, and I don't think it was only that this particular form of divertissement is occurring right at the moment. This was a matter of serious concern about governmental problems; and you remember they had thoughts about regional primaries and the like, all of which are interesting.

But the thing that surprised me was that there was not a single voice that considered that changes in the basic constitutional method of presidential choice were worthy of consideration. I don't have in mind now merely the old issue of the electoral college, which really has ceased to be much of an issue, because, really, what difference does it make if you count up state choices by counting real people in the electoral college or using a mathematical formula allotting the same weight to the voters in each of the several states? But what I should have thought terribly important to focus on is that provision of the Twelfth Amendment, going back really to the original plan, that throws the choice of a president to the House of Representatives, in the event that no candidate receives a majority of the electoral votes, and that calls for voting in the House of Representatives by states rather than per capita, so that the vote of Nevada would have the same weight in the presidential choice by the House as the voice of Pennsylvania or California or New York.

Now, of course, you can say that that's an abstract concern. But I'm surely not alone here in remembering the election of 1948, in which the Dixiecrat candidate got, as I recall, 39 electoral votes, and a shift of 25,000 or so popular votes in Ohio and California would have thrown the election to the House. And what would the position then have been on the House delegations? The names before the House would have been, of course, Truman, Dewey, and Senator Thurmond.

Well, I don't suppose Thurmond could have been elected, but he might have had enough delegations to support him to prevent a majority vote of states in the House and permit Alben Barkley, the vice-presidential candidate who would have been elected by the Senate, to succeed to the presidency. That was, at least, one of the game plans of that time and there, of course, were others. I am not privy to the deliberations of the Wallace campaign, but could it be that such thoughts may, from time to time, have been ventilated in those quarters?

In any event, I say that I was rather surprised that this matter did not receive attention, the more so, since President Lyndon Johnson did propose that there be a change on that score and that, in the event of failure of majority, the choice fall to a per capita vote of both houses, as it does under the Twenty-Fifth Amendment now, when there's a vacancy in the vice-presidency and a nomination is made by the president in office.

To be sure, Arthur Schlesinger and Senator Kennedy seem to think that the Twenty-Fifth Amendment was a failure and ought to be reexamined. I regard it as one of the great constitutional achievements of the recent past; and I should suppose that the succession of President Ford, far from demonstrating that some other plan was needed, shows what a great success it was—not that I am announcing my support for President Ford, but I am announcing my happiness that a succession was achieved and achieved as peacefully and easily as it was.

I am not disposed to feel greater pleasure in the vote of the parliamentary Labor party to supplant Prime Minister Wilson by Mr. Callahan, simply by that vote, than in a process in which the entire Congress of the United States takes part. After all, it was just the barest accident that the Constitution came out of Philadelphia without a plan for the president to be chosen by Congress. That was the plan until very near the end, and it was only the desire for greater presidential independence of Congress that led to the provisions that developed.

I guess the one thing that present experience teaches us is that you can have a president confirmed by vote of both houses who doesn't suffer from undue reliance or dependence on the Congress. Whatever else one may think of Gerald Ford, I don't think the historians will say that he suffered from subservience to Congress.

The main contribution of the conference was, of course, the conclusion which has been expressed earlier, that, despite the wealth of reflection given to our current governmental problems, there was a close approach to a consensus that they are soluble within the present framework. One might say that the lesson was embodied in the words that Shakespeare has Julius Ceasar address to Brutus: "the fault . . . is not in our stars but in ourselves. . . ."

And I think it is splendid for the Academy to carry that message to the American people, that despite the magnitude of our problems, domestic, foreign, scientific, cultural, economic, ethnic, and moral, the future lies within our grasp as a nation and its shape will depend upon ourselves.

Report of the Board of Directors to the Members of the American Academy of Political and Social Science for the Year 1975

MEMBERSHIP

MEMBERSHIP AS OF DECEMBER 31

Year	Number
1965	20,071
1966	21,043
1967	23,440
1968	25,158
1969	24,597
1970	24,544
1971	23,413
1972	21,963
1973	21,070
1974	19,473
1975	16,923

FINANCES

Our bank balance at the end of 1975 was $52,038.65.

SIZE OF SECURITIES PORTFOLIO

MARKET VALUE AS OF DECEMBER 31

1966	$462,675
1967	481,123
1968	566,681
1969	539,083
1970	616,429
1971	612,046
1972	642,808
1973	533,024
1974	371,004
1975	440,450

STATEMENT OF REVENUE, EXPENSE AND SURPLUS FOR THE YEAR ENDED DECEMBER 31, 1975

REVENUES:	1975	1974
Dues and subscriptions, net of agents' commissions and refunds	$235,655.21	$238,804.57
Sales of publications, net of discounts and refunds	35,435.67	30,435.04
Advertising, net of discounts	7,035.12	10,689.83
Royalty and reprint permissions	9,803.64	7,672.49
Annual meeting, net of refunds	7,224.76	5,209.00
List rental	2,000.00	3,432.65
Sale of review books	2,610.00	1,594.00
Miscellaneous	272.35	318.55
TOTAL REVENUES	$300,036.75	$298,156.13

OPERATING EXPENSES:

	1975	1974
Annals printing, binding and mailing	$ 96,866.45	$ 99,948.23
Shipping and cost of publications sold	8,539.19	9,273.83
Salaries and related benefits	176,177.65	174,249.75
Annual meeting	9,505.08	10,117.88
Depreciation	564.00	564.00
Insurance	1,885.50	1,488.05
List rental and exchange	3,642.29	1,943.26
Postage	8,236.34	9,987.52
Printing, duplicating and stationery	15,951.61	20,402.90
Supplies	1,646.31	2,938.75
Telephone	1,495.24	1,553.33
Repairs, maintenance and utilities	8,511.63	9,423.85
Miscellaneous	7,707.24	7,469.12
TOTAL OPERATING EXPENSES	$340,728.53	$349,360.47
INCOME (LOSS) BEFORE MONOGRAPH REVENUE	($ 40,691.78)	($ 51,204.34)
MONOGRAPH REVENUE, NET OF COSTS	1,728.31	2,700.99
OPERATING INCOME (LOSS)	($ 38,963.47)	($ 48,503.35)

OTHER REVENUE (EXPENSE):

	1975	1974
Dividends and interest	$ 24,066.57	$ 24,353.25
Investment fees	(964.52)	(1,038.14)
Loss on sale of investments	—	(18,551.97)
Bicentennial	11,122.00	—
TOTAL OTHER REVENUE (EXPENSE)	$ 34,224.05	$ 4,763.14
EXCESS OF REVENUE OVER EXPENSE	($ 4,739.42)	($ 43,740.21)
SURPLUS, BEGINNING OF YEAR	346,895.92	390,636.13
SURPLUS, END OF YEAR	$342,156.50	$346,895.92

PUBLICATIONS

<table>
<tr><td colspan="2" align="center">Number of Volumes of The Annals Printed</td><td colspan="2" align="center">Number of Volumes of The Annals Sold</td></tr>
<tr><td colspan="2" align="center">(6 per year)</td><td colspan="2" align="center">(in addition to memberships
and subscriptions)</td></tr>
<tr><td>1965</td><td>119,681</td><td>1965</td><td>12,492</td></tr>
<tr><td>1966</td><td>133,056</td><td>1966</td><td>18,063</td></tr>
<tr><td>1967</td><td>134,788</td><td>1967</td><td>19,061</td></tr>
<tr><td>1968</td><td>147,631</td><td>1968</td><td>13,072</td></tr>
<tr><td>1969</td><td>154,153</td><td>1969</td><td>15,610</td></tr>
<tr><td>1970</td><td>145,456</td><td>1970</td><td>14,143</td></tr>
<tr><td>1971</td><td>139,450</td><td>1971</td><td>10,046</td></tr>
<tr><td>1972</td><td>143,360</td><td>1972</td><td>16,721</td></tr>
<tr><td>1973</td><td>132,709</td><td>1973</td><td>12,430</td></tr>
<tr><td>1974</td><td>120,397</td><td>1974</td><td>13,153</td></tr>
<tr><td>1975</td><td>104,049</td><td>1975</td><td>13,034</td></tr>
</table>

Monographs Published

Date	Subject	Number Printed	Number Sold	Complimentary Distribution
1962	#1–Behavioralism	15,225	5,402	9,764
1963	2–Mathematics	30,725	2,564	28,162
1963	3–Public Service	17,230	1,140	16,105
1964	4–Leisure	37,488	3,645	33,844
1965	5–Functionalism	44,459	2,631	41,828
1966	6–Political Science	21,067	5,646	15,421
1967	7–Urban Society	22,578	1,506	21,073
1968	8–Public Administration	25,311	2,188	23,154
1969	9–Design for Sociology	16,191	3,752	12,540
1970	10–International Relations Research	10,055	1,303	5,823
1971	11–Technology	12,167	407	3,217
1971	12–International Studies	7,609	390	3,802
1972	13–Diplomacy	7,090	292	3,021
1972	14–Integration	8,096	347	7,000
1973	15–Public Interest	8,001	252	6,865
1973	16–Urban Administration	20,066	513	17,699
1973	17–Language Studies	5,109	528	837

During 1975, the six volumes of THE ANNALS dealt with the following subjects:

January   *Drugs and Social Policy*, edited by Ralph M. Susman, former Associate Director, National Commission on Marihuana and Drug Abuse, and Lenore R. Kupperstein, former Assistant Director, National Commission on Marihuana and Drug Abuse.

March   *Planning for Full Employment*, edited by Stanley Moses, Assistant Professor, Department of Urban Affairs, Hunter College, City University of New York.

May   *General Revenue Sharing and Federalism*, edited by David A. Caputo, Associate Professor of Political Science, Purdue University, West Lafayette, Indiana.

July   *Adjusting to Scarcity*, edited by Marvin E. Wolfgang, President of this Academy.

September   *Perspectives on Publishing*, edited by Philip G. Altbach, Professor, Faculty of Educational Studies, State University of New York, Buffalo, New York, and Sheila McVey, Ph.D., Educational Policy Studies, University of Wisconsin, Madison, Wisconsin.

November *The Suburban Seventies*, edited by Louis H. Masotti, Director, Center for Urban Affairs, Professor of Political Science and Urban Affairs, Northwestern University, Evanston, Illinois.

The publication program for 1976 includes the following volumes:

January *Crime and Justice in America: 1776–1976*, edited by Graeme R. Newman, Professor, School of Criminal Justice, State University of New York at Albany.

March *International Exchange of Persons: A Reassessment*, edited by Kenneth Holland, President Emeritus, Institute of International Education, United Nations Plaza, New York, New York.

May *Political Finance: Reform and Reality*, edited by Herbert E. Alexander, Director, Citizens' Research Foundation, Princeton, New Jersey.

July *Bicentennial Conference on the Constitution: A Report to the Academy*, edited by Marvin E. Wolfgang, President of this Academy.

September *Role of the Mass Media in American Politics*, edited by L. John Martin, Professor of Journalism, College of Journalism, University of Maryland, College Park, Maryland.

November *The American Revolution Abroad*, edited by Richard L. Park, Professor of Political Science, University of Michigan, Ann Arbor, Michigan.

The rotating summaries of social sciences disciplines, established in 1961, are being continued.

During 1975, the Book Department of THE ANNALS published 389 reviews. More than three-fourths of these reviews were written by professors, and the others by college or university presidents, members of private and university-sponsored organizations, government and public officials, military personnel, and business professionals. Most reviewers were residents of the United States, but some were residents of Great Britain, Canada, Scotland, Ireland, Ghana, Japan, Thailand and the West Indies. One thousand two hundred and thirty-five books were listed in the Other Books section.

One hundred and forty-eight requests were granted to reprint material from THE ANNALS. Most of these went to professors and other authors for use in books under preparation.

MEETINGS

The seventy-ninth annual meeting, which was held in April 1975, had as its subject *Adjusting to Scarcity*, and continued the tradition of our gatherings with respect to the diversity of organizations represented by delegates, the size of the audiences and the interest displayed. Twenty-two embassies sent official delegations, as did 13 United Nations missions and 14 states, cities and agencies of the federal government. Delegates were also sent by 112 American and foreign universities and colleges and 83 international, civic, scientific and commercial organizations. Nearly 600 persons attended one or more of the sessions. The average attendance for a session was 500.

The theme of the eightieth annual meeting, held April 9 and 10, 1976, at the Benjamin Franklin Hotel, Philadelphia, was *Bicentennial Conference on the Constitution: A Report to the Academy*. This volume of THE ANNALS contains the papers presented at the meeting.

OFFICERS AND STAFF

Marvin E. Wolfgang and Norman D. Palmer were reelected for another three-year term.

The Board also renewed the terms of its counsel, Henry W. Sawyer, III, accepted the resignation of its auditor, John H. McMichael, and appointed the firm of Cionci, Mazen & Company.

All of the Board officers were reelected, and both the Editor and Assistant Editor were reappointed.

Respectfully submitted,

THE BOARD OF DIRECTORS

Norman D. Palmer
Howard C. Petersen
Walter M. Phillips
Paul R. Anderson
Karl R. Bopp
Elmer B. Staats
Marvin E. Wolfgang
Lee Benson
A. Leon Higgenbotham, Jr.
Richard D. Lambert
Rebecca Jean Brownlee
Covey T. Oliver

Philadelphia, Pennsylvania
1 June 1976

Book Department

INTERNATIONAL RELATIONS AND POLITICAL SCIENCE

SYDNEY D. BAILEY. *The Procedure of the U.N. Security Council.* Pp. vii, 424. New York: Oxford University Press, 1975. $26.00.

The Procedure of the U.N. Security Council, a welcome contribution to the study of international relations, seeks to "examine the procedure and practice of the Security Council as it was at a particular point in time: March 1974" (p. 18). It is the second of a triology on the Security Council which its author, Sydney D. Bailey who is an expert on the United Nations, is attempting to complete. *Voting in the Security Council* was published in 1970, and in the other volume he will deal with aspects of the Council's primary responsibility for "peace-making and peace-keeping."

The work exhibits three major levels of analysis: a descriptive, a normative, and a prescriptive. And one of its weaknesses is that as the author examines the procedure and practice of the Council within the framework of the history and general purposes of the United Nations, the Provisional Rules of Procedure of the Security Council—as amended 17 January 1974—and the customs of the latter organ, transitions from one level of analysis to the other are sometimes unclear.

The author also runs into difficulties in his normative and prescriptive analysis. He changes standards in evaluating the same phenomenon. In judging whether the Security Council should continue the practice of "holding meetings" at "places other than the seat of the organization," he employs the criterion of whether the meetings did "best facilitate" the councils's work when they were held in London and Paris and whether they were "overwhelmingly successful" (p. 291) in Ethiopia and Panama. Also, unarticulated assumptions plague many of his conclusions—including his works, "Veto in the Security Council" and *The General Assembly of the United Nations*: he assumes that structure does not substantially determine attitude and behavior. Thus in evaluating the veto, he concludes: it is "a consequence rather than a cause of disagreements" (p. 35).

The work is comprehensive. It does not only examine the practices and procedures of the Security Council, but as they relate to every aspect of that body's relationship to other major and subsidiary organs of the United Nations. The study also reflects a familiarity with major conclusions of pertinent, recent works such as F. Y. Chai's *Consultation and Consensus in the Security Council* (1971) and Arthur Lall's *The Security Council in a Universal United Nations* (1971).

The book is well written, richly documented and amply supplied with graphs, tables and appendices. And despite the aforementioned weaknesses, it will prove very useful to all who are interested in international relations. In particular, scholars will find the suggestions for procedural changes which do not require amendments significant. Professors will find it useful as a reference and for courses in international relations. And would-be and current diplomats as well as all students of international organizations will find it instructive.

W. E. LANGLEY

Boston State College
Massachusetts

ROBERT M. BATSCHA. *Foreign Affairs News and the Broadcast Journalist*. Pp. v, 254. New York: Praeger, 1975. $15.00.

There are those among the journalism profession who would argue strongly that news is something specific, definable and is dealt with by the mass media. There are students of the mass media who would argue equally as strongly that news is whatever the commercial media defines it to be and that each medium defines news to fit its particular capabilities.

Robert M. Batscha in *Foreign Affairs News and the Broadcast Journalist* offers some interesting insights into the manner in which mechanical and structural considerations become the primary focus of news broadcasts and the substance and thought of the correspondent become secondary. Stories and ideas which do not lend themselves well to visual treatment, Batscha concludes, are more difficult to cover and therefore receive less attention.

Foreign news particularly suffers because of this orientation, Batscha concludes. "Too often the African or Asian story becomes a pictorial guide to the natural wonders of the area rather than a discourse on the ideas of nation-building, emerging nationalism, socialism and modernization that are the forces actually affecting these continents."

This emphasis on the visual, along with the time factors, encourages the presentation of many stories which are severely limited in duration. This combined with the cost considerations connected with reporting foreign news forces competent reporters to focus only on events which photograph well, can be told in a few words, and can be handled within the budget limitations.

Information for Batscha's study was obtained through extensive interviews with foreign correspondents, producers and executives of the three United States commercial television networks. He concludes that foreign correspondents generally deserve admiration for the professional work and the limitations of broadcast news lie much more with the producers than the reporters. He finds that many producers have faulty understanding of the news functions and the affected audiences.

If those providing the daily television news fare for the nation understand the functions and implications of providing information to the nation, then the Batscha study offers some interesting insights. Unfortunately, scholars who are not practicing television correspondents or producers have been little consulted or used in this attempt to gain an understanding of how the networks relate foreign happenings to an American audience.

WILLIAM E. AMES

University of Washington
Seattle

DAVID CARLTON and CARLO SCHAERF, eds. *International Terrorism and World Security*. Pp. 332. New York: Halsted Press, 1975. $19.75.

FRANK BARNABY and RONALD HUISKEN. *Arms Uncontrolled*. Pp. xiii, 232. Lawrence, Mass.: Harvard University Press, 1975. $12.50

The Carlton and Schaerf book contains the twenty papers presented to the fifth course at the International School on Disarmament and Research held in Urbino, Italy, during the summer of 1974. Four major topics provide the foci within which the contributors concentrate, namely, international terrorism, the arms race, European and Middle East security, and, peace teaching and the study of conflict.

Three themes comprise the focus on international terrorism; international terrorism in its historical context; the problem of definition; and, how to deal with terrorism. Efforts at deterrence and control by the world and regional communities have been agonizingly slow. While it is obvious that the legal solutions proposed will curtail certain of these nefarious activities the mélange of underlying motives appears to be seeded in political causes. Existent gray areas in the legal solutions offer little prospect of eliminating such behavior.

The second and third main foci concern the arms race, nuclear weapons, the diffusion of nuclear technology, European security and the Middle East question. Herein the reader explores major power deterrence and minor power proliferation.

One finds stimulating discussion concerning the potential use of nuclear weapons in Central Europe and the Middle East. A variety of arguments are adduced concerning the possible strategies. The recent American offer of peaceful nuclear facilities to both Egypt and Israel might add nuclear fuel to the ongoing arms race. This leads of course to a discussion on the merits of minor power nuclear proliferation for peaceful purposes and the dangers of nuclear weapons proliferation. There are problems underscored which accompany the spread of nuclear technology including the dangers of clandestine production, potential diversion of fissile material and the danger of theft of fissile material. An analysis of the unilateral disarmament, the NATO consultations during and after the Arab-Israeli October 1973 war, arms control in the Mediterranean and compromise solutions so as to denuclearize and limit proliferation are ably presented.

Because of the affinity of subject-matter in the second book under review, I digress to its contents. The data in *Arms Uncontrolled* are based on the publica-

tions of the Stockholm International Peace Research Institute. For the neophyte reader first encountering the subject of the arms race, this book is an excellent starting point. For the veteran steeped in knowledge of the subject there is the update from where we have been since the end of World War II through to the ominous nuclear future. Herein is a description of world military expenditures on arms research and development, and the global arms trade. Military technology has influenced tactical weapon system development. Specific attention is devoted to the automated battlefield, antisubmarine warfare, the chemical and biological weapon arsenal, and, the recent weapon development utilized in Vietnam and the most recent Middle East war.

Recent qualitative advances in strategic nuclear weapons are described, followed by an analysis of the current debate on nuclear policies. The link between the spread of nuclear technology for peaceful purposes and potential nuclear weapon proliferation is demonstrated with the prevention of this proliferation possible through the universal application of International Atomic Energy Agency safeguards to all peaceful nuclear activities within a state. The book concludes with a review of the treaty law and negotiations to limit arms build up with a stress on nuclear disarmament.

In returning to the first title the final segment of *International Terrorism and World Security* is devoted to peace teaching and the study of conflict. I am in agreement with the sceptic's view of peace education. One encounters the amorphous concepts of peace, peace research and peace teaching, but the permutations of meaning are recognizable. There follows an explanation for the current arms control attitudes and how the public can gain a broader perspective. Finally, there is a most interesting analysis of the psychological factors and personality characteristics of negotiators. How does information in the bargaining environment influence the negotiator's tolerance of ambiguity?

Both titles are topical and of course

leave the reader to reflect upon the myriad of issues open to future resolution.

Daniel C. Turack
Capital University
Columbus
Ohio

Harry Eckstein and Ted Robert Gurr. *Patterns of Authority: A Structural Basis for Political Inquiry.* Pp. vii, 488. New York: John Wiley & Sons, 1975. $19.95.

This is a long (488 pages including index), generally well-reasoned and well-written, and highly theoretical work that grew out of an attempt to test Eckstein's "congruence" theory of political performance by members of the Workshop in Comparative Politics at Princeton University. "The gist of this theory is that high performance by any political system requires that the authority patterns of governmental institutions closely resemble those of less inclusive social units, notably those that socialize citizens and recruit and train political cadres and elites" (p. ix). It was concluded that the theory could not be tested because no adequate conceptual scheme for analyzing authority relations had been developed. The authors, therefore, first had to develop such a scheme, and this was their basic purpose in writing the book.

The book may be seen as dealing with three chief topics. The first, and surely to be most controversial, is an attempt to re-define the scope of political science. Arguing from the premise that political scientists are not unanimous about what it is they study, the authors reject the traditional structural approach as too narrow and the newer functional approach as too broad. They then propose a new approach based on the cornerstone of "asymmetric relations," that is "interactions in which abilities to produce intended effects and derive benefits are unequally distributed" (p. 9). Political relations are defined as the subset of asymmetric relations that occur in hierarchically ordered social units and that are concerned with the direction of such units (pp. 15–18). It is then said that these criteria define *authority patterns* (p. 20), from which it follows that politics equals authority patterns. The authors believe this represents "a sensible point at which a decent tradeoff between inclusiveness and homogeneity can be struck" (p.23).

If this scheme could be and were implemented, political scientists would find themselves studying some strange things indeed, namely nongovernmental authority patterns (p. 26), that is "private governments" such as business organizations, hospitals, some components of organized religion and, in some societies, the family, to name a few. Indeed, the authors assert that there are two fundamental sciences of society: (1) "economics," dealing with symmetrical social relationships, "those in which humans are equals and exchange"; and (2) "politics," dealing with asymmetric social relationships, where people are "hierarchically ordered and direct or are directed" (pp. 32–33). While such neatness is appealing, they admit that the traditional topic of international relations would fit under their rubric only with difficulty and suggest that those scholars might be better off going it alone (pp.29–30). On the other hand, other traditional aspects of politics such as bargaining and coalition formation are not to be excluded even if they involve symmetric relations *provided* those relations concern direction (p. 31).

A second important aspect of the book deals with classification. Political scientists are said to have been very "casual" in constructing their classification systems (pp.351–56) and for reform, the authors suggest "progressive differentiation," a system which parallels that used in the biological sciences.

The third and for some the best aspect of the book is its theoretical analysis of authority patterns. This is done in two parts: (1) *elements*, consisting of influence, inequality, direction, recruitment, and legitimacy; and (2) a tentative *typology*, based on recruitment (regulated versus unregulated and closed versus open), and decision rules and decision behavior (directiveness, participation, and responsiveness).

In sum, this is a pioneering book but it probably will have little readership outside of social science academics. It is worth noting that the authors have attempted to test their hypotheses empirically in the field. On the other hand, the degree to which they are obviously well pleased with themselves may not be fully warranted. The book is jargon-laden and redundant at times, and it has the expected trait of a theoretical work in that the authors attempt to anticipate all possible exceptions to their arguments and refute them in advance. Their proposed re-definition of political science raises serious problems, and the obvious reorganization of academe it would require will alone preclude its implementation. Finally and most seriously, we must ask if the study of politics as asymmetric authority patterns would encompass all about which we should be concerned, and this question need not be restricted to values alone.

WINFIELD H. ROSE
East Texas State University
Commerce

DORIS GRABER. *Verbal Behavior and Politics*. Pp. xiii, 377. Urbana, Ill.: University of Chicago Press, 1976. $12.95.

Sometimes it appears that political talk is almost as meaningless as deodorant commercials. Content seems to have been drained away to be replaced by plastic personality images and empty style. Terms such as "detente" and "escalation," "freedom" and "progress" seem to evaporate into the murky atmosphere. Lest we despair that political verbal behavior bears no relationship to actual events, this book forcefully reminds us that words help shape reality and political promises are often fulfilled. In a powerfully presented survey of social science literature derived from numerous disciplines, Professor Doris Graber demonstrates that words count in politics, that words can be counted and

that political words may often be counted upon in the real world of policymaking.

Although Richard Nixon warned us to watch what he did rather than what he said, there was a relationship between the two, however slender. The various uses to which political words may be put are reviewed in painstaking detail in this excellent book. Verbal manipulation, words as triggers to policy and words as myths, symbols, ritual, bargaining tools and control techniques are panoramically considered by the author. The whole is thoughtfully organized, including chapter summaries and a generous bibliographical essay.

This formidable collage of communications theory, propaganda analysis, content analysis, small group theory, elite analysis and semantics is not without flaws. The physiological, psychological and philosophical roots of political language are undervalued. There is a moral obtuseness in failing to observe the decline of political discourse from the *Federalist Papers* to contemporary doublespeak. In addition, it is never quite clear when political words are cues to action, substitutes for action or a form of incantation, while verbal power is frequently overrated.

Even so, this is the best work of its kind. This book should inspire many to explore further the theoretical paths cleared by the author. Increasingly, our lives are wrapped in political words and the author proposes ways to help make us masters of our words and our future. Like all good books, this changes our way of perceiving reality.

JAY A. SIGLER
Rutgers University
Camden, N. J.

JEROME H. KAHAN. *Security in the Nuclear Age: Developing U. S. Strategic Arms Policy*. Pp. vii, 361. Washington, D. C.: The Brookings Institution, 1975. $12.50.

Jerome H. Kahan, a former senior fellow in the Brookings Foreign Policy Studies program and now a member of the Policy Planning Staff of the State Department has written a very good book about U. S. strategic arms policy. The book is divided into two parts. Part One examines the issues of strategic power and massive retaliation (1953–1960); assured destruction (1961–1968); and parity, sufficiency, and SALT (1969–1974). Part Two deals with future strategic policy issues.

The author has set forth the analytical outlooks of policy planners, the strategic doctrine of military experts, and the actual size and sophistication of the American nuclear arsenal with great clarity and in considerable detail. The analysis of the complex interaction between the innumberable factors which correlate to make strategic decisions in the nuclear age is clear and enlightening, and the reader is left with a large fund of knowledge as well as considerable insights after reading this book.

It is not possible to analyze decision-making in the strategic arms field without reference to the broader aspects of U. S. foreign policy, or the external variables of general *Soviet* foreign policy and strategic decision-making. In these fields, the book is considerably weaker than in the treatment of U. S. decision-making. This is not really a very serious criticism, since the author is well aware of the shortcomings here, and in fact draws the reader's attention to them in the introduction (pp.5–6). It is true, of course, that no volume can exhaust the many fields of interaction in a problem area as complicated as security in the nuclear age, and the author has wisely decided against a *detailed* examination of the broader fields of U. S. and Soviet foreign policy, but it might have been worthwhile to do a little more than the author has done here, as an informational overview of the parameters within which decision-making for strategic arms policy takes place. But this comment is really merely a structural suggestion rather than an important criticism of the book; as stated, I find this volume to be very well researched and lucidly written—in short, a considerable contribution to our knowledge in a complex field.

The book is well footnoted and has a fairly detailed index, but there is no bibliography.

TROND GILBERG
The Pennsylvania State University
University Park

RICHARD LITTLE. *Intervention: External Involvement in Civil Wars.* Pp. xii, 236. Totowa, N. J.: Rowman and Littlefield, 1975. $18.75.

Despite the great outpouring of books about specific interventions in recent history—notably the Vietnam literature—there is a distinct lack of systematic inquiry into the theoretical framework of intervention. Indeed with the exception of Marxist theory, there seems to be no major body of thought which could be identified as a theory of intervention. The author of this treatise has directed his research toward a preliminary effort to fill this gap.

The reasons for the gap lie partly in the character of the leading schools of academic scholarship in international relations. The behavioralism approach has studied activity within a state or, at most, relations between states. Only recently have a few scholars focused on the interaction between internal and external politics. The "realism" paradigm, on the other hand, concentrates on great power relations, with only secondary attention to interventions which do not become involved in the arena of power politics.

On the basis of some preliminary study, the author had developed a series of propositions about what happens when a state is confronted with an "interventionary situation." These he tested by intensive research into four selected British cases: the intervention in Portugal (1826–28), the non-intervention in the American Civil War, the collective intervention in the Russian Civil War (1918–20), and the collective non-intervention in the Spanish Civil War (1936–39). Convenience of British archival resources dictated this choice of cases, so that critics might argue the author has in fact developed a theoretical model of British intervention rather than a general model. The trade-off for this disadvantage is that he was able to do an exhaustive study of the decision-making process in the four cases.

With the results of his research in hand, the author then revised his original set of propositions into a new set; in turn, he suggests, others may build on these with their own research into other cases, thus constructing incrementally a truly general theory.

Though a brief summary does injustice to the author's carefully developed study, it is worth the attempt because the book is not likely to be widely available to students of international relations and international ethics. His eight "propositions" are applicable only to a formally defined interventionary situation: one in which "conflict develops between the units in a bifurcated actor, creating a potential for system transformation." Intervention occurs when an outside power takes sides; non-intervention occurs when an outside power maintains relations with both sides. The eight propositions, here paraphrased at some risk to the meaning, are: there is an international norm against intervention; the intervenor will encounter internal divergence; the intervenor will define the situation as involving systemic conflict whereas the non-intervenor will define it as non-systemic; both an intervenor and a non-intervenor will seek international approval; the intervention response reflects a false consensus; in an intervention situation, decision-makers will in fact be in conflict; such conflict will increase with the costs of intervention: those originally favoring it will escalate its importance and presumed gains, while those giving it only lip-service will seek to prevent such escalation; finally, decommitment occurs when the situation is redefined as no longer bifurcated.

For each of these themes, the author finds rather convincing supporting evidence in the archival record. The result is a fascinating exercise in reasoning similar to the thesis-antithesis-synthesis pattern. It would be especially valuable if the author's model could be applied in

a similarly systematic study of totalitarian interventions.

OLIVER BENSON
University of Oklahoma
Norman

DREW MIDDLETON. *Can America Win the Next War?* Pp. 271. New York: Charles Scribner's Sons, 1975. $8.95.

Drew Middleton, distinguished military correspondent for *The New York Times* and author of *The Struggle for Germany, The Atlantic Community*, and other books, has just published a most significant study on the controversial subject of America's role in a hypothetical "next war." While the title is somewhat lurid and carries with it a dangerous connotation, the book itself is actually a scholarly and up-to-date analysis of recent developments in Soviet-American relations. The basic topic, namely the author's systematic thinking about war, is both provocative and occasionally, by necessity, unpleasant. Drew Middleton himself realizes this feature of his study and observes in the brief Foreword that the conclusions he has reached will be unpalatable to many, but that he has written "about things as they are, not as we would wish them to be." As Professor Brzezinski phrased it in a brief comment on this book: "Since we desire peace, we must think about war. Middleton's analysis is thus a vital contribution to peace."

To this reviewer one of the most interesting features of the book was a detailed and colorful survey of America's current military posture including on-the-scene observations of U. S. military forces abroad (particularly in West Germany, but also in Korea) as a general prelude to the author's theorizing about future possibilities of direct military confrontations between the U. S. S. R. and the U. S. A. The military summary not only includes excellent historical perceptions like the analysis of the "elite unit idea" (pp. 93–94), but also a sound review of the industrial backing of our military capabilities. U. S. Naval activities, Marine Corps degrees of preparedness and Air Force striking power are presented in an able and picturesque manner. In ideological terms, one of the author's principal conclusions seems to be that in a politico-military contest before us, the Soviets would be in a far better situation. "There is a controlled dissidence in Russia but no powerful opposition to the governmental or social system," observes Mr. Middleton (p. 184). He also is convinced that the Soviet Union is infinitely better prepared in most respects to conduct a war; the Russians' political and social advantages —in the author's opinion—primarily an authoritarian government ruling a basically stable society, appear to outweigh the technical advantages of the United States (p. 185). In his over-all assessment, the author feels that we could win a limited war against a weak opponent *if* the Russians don't intervene in force and *if* the American public, disillusioned as it is after the Vietnam experience, actually supports the war.

The book also has fascinating geopolitical vignettes, particularly on the European continent, which has always been one of Drew Middleton's major areas of intellectual concentration (he served as Bureau Chief for *The New York Times* in the Soviet Union, Germany, England, France and at the U. N.). This reviewer found the remark made in Chapter 9 (p. 187) particularly challenging:

Bismarck in his old age said, with singular prescience, that the next great European war would probably arise from some damned silly thing in the Balkans. This is a more complex world than that Iron Chancellor knew. But it does appear likely that the next military confrontation with the Soviet Union will be some variety of Class A.

It cannot be emphasized too often that the Soviet Union does not regard its policy of peaceful coexistence, which we call detente, as insuring world peace.

In the current nationwide debate on the pros and cons of detente, Middleton firmly and squarely takes the side of former Defense Secretary James Schlesinger. In his opinion even if detente worked, which might be very doubtful, it can never be looked upon as an insurance of world peace. Peaceful coexistence does not imply the end of the struggle of the two world systems, as *Pravda* has so often observed. Middleton discusses in detail the Soviet's current ideological-military strategy (pp. 188 to 230). Most recent events in Angola have spectacularly supported the author's prophetic remarks concerning the immediate dangers of the Soviet's pseudo-detente strategy.

This is a very pessimistic book. The last 30 pages talk about a number of obvious danger signals fluttering at various mastheads, as Middleton phrases it, including signs of military malaise among our key NATO allies. He offers a perceptive discussion of the United Kingdom, West Germany, Canada, as well as our French, Italian, Belgian and Dutch allies. This is a thoughtful book and a powerful warning signal. As such it should be carefully studied not only by the interested and specialized students of international politics but also by the top level decision-makers in the American Defense and Foreign Policy-making processes. At this crucial moment of detente in negotiations between the Soviet Union and the United States, the author's advice and warning should be taken most seriously. An important if sobering study.

ANDREW GYORGY
Institute for Sino-Soviet Studies
The George Wasington University
Washington, D. C.

HENRY T. NASH. *Nuclear Weapons and International Behavior*. Pp. vii, 172. Leyden, The Netherlands: A. W. Sijthoff, 1975. No price.

Since August 14, 1945 the problems of controlling the impact of nuclear weapons on international behavior have been a subject of constant discussion. Rather than trying to answer the question of *how* nuclear weapons actually affect international behavior, most analysis dealing with the linkage between these two subjects has resulted in prescription of what the effects should be in order to maximize national security. Certainly the Kissinger-Schlesinger exchange over defining strategic superiority and what nations might do with it comes to mind as a significant example of this approach. Nash, a professor of politics at Hollins College, is less prescriptive as he applies a problem-solving approach to explain how identification of these behavioral changes can contribute to a more stable international environment.

Using basic concepts of international relations, Nash examines the interaction between nuclear weapons and the balance of power, alliances, and war to identify how nuclear weapons have affected these concepts of international behavior. In analyzing the balance of power, he notes that it failed in both nuclear and pre-nuclear situations. And, today only nuclear superpowers can provide security for the lesser nations, but alliance security has a very high price. The superpowers undermine national sovereignty, force greater interdependence, and limit the self-sufficiency of the protected nation. Waging war is viewed through the perspectives of national nuclear deterrence and its creation of "permanent mobilization" and the unrelenting atmosphere of superpower hostility. This interaction creates a tautological impact in which "deterrence is the only available defense, security resting with the ability to deter" (p. 69). This, in turn, impacts on techniques of deterrence, particularly the credibility of using military capability.

Using three case studies, Nash considers the familiar series of talks that are a direct product of the impact of nuclear weapons on international behavior in the nuclear era—SALT, MBFR, and CSCE. After providing useful background, he distinguishes between key factors affecting each international conference: objectives of the participants, significant events in the negotiating process, and actual results through mid-1974. His discussion echoes the concern of national leaders, while dealing with national perspectives, for maintaining national security.

Nash demonstrates how relationships between nuclear weapons and international behavior have changed from the pre-nuclear to the contemporary setting, while evaluating key factors that have been skillfully used to reduce threat perceptions and strengthen national security. Result: a thoughtful book for the general reader that is adequate supplementary reading for contemporary courses in international affairs.

JOHN D. ELLIOTT
The George Washington University
Washington, D. C.

HENRY R. NAU. *National Politics and International Technology: Nuclear Reactor Development in Western Europe.* Pp. v, 287. Baltimore, Md.: The Johns Hopkins University Press, 1974. $12.50.

Henry Nau's book, while, on the one hand, highly specialized, offers, on the other, a comprehensive overview of nuclear reactor development in Western Europe. In addition, the book—and here is where it will be of greatest use to the international relations scholar—attempts to place his more specialized study within the much broader theoretical context of nationalism, internationalism, and functionalism. On the very first page, Nau introduces the two basic points which will permeate the entire manuscript: the first is that the nation-state perspective offers the best approach to understanding international technological development; and the second is that functionalist theory is not very useful in bringing about such an understanding because functionalism posits a spill-over effect and such a spill-over is not occurring in the technological area.

According to Nau, the relationship between international politics and technology "is often perceived in terms of conflict between the emerging global scope of technology and the persisting nation-state organization of politics. Technology is viewed as an ineluctable force making the territorial unit of the nation-state increasingly obsolete" (p. 1). Throughout his book, Nau counters this argument with a detailed examination of how nation-states have "sought to accommodate *civilian* technologies to national aims." His study "deliberately emphasizes the impact of national structures of interest on international technological and economic activities" (p. 1).

The book is divided into four parts. Part I is basically a review of the theoretical literature on technology and international politics. Nau analyzes two basic approaches to the subject: the first, a technical perspective, "stressing the impact of technological progress on the political and social organization of the international system." The second, a political perspective, emphasizes "the impact of political structures on the content and direction of technological progress" (p. 9). Nau is clearly drawn to the latter for a number of reasons, including "the practical utility of an analytical approach which emphasizes leadership, and the normative advantages of a direct focus on national (human) purpose" (p. 33), as well as the fact that "the nation-state is still the most powerful unit of action in international affairs" (p. 37).

Part II takes an historical view of the development of atomic energy in Europe from a national, a regional, and an Atlantic perspective. This may well be the most interesting part of Nau's book; in it, he discusses European reactions to the American technological and economic invasion, the domestic determinants of international technological interaction, the politicization of scientific endeavors, the political origins and evolution of Euratom, and the logical conclusion that, in the future, "national governments, not the Community, will be the key actors in negotiations to fashion common programs from a set of internally integrated national programs" (p. 122).

Part III is made up of a series of four case studies of European nuclear reactor projects. Fortunately for the lay reader, Nau has been thoughtful enough to include a sample five-page appendix explaining the different nuclear power systems. All four of the case studies illustrate "how internal European rival-ries continue to complicate efforts to consolidate European resources in competition with the United States" (p.211).

In the last part of the book, Nau offers a number of propositions concerning how states " 'use' scientific and technological processes to implement specific group or national purposes . . . " (p. 239). He reasons that, "until we know the saintly or selfish purposes for which men apply the advances of technology, we cannot know how to promote or parry these purposes in the interest of world peace" (p. 239). Unfortunately Nau, after mentioning this latter objective, immediately proceeds to drop it. His conclusion, then, is a rather expected one: "The expanding scale and cost of technological activities have reinforced rather than weakened the significance of national policies. . . . Contemporary international politics, therefore, reflects an ongoing tension between national consolidation and international specialization, not a unidimensional trend toward increasing global interdependence" (pp. 266–67).

Environmentalists might chide Nau for only three brief and passing references to the environmental impact of nuclear power plants. His justification— perhaps a poor one—is that "environmental considerations do not figure into the story of nuclear power development in Europe until very recently and, even then, only in muted fashion compared to the protests of ecological groups in the United States" (p. 4).

Perhaps the best statement summarizing Nau's excellent study is one made by him regarding the European Community nuclear laboratory at Ispra, Italy. He says (p. 183): "Leaving Ispra in May 1970, this writer was struck by the overgrown and unkempt conditions of the roads and landscape. In comparison to the manicured lawns of the numerous national centers he had visited, this seemed a fitting reminder of the gap between the visions and vicissitudes of research cooperation in Western Europe."

RICHARD C. GIARDINA
Bowling Green State University
Ohio

ROBERTO MANGABEIRA UNGER. *Knowledge and Politics*. Pp. x, 336. New York: The Free Press, 1975. $12.95.

By defining politics broadly ("... some matters are properly beyond politics, but nothing is beyond it inherently or forever," p. 274), Professor Unger anticipates a wide audience. He makes effective use of classical British, French, German, and Greek works to devise a theoretical framework summarized in eleven propositions (see pp. 6–7).

The thrust of Unger's thought is moral, asking where humans fit into the welfare-corporate state, how those who separate themselves from the world find meaning, and in what sense "the contemporary state might be changed ... to achieve the good more perfectly" (p. 23).

Unger's methodology is consistently linguistic, with helpful definitions, from antinomy to will. His approach is almost timeless, with only occasional analogic diversions, such as his citations from Schopenhauer (p. 156) and from Rousseau (p. 192): "When Archimedes ran naked through the streets of Syracuse to announce his findings, what he said was no less true because of the way it was communicated."

Knowledge and Politics is, in essence, a legalistic critique of liberal political theory. It encourages assessment of our thinking processes. Too often, reason is expected to be confined to one's public life and emotion to one's private activities, whereas hope should be "a form of knowledge" (p. 28). Unger stresses that men should elevate their level of concern beyond the particular to the universal, that they seek the vantage point of inter-disciplinary work (see p. 47), looking to universality as "the only kind of objectivity" (p. 34). To support viewing the world in different ways, Unger differentiates an abstract "quality of stoneness" from "concrete things" (p. 28).

In light of recent systemic changes, many international relations scholars would not agree that "the state . . . is to society what God is to the world" (p. 161) or that corporations are part of "a corporate state" (p. 175). They would point instead to a separate community role for multinational corporations, *á la* Unger's statement that "the corporation and the factory itself increasingly turn into states in their own right" (p. 185). Other comments which reflect modern society include "the control of labor is the most direct form of power" (p. 65)—consider India—and "terrorism... the seduction of violence . . ." (p. 75) —note both IRA and PLO.

The reviewer acknowledges that "to interpret the work . . .," he "looks in, as it were, from the outside" (p. 109). In doing so, he appreciates Unger's historical view of knowledge about humanity (p. 234): "Man cannot yet be fully known, because, in a sense, he does not yet fully exist."

CHARLES T. BARBER
Indiana State University
Evansville

*ASIA, LATIN AMERICA
AND THE MIDDLE EAST*

CYRIL E. BLACK et al. *The Modernization of Japan and Russia*. Pp. xi, 386. New York: The Free Press, 1975. $17.95.

It is rare to find a book written by a galaxy of experts in various disciplines on the comparative development of two major countries such as Japan and Russia. Here is a pathfinder type of work which should stimulate other comparative studies by teams of experts, as these authors suggest in their concluding chapter titled "Implications for Modernization." The authors conferred during the research and writing, but pooled their talents and are not identified inside the text as the chapters are all a combined effort.

The work begins with an introductory chapter on the "problem" of analyzing modernization through its stages, definitions, and why the two nations were selected (both began late, adopted much from the West, but retained much traditional culture—Russia the authoritarian political style and Japan a greater measure of democracy and consumerism). Part I deals with the heritage of the two nations' past—Byzantine for Russia and China for Japan, but both were selective in their borrowing and retained much native tradition. Contrasts between Russia and Japan are made on almost every page, as the topical discussion lends itself to paragraph-by-paragraph comparisons. Successively, the authors deal with the international context, political structures, economic growth, social interdependence, knowledge and education, and a concluding section.

Parts II and III, covering respectively the Transformation (modernizing decades from the late nineteenth century to World War II) and the Contemporary Era, use the same topical segments as Part I, and the conclusions of each help the reader to summarize his view of the section. In fact, the thousands of comparisons between Russia and Japan sometimes cause confusion, as there is occasional repetition and uncertainty, but the conclusions at the ends of the three major parts clarify this. Statistical tables also assist.

The wealth of data defies inclusion in any review, but we can make a few comparisons that generally favor Japan over Russia in terms of political democratization, economic and educational growth at the mass level which give Japan a greater per capita income than Russia over the past few decades, and a greater willingness to learn from abroad. The authors fail to mention that all postwar Japanese polls show that Russia is the most unpopular foreign country to the Japanese public, while in recent years the image of the U. S. has risen and that of the People's Republic of China has fallen. The authors make some flattering comments about the ability of China to learn from both their neighbors and serve as a late twentieth century modernizing nation, but it seems more appropriate to follow the book's final chapter suggestion to study the late

modernization of Korea and Taiwan, whose living standards are much higher than mainland China.

The authors claim that both Russia and Japan had effective governments of a centralized nature before modernization, which helped them progress better than many other late modernizers. Japan used more foreign help in the 1870–1914 period while Russia used them more in 1922–1938, as Stalin himself is quoted as saying in 1944 that two-thirds of all big industrial plants of the 1930s had been built with American help (p.184). It is advisable for a developing nation to take the best it can from all sources but never allow the foreign donor nation to become too influential—such nationalism was evident in both Japan and Russia, as it is in China today. The book also comments on the low service levels in Russia compared with Japan, due to Marxist distaste for service work, and every Japanese visitor to the U. S. S. R. makes the same point, although services in Japan have declined recently too. The Soviet labor force share in education and science is double that in Japan, partly due to huge Russian military budgets to the neglect of consumers—the opposite of Japan.

Finally, the book serves as a good guide to the study of other nations' modernization because of its categories and reluctance to cite Japan or Russia as models.

DOUGLAS H. MENDEL, JR.
University of Wisconsin
Milwaukee

VIVIAN A. BULL. *The West Bank—Is It Viable?* Pp. vii, 170. Lexington, Mass.: Lexington Books, 1975. $14.00.

This brief work, which raises some very fundamental questions about the West Bank of the Jordan River, occupied by Israeli forces in 1967, including that of economic viability, originally was submitted as a doctoral dissertation to the Graduate School of Business at New York University. The author is well aware of the difficulties in the use of precise terms. She observes that a country can be considered economically viable if its economic characteristics permit it to experience economic growth and rising welfare per capita.

Mrs. Bull considers three possible alternative solutions in testing the problems of viability: (1) close relations or federation of the West Bank with Israel, which she considers economically, but not politically, feasible; (2) renewed affiliation of the West Bank with the Hashemite Kingdom of Jordan, politically, but not economically, feasible; and (3) the creation of a political region or entity, in cooperation with both Israel and Jordan—an area which might include the Gaza Strip. While the latter might not render full justice to the Palestinians, the author considers it to be a step in the right direction which might lead to further constructive moves in the area.

The book opens with an introductory examination of development theory and its bearing on the economic prospects of the West Bank, an area of some 2,350 square miles, about the size of the state of Delaware. A brief discussion of the history, geography and cultural development of the West Bank follows. Then come brief chapters on the general development of the West Bank and detailed analyses of the agricultural and industrial sectors of the economy of the area, human resources and the labor force and some sociopolitical problems of the West Bank. In the latter instance, there are very brief examinations of the problems of Jerusalem, and Arab refugee problem, and the Jordan Valley settlements (agro-military) of the Israelis. The author considers it difficult to imagine any solution of the problem of Jerusalem, in view of the religious factors involved. She is also very dubious about the Israeli settlements in the West Bank area.

The author, a Professor of Economics at Drew University, first visited the Middle East in 1957, and subsequently revisited the area ten times in furtherance of her research. While Mrs. Bull discussed her problems with a number of scholars at Hebrew University, Tel Aviv and New York University, she does not seem to have engaged *au fond* in discussions with competent Arab schol-ars. Nor does her bibliography reflect extensive study of materials, archival or published, of UNRWA data. She might well have examined some of the voluminous UNRWA material dealing with economic development of the Jordan Valley, and given more attention to the development of the UNRWA programs for vocational and technical training. The questions which she raises as to viability are fair ones, nevertheless, even if precise answers cannot always be given in a complex situation like the one with which she deals. Is Israel a viable state—or Jordan—without massive external assistance?

HARRY N. HOWARD

Bethesda
Maryland

HSI-SHENG CH'I. *Warlord Politics in China, 1916–1928.* Pp. 282. Stanford, Calif.: Stanford University Press, 1976. $11.50.

The warlord period in contemporary China, 1916 to 1928 (or 1937), continues to excite scholarly attention. Three crucial issues involve most researchers. First, can anything more be learned about why the 1911 republican revolution, which overthrew China's 2,000-year-old monarchy, did not ultimately succeed? Second, can one throw new light on why Chiang Kai-shek's National Party could not better turn the chaos and strife of that warlord era to its own advantage? Finally, why were the revolutionary forces led by Mao Tse-tung able to deal so creatively with the ultimate insecurities which plagued China?

Professor Ch'i eschews all these broad approaches. Instead he studies the various military groups of this period for their own sake. All the other approaches, he claims, lose sight of concrete realities by taking one position or another on the larger issues as a basis for making sense of the vagaries of the warlord period. Professor Ch'i essays a ground-clearing operation to unearth the historical reality, a dynamic pattern of interaction among various militarists.

Warlord Politics in China is a well

written, judiciously argued, informed study of environmental factors—the differential resource bases of geography, wealth, military capability (arsenals, training, railroads) and political support—which shaped the military strife. The battles at the outset involved armies rooted in the resources of the southwest, southeast and north. Given China's economic geography, a major battlefield, camping ground, marching route and prize thus became, as Ch'i's data show, the central province of Hunan. Although Ch'i doesn't mention it, the havoc wrought upon the people of Hunan—accompanied by a worthless paper currency issue, natural calamities and war among Hunan military groups—were a major cause of the revolutionary upheavals and mobilizations which subsequently rocked the province and helped launch the Hunan peasant movement and China's earth-shaking rural revolution.

The patterns that interest Ch'i, however, are not of this larger type. There is no investigation of agricultural surpluses, depressions, world prices, and the like in terms of a variegated China. Rather, Ch'i persuasively concludes that territorially based militarists could oust non-territorially based ones, that small ones gave way to large ones, that fighting became fiercer over time, that with secured foreign loans claiming customs and other revenues, and with Chinese capital seeking security in foreign-protected areas, the financial burden of armies fell, in general, ever more heavily on the vulnerable tillers of the soil who had ever-decreasing opportunities to earn money in disrupted markets. Without my in the least questioning the importance of these trends, it must be pointed out that Ch'i often also explains warlord politics in the traditional manner—personalities, cliques, betrayals, arrogance—arguing that "the particular characteristics of individual actors must be given special attention" (p. 202).

After offering up most of the National Party's self-justification—honest, kind to the peasants, betrayed by the Communists, kept from victory mainly by the limited scale of its territorial base—Ch'i concludes by applying with caution and critical awareness a Morton Kaplan notion of balance of power to warlord China. Since China was anything but a self-contained system, since it was decisively penetrated by everything from the impact of the First World War (loss of loan money from Europe, increased power of Japan and groups tied to Japan, increased difficulty in getting European arms, increased importance of Chinese arsenals), the Bolshevik revolution (influx of Soviet advisors, weapons, money) and post war international agricultural depression ruining certain commercialized areas, it is difficult to take such a logical systematic analysis very far. It does, however, most usefully force the reader to see the maneuvers of the militarists as formally rational: "the wars were the outcome of cool-headed deliberation and negotiation," (p. 220) and the destruction of the warlord system as resulting from new nationalistic militaries which had no common frame of reference with the traditionalist militaries (p. 230). This explanation would be more persuasive if Ch'i could show that traditionalists weren't nationalists. They were.

Nonetheless, the specialist will find the difficulties of Professor Ch'i's argument matters of secondary concern. What is impressive is his command of complex detail, his evaluation of action and alliances in terms of traditional personalistic ties or China's little tradition, his elucidation of the internal structure of factions, his confirmation of the importance of the north-south distinction and much more of similar magnitude. Still, something remains of the old-fashioned "comic opera" (p. 137) view of warlords:

[D]uring the height of the 1924 war, planes of the Fengtien faction made 24 sorties in eight days . . . where large Chihli forces were concentrated. The bombs killed five soldiers, felled two trees, and partially damaged one hotel. And Fengtien even managed to lose two planes (p. 259).

EDWARD FRIEDMAN
University of Wisconsin
Madison

PETER WARD FAY. *The Opium War, 1840–1842: Barbarians in the Celestial Empire in the Early Part of the Nineteenth Century and the War by which they Forced Her Gates Ajar.* Pp. xxi, 406. Chapel Hill: The University of North Carolina Press, 1975. $14.95.

Professor Fay has written a superbly styled study dealing with "westerners in China in the third decade of the nineteenth century and of the opium war that they brought on." This is narrative history at its best and the value of this traditional sort of study is readily evident. One is able to grasp the size and scope of the early period of western penetration in China. The pulse of everyday life in Portuguese Macao and in the largely British run factories outside of Canton is depicted. The campaigns of the British war against China which was at least the indirect product of the opium trade are clearly recited.

The story of missionary activity in China in the 1830s constitutes a significant part of Fay's study. A nucleus of Protestant missionaries, British and American, established themselves in the Canton factories and in Macao, their work frustrated by Chinese refusal to allow them beyond these restrictive enclaves. Fay adds a fascinating description of the work of the Catholic missionaries. French Lazarists and the priests of the Mission Etrangères, in spite of the watchful Chinese, were able to infiltrate the inner provinces of China and minister to secret christian communities.

On the political side, Fay analyzes Lord Palmerston's decision for war against China. He argues that the British sought to gain satisfaction from China for its "unjust and humiliating" conduct in imprisoning British subjects until their opium chests were turned over to the Chinese for destruction. Undoubtedly Palmerston chose to think in terms of defending British honor. But Fay's own description of the extensive productive and commercial mechanism created for the sale of opium and the fear generated by the prospect of its complete collapse must be taken into account here. This was certainly the deeper force leading to London's decision for war. Fay might have been more explicit in linking this economic connection to political decisions.

Students of Asian affairs are indebted to Fay for the most detailed and illuminating description available of Britain's military operations against China. The naval bombardment of Chinese forts and towns, their capture and occupation, are forcefully told. The British soldier's practice of taking no prisoners foretells the conduct of later western wars in Asia. The meaning of western technical military superiority is effectively blended into Fay's narrative. Thus it is perplexing, and slightly disappointing, that Fay declines to draw any broad conclusions: "Whether the West went about the job properly, or ought even to have attempted it, is for us a moot question." My criticism, however, is that of a greedy reader who desires a more fitting conclusion to a clearly brilliant book.

EDMUND S. WEHRLE
The University of Connecticut
Storrs

STANLEY E. HILTON. *Brazil and the Great Powers, 1930–1939: The Politics of Trade Rivalry.* Pp. xv, 304. Austin: University of Texas Press, 1975. $9.95.

Stanley Hilton's *Brazil and the Great Powers, 1930–1939* is an impressive monograph. Written with limitless confidence, its arguments are substantiated by primary materials and especially archival materials well above the ordinary in quantity and quality. Not satisfied with Brazilian sources, Hilton has plunged into U.S., British and especially German archives. The research always exceeds expectations, and the monograph as a whole is a model of professional historical scholarship.

Having praised what is praiseworthy, it is necessary to point out that there will be plenty of ground for controversy over matters of interpretation. For it is Hilton's view that Vargas and his advisors, while frequently differing over particular questions, possessed a unified, comprehensive view of Brazil's developmental needs and political vulnerability. Brazil was a militarily naked, politically fragmented and economically underdeveloped nation in a world of aggressive and powerful imperialist powers. Shrewdly maneuvered national interest politics were the order of the decade if Brazil were to prosper in this dangerous world. Yet, it is over this major point of a consciously unified national interest politics that argument will arise. The problem begins when Hilton accepts at face value his evidence that Hitler's Germany was an essentially martial, expansionist, predatory nation. At the same time, he favors a generous interpretation of Roosevelt's Good Neighborliness in which U.S. reciprocal trade aims are seen from Cordell Hull's point of view as nothing more than an effort to expand depressed world trade presumably to everyone's benefit. Why then did Vargas favor a barter agreement with a menacing Germany over the liberal trade principles of a benign United States? The obvious answer is national interest, an argument which Hilton might have strengthened had he been willing to accept the imperialism of free trade insight. As it stands, the argument is that Germany offered a lucrative market for Brazilian primary products, especially low grade cotton from the Northeast, while German industrial goods, particularly military hardware, were desired in return. Of course, Brazil could not afford to forego coffee exports to the United States, but the U.S. was not willing to lose its traditional friendship and economic opportunities in Brazil by adopting reprisals. Therefore, Brazil could have its barter agreement with Germany while keeping its coffee market in the United States. The success of this policy, according to Hilton, resulted from a skillful and daring application of national interest politics. But did it? John D. Wirth in his *Politics of Brazilian Development* has argued that Brazilian trade policy in the 1930s was diffuse with different policy makers at cross purposes and with conflicting domestic pressures pulling and hauling Vargas and his Foreign Trade Council as if they were

made of silly putty. Hilton's evidence confirms that such pressures existed with the military applying the greatest leverage. Rather than consistent national interest politics, the evidence could easily lead to a Wirth-like conclusion that over-weening military influence combined with the clamor of special economic groups to force the barter arrangement with Germany, or at least to maintain it after 1935. Hilton would doubtless reject this interpretation, but the fact is that his brilliantly documented monograph shows time and again how special interests and perceptions whether they be the economic interests of such groups as coffee and cotton growers or the institutional interests of the military can be made to masquerade as quintessential national interests.

PHILIP EVANSON

Temple University
Philadelphia
Pennsylvania

JOYCE PETTIGREW. *Robber Noblemen: A Study of the Political System of the Sikh Jats*. Pp. 225. London: Routledge & Kegan Paul, 1975. No price.

Dr. Pettigrew's book is a study of political factionalism in the Punjab (India's northern-most plains state, on the frontier with Pakistan) and therefore of wide interest for everyone concerned with economic development and social change in the third world. Factional conflict—at the village, sub-regional, and state levels; within, between, and in relation of official political parties; and always for its own sake with little or no apparent ideological basis—is a widely reported characteristic of the Indian political scene, past and present. Among its consequences are frequent changes in leadership, governmental weakness and instability, and a concentration of attention and energy on the maintenance of power rather than the development and implementation of the programs considered to be central to the nation building process by most theorists. In a political system dominated by factionalism, the domain of politics is radically enlarged if not all encompassing; few aspects of individual, family, and institutional activity are devoid of political meaning and motivation. Pettigrew is not the first to study factional conflict in contemporary South Asia. But her emphasis on the linkage and generative consequences of factions at the local, sub-regional, and state level; and examination of the cultural and historical foundations of the system make her book an important and original contribution to the literature which will take its place along side two other classics: Paul Brass' *Factional Politics in an Indian State*, and F.G. Bailey's *Politics and Social Change*.

Party politicians participate in the factional system because they are Jats, and because Jats dominate rural Punjab controlling large blocks of rural votes through their patronage networks. An aspirant for state office must therefore look for local strongmen; men with large landholdings (over fifty acres, and more likely more than one hundred—the average in the area is four) and a large family; the resources; and physical power to protect them through intimidation and murder.

It is difficult to fault Pettigrew's data and analysis of factional politics in the period covered by *Robber Noblemen*. But the claims she makes for the durability and relevance of the system are quite another matter. There is superficial similarity to eighteenth century political organization, but the differences in the resources at stake and the larger context of politics are so great that they have little meaning. Pettigrew's analysis is consciously timeless, and therefore overlooks significant changes—a point made by Cluckman in his foreword, although with reference to the period 1947–60. It is difficult to trace even superficial similarities through the British period 1849–1947 (about which she says nothing). I am also troubled by the pervasive sense of insecurity which Pettigrew stresses as the reason for the existence of the faction; insecurity either from the numerous conquests or from the depredations of powerful men in the locale. Invasions often brought new regimes and new tax collectors, but there is little evidence of massive displacement of

cultivators in the last five hundred years; and little evidence from the beginning of British rule into the early 1960s of the kind of concentration of property in the hands of a few big landlords at the expense of small cultivators (the kind of men owning four acres in her area at present) that her formulation would suggest. It is well known that landlords used wealth, political influence, and debt bondage, to control others, but for reasons that Pettigrew does not reveal for the present or the past, "peasant proprietors" retained their foothold in the Punjab.

Her emphasis on family rather than caste, and the ethic of achievement rather than ascribed status is very valuable. But to state that Jats believe in equality is misleading in that their motivating concern is dominance. Equality among the Jats only means that no one is accepted as innately superior— a man must prove his claim. Non-Jats can do this as well, but only by assimilating to Jat standards.

Finally I am ultimately unsatisfied by an explanation of factionalism in the Punjab which consists of factors unique to the region—repeated invasion, and Sikh Jat ideology, social structure, and history—when factional politics is equally pervasive in other parts of South Asia. While understanding the Sikh Jats' own perceptions of the functioning of their political system is essential, there must be a more general level of explanation which is applicable to other regions as well.

THOMAS J. RICE
Denison University
Granville
Ohio

G. REICHEL-DOLMATOFF. *The Shaman and the Jaguar: A Study of Narcotic Drugs Among the Indians of Colombia.* Pp. vii, 280. Philadelphia, Pa.: Temple University Press, 1975. $15.00.

G. Reichel-Dolmatoff's book, *The Shaman and the Jaguar*, provides excellent descriptions of drug usage, and the reasons for this usage, among the Tukano Indians in the Vaupés region of Colombia. The book is attractively presented with numerous photographs which visually augment the years of serious field work undertaken by Dr. Reichel-Dolmatoff. The account is scholarly and it bridges the gap between the scientific approach toward hallucinogenic drugs of Richard Evans Schultes and the popular studies of Carlos Castaneda. *The Shaman and the Jaguar* is a clear contribution to ethnologists and researchers of narcotic drugs and their effects.

Dr. Reichel-Dolmatoff began by surveying the printed primary and secondary literature concerning drug usage among the Indians of the Americas and to the identification of narcotic substances in technical terms. The historical account of European experimentation with American narcotics includes lengthy descriptions and quotations from chroniclers and travelers in Latin America. Later, Dr. Reichel-Dolmatoff recounts his personal experiences with narcotics in the Vaupés region. This first section is filled with collected bits of information and gives the historical background for Indian drug usage so lacking in Castaneda's studies. This reader was amused to learn that many of the early Spanish explorers were not only confused by the narcotic drugs they encountered, but also frequently had difficulty distinguishing between "narcotic drugs" and tobacco.

Following this historical background, the author focuses on the major region of his research and field study—the Vaupés Territory of Colombia on the upper Amazon River basin. The Tukano Indians of this region are described as a peaceful people who frequently talk of violent vengeance but find an outlet for aggression through drugs rather than physical violence. "All aggressiveness . . . is acted out in the hallucinatory dimension . . . and tensions are relieved that would otherwise be intolerable" (pp. 104–105).

Individuals on all levels of Tukano society carefully study the proper procedures (usually drug related) for relating to others and solving problems. "Drug related ecstasy seems to have two main objectives in Tukano shamanism: to find cures for diseases and ways to punish one's enemies" (p. 103). Most important is the close association between the shaman and the jaguar. The Indians believe that the shaman can literally become a jaguar serving as a helper, protector, or an aggressor.

Reichel-Dolmatoff's major conclusion is that virtually all personal enemies and tensions among the Tukanos result from sexual problems, both imagined and real. Everything has a sexual connection. Food and sex are closely related, many animals have sexual connotations, and enemies result from sexual jealousies. Therefore, the bulk of Dr. Reichel-Dolmatoff's observations fall into a straightforward Freudian interpretation of Tukano culture and drug usage.

WILLIAM F. SHARP

Temple University
Philadelphia
Pennsylvania

FREDERIC WAKEMAN, JR. *The Fall of Imperial China.* Pp. xi, 276. New York: The Free Press, 1975. $10.95.

JAMES E. SHERIDAN. *China in Disintegration: The Republican Era in Chinese History.* Pp. ix, 338. New York: The Free Press, 1975. $12.95.

These two books are the first in a series of four in a new series "The Transformation of Modern China" under the general editorship of James Sheridan. Wakeman's is the initial contribution and focuses on the social change in China that engendered the fall of the imperial system. The period covered is from the 16th century to the fall of the last dynasty in 1911. Sheridan's book is next in the series and covers the Republican Era from 1911 to 1949. His work is also an assessment of social forces and the relationship between the turmoil in Chinese society and the failure of the republican movement. The last two books in the set, *The People's Republic of China: An Interpretive History of the First Twenty-five Years* and *Chinese Foreign Policy: A Conceptual History,* are still in preparation.

The two books under review here, *The Fall of Imperial China* and *China in Disintegration*, are essentially social histories. They are well-written, and, considering the fact that they were produced by different authors, fit together very well, not only in chronology, but also in style and direction of analysis. Both are replete with in-depth analyses of specific events and generalizations which events afford. In short, each book represents the effort of a brilliant historian, yet the two works form a well-connected one-half of the series.

Especially noteworthy in both of these books is the fact that the authors present an astute assessment of the complicated undercurrents at work in Chinese society and answer the questions why the dynastic system fell and why republicanism and democratic institutions did not supplant the traditional system. Finally, they are able to fit events in China into the framework of world events: the impact of the West is a constant theme in their presentations.

Wakeman begins with an analysis of three major social classes in China: peasants, merchants and gentry. This the author handles well; however, the reader cannot help but wonder why China's other two social classes are not included—soldiers and workers. The military played a particularly important role in events which the author narrates and analyzes in subsequent chapters. Wakeman then examines the dynastic cycle in relation to forces generated by social change and class dissatisfactions. The nadir of the cycle—the withdrawal of Heaven's Mandate—is discussed in the context of the fall of the Ming Dynasty in the 17th century and then the collapse of the Ch'ing in the early 20th century. Wakeman grasps the causative factors with ease and gives a well-done exegesis on the relationship between central governmental authority and local power in the hands of the gentry. Especially insightful is his discussion of the political system which was unitary in theory and generally confederate in practice, though the proportion varied with social stability. Wakeman concludes with suggestions why the Ch'ing

Dynasty fell when it did. He also describes the foundations laid for a new political system and offers preliminary reasons for the failure of the republicans based on the problems that existed with their debut.

Sheridan begins by describing the concept of social integration, which he then adapts to analyze the Republican Period. He elucidates the centrifugal forces in Chinese society and the degree of disunity, which, he argues, explains the failure of Chiang Kai-shek: Chiang failed to promote social integration, did not develop an ideology and was particularly remiss in perceiving the gap between city and countryside. Sheridan supplies a superb analysis of the warlords in terms of the social causes for their dominance during the period and their conflict with the Nationalists' aim of unifying China. He also presents a refreshingly objective account of the role of Yuan Shih-kai during the early part of the period. The last part of *China in Disintegration* deals with the Communist takeover, which Sheridan argues was a natural consequence of years of social turmoil and unrest, though it was in its last analysis a military victory. He gives less attention to the organizational techniques of the Chinese Communists and Mao's military tactics and greater weight to the failure of the Nationalists in the realm of ideology.

Both of these books are well-researched and well-documented. The analysis in each is directed toward explicating the fall of two political systems—the traditional imperial system and republican government. Both lay the groundwork for the Communist victory. The role of the intellectual also occupies a central position in each book. Wakeman's work embodies more general historical themes and presents a broader interpretation of social forces in China. However, this is natural since his book covers a greater time span. Sheridan's work gives greater emphasis to events and people. Either volume highly qualifies as a text in an undergraduate course in Chinese history, or they could be used together. They are highly readable and can be grasped by the intelligent layman as well as appreciated by the Asian scholar.

JOHN F. COPPER
University of Maryland
Far East Division

EUROPE

JON D. GLASSMAN. *Arms for the Arabs: The Soviet Union and War in the Middle East.* Pp. viii, 243. Baltimore, Md.: The Johns Hopkins University Press, 1975. $12.50.

John D. Glassman is a career Foreign Service Officer whose one-year leave of absence at the Harvard University Program on Science and International Affairs enabled him to research and write *Arms for the Arabs.* This timely and provocative study of Soviet arms transfers and diplomacy in the Middle East since 1955 focuses especially on the three Arab-Israeli wars of 1956, 1967, and 1973.

Glassman's thesis, propounded vigorously throughout the volume, is that Soviet policy in the Middle East has manifested the basic dilemma of Soviet global strategy: how to reconcile its commitment to support "revolutionary" and "progressive" forces with the seemingly contradictory pursuit of "peaceful coexistence" or "detente." This dualism in Soviet foreign policy has forced Moscow to seek to balance or harmonize these polar objectives. This balance defines the limiting conditions of Soviet military aid and diplomatic support for the Arabs during the last two decades.

However, this "balance" has not been static but rather fluctuating, and the fact that Soviet military involvement in the Middle East has tended to escalate during periods of increased manifestations of detente suggests that movement toward the one extreme generates compensating forces in the other direction. Furthermore, as the Soviet restraints on military and diplomatic assistance have been progressively eroded with each outbreak of war in the Middle East, the long-term "balance" has shifted toward the "revolutionary" pole. In sum, Soviet policy in the Middle East has been opportunistic yet cautious, assertive yet restrained, always striking a delicate balance between support for the "progressive" Arab states and the overriding concern to avoid open hostilities with the United States.

Although Glassman's general analysis is not novel, his distinctive contribution is the elaboration of this thesis on Soviet foreign policy behavior in a specific case study context. His detailed inquiry defines more precisely the changing dimensions and implications of the Soviet balancing act in the Middle East. Additionally, he has developed a useful methodology (explained in an appendix) for assessing arms transfers which includes (1) the number and types of weapons delivered, (2) the forms of Soviet military equipment withheld, (3) the capabilities and purpose of Soviet weapons supplied, and (4) discernible shifts, changes, and trends in the long-run pattern of Russian arms transfers.

Glassman's documentation is meticulous, as indicated by almost 700 footnotes in the 170 pages of the four core chapters. His research was based largely on published literature, especially serials and newspapers. The various Soviet organs such as *Izvestiya, Pravda,* and *Trud* proved particularly useful, as did a series of interviews with senior Israeli government officials and prominent academic figures.

The policy implications of Glassman's analysis are intriguing. For the Soviets, the main "lesson" of the three Arab-Israeli wars is that the threats of armed intervention have been effective in maintaining its credibility as the champion of "progressive" forces and at the same time forcing the United States to restrain Israeli actions. But what has the U.S. learned? Unfortunately, Glassman chose not to address such questions.

JOSEPH P. SMALDONE
University of Maryland
College Park

LAWRENCE R. PRATT. *East of Malta, West of Suez: Britain's Mediterranean Crisis, 1936–1939*. Pp. 215. New York: Cambridge University Press, 1975. $17.95.

This reviewer once had the enlightening experience of being a major participant in an all-day seminar, at the end of which, a competent rapporteur summarized lengthy observations in two minutes. Pratt's work, and he has done a lot of it, is sorely in need of such compression.

In his "conclusions" he says, "It has been argued, probably at too much length and with an excess of emphasis (and one can only agree) that Britain's pre-war Mediterranean policies . . . can only be understood against the background of an ever-deepening global predicament and an ever-diminishing margin of relative power." Repeatedly, Pratt makes the point that simultaneous potential threats from Germany, Italy and Japan forced English diplomats under pressure of a harassed and sometimes timid Admiralty to try to appease Italy in the vulnerable Mediterranean. Uncertain as were the United States and France as willing or effective allies, the fleet would have to place primary emphasis upon protecting home waters and Singapore. The far East—including Australia, New Zealand, China—had influential supporters in Admiral Sir Ernle Chatfield and Sir Maurice Hankey. The latter "presided over the inner machinery of the British cabinet and Committee of Imperial Defence." He was "perhaps the most powerful bureaucrat of recent Western history" (p. 25). He even took his vacation in Mussolini's Italy and was impressed with its order. "As a source of trade, markets, investment and raw materials the British Empire east of Suez was of vastly greater significance than the undeveloped and apparently unpromising Mediterranean" (p. 11). He does acknowledge the value of Middle Eastern oil. Consequently, after Mussolini's invasion of Abyssinia, despite adverse public opinion in England, Italy was courted. Not until the fleet had been strengthened, and that would not come fully until 1939 at the earliest, could England contend with multiple enemies.

This study deals with the innumerable ripples of the diplomatic currents of the day. Petty alarums are gone into excessively. What Pratt does make clear is that "appeasement of the Axis was in part the result of failure of the will, partly the result of over-rating Mussolini's power, but also a sober recognition of England's constricted options."

While in this apparent doctoral thesis (published in cooperation with the London School of Economics and Political Science), Pratt eschews passing judgment upon those in power, and he does stress that the British had over-extended themselves in empire. Let the United States, the Soviet Union and China take heed.

The author shows promise of being a very fine historian. However, the price of this book in terms of time and dollars is a bit too high.

WALLACE SOKOLSKY
Bronx Community College
City University of New York

S. SERGEICHUK. *Through Russian Eyes: American-Chinese Relations*. Pp. vi, 220. Arlington, Va.: International Library Book Publishers, 1975. $11.95.

In commending this volume to American readers, Professor N. Molchanov of the Soviet Ministry of Foreign Affairs in a brief preface expresses a hope that "it will enhance the understanding in the United States of the Soviet community's attitude toward one of the most important aspects of U.S. foreign policy, and thereby promote mutual understanding between our peoples" (p. ix). The idea of promoting better understanding between Americans and Russians is, of course, exemplary—whatever one may feel about detente—but whether this volume is likely to accomplish the objective is a question which we must consider. First, however, the message of Sergeichuk's volume and its format (Sergeichuk is a pseudonym of a Soviet Sinologist, trained at the Moscow Institute of Oriental Studies and author of several volumes on Chinese history and literature).

The book proceeds chronologically from the post-World War II era, with a brief glance backward to the 1930s, tracing the course of American and Chinese Communist policies towards each other. There is considerable detail, especially relating to American policy, and the bulk of it is recognizable. Once the reader surmounts the tendentious formulations that normally precede any scholarly or journalistic publication in the Soviet Union (for example "Western reactionary circles—above all, the bosses of the American military-industrial complex and the NATO militarists—are opposing with all their strength the process of relaxation of international tension . . . "—author's Introduction, p. xii) he will find few surprises in Sergeichuk's account. The revelations of the 1948 "White Paper," the Congressional debates on America's "loss" of China, the demoralization of the State Department during the McCarthy era, the persistent efforts of the "China Lobby" to preserve a pro-Nationalist orientation to American policy—all these episodes are treated in much the same way they were treated at the time in Soviet publications. In this sense, then, there are no surprising revelations in Sergeichuk's "research." He presents a coherent picture of American attitudes toward China—and to a lesser degree of Peking's attitude toward the United States—from the perspective of Soviet foreign policy. In essence, Sergeichuk sees American policy toward China softening from the time the Sino-Soviet dispute came into the open—in 1963—and therefore a conscious device to widen the split; China's receptivity to American probes is seen as evidence of "nationalist" ascendancy over "internationalists" in the Chinese party and the perfidy of Marxist leadership. Sergeichuk finds the Chinese the most pernicious of Russia's two rivals and he

misses no opportunity to emphasize the point. The reader will come away from this volume with a keener sense of Moscow's concern over Sino-American rapprochement than of the rapprochement itself. This indeed is the book's *raison d'être*.

One must question how much Sergeichuk's volume contributes to "mutual understanding" between Americans and Russians. Specialists in Soviet affairs are familiar with the rigidity of Russian scholarship in foreign affairs and follow it for the indications it gives of shifts in policy or reaffirmation of existing attitudes; the arguments used to justify policies are not, as a rule, taken very seriously. For these purposes an article by an authoritative Soviet spokesman in, say, the Party's theoretical journal *Kommunist* is more useful than a book of this length. What the nonspecialist reader of this book will find most disturbing, I think, is the dubious level of its "scholarship." It is not simply that the book lacks footnotes or a Bibliography to show where the author gathered his information—many perceptive studies in international affairs are written without these scholarly hallmarks —but Sergeichuk's frequent failure to identify crucial sources is a serious shortcoming: he devotes several pages (pp. 19–22), for instance, to a "secret conference" of American specialists on China, held in Washington in October 1949, without once indicating the source of his evidently detailed knowledge of the deliberations; he repeatedly cites journals like *Foreign Affairs* as the source of a given point of view without indicating which *author* in these publications expressed it. Indeed, Sergeichuk's persistent view of the American press is that its role is to reflect, justify and cushion shifts in official policy. "As if on command," Sergeichuk writes of the 1969 era (and the "as if" he probably thought gratuitous), "the American press began intensive efforts to persuade the ordinary American that the Chinese threat . . . was not really so terrible after all" (p. 169). Although he quotes copiously from the American media, his principal source of information, and shows a broad familiarity with American personalities—no fewer than 250 "policy makers" (government officials, politicians, journalists and scholars) are listed in his Index—he persists in seeing the American decision-making process as monolithic, like Russia's. The nuances of American policy, accordingly, the degree to which it is shaped by multiple forces and multiple interests and the compromises that inevitably go into policy-formulation are lost in Sergeichuk's inflexible analysis of inexorable Sino-American détente.

These shortcomings in the volume under review cast grave doubts on the usefulness of such studies in furthering "mutual understanding"—at least in the arena of foreign affairs. If "mutual understanding" is the goal, Soviet scholars are better advised to offer us studies in areas less charged with national interest and less susceptible to ideological overtones.

CHARLES B. MCLANE
Dartmouth College
Hanover, N.H.

HEDRICK SMITH. *The Russians*. Pp. 527. New York: Quadrangle, 1976. $12.50.

The Russians is a fascinating and very informative study of Soviet society based on the first-hand observations of Hedrick Smith, a Russian-speaking reporter, during his recent four-year assignment in the USSR.

It is an interesting book because it footnotes in a clear manner what specialists on the USSR have known for decades but which far too often is presented in a rather dry or theoretical manner in the standard academic publications and textbooks about the Soviet system. Although many of the specific vignettes Smith provides are already familiar to Western Sovietologists, many others appear in print for the first time, and taken together they provide both layman and scholar with an enlightening picture of Soviet society.

Smith's most interesting chapters describe the highly privileged class structure in the Soviet Union. In itself this is hardly a new subject. Djilas among others has written about it in some detail. Smith, however, provides specific down-to-earth details regarding such class privileges as: the extra pay envelopes given Party and government officials, the special stores for the elite with rows of chauffeur-driven Chaikas and Volgas parked in front, the highly coveted permits for travel abroad, the tickets to sanatoria or special cultural and sporting events, the right to quickly purchase automobiles or other scarce commodities, or even the ability to return uninspected through Soviet customs with suitcases loaded with prohibited purchases from the West.

What might puzzle the average Westerner is how the Soviet elite get away with such class inequities. If the United States were officially committed to the sort of economic equality that the USSR professes to have already achieved, it would be very difficult to hide the wealth and privileges of America's well-to-do from the rest of society. Russian elite classes, unlike their Western counterparts, however, lead lives of sheltered rather than conspicuous consumption. Access to stores selling luxury goods is only by special permit. The opulent life-styles in the U.S. that can be easily seen on a visit to New York's Fifth Avenue are not readily visible in the USSR. Russia is still a closed society, not just to Western observers but to the Soviet population as a whole. This is perhaps why, as Smith so aptly notes, the Soviet masses are not greatly perturbed by the privileges enjoyed by the Soviet elite—in most cases they don't even know anything about them.

Much attention is given in the West to the travails of Soviet dissidents. Unfortunately, for most Western readers, this term has usually meant Solzhenitsyn, Sakharov and perhaps Medvedev. After that, general Western knowledge on this subject is quite vague. Smith's book helps to fill this information gap by explaining why dissent is not really very widespread among ordinary Russians and why lesser-known dissidents find it difficult to survive as successfully as their internationally famous colleagues who rely heavily on Western public opinion for support and protection from the KGB. Given the all-encompassing controls by the Soviet government over employment, education and other key aspects of life, the lesser-known critics of the Soviet regime are in danger of losing their residence permits or even the very means of economic sustenance when they speak out. It is no wonder, therefore, Smith points out, that so many Soviet dissenters emigrate internally, reserving their honest criticism for private gatherings with trusted friends, while at the same time learning to survive by outwardly conforming to the demands of the Party.

I was somewhat disappointed that a book of this scope and size, relying as it does so much on personal interviews and word-of-mouth comments by knowledgeable Russians, devotes so little space to the question of who might be the future Soviet leaders. Admittedly, as Smith states, many thinking Russians blot out of their minds topics that intrigue Kremlinologists, namely who is on the way up or who will succeed Brezhnev; but surely some of the people Smith talked to had interesting and worthwhile opinions regarding the next generation of Soviet leaders. It would have been fascinating to learn what some of Smith's sources thought about Romanov, Dolgikh, or even Andropov, whom Smith refers to as the most intelligent of the current Politburo members.

One could continue for quite some time commenting on Smith's excellent study, for it is broad in scope and rich in the sort of details that help clarify some of the questions that many Americans have about the Soviet system. One last comment in this regard may be worthwhile. Smith's book helps to deflate some of the more optimistic rhetoric that has been recently emerging to the effect that détente is having a liberalizing impact upon the Soviet system. This, he points out, is not necessarily so. Too many other factors prevent rapid change from taking place in Soviet society. Cultural and social traditions inherited over the centuries combined with the totalitarian control that the Party cur-

rently maintains over Soviet society play a key role in impeding Western-type democratization of the USSR. "The weight of the Russian past on the Soviet present," Smith concludes, is still very powerful.

ANDREW SWATKOVSKY
Hubbardsville
New York

DALE VAN KLEY. *The Jansenists and the Expulsion of the Jesuits from France, 1757–1765.* Pp. ix, 270. New Haven, Conn.: Yale University Press, 1975. $15.00.

It is the thesis of this carefully researched and well-argued book "that it was the Jansenists who principally engineered the suppression of the Jesuits in France, and that they did so at least partly because of their Jansenism," (p. ix) rather than the expulsion being a victory of the Enlightenment over traditional religion. As the book unfolds, Van Kley shows how Jesuit and Jansenist developed in seventeenth-century France as two distinct versions of Catholic piety and morality; how they conflicted over the doctrine of grace; how there arose a convergence of interests between Jansenism and the Parlement of Paris built upon their common anti-Jesuitical Gallicanism; and how all of this shaped into a bitter attack which publicized charges against the Jesuits of blind obedience, tyrannicide and moral laxity which had long circulated, leading finally to the expulsion of the Jesuit order by the Parlement of Paris and many provincial parlements, the king finally acquiescing because he feared to antagonize a court which exercised considerable control over his finances. The last chapter recounts the attempt by one of the philosophes, D'Alembert, to claim credit for the destruction of the Jesuits and the Jansenist response.

There perhaps still remains some question whether a strong enough case has been made for the distinctly "religious" Jansenist character and motivation of the latter phases of the anti-Jesuit activity of the Parlement, a matter of importance for the initial thesis; however, the book is to be commended for the skill with which it threads its way through the complex interconnections of politics and religious faith, avoiding the temptation to subsume either under the other—like some other important recent works of religious history, it takes theological ideas seriously and tries to determine their sociopolitical impact. The long first chapter is an excellent introduction to the early history and theology of Jansenism, though one might argue that the description of probabilism (p. 16) is a bit oversimplified or that it is not quite accurate to describe Calvinism as a revolt against humanism (pp. 9–10)—the relationship of Calvin and even of some later phases of Calvinism to Renaissance humanism has received significant revision of late.

Of greatest interest to this reviewer because of its ramifications for the understanding of the religious history of the eighteenth century as a whole is what the author has to say about the relationship of Jansenism to the Enlightenment. At least since Robert R. Palmer's *Catholics and Unbelievers in Eighteenth Century France* we have been made conscious of a greater complexity in the French Enlightenment than older views of enlightened philosophe versus benighted churchman would suggest, with especially the Jesuits playing an ambivalent role in the Age of Reason, not surprising granted their optimistic view of man's nature and reason. But Van Kley detects an important influence of the enthusiastic religion of the Jansenists in the bringing down of the ancien régime, especially as it was a force shaping and publicizing to the masses anticlerical ideas; where the interests of philosophes and Jansenists converged they could make common cause, as in the destruction of the Jesuits. As studies in Methodism in England and evangelicalism in the American colonies have recently shown, the sometimes revolutionary changes in European society and culture which we have routinely associated with the Enlightenment also had an important component of pietistic and enthusiastic religion within them, often providing a popular base they

would not otherwise have had, and now we should begin to consider the Jansenist influence in pre-Revolutionary France in the same light.

DEWEY D. WALLACE, JR.
George Washington University
Washington, D. C.

JOHN P. VLOYANTES. *Silk Glove Hegemony: Finnish-Soviet Relations, 1944–1974.* Pp. xiii, 208. Kent, Ohio: Kent State University Press, 1975. $10.00.

Professor Vloyantes sets out to define and illustrate a concept of the "soft sphere of influence," using the example of the Soviet Union's relations with Finland since World War II. His treatment is straightforwardly chronological, and focuses on a number of instances, such as the "nightfrost" of 1958 and the "note crisis" of 1961–1962, in which strain appeared in Finnish-Soviet relations, and in which the principles underlying the "soft sphere of influence" were put to the test.

Now, if the author had confined himself to the writing of history, all would have been relatively well, even though his research plan is asymmetrical, including detailed interviews with Finnish leaders and journalists, but none on the Soviet side. The facts are accurate as far as I can see and logically laid out. If one is interested in "Nordic" diplomacy and in the mechanics of the Cold War one will find this book sound and interesting enough. However, anyone who lays claim to the role of "scientist," political or any other kind, assumes an obligation to quantify and measure which Professor Vloyantes has made no attempt to fulfill. The concept of "spheres of influence" is a slippery one: after all, it might be claimed that the American sphere of influence extended to the Soviet Union (vide the release of Solzhenitsyn and others), or that the Soviet sphere of influence extended to Washington (vide President Ford's failure to receive Solzhenitsyn). Vloyantes defines spheres of influence as a manifestation of imperialism, which in my view is an unconscionable stretching of terms: imperialism must have an economic content, otherwise it is only a curseword.

In brief, this is an interesting and useful work (in a very limited way) but it is misleadingly labelled.

STEPHEN P. DUNN
Highgate Road Social Science Research Station
Berkeley
California

UNITED STATES

MICHAEL LES BENEDICT. *A Compromise of Principle: Congressional Republicans and Reconstruction, 1863–1869.* Pp. 493. New York: W.W. Norton, 1974. No price.

"Radical Reconstruction" was that program of legislative regulation, military occupation, and constitutional prescription by which a Republican Congress, in the five years after Appomattox, attempted to impose a "new deal" for southern black Americans on the defeated Confederacy. Embodied in Congressional statute and the 14th and 15th amendments, "Radical Reconstruction" reflected a desire to protect the ex-slave against exploitation and terror in a South which seemed bent on reducing him if not to actual slavery at least to social and legal subordination and economic dependency. A bold, even visionary attempt to create a more racially just and equal society, "Radical Reconstruction" was sabotaged by President Andrew Johnson who for two bitter years worked stubbornly to destroy the program by nearly every executive resource at his command. Although yielding at last in order to escape conviction by the Senate for "high crimes and misdemeanors," Johnson, by the very process of his obstruction, so encouraged and so aroused hostile Southern opposition that the final defeat of "Radical Reconstruction" by a white supremacist South became only a matter of time.

In this detailed study of Congressional Republicans and Reconstruction, Michael L. Benedict shows once again how re-examination of familiar subject matter can yield new information. An assistant professor of history at Ohio State University, Benedict is the author of the well-known study, *The Impeachment and Trial of Andrew Johnson,* which attracted such interest during the impeachment hearings on Richard Nixon. An outgrowth of the author's Rice University dissertation written under Harold Hyman, this book is too heavy with data and too technical to reach the same general audience. Nevertheless, it will interest Reconstruction specialists and political scientists whose field is Congress or the Presidency.

Using scale analysis and other statistical techniques as well as traditional research, Benedict has unearthed a mass of information about the composition and political behavior of Congressional Republicans. Two themes emerge from his densely packed discussion. First, most Republicans—"Radicals," "Moderates," and "Conservatives" alike—were much closer in sympathy towards the black man than has commonly been realized. Discounting Thaddeus Stevens, Charles Sumner, and Benjamin Wade who championed land distribution and public education for blacks, most Republicans across the political spectrum did favor at least equal legal and political rights for freedmen. At the same time "Moderates" and "Conservatives" feared that their party (with whose fortunes they identified a successful Reconstruction) might lose control of Congress to the Democrats if they went too far too fast and were far less militant in pressing for action than their "Radical" colleagues. Second, "Radical Reconstruction" as it finally became incorporated into concrete legislation and constitutional amendment was far more the creation of "Moderates" and "Conservatives" than of "Radicals." Less stern and far-reaching than "Radicals" would have liked, such laws as the Civil Rights Act, the Second Freedman's Bureau Act, and the Military Reconstruction Act, as well as the 14th and 15th amendments, were enacted by "Moderates" and "Conservatives" *after* they realized the extent of Southern white exploitation and terror of the black man, after their break with Johnson, and after they realized that they must do something to protect Southern blacks against a resurgent white South and an obstructionist president.

These themes, summarized but not developed in Benedict's *Impeachment and Trial of Andrew Johnson,* here receive extensive and detailed elaboration. On the subject of Johnson's impeachment itself, the present book also affirms conclusions reached in the previous study. By systematically obstructing and nullifying "Radical Reconstruction," Johnson drove a reluctant and frustrated Republican majority into impeachment and near-conviction. More explicitly than any previous historian, Benedict has shown in these two books that Johnson's Congressional impeachment managers were not "mad dogs" thirsting for revenge on a hated president, but principled, well-meaning men who were convinced that Johnson, in his war against Congressional Reconstruction, had violated the Constitution, his oath of office, and federal statute. As Benedict shows convincingly, they had a good case, much stronger indeed than any historian before him had recognized.

ROGER H. BROWN
The American University
Washington, D. C.

W. AVERELL HARRIMAN and ELIE ABEL. *Special Envoy to Churchill and Stalin, 1941–1946.* Pp. xii, 595. New York: Random House, 1975. $15.00.

During World War II W. Averell Harriman served in several of the most difficult and taxing positions in public service. Principally, as Ambassador to the Soviet Union during almost the entire course of the War, Harriman was present at and participated in all of the meetings of Roosevelt, Churchill and Stalin and was instrumental in presenting to the Soviet Union American proposals on lend lease, war strategy and the United Nations.

In this long and involving memoir, Harriman and co-author Elie Abel make clear that the perplexities of attitude and experience that now beset the United States and the USSR were existent even as these allied countries were straining to defeat Germany during the War. Stalin's distrust of the Western powers and the Soviet Union's insecurity are presented as the primary bases for much of the Russian intransigence over diplomatic compromise at the close of hostilities and until Harriman's appointment as Truman's Secretary of Commerce in 1946.

Part of what is intriguing about Harriman's characterizations of the great leaders during war-time is his easy and familiar acceptance by each of these participants. Not only had he known Roosevelt since childhood, but in dealing with Stalin, Churchill, Eisenhower, Chiang Kai-shek and Molotov, he was accorded an almost unique position as a necessary and trusted party to negotiations.

Of particular note is Harriman's experience with Stalin, who is pictured, at least in personal and diplomatic settings, as polite, intelligent and concerned. The conflict between this description of Stalin and his acknowledged barbarous treatment of domestic dissidents is something that *Special Envoy* never reconciles. As Harriman notes, "I found [Stalin] better informed than Roosevelt, more realistic than Churchill, in some ways the most effective of the war leaders. At the same time he was, of course, a murderous tyrant. I must confess that for me Stalin remains the most inscrutable and contradictory character I have known—and leave the final judgment to history."

Amazingly with all the detail that accompanies Harriman's descriptions of leaders and events during this turbulent time, there is extremely little that emerges about Harriman himself. It is quite easy to hear the tones and cadences of his voice in this quite literate work, but there is none of the personal revelation that usually accompanies contemporary letters. Frequent mention is made of Harriman's daughter, Kathleen, and her letters are quoted to particular advantage, but there is no feeling in *Special Envoy* either for the personal problems that might have grown out of

Harriman's continued absence from the United States or for the discomforts associated with war-time life in Moscow (the latter of which George Kennan describes quite well elsewhere).

Perhaps the principal insight of this work, in addition to its analysis of the personalities and motives of the Allied leaders, is its evocation of the enigmatic character of diplomacy during this period. Negotiators were continually left in the dark as to the policies of their governments, confusion and anger were often allowed to intrude into conflict resolution (because of the fatigue of the parties) and domestic pressures frequently disrupted carefully balanced diplomatic planning. Even when good intentions existed for all the parties, Harriman insists on the inevitability of discord because of the hugely varying emotional and ideological premises of the United States and Russia.

Much of the historical account that Harriman and Abel present is of some familiarity to writers concerned with this field, but the lucidity of expression and keenness of insight presented here are far beyond the commonplace. Much of the basis for the international acrimony and tumult of the past twenty-five years, through all of which Harriman has continued to participate in public service, is reconstructed here in perhaps the most thoughtful account of the War years available.

JAMES R. SILKENAT
Member of the New York Bar
New York City

ROBERT C. MCMATH, JR. *Populist Vanguard: A History of the Southern Farmers' Alliance.* Pp. xiv, 221. Chapel Hill: The University of North Carolina Press, 1975. $13.95.

Sympathetic but not uncritical, this study examines nineteenth-century America's leading farm organization which became the wellspring for Populism. McMath sees southern Alliancemen as neither Marxist revolutionaries nor reactionaries seeking to restore agriculture's supposedly palmy days; they were "earnest, God-fearing" agrarians responding reasonably to inexorable market-place forces. Beginning on the near-frontier, they followed national traditions of voluntary associations for socializing and group help in difficult times. With few large planters and no concerted effort among impoverished tenants, the rural middle-class Farmers' Alliance absorbed many Democratic politicians, genteel agricultural societies, and more assertive small-farmer organizations alike.

Soon the order (with evangelical rhetoric and "lecturers" promulgating its gospel) came to stress producers' cooperatives in appealing to the economically pinched. This furthered rapid Alliance expansion to the Southeast and then the Plains states; it also produced difficulties. Purchasing and marketing cooperatives, perpetually short of capital, clashed with the South's established credit system. When, after arousing inflated expectations, they were by themselves inadequate to cure complexly adverse conditions, the Alliance was compelled to turn to political panaceas.

But the basically patch-work order's cohesion was more apparent than real. Genteel and "mudsill" practices differed over a proper political role; Democratic leaders opposed any hint of voter insurgency; Midwestern "southern" members and those of the rival "northern" Alliance disliked racial segregation or cotton-raisers' economic emphases; and in the South struggles for domination between Lafayette Polk and Charles Macune rent the organization. Its dream of a classless rural society proved unrealizable.

Macune's remedy was his famed "sub-treasury plan." Endorsement of it was made the test for political candidates desiring Alliancemen's votes in 1890, and through pressure within the Democratic party the plan's proponents seemed briefly to triumph in southern elections. Party chieftains, however, denounced the proposal, gentleman farmers were dubious, and the national convention rejected it. While Macune fought to keep the Alliance non-partisan, to many a third party appeared the only answer. In short, Populists siphoned off thousands of members and replaced the order as focus for reform; Alliancemen unable to break with their Democratic heritage also lost interest in the organization. Not enough farmers supported Populism in 1892 to carry the South; the decimated Alliance saw even cooperatives dying, and drifted into desuetude.

McMath's work portrays the organizational basis for Populism, together with a major explanation for its failure. The volume shows the revivalistic fervor permeating both Alliance and Populist movements, rescues multitudinous names from near-obscurity, and demonstrates how sober, essentially logical agrarians were reluctantly swept into political dissidence. Scarcely easy reading despite a certain lucidity of style, its significance for students of Populism seems indisputable.

DONALD H. STEWART
State University of New York
Cortland

CLARK R. MOLLENHOFF. *Game Plan for Disaster: An Ombudsman's Report on the Nixon Years.* Pp. 384. New York: W.W. Norton, 1976. $9.95.

The deluge of Nixon-Watergate books flooding the marketplace obligates each new author to justify yet another version. There ought to be some claim to originality, rather than mere novelty, based either on significant new information or insights gleaned from a unique personal or theoretical vantage point. Unfortunately, Mollenhoff's report is basically a journalistic expose of what has already been well exposed. However praiseworthy its passionate plea for openness and honesty in government, the book adds little to our knowledge of the Nixon administration and offers no new theories on why it came to such a sorry end.

The ironic novelty offered in the first third of the book is a report on Mollenhoff's service as an "ombudsman" for the president between 1969 and 1970. His assignment was to keep the administration honest by investigating past and potential scandals and reporting his findings to the president for remedial action. Hampered in his work and unable to penetrate "the Berlin Wall" surrounding the president, Mollenhoff resigned in disillusionment. The remainder of the book is given to superficial accounts of miscellaneous affairs and the Watergate story.

The thesis is that secrecy and executive privilege lead to disaster, if not dictatorship, while honesty and openness lead to success and good government. But the analysis of secrecy is anecdotal and does not extend, for example, to some of the administration's more subtle efforts to buttress "national security" secrecy with judicial and legislative underpinnings through the unprecedented prosecution of Daniel Ellsberg and Anthony Russo and the Nixon-Mitchell secrecy proposals incorporated in the pending Criminal Justice Reform Act. After a dreary and somewhat disjointed recitation of scandal after scandal which almost defeats any hope for believing that honesty can ever become public policy, Mollenhoff abruptly concludes that: "Unless we establish a statutory independent ombudsman, a permanent special prosecutor, and an office of congressional legal counsel, this nation could be easy prey for a president set on dictatorship."

JOHN KINCAID
Temple University
Philadelphia
Pennsylvania

WILLIAM E. NELSON. *The Americanization of the Common Law: The Impact of Legal Change on Massachusetts Society, 1760–1830.* Pp. viii, 269. Cambridge, Mass.: Harvard University Press, 1975. $14.00.

This book tells of the legal contribution to, and the legal response to, the acceptance of Henry Sidgwick's dictum of 1822 that "mutability is the grand law of human life." Two "fundamental shifts" in Massachusetts culture are examined: the replacement of "essentially religious, other worldly" by "materialistic, worldly values," and the establishment of the notion that "individuals were free to choose their own values." "The law" chose to promote those "who decided to pursue earthly riches." By 1827, the ideas behind the grant to the Charles River Bridge proprietors were held to have been "generally exploded." Property was no longer merely the means of securing liberty, that it had so largely been to the Revolutionary generation: its role was dynamic rather than defensive, its connotations economic rather than political. In the 1820s, Courts tried to underwrite "rational economic planning and resource allocation," yet many cases sprang from the very unpredictability of "circumstances in the market place."

Nelson's argument is qualified by the recognition that changes were "not sharp and clear-cut but slow and, even then, only partial." Further investigation is needed to turn such qualification into clarification. The conclusion, that "the law came to be a tool by which those interest groups that had emerged victorious in the competition for the control of lawmaking institutions could seize most of society's wealth for themselves and enforce their seizure upon the losers," is extravagant. Legislation frequently lagged behind judicial ruling. The particular concerns and roles of those groups—juries, lawyers, judges, and legislators—who contributed to "the law" require elucidation. The use of the terms "community" (or "communities"), and "ethical unity," is not completely convincing: divisions in pre-Revolutionary society, which cannot be totally understood in the context of "the continuing vitality of lingering puritanical standards," are understated.

Mr. Nelson's book prompts questions and doubts about his notion of the relationship between a society and its legal 'system'. On the evolution of the legal process itself, he is superb. Changes in legal ritual and procedure are explained crisply and clearly: discussions of individual cases are sharply focused. The footnotes reveal a mass of intriguing material to which scholars of many interests will wish to address themselves. This is a most stimulating book, to be set alongside *Common-*

wealth by the Handlins, and J.W. Hurst's *Law and the Conditions of Freedom* as essential reading for students of the young Republic, and for those interested in a society's legal expression of its hopes and fears for its future.

COLIN BROOKS
University of Sussex
England

CHARLES P. ROLAND. *The Improbable Era: The South Since World War II.* Pp. 228. Lexington: The University Press of Kentucky, 1975. $11.95.

Professor Roland has produced a readable text, but not one that contains any new or unique conclusions. It has all been said before, and in one instance probably better, by George Mowry in *Another Look at the Twentieth Century South.* The South in too many ways is still the South of the nineteenth century, and the author does recognize that fact.

The book throughout leaves the reader with the feeling that the author was most careful not to offend anyone, when presenting subjects open to controversy. His twelve page chapter on the "Challenge to Racial Inequality," concludes that "The preeminent black heroes in the drama (integration) were a handful of children who first actually attended the white schools . . ." (p. 42). The truth of the statement is not questioned, but there were many black leaders (in the struggle) who deserved the author's attention. The Brown decision is considered by Dr. Roland as "the most momentous judicial decision in the nation's entire history" (p. 35). This reviewer would have expected that the author would have then gone on to give that decision its proper weight and significance.

In a chapter on religion, Professor Roland devotes twelve lines to the Roman Catholic Church. It is true that the Catholic Church has not had the influence in the South that it has had elsewhere in the nation. However, the author fails to note that integration came first in parochial schools, and that it was the Catholic clergy who decried the treatment, (afforded to blacks) long before the Brown decision. As Dr. Roland states, there are also many southern towns without a Catholic church. There are also many Irish towns without Protestant churches. Shame on both places. There are over 1,500,000 Catholics in the South—they can't be dismissed in twelve lines.

It is in the area of the fine arts that this book makes its most significant contribution. In two interesting and enlightening chapters we learn of the progress made, and of those responsible for, a southern school of writers and performers. The new architecture of the South is carefully and clearly discussed in a manner that is most interesting. The South has come into its own in contributions to the fine arts. However, Southerners have a long way to go if, as in so many instances, they continue to prefer their "folkways to the fine arts" (p. 167).

There is much to be said for this book in spite of some of its obvious shortcomings. Dr. Roland has put together a clear, well written analysis of the South since 1945. Your reviewer believes that anyone seeking a concise summary of what has been taking place in the old Confederacy could not find a better presentation than in this small volume.

JAMES J. FLYNN
St. Francis College
New York

BRUCE M. RUSSETT and ELIZABETH C. HANSON. *Interest and Ideology: The Foreign Policy Beliefs of American Businessmen*. Pp. xiv, 296. San Francisco, Calif.: W.H. Freeman & Co., 1975. $10.95. Paperbound, $4.95.

This meticulously produced book purports to explore the foreign policy beliefs of American businessmen in order to delineate the assumptions underlying the American policy of intervention abroad and, subsequently, to advance an explanation of the U.S. foreign policy. Basically, the authors have tried to explore the role of the economic motives in determining the course of American action in the international arena. The authors believe that the philosophical foundation of the Ameri-

can foreign relations is moving from long established moorings to new realities and new values thus making it imperative to focus attention on the roots of the American foreign policy. It is through an analysis of the attitudes and perceptions of the corporate executive that the authors attempt to assess "the importance of ideological and economic influences" on the structure of the American foreign relations and to determine whether the international behavior of the United States is motivated by a desire to halt the advance of communism or by a search for new markets and the need for greater investment opportunities in foreign countries.

Although beliefs and attitudes of a number of the politically relevant "elites" on several issues are identified, it is the business and the military perspectives which are examined in considerable detail. The views of the businessmen are given even greater emphasis than the military, no doubt because "many senior government officials are customarily recruited from the ranks of senior business executives" (p. 24) who are instrumental in formulating governmental policies. The authors contend that the question of the economic influence on the American foreign policy can most adequately be answered by the businessmen themselves since they are the ones who allegedly exert pressures impelling American intervention in foreign affairs in order to realize economic gains for themselves and for the United States. The authors argue that if the economic theories of American intervention in world affairs are proven true, then it is possible that under appropriate conditions of cost/benefit ratio intervention could be expected again, and perhaps even rivalry in international relations in the future with some economically motivated major power.

Collecting data through a variety of methods, guided in their endeavors by a conceptual framework, the authors find the military, on the whole, to be consistently and predictably more hawkish on the intervention issue than the businessmen. The business espousal of an expansionist and aggressive foreign policy is discounted, because, the authors claim that on the basis of their data the analysis shows that "the support for the economic interest theories, the relative explanatory power, when compared with that of strategic and ideological theories, is not impressive" (p. 250).

Although the authors have tried to refute the economic motivation argument as a basis for the American intervention abroad, the evidence they have presented on this issue seems to be less than clearcut. As a matter of fact the authors even acknowledge that "the needs of a capitalist system probably do make *some* contribution to producing an activist, globalist, interventionist United States foreign policy" (p. 252). This is all the more confusing when the authors conclude that they did not "find substantial economically based enthusiasm for Vietnam or other military interventions at any point during the cold war" (p. 264). The international behavior of the United States could really be understood, argue the authors, through an ideological explanation, rather than an economic one. In their estimation, then, the cause of the American action abroad is due not to the pursuit of economic advantages but a crusading desire to turn the tide of communism.

This is indeed an interesting volume, both for its substantive discussion and its use of sophisticated scientific methodology for the collection and analysis of data within a theoretical scheme. As a thoroughly detailed empirical study this monograph is not for the light reader; though the careful student of world affairs would find in it a significant contribution towards an understanding of the American foreign policy.

GHULAM M. HANIFF
St. Cloud State University
Minnesota

DWIGHT C. SMITH, JR. *The Mafia Mystique*. Pp. 400. New York: Basic Books, 1975. $15.00.

The Mafia Mystique by criminologist Dwight C. Smith is a 400 page tour-de-force exposition of the evolution of the Mafia image in America. Starting with a detailed accounting of the origins of the Mafia in post-feudal Italy and its subsequent arrival in the United States, Smith convincingly shows how various agencies of government as well as a cadre of public prosecutors, investigators, scholars and literary figures (whom Smith describes as "moral and literary entrepreneurs") sought to foist the Mafia image upon a reluctant public as a catch-all label for organized crime. In rank order, the author levels indictments for perpetuating the Mafia imagery against the Federal Bureau of Narcotics (FBN), The Kefaufer and McClellan Senate Committees, The Crime Commission Report and Mario Puzo whose bestseller *The Godfather* is credited with elevating the label to a high vogue. Their reasons for doing this were, according to Smith, self-serving. Thus, the FBN needed to blame their failure to control narcotics traffic on a "supercriminal" organization with international ties; the Justice Department needed legislation for wire tapping; the novelists and pop-historians needed a topic to sensationalize. In each instance, therefore concludes Smith, the Mafia image was a convenient rubric under which a variety of expressions of crime could be subsumed.

Readers primarily interested in discovering once and for all if the Mafia is real or not and whether it poses a formidable threat to the nation will find Smith's answer in the last part of the book. It is not an unequivocal answer to be sure; however, after assessing the evidence from the three sources (moral entrepreneurs, literary entrepreneurs and scholars) of our present-day images of crime, he concludes that three-quarters of what has been written or said about the Mafia and organized crime has been "noted for its emotional content rather than its disciplined objectivity." Though Smith sees the noted sociologist-criminologist Cressey as standing on the periphery of this indictment, the recent scholarly works of Albini and Ianni are credited with turning the tide of our thinking about organized crime from the stereotype Mafia images to a more plausible and easily substantiated view of organized crime as a reaction-formation of immigrants, many of whom, incidentally, came from Sicilian backgrounds, who turned to crime because the normal routes of mobility were denied to them by a hostile society. Smith's final contention is that the real threat to the nation is not the Mafia or Mafiosi but the mania that has seized our consciousness over the last decade and has, in turn, "seized-up" our ability to bring new perspectives to the problem of organized crime. As an antidote to this, Smith proposes a new approach to looking at crime which he calls a "Theory of Illicit Enterprise."

The Mafia Mystique is unquestionably an important book and is sure to become a standard reference for serious students of crime, mass communications and ethnicity for years to come. The exposition is scrupulously documented and is replete with a jumble of names, places and events that will surely titillate the sensibilities of the criminologist-scholar but very likely tax the patience of the general reader who is not conversant with these references. Repetitiousness is, to this reviewer, the book's most serious defect: many of the allusions that are cited to explain the present state of the Mafia imagery are repeated to the point of becoming a litany. In all fairness to Smith, however, the repetition that will surely occasion some measure of annoyance to the reader may be justified lest one lose track of the narrative in the labyrinth of events and characters that are integral to his exposition. To fully appreciate the tapestry of Smith's arguments, therefore, requires a reader with a practiced capacity to store a welter of detail in his mind as he moves from chapter to chapter.

ALFRED AVERSA, JR.
Fairleigh Dickinson University
Teaneck, N. J.

ERIC VEBLEN. The Manchester Union Leader in New Hampshire Elections. Pp. xi, 205. Hanover, N.H.: University Press of New England, 1975. $9.00.

William Loeb's Manchester Union Leader holds a uniquely influential position: not only does it enjoy the largest daily circulation in New Hampshire (40 percent of the state's newspaper market), but the absence of any in-state television competition gives the Union Leader the predominant position in providing local news to the state's residents. Since New Hampshire's presidential primary is the first in the nation, the potential political impact of the paper is wider than the state. The New Hampshire primary hurt the presidential aspirations of Nelson Rockefeller in 1964, and ended those of George Romney in 1968 and Edmund Muskie in 1972. Loeb's strident editorial policy and involvement with national political figures has itself become news.

The question to be answered is, to what extent is William Loeb responsible for the results of New Hampshire elections? To examine Union Leader influence, Veblen concentrated on elections for governor and United States senator between 1960 and 1972. Examining local elections minimized out-of-state influences. Veblen conducted extensive interviews with candidates and campaign managers, evaluated newspaper coverage of candidates and elections, and studied voting patterns in these contests.

The study concludes the Union Leader has had significant impact on local elections in New Hampshire (and possibly on national elections). In some cases, candidates have decided to run or not to run based on the paper's support or opposition. The paper's impact may be negative, supporting weak candidates to primary victories and general election defeats. But the Union Leader has been able to build support for previously unknown candidates. Campaign planners believe that the paper has a wide influence, and strategy is conceived and executed with Loeb in mind. To some extent Loeb is able to define issues, and to focus public attention on some issues to the exclusion of others. For example, Loeb's opposition to sales and income taxes have made that issue a major one in every local election from 1960 to 1972, never as "tax reform," but always as "vetoing new taxes."

Veblen's study is thoroughly researched and well documented. Informative appendices reinforce the narrative and provide the statistical backing for the voting analysis. His subjective judgments on the content of newspaper stories and editorials are supported by numerous examples. The author has accomplished a very difficult task: he has provided an even and unemotional account of a very controversial figure and newspaper.

DONALD B. SCHEWE
Franklin D. Roosevelt Library
Hyde Park, N. Y.

SOCIOLOGY

GENE E. CARTE and ELAINE H. CARTE. *Police Reform in the United States: The Era of August Vollmer.* Pp. x, 137. Berkeley: University of California Press, 1975. $7.95.

In that semi-structured era between the two world wars, the ambitious reformer was an amazing triumph of vision over limited knowledge, of morality over expediency. The nature of reform, however, was highly personal, fitful, fractionated, and distressingly temporary. But an implicit strategy of reform now seems clear: a focus on specific deficiencies of urban areas.

It is instructive to be reminded that the need for revision of city police forces in the U.S. was clearly recognized and acted upon well before World War I, not by professional reformers or social scientists, but by police administrators such as the acknowledged pioneer, Chief Vollmer in California. After almost fifty years of virtual neglect, social scientists are beginning to analyze the less visible but significant role of policemen and police organization in modern metropolitan areas.

Police Reform in the United States is a brief, sympathetic account of the once famous August Vollmer, who emerged from obscurity to become a very effective public official, educator, speaker, researcher, and consultant on crime control. From 1909 till well into the 1940s,

Vollmer either initiated or forcefully advocated numerous changes in law enforcement. Among these were: effective separation of the police force from "political" interference; recruitment of college students to the police profession; the development of a central record-keeping system of crimes (a precursor of the Uniform Crime Reports of the FBI); practical rather than moral opposition to capital punishment; the use of the lie-detector; radio communication in police cars; and the development of a police curriculum at the university level.

Vollmer is rarely discussed in the crowded textbooks of criminology and penology, but in retrospect he was and is important in the arduous and still incompleted process of developing police work as a dignified profession in the urban areas of the U.S. In that comparatively simple period before World War II, political corruption, limited public funds, and the insulated views of most citizens largely prevented the development of crime control systems comparable to those of Western Europe. Police in the U.S. were rather low in prestige, disdained rather than vilified or distrusted. Organized crime, stimulated by Prohibition and yet octopally powerful only after the end of war and the succeeding prosperity, became still another ordeal for police systems. Vollmer's quest for professionalism, however, probably approximated success in the late '50s and early '60s, when, paradoxically, the demographic and status complexities of urban communities were translated into tensions and violence—with understandable hostility toward any development in police "efficiency." Thus, Vollmer's ideal of professionalism is again in contention, the victim of changes he could not have anticipated.

The authors briefly discuss the dilemmas of police functions and "styles" in their last chapter, without arriving at very firm conclusions. But they have unpretentiously filled in one portion of the social history of crime control by focusing on one colorful and impressive career. In addition, they have compiled a detailed chronology of Vollmer's activities and a bibliography of his writings in various journals and newspapers.

ALVIN BOSKOFF

Emory University
Atlanta
Georgia

NATHAN GLAZER. *Affirmative Discrimination: Ethnic Inequality and Public Policy.* Pp. 248. New York: Basic Books, 1976. $10.95.

Glazer argues that "affirmative action," the recent government policy prescribing educational and business institutions to actively favor members of discriminated minorities in the areas of employment (Chapter 2), education (Chapter 3) and housing (Chapter 4) is incompatible with a major thrust of our historical tradition (Chapter 1) and that it favors only privileged strata within these minorities.

One doesn't see why the American tradition of guaranteeing equal opportunity to *individuals* conflicts with efforts to foster equal opportunity to *groups*, if one grants, as Glazer does, that it is part of our historical heritage to guarantee not only everybody's access to what society makes possible but also everybody's right to maintain group identity and allegiance (p. 7) and to prevent that no group becomes subordinate to another (p. 5). Should a purely individualistic interpretation of our Constitution prevail, it would certainly be too restrictive and not easily reconcilable with our tradition, since differential group opportunities in the long run undermine the individual's right to ethnic allegiances. At any rate, the argument which fosters *individual* opportunity and opposes *group* opportunity is highly questionable on sociological grounds, since in no society are individuals able to foster their own opportunity independently of some sort of group affiliation.

The pragmatic argument that affirmative action came at a time when blacks were making real progress under the old policy of equal opportunity seems to be undermined by the rest of Glazer's own analysis of the economic situation of Blacks (see p. 43). He argues that the previous policy of equal opportunity ensured the broadest possible political consensus in an multiethnic society and now this political consensus is threatened by affirmative action (p. 168). This argument seems to place the present form of political stability above the issue of social justice. The same can be said of the argument against the policy of affirmative action based on the presumed political backlash it has created on the part of ethnic groups (Chapter 5). The book is filled with other questionable assumptions and views, like those concerning the role of the courts and the cultural climate created by the judges, sociologists and liberal intellectual elites (Chapter 6). The book certainly proves to be a highly stimulating, although not sociologically cogent or clarifying, reading on a controversial and often confusedly framed issue.

INO ROSSI

St. John's University
Jamaica, N.Y.

JOHN HELMER. *Drugs and Minority Oppression.* Pp. 192. New York: Seabury Press, 1975. $9.95.

Drugs and Minority Oppression by John Helmer, a staff member at the Research Center for Economic Planning in New York, is "the third [book] in a series on the social and economic dynamics of class conflict in America." Based on a study commissioned by the Drug Abuse Council in Washington, D.C., the book generally explores "the relationships between broad changes in market conditions and changes in public *policy* on drugs." More specifically, Dr. Helmer looks at police crackdowns on the Chinese and opium, Blacks and cocaine, Mexicans and marijuana and concludes that class conflict accounts for the selectivity in drug law enforcement.

The main points in Dr. Helmer's interpretation of his findings may be summarized as follows. A mythology of narcotics has grown up in the United

States during the past century. Part of this mythology says that "scientific knowledge has replaced lay ignorance and prejudice about narcotic drugs. . . ." The truth is that an antiworking class bias—rather than any real threat to public health and safety—underlies America's drug policy. As one Oregon district court noted: "Smoking opium is not our vice, and therefore it may be that this legislation proceeds more from a desire to vex and annoy the 'Heathen Chinese' . . . than to protect the people from the evil habit." The truth is that middle class Americans have used the drug issue as a rationalization to keep working class Americans in their proper economic place. Evidence for this position can be found in the connection between drug crackdowns among minority groups and radical downturns in the business cycle as well as surplus conditions in secondary labor markets. And evidence for this position as a class, rather than a race, related phenomenon can be found in the drug crackdowns initiated against white, working class youth fighting in the Vietnam War.

Despite the book's brevity, Dr. Helmer's interpretation of America's drug policy is documented by a wealth of statistics, figures, tables and citations. Of special interest is his compact history of drug use among U.S. Army personnel in every American war from the Revolution to Vietnam. If the book has any flaw, it may be in organization. Some information seems out of place. For example, the quotation from the Oregon district court about the Chinese and opium (above) appears in the chapter "Blacks and Cocaine." Wherever his information appears, though, future critics of and apologists for America's drug policy will have to contend with John Helmer's strongly argued class interpretation.

DONALD J. ROGERS
New Trier West
Northfield
Illinois

CURT LAMB. *Political Power in Poor Neighborhoods*. Pp. 315. New York: Halsted Press, 1975. $19.50. Paperbound, $9.50.

In 1967 the Office of Economic Opportunity (OEO) commissioned a research organization to investigate the question of whether its Community Action Program (CAP) was bringing about any "actual change in the institutional environment of poor Americans." Three years later the results of a study of 100 poor neighborhoods, the Local Change Survey, were delivered to officials in the Nixon administration who were dismantling the OEO and cared little about the poor. The cost of the survey was over one million dollars. Since the results were ignored, it was another expensive, bitter joke at the hands of those who can least afford to laugh.

Now an unusual scholar, Curt Lamb, who manages to be both an empirical political scientist and a committed man with a heart, has come along to make new use of this study. Noting that it is "a perverse priority which gives research professionals a million dollars to investigate a policy itself starving for funds," he has reevaluated the data from the 8,000 interviews of the Local Change Survey in an attempt to reclaim some of the original promise of both the study and the whole War on Poverty. His main interest is the capacity of the poor for "political revitalization," that is, for guiding and directing the destinies of their own communities.

The resulting work, *Political Power in Poor Neighborhoods*, has unfortunately been produced for an elite. The book's complicated tables, figures, charts, footnotes and appendices are aimed at the specialist and its formidable price may keep it out of the hands of those who might most benefit from it, the leaders of the poor. Yet its results should be made available to those concerned with organizing and improving the lot of poor neighborhoods. For if it documents the dreary picture of alienation we already associate with the urban poor, it also provides some hope that change can come. A few neighborhoods under the spur of the CAP changed just enough to allow Lamb to suggest the kinds of strategies and activities that other poor communities might emulate. He convincingly documents how certain kinds of radicalism, direct action and ethnic identification have produced real alterations both in the consciousness of poor people and in the objective policies of public and private agencies that minister to them. This leads Lamb to agree that those social planners who insisted the government should support organization among the poor were on the right track. Deploring the abandonment of the War on Poverty, he concludes: "It is not social disorganization among the poor that has frustrated poverty policy, but the failure of a timid country to act."

ROBERT A. ROSENSTONE
California Institute of Technology
Pasadena

SAR A. LEVITAN and KAREN CLEARY ALDERMAN. *Child Care and ABC's Too*. Pp. vii, 125. Baltimore, Md.: The Johns Hopkins University Press, 1976. $8.50.

As economic, social and personal forces continue to demolish barriers preventing women from entering the labor market, provisions for day care facilities for increasing numbers of pre-schoolers will be needed. Social planners attempting to develop a structure within which this need can be met will be faced with a number of thorny problems. For example, how will child care and pre-school education be financed? What are the relative costs of plans which feature private, public and mixed financing schemes? How does one determine which services are necessary for pre-schoolers, which are desirable, and which are expendable? These questions illustrate some of the kinds of data which will be needed in rational decision-making in this pressing policy area. It is to this need that Levitan and Alderman seem to be addressing themselves.

Following a brief description of the "American child-care system," one dominated by private arrangements with non- or semi-professional baby sitters, the authors consider a wide range of topics. Some examples are trends in female employment, characteristics of working mothers, the effect of the in-creasing number of female-headed households upon the demand for child care and tax credits available to those using child-care services.

With respect to two of the major variables influencing procurement of child care, availability of care and cost, the authors find a general preference for informal rather than institutional care and they find that child care is relatively expensive for the working mother. The informal situation apparently provides greater flexibility and economics than the more formal. The cost of child care is higher for the middle income families than for low income families because of the availability of public aid for the latter.

In the final chapter, a growing use of child-care facilities is predicted and the future needs are considered, among them public support of these facilities. The authors expect that demand for informal baby-sitting arrangements will outstrip supply, hence the need for more high-density centers. Local school systems may be in a position to absorb part of this function, especially since the dropping birth rate might otherwise lead to major employment cutbacks in primary and secondary schools.

Levitan and Alderman have produced a well-written and nicely organized book. It is largely a catalog of empirical data garnered from public documents such as special reports from the Bureau of the Census and the Department of Health, Education and Welfare. This emphasis will be applauded by those writing policy and grant proposals. General readers, however, will find this book of limited interest.

In summary, the authors have produced a documented and unembellished profile of the socioeconomic situation of working women, their children and the resources they call upon for baby-sitting and pre-primary school education.

THOMAS F. GARRITY
College of Medicine
University of Kentucky
Lexington

GRANT NOBLE. *Children in Front of the Small Screen*. Pp. 256. Beverly

Hills, Calif.: Sage Publications, 1975. $15.00.

Reading this book has been an interesting experience, permitting contact with a resourceful investigator and wide-ranging thinker who has aims with which it is easy to concur. The author, moreover, is in many ways unlike the typical American Psychologist, being very British in his vocabulary (a few words are quite incomprehensible) and spelling, and in his conception of what a psychologist should be, and seems possibly to be British in certain assumptions on which his conclusions implicitly depend. He is also somewhat of a rebel, to use one of his own terms, and in his urgency to oppose what he sees as stultifying traditional views advocates alternatives which seem to have flaws of their own.

The book asserts as its major thesis that in a complex industrialized civilization like that of Western Europe, the United States, and Canada, television, or TV, performs a useful, almost a necessary function. This is to provide what the "village" and the extended family provided in the past for the people of these same lands and what they still provide in many other lands: first, a social mirror which teaches each new individual how he is seen by many others and so gives him a consistent, integrated "self," and secondly, intimate first-hand knowledge of most of that society's statuses and life-patterns, into which he may some day enter. The vastly more complex society of today deprives many of its members both of the mirror and of first-hand knowledge of all but a very few of its existing life patterns. TV, however, in part provides or can provide both, and so enables modern youth to repair inconsistent or fragmented self images and to avoid social alienation; it provides models and a social context, transmits standards, and promotes comradeship and mutual helpfulness.

Noble thus in effect defends TV, including its so-called "violent" programs, and rejects out of hand the conclusions of highly regarded psychologists that it promotes violent behavior among its viewers. He champions the Freudian concept of catharsis, in this case the idea that watching aggressive TV programs discharges pent-up aggression in viewers who suffer from frustrations and conflicts, and thus usefully prevents their engaging in practical aggression, and in one chapter uses the Piagetian theory of stages in a child's logical development to explain the inability of young children to see things from another person's viewpoint or to grasp a story line as a unity, which he thinks he has observed but which TV program designers generally do not recognize.

There are many good things in the book, of which one example is Noble's tripartite classification of 37 delinquent teenaged boys in a detention home into problem boys with poorly integrated self images; rebels, who reject the self images reflected upon them by their parents and teachers, wishing to be seen as worthy, and during their teen years scornfully oppose accepted standards; and conformists. The first tend to be social isolates, the second are leaders among the boys but have little to do with their own parents, and the third, the conformists, have friends among the boys and do talk with their parents. For the first, the author says, TV provides a small community of familiar persons (characters) which gives them security; for the second, it portrays the holders of respected social positions which they hope some day to attain; and for the third it provides information about the real world and opportunity to see the funny side of life.

Noble strongly rejects the findings of research done in psychological laboratories, seeing it as too artificial to be relevant to the real world and especially to current social problems, and thus at times rejects even experiments which do use subjects and situations closely similar to those found in the community. In such contexts he at times ascribes the findings to the "demand characteristics" of the laboratory situation, but seldom mentions the same possibility or other vitiating factors in relation to his own investigations. By avowed intention, he seldom reports the significance levels of differences on which his argument depends, but this practice robs him to some extent of ability to convince a skeptical reader. In at least one case the table representing his findings so lacks clarity of meaning as to disprove the supposed superiority of tables in ability to communicate.

The possibility that Mr. Noble is British also in some of his assumptions is suggested to this reviewer by his general approval of the TV programs whose effects on viewers he investigates. In one passage he does speak unfavorably of United States television programs, saying that they simply use Hollywood methods and do not depict life situations as they really are, but in general he seems to see only desirable qualities in the TV programs for children with which he deals, including those watched by his delinquent adolescents. This may be because in Britain at least, and perhaps in Canada and Ireland where many of the field experiments he reports were conducted, public television is much more dominant and TV is more oriented to benefiting child viewers. Certainly this reviewer has seen in the U.S. too many blatantly commercially motivated programs and programs seemingly designed to attract mass audiences to particular TV stations for advertising purposes, to feel that children are chiefly benefited by watching. Noble regrets the affluent surroundings seen in TV programs by viewers who do not share in such affluence, but seems entirely unconcerned about the sentimentalized family life or tawdry affairs of the heart, or about the violent criminality and self-righteous activism of the law enforcers, which may or may not serve as guides to their child viewers' own future behavior but which (in the U.S. at least) are apparently taken by these viewers as true depictions of the surrounding society.

The book is bound in a material which immediately shrinks, so that the book will not lie flat, a fault of the publisher's, but it has also an excellent index and an extensive bibliography which includes many American references. Especially it does discuss real and important issues and does illustrate the advantages of the newly acquired right of psychologists even in America to take account of inner experience and to deal openly with cognitive processes and feelings. It can also introduce its readers, through its bibliography and citations, to many writers and publications generally unknown to Americans.

ELIZABETH J. LEVINSON
American Board of Professional
  Psychology
Orono
Maine

DAVID J. O'BRIEN. *Neighborhood Organization and Interest-Group Processes.* Pp. ix, 263. Princeton, N.J.: Princeton University Press, 1976. $13.50.

RUTH R. MIDDLEMAN and GALE GOLDBERG. *Social Service Delivery: A Structural Approach to Social Work Practice.* Pp. 233. New York: Columbia University Press, 1974. $10.00.

O'Brien's study is a highly welcome, sympathetic but sober review of efforts to organize the urban poor in their own behalf. He develops a carefully reasoned theoretical framework and posits a number of critical issues with which organizers are confronted. The urban applications of the community development approach, the social action and protest strategies of Saul Alinsky, and the federally initiated community action program are reviewed.

O'Brien draws heavily from economic theory in posing a central dilemma confronted by organizers. A potential neighborhood organization may be able to achieve collective benefits but the benefits are largely indivisible. If self-interested individuals are to be induced to contribute to a collective effort, additional divisible incentives must be offered. Analyzing American labor union history, O'Brien observes that, only when federal legislation made it legitimate for unions to use coercion as an incentive for membership, were unions able to achieve mass membership. O'Brien is also impressed with the resource problems which face the poor when they attempt to organize. Compared to the society at large, they have limited resources to pool and, consequently, limited potential benefits to offer to those who join their cause. O'Brien also notes that in some instances where organizations of the poor have found a way to be responsive to needs of their constituencies, they have been readily outflanked subsequently by large corporations or units of government which were able to offer richer services in the same domain.

Although the book is primarily theoretical and analytic, O'Brien concludes by offering some advice. If neighborhood organizations are to gain substantial resources or if they are to gain the legitimation needed to use coercion in seeking membership, it is essential for them to make themselves attractive to organizations of the larger society which control the resources and legitimacy which they need. O'Brien is intrigued by limited decentralization of government which would give neighborhood groups control over services such as recreation and peace-keeping aspects of police work. Voucher systems for education and other forms of local service are also suggested. Above all, O'Brien urges that local organizations find ways to offer immediate benefits to individuals with diverse private interests. In making these suggestions, O'Brien is guided by a keen sense of intellectual honesty which obliges him to acknowledge problems which must be expected by those who pursue the directions he recommends.

The study can be faulted for missing some fertile areas such as experiences of urban political machines in building neighborhood constituencies and illegitimate development of local power based on the provision of such attractive services as drugs, gambling, and prostitution, reinforced by protection schemes. In reviewing a broad range of organizing efforts, O'Brien often draws

sharp interpretations of complex events about which complete information is not available. It will be argued, consequently, that some of his inferences from the case material are forced and exaggerated.

The struggle to develop and refine institutions which permit effective response to local concerns, particularly on the part of the poor, in a society in which money and communication are increasingly centralized, is a basic issue in an urban society. O'Brien's study is a major contribution to the literature on this theme.

Middleman and Goldberg offer an introduction to social work practice which is an indicator of the ferment and change which have taken place in recent years in social work education and practice. Their thesis is that social work practice should be seen as intimately linked to issues of social structure and social policy. Fundamentally, they see that social work practice can be organized according to four major categories: (1) Direct work with "sufferers" in their own behalf, (2) Work with "non-sufferers" out of concern with a specific "sufferer," (3) Work with specific "sufferers" in behalf of a category of "sufferers," and, finally, (4) work with "non-sufferers" in behalf of a category of "sufferers." The underlying premise is that individual problems are a reflection of alterable social conditions. The perspective urges workers to be concerned not only with the alleviation of the problems presented by individuals, but with the conditions which underlie the problems and which also affect unseen sufferers. Consequently, changes in the structural conditions which lead to individual suffering are as much the business of the social worker as the alleviation of individual problems.

Middleman and Goldberg's perspective is, of course, conventional wisdom for sociologists, economists, and political scientists, but it reflects an important change of direction for a field long dominated by a concern with individual adjustment and based on psychoanalytic theory.

For those who are concerned directly with social work practice or who study it, the authors offer useful distinction among basic practice roles. The social worker is an advocate when representing a party in a conflict of interest; a mediator where underlying interests are complementary, but there is surface conflict; or a broker where bringing together individuals with complementary interests.

Considerable emphasis is placed in the text on individual practice. General prescriptions are offered in such matters as setting the stage for interaction and managing interaction. Advice is offered on the use of spatial arrangements and gestures in interacting with clients. Interestingly, more than anyone else, the authors draw upon Erving Goffman in support of the practice prescriptions offered.

A fundamental limitation of the book is that much less is said about social structure, social change, and principles of organization than is said about work with individuals. The book would be stronger if it had been extended, for example, to cover some of the approaches to organizing client groups in their own behalf which O'Brien analyzes so effectively.

FRANCIS G. CARO
Community Service Society
New York City

LEONARD ORLAND. *Prisons: Houses of Darkness*. Pp. xv, 224. New York: The Free Press, 1975. $10.00.

This is a lawyer's book on prisons, strong on the emergence of correctional law through court decisions in the past decade, solid on the need for increasing rationality and due process in sentencing and parole, but somewhat frail on social science studies of the prison experience.

Orland is no ordinary law professor. Not content with experiencing prison as a visiting parole board member, he had himself locked up as though an inmate for a weekend, including 24 hours in "the hole." He sends his students through this ordeal also, as part of a course.

The book opens with a short but unusually good history of prisons. A chapter on "Theoretical Justifications for Prison" cites glib conclusions of some atheoretical writings on rehabilitation and deterrence, a chapter on "Prison Profiles" summarizes statistics and simplistic theories on prison conditions, while a chapter on "Prison Realities" gives grim details on the regimentation of the inmate's daily life and the horrors in prison disciplinary punishment. The recent reversal of the traditional "hands off" policy of courts towards abuse of prisoner rights is dramatically detailed in a chapter called "Institutions in Conflict." The irrationalities of sentencing and the haphazardness of parole decisions are well summarized in a chapter on "Imprisonment and Release."

A concluding chapter proposes "Establishing the Rule of Law in Prison" by: sentences limited to five years; judges writing justifications for their sentences, under legislative guidelines; appellate review of sentences, including possible appeal by the state after five years that confinement be prolonged because of the inmate's dangerousness; "good time" of up to two months per year instead of parole. An alternative "reformist" approach would provide written records of all that transpires in plea bargaining plus a description of the offense stated for the record in open court, as well as parole hearing procedures assuring more rule of law. Also proposed are detailed rules for prison management, such as those in the book's appendices, which include the United Nations rules, a model disciplinary code and a model correctional ombudsman agreement. Much more could have been said on economic and other assistance as recidivism reducing for many offenders, and cost beneficial to the taxpayer. For identifying and correcting procedural abuses, however, this book is a great contribution, nicely complementing Norval Morris' *The Future of Imprisonment*.

DANIEL GLASER
University of Southern California
Los Angeles

EDWARD SHORTER. *The Making of the Modern Family*. Pp. 369. New York: Basic Books, 1975. $15.00.

Professor Shorter's latest book is a brilliant comparative study of the changing role of the family in the United States, England, and the Western, Central and Northern countries of Europe. With an outstanding sense of fine humor and in excellent, stimulating style, the author describes the changes in the relations between the members of the family. Its emphasis on choosing common people instead of kings, dukes, aristocrats and the wealthy elites as most earlier history books did, distinguishes this new study which analyzes the life styles of peasants, common workers, artisans and industrial workers in the period from 1700 to the present. If we remember Barett Wendell's characteristics of excellence, Professor Shorter meets their request of clarity, elegance and force of style and combines them with his excellent humor, his courageous criticism, his modesty as to his conclusions and his warm understanding of the decisive value of love and mutual respect between the members of the family. Undergraduate and graduate students of history, anthropology, sociology and social work will welcome Shorter's clear and stimulating analysis of the changing character and functions of the family here and in Europe during the past three centuries. Of special interest in this study is the explanation about the changing position of women, young and adolescent children, of persons helping in the household and of the different roles which romantic love is playing in the choice of marital partners. Also revealing is the disclosure of the importance of class divisions and their influence in the different types of societies and historical periods covered during this time.

In respect to the present growing divorce rate in most countries and the actual interest in comparative studies, the book also encourages further research for which the carefully selected bibliographical notes and references offer valuable stimulation.

The chapters of the book dealing with the fundamental questions about the role of the family in society, in history, household and community, men and women, mothers and small children in the traditional society and in the changing centuries, the sexual revolutions, the specific causes of change in different countries and the development of the post-modern family offer ample stimulation for new research. Five appendices supplement information on fertility rates distinguished between social classes, explaining the present high interest in the study of population trends and limitations, the questions of illegitimacy and prevention of pregnancy, age differences between spouses different in countries and centuries, and periods of conception and infant mortality. A carefully selected index and a list of special suggestions for further study complete this outstanding book. *The Making of the Family* can be highly recommended as a useful text for courses in history, anthropology, sociology, political science and social work.

WALTER FRIEDLANDER
University of California
Berkeley

JOSEPH WEIZENBAUM. *Computer Power and Human Reason: From Judgment to Calculation*. Pp. xii, 300. San Francisco, Calif.: W. H. Freeman & Co., 1976. $9.95.

Joseph Weizenbaum, Professor of Computer Science at MIT, has made distinguished contributions to the science he professes, including a language analysis program named ELIZA with which one can "converse" with a computer in English. In this program a young lady plays the role of a patient and the computer that of a psychotherapist in his initial interview with her. The "conversation" is startling in its plausibility and for that reason it won national recognition for its creator and stimulated a number of extravagant reactions. One writer, full of admiration, predicted that the technique could become an automatic form of psychotherapy and that the computer, far superior to a human psychotherapist, would be able to handle several hundred patients an hour. Some who conversed with the computer became emotionally involved with it. Still others concluded that the problem of computer understanding of a natural language had been solved.

These reactions disturbed ELIZA's creator. He accordingly decided to write this book and to indicate as clearly as he could what computers can and cannot do. He concedes that they have become indispensable for the stock market, the armed services, the banking system, and large corporations. His message, however, is a cautionary one. He has no patience with "compulsive programmers" and the "artificial intelligentsia" who assert that computers can do anything, if not now then certainly in the future.

Weizenbaum believes in fact that computers have rigidified social and political institutions that were otherwise ripe for change, opposes those who regard man himself as only an information processor, suggests a number of things that computers cannot do (they cannot hope, for example), and says there are things in addition that they ought not to be asked to do. He himself stands squarely on the side of a rational humanism and deplores any kind of technology—including computer technology—that endangers a humanistic view of man. His book is a refreshing antidote to those who like to think that man himself is only an inferior computer.

ROBERT BIERSTEDT
University of Virginia
Charlottesville

CHRISTOPHER WHEELER. *White Collar Power*. Pp. vii, 210. Urbana: University of Illinois Press, 1975. $12.00.

In Sweden, physicians, university professors, army officers, high civil service officials, engineers, retail clerks and postal carriers are all included in the category of "white collar" workers, and are accordingly organized into four white-collar federations. At the same time, the differences between the lower level of white-collar workers and the blue-collar workers is of minor significance. With the rise of industrialization, organization and government, white-collar employment has risen noticeably faster than that of blue-collar positions. Between 1900 and 1960, white-collar employment increased more than five times, while blue-collar jobs decreased from 56.9 percent of the work force to less than 50 percent.

The largest number of white-collar workers are employed in transportation, communications and commerce, followed by those in public administration and the professions. Even in manufacturing, 23 percent of all the workers are white-collar.

Seventy percent of all white-collar workers in Sweden are organized, and "at most firms, in fact, it has become standard operating practice to make sure that a new employee meets the trade union representative during the introductory rounds at the office" (p. 19). While in the early part of this century unionism for white-collar workers was frowned upon, at present it is accepted as a legitimate group activity by both employers and the population in general.

The ideology of free trade in the nineteenth century laid the basis for later trade unionism by abolishing governmental restrictions on the labor market and destroying the power of the guilds to regulate the activities of both journeymen and apprentices. By 1909, both industry and the law accepted the right of blue-collar workers to unionize. White-collar workers had a more difficult job in unionizing themselves because of their traditional identification with management—and thus did not gain complete acceptance until 1936, when legislation spelled out the rights of white-collar unions to deal with employers concerning working conditions, unemployment benefits and pensions.

Along with these rights, Sweden also gave white-collar workers, as well as other categories of employees, a social security system that has few equals anywhere in the world. Trade unions as interest groups have played important roles in pushing through "womb to tomb" social welfare benefits (though Sweden is now one of the most expensive countries in the world to live in, and certainly one of the most highly taxed). Large numbers of union officials do nothing else but devote themselves to a concern with public policy.

White Collar Power is an extension of a doctoral dissertation, and is replete with data on the organization of the various white-collar unions in Sweden. Its theme hinges on the different interpretation which is given to the meaning of "white collar" in Sweden and in the United States. Since in the former country this group includes a much larger percentage of the professional, teaching, technical and administrative staffs, one can assume that it possesses leverage in exerting effective political power. The author undertakes to analyze some of the techniques for doing so on the group level, with comments on the more recent development of the individual level.

DAVID RODNICK
University of Hamburg
Germany

ECONOMICS

RONALD ANDERSEN, JOANNA KRAVITS and ODIN W. ANDERSON, eds. *Equity in Health Services: Empirical Analysis in Social Policy.* Pp. xxiii, 295. Cambridge, Mass.: Ballinger, 1975. No Price.

HELEN M. WALLACE, ed. *Health Care of Mothers and Children in National Health Services: Implications for the United States.* Pp. x, 330. Cambridge, Mass.: Ballinger, 1975. No price.

The Andersen-Kravits-Anderson book brings social survey data to bear upon the issue of equity in health care in the United States and how it can be achieved. The chapters are organized about (1) the predisposition of persons to seek health care (involving demographic, social and attitudinal variables), (2) factors enabling persons to secure health care (including payment resources and the accessibility of services), (3) the need for health care (as indicated by perception of illness, symptoms experienced, and disability incurred), (4) the effects of medical care (on utilization of services, on health status) and (5) implications. Each chapter was written by an author whose discipline was appropriate to the variables under consideration, utilizing analytic techniques and concepts from his or her field.

Primarily, data were derived from the 1971 social survey of a national sample concerning its utilization of health services conducted by the Center for Health Administration Studies and the National Opinion Research Center of the University of Chicago. Information also came from health care providers, insurers and employers.

Each chapter begins with a brief abstract and ends with a summary or conclusion. There is also one chapter which summarizes the findings and another which utilizes the findings by indicating their implications for public policy.

The Andersen-Kravits-Anderson book is well-structured and well-written, as well as sophisticated methodologically and appropriately multi-disciplinary. Indeed, it could serve as a model for the way in which policy-related social research should be planned, conducted, utilized and reported upon.

Both the United Kingdom and Sweden have national health insurance programs and national health services. These systems are described, along with the place of maternal and child health within them, in the book of papers edited by Helen M. Wallace. Included are sections on family planning, abortion, perinatal care, and services for infants, handicapped children and adolescents. There are four papers worthy of special note: one on social pediatrics and another on longitudinal studies in the United Kingdom; and one on day care for children and another on sex education in Sweden.

It is in her chapter on implications for the United States that Dr. Wallace makes her statement. This includes a set of principles about what, in her opinion, ought to be (for example, health care is a right, government is responsible for seeing that it is provided, preventive services should be free of charge), and about which others might differ. Using the experience of the United Kindom and Sweden, Dr. Wallace describes how she believes maternal and child health services in the United States should be planned (regionally), focused (special provision for preventive services and for high risk groups), organized (one MCH agency at each level of government), evaluated, and funded. The relevant differences — socio-cultural, political, and demographic, among others — between these two nations and the federated sub-continent that is the U.S. are not discussed sufficiently. As a consequence, the case is not adequately made that these are necessary implications; they may be a series of informed and valuable, but nevertheless personal, opinions. However, the presentations of the programs of coverage and care in the United Kingdom and Sweden are worth reading, whether or not one accepts Dr. Wallace's view of what implications their experience has for the United States.

LAWRENCE PODELL
Office of Program and Policy Research
City University of New York

RALPH L. BEALS. *The Peasant Marketing System in Oaxaca, Mexico*. Pp. ix, 419. Berkeley: University of California Press, 1975. $20.00.

Economists should welcome this gift from the anthropologists. It is intended to be a reliable guide for adapting western economic analysis to non-western cultures and is the chief work so far from the "Oaxaca school" of social

scientists. Written by a senior scholar and based on more than a decade of work by a large team of investigators, the book utilizes also the work of earlier scholars and observers in the Oaxaca area. It demonstrates the philosophical position that culture, even if exotic or apparently anomalous, can be analyzed quantitatively and meaningfully through patience, method and imagination. Thus its scholarly apparatus is massive, containing 45 appendices in 114 pages and many graphs and lists incorporated in the text—including, for example, four patterns of haggling ("negotiated prices"). Chapter titles indicate the categories of analysis: setting and extent of the Oaxaca market system, the production system, the consumption and expenditure system, the structure of the marketing system, dynamics of the market system (traditional and modern), price making and market results, and finally, growth and change.

Completion of the Pan-American highway to Oaxaca in 1938 opened the area to new and modern trade influences. Reliable statistics for a number of activities in the Oaxaca market have been established from that date to 1966, and much of the book is devoted to analyzing the adaptation of the traditional peasant marketing system, 1938–1966, to those modern influences. The main point demonstrated in the book is the durability and elasticity of the peasant market as a social mechanism. This is accomplished through relentless analysis of the relationship of subsistence and market economies. The author's concluding observation should shake any convictions about the inevitable wisdom of modern economic practice. Synthesizing the rich data presented he asserts that "it is at least an open question whether planners and 'developers' should concentrate their efforts on promoting and accelerating changes in [the peasant market] sector of the distribution system. It may well be that in the long run they should devote their efforts to curbing or eliminating undesirable features in the modern distribution systems" (p. 282).

This book deserves the benchmark

label, for it will undoubtedly remain a solid reference point in scholarly literature.

WAYNE M. CLEGERN
Colorado State University
Fort Collins

SAMUEL BOWLES and HERBERT GINTIS. *Schooling in Capitalist America: Educational Reform and the Contradictions of Economic Life.* Pp. 340. New York: Basic Books, 1976. $13.95.

In America, education has repeatedly been proposed as a cure for social evils and a guarantee of social democracy. Nevertheless, studies of the relationships between "cognitive intelligence" and income demonstrate that intelligence, whether innate or acquired, is not an important determinant of social position; even when it seems to have been influential, closer inspection of the data reveals that it has been a corollary of class and status rather than their cause. These findings indicate that innovations in school and college will not encourage democracy understood either as self-determination or as personal development. Instead, achieving it depends upon remaking the society and the economy; in particular, upon substituting democratic socialism for capitalism, which has generated most of the characteristic shortcomings of American education. At the same time, the inherent contradictions between the system and the objectives college students now pursue—better jobs, self-expression, humanistic values—are producing an explosive and potentially revolutionary situation, which those who understand it can help bring to fruition in radical social change.

Here is the basic argument of this tendentious book, an argument supported in its empirical aspects by sophisticated statistical analysis and an up-to-the-minute acquaintance with revisionist studies of education in the United States. It will be persuasive to the intelligent reader in approximately the same measure as he or she values the social and economic paradigms of Marxism. To Bowles and Gintis it is all but self-evident that the defects in American education are attributable to the capitalist system, that American education has long served unworthy social purposes, and that even the most venturesome educational reformers (among whom they would list John Dewey) have been unable and in some degree unwilling to propose the radical social changes that are necessary to make their educational ideals plausible.

The effect of this argument is to hold up progressive educational ideals as a criterion for the good society but to use them as an occasion for conscious radicalism. Instead of asking whether those ideals are attainable in modern society, or whether any educational system can fully honor their commitment to individual self-determination and personal development, the authors simply reiterate an *a priori* belief that the evils they describe will disappear with the substitution of an alternative economic system that has no known precedent. (Significantly, they brush aside as irrelevant most of the practices of communist nations.) Hence all of their insights, all of their incisive challenges to business as usual, are finally irritating rather than persuasive. The twin concerns of social amelioration and improved education deserve more thoughtful champions.

RUSH WELTER
Bennington College
Vermont

HYMAN P. MINSKY. *John Maynard Keynes.* Pp. vi, 169. New York: Columbia University Press, 1975. $12.00. Paperbound, $2.95.

This is a wonderful little book. Its analysis, its polemics, its penetrating insights, are a delight to read. The contrast is most welcome in this day of mammoth textbooks testing a student's weight-lifting prowess while reiterating interminable stale and superficial 'Keynesian' dogmas—usually perpetrating a hoax on Keynes—or inept monetarist slogans which qualify as recipes for exorcising the inflation mess through the trauma of unemployment.

Minsky, like too few others, has uncovered the breach that threatens to reduce economics to the art of futility. There has been a travesty in interpreting Keynes on the theory of capital investment decisions, on financial behavior, on money, and on inflation—a short but overwhelming list! Most of the confusion is attributable to Keynesians purporting to write in Keynes's spirit, and sustained by second and third hand resumes of the subject himself. Result: a specious regression to 'equilibrium' models *sans* the uncertainty in decision-making in which Keynes's theories were wrapped; the interplay of financial contracts and job markets was ignored in a flight to Walrasian fancies. It was this lifeless rendition of Keynes that opened the wedge for the monetarist assault that "money mattered," containing miniscule prescriptive content effectively concealed behind diversionary statistical rhetoric.

Entrepreneurs must take actions today to run over the unknowable future in seeking profits which may emerge as losses: the scan of the 'tomorrows' is vague because it is unknowable. There is no escape from the human condition. Mechanical econometric models premise that if enough information is computerized in yesterday's data, then tomorrow will be revealed—where 'tomorrow' means a 10 to 20 year vista. Would that it were so—as many a Wall Street speculator or race track bettor has moaned in tallying his losses in a shorter streak.

Minsky, in an encouraging and exciting departure from orthodoxy, returns to Keynes's *General Theory* to revive its dynamic essence. Due weight is attached to the gobs of uncertainty that pervade all forward-looking decisions conditioned by erratic cyclical spells inherent in the economic process. In reaching back to Keynes, the one qualified theorist since David Ricardo with

important first hand experience in financial markets as an actor and close observer, Minsky develops an important theory of the 'layering of financial claims' on which a capitalist production system depends. Ramifications extend to job markets and production efficiency. The systemic fragility is disclosed, whereby small upsets can engender a contagious and devastating set of corrections which can be complicated by Federal Reserve action—or inaction. Monetary responses ordinarily have more than a bit of routinized ideology masquerading as 'judgment'.

I think that Minsky can be criticized for underplaying the importance of money wage inflation in engendering the recent disorders, and prolonged by timid monetary response fostered by the lack of an effective Incomes Policy. To be sure, he recognizes the origins of the malaise but it is paramount to his theme. Also, his laudable humanistic sentiments for a fairer income shake skip the destructiveness of union-management combinatorial solutions by way of far-fetched wage and salary advances that guarantee the inflation-unemployment morass.

But this is to carp at an outstanding analytic event. Alongside the book by Professor Paul Davidson, on *Money in the Real World*, and with constant reference to early and late Keynes, monetary and economic theory—the two are inseparable—are primed for a giant leap forward. Supplements would come from a short list of other contributors.

Quotable passages abound in what is generally a literary and stylistic triumph—if only a few sentences were shorter! The book is itself a telling argument for an academic press, relieved of the textbook drivel based on the principle that what once sold must sell again, in a 'safe' volume. Detroit, with a fifteen-year model lag, has responded to events with alacrity compared to commercial publishers.

It is mind-boggling that in returning to the best covered figure in the history of economics Minsky has been able to capture Keynes's vision in a fresh, timely perspective. He has a truly *new* book and he deserves a salute for service *far* 'above and beyond' the prevalent pseudo-Keynesianism.

The Columbia University Press also deserves our gratitude.

SIDNEY WEINTRAUB
University of Pennsylvania
Philadelphia

JEFFERY M. PAIGE. *Agrarian Revolution: Social Movements and Export Agriculture in the Underdeveloped World.* Pp. vii, 435. New York: The Free Press, 1975. $15.95.

This study by Professor Paige of Berkeley is massively valuable. Its closely though clearly printed pages, with long paragraphs and small margins, are densely packed with information and reasoning, giving a commendably exhaustive—and correspondingly exhausting—examination of this wide, complex and fateful field of socioeconomic and political change in the modern world. It is not possible to cover this in a short review, limited (for instance) to about one hundredth of the wordage of the author's own summary of "Conclusions" (pp. 334–376). The book's discussion ranges literally from China to Peru (via Angola) and from abaca to zero-sum games (via irrigation), with a myriad of cross-references (which are helped by a good index). The bibliographical appendix cites over 600 works dealing with nearly 70 countries.

The author derives a theory of rural class conflict (Chapter I, 71 pages): "The social movements associated with various types of agricultural organization are fundamentally a result of the interaction between the political behavior associated with the principal source of income of the upper and lower agricultural classes," in various "combinations." (A) If both cultivators and non-cultivators depend on income from land, the outcome is agrarian revolt. (B) If the non-cultivators depend on income from commerce, the resultant movement is for

market- or price-control, demanding "neither the redistribution of property nor the seizure of State power," only a "limited economic protest." (C) If the non-cultivators depend on income from capital, as in "industrial plantation systems," demands are similarly limited to pressure for higher wages and better working conditions rather than expropriation or political overturn. However, (D) "A combination of non-cultivators dependent on income from land and cultivators dependent on income from wages leads to revolution." In decentralized share-cropping systems such revolution is likely to be communist, in settler-estate or migratory systems nationalist (pp. 70–71).

Chapter II (52 pages) on "World Patterns" presents a generalized theory on this basis. The rest of the book goes into case-studies of agricultural export sectors in Peru (where both agrarian and labor movements are considered, in a "reformist" period under a government committed to land reform), in Angola (the settler-based coffee industry engendering a revolutionary nationalist movement) and in Vietnam (where the war evidently instances a revolutionary socialist movement). The correlations between assassinations and other revolutionary activities with the production and export of rice and with the local systems of land tenure, for each Province of Vietnam (pp. 330–1) are most interesting; but there is a wealth of other descriptive, analytical and indicative material in this highly relevant book.

E. STUART KIRBY
Asian Institute of Technology
Bangkok
Thailand

OTHER BOOKS

ABERCROMBIE, NIGEL. *Artists and Their Public.* Pp. 123. New York: UNIPUB, 1975. $4.95. Paperbound.

ADAMS, LAURA. *Existential Battles: The Growth of Norman Mailer.* Pp. vii, 192. Athens: Ohio University Press, 1976. No price.

AGARWAL, A.N. *Indian Economy*. Pp. vi, 672. New York: International Publications Service, 1975. $15.00.

ALDERFER, CLAYTON P. and L. DAVE BROWN. *Learning from Changing: Organizational Diagnosis and Development*. Vol. 19. Sage Library of Social Research. Pp. 256. Beverly Hills, Calif.: Sage, 1975. $12.00. Paperbound, $7.00.

ALLEN, V.L. *Social Analysis: A Marxist Critique and Alternative*. Pp. vi, 316. New York: Longman, 1975. $19.00. Paperbound, $13.50.

ALTBACH, PHILIP G. *Publishing in India: An Analysis*. Pp. vii, 115. New York: Oxford University Press, 1976. $3.25. Paperbound.

ANDERS, LESLIE. *The Twenty-First Missouri: From Home Guard to Union Regiment*. Contributions in Military History, no. 11. Pp. x, 298. Westport, Conn.: Greenwood Press, 1975. $17.50.

ANTHONY, J. GARNER. *Hawaii under Army Rule*. Pp. xi, 203. Honolulu: University of Hawaii Press, 1975. $3.95. Paperbound.

ASHTOR, E. *A Social and Economic History of the Near East in the Middle Ages*. Pp. 384. Berkeley: University of California Press, 1976. $18.50.

AS-SAID, LABIB. *The Recited Koran*. Pp. 156. Princeton, N.J.: Darwin Press, 1976. $10.00.

AVAKUMOVIC, IVAN. *The Communist Party in Canada: A History*. Pp. v, 309. Toronto, Canada: McClelland and Stewart Limited, 1975. $5.95. Paperbound.

AYLMER, G.E., ed. *The Levellers in the English Revolution*. Pp. 180. Ithaca, N.Y.: Cornell University Press, 1975. $9.50. Paperbound, $2.95.

BAKER, DEREK, ed. *The Materials, Sources and Methods of Ecclesiastical History*. Vol. II. Pp. vii, 370. New York: Barnes & Noble, 1976. $20.00.

BARRACLOUGH, GEOFFREY. *The Crucible of Europe: The Ninth and Tenth Centuries in European History*. Pp. 180. Berkeley: University of California Press, 1976. $14.95.

BEARD, EDMUND and STEPHEN HORN. *Congressional Ethics: The View from the House*. Pp. 87. Washington, D.C.: Brookings Institution, 1975. $2.50. Paperbound.

BEASLEY, W.G., ed. *Modern Japan: Aspects of History, Literature and Society*. Pp. 296. Berkeley: University of California Press, 1975. $17.50.

BECKER, GARY S. *Human Capital*. 2nd ed. Human Behavior and Social Institutions, no. 5. Pp. ix, 268. New York: Columbia University Press, 1975. $10.00.

BERTSCH, GARY K. and THOMAS W. GANSCHOW. *Comparative Communism: The Soviet, Chinese, and Yugoslav Models*. Pp. v, 463. San Francisco, Calif.: W.H. Freeman, 1975. $12.95. Paperbound, $6.95.

BINKIN, MARTIN and JEFFREY RECORD. *Where Does the Marine Corps Go From Here?* Studies in Defense Policy. Pp. vii, 93. Washington, D.C.: The Brookings Institution, 1976. $2.95. Paperbound.

BLACK, CYRIL E., ed. *Comparative Modernization: A Reader*. Pp. v, 441. New York: Free Press, 1976. $12.95.

BLACKMER, DONALD L. M. and SIDNEY TARROW, eds. *Communism in Italy and France*. Pp. v, 651. Princeton, N.J.: Princeton University Press, 1975. $25.00.

BONE, HUGH A. and AUSTIN RANNEY. *Politics and Voters*. Pp. v, 135. New York: McGraw-Hill, 1976. No price.

BORISOV, O.B. and B.T. KOLOSKOV. *Soviet-Chinese Relations, 1945–1970*. Edited by Bladimir Petrov. Pp. vii, 364. Bloomington: Indiana University Press, 1975. $12.50.

BURGESS, KEITH. *The Origins of British Industrial Relations*. Pp. 331. Totowa, N.J.: Rowman and Littlefield, 1975. $19.50.

BURNER, DAVID. *The Politics of Provincialism: The Democratic Party in Transition, 1918–1932*. Pp. xi, 293. New York: W.W. Norton, 1975. $3.95. Paperbound.

CALLOW, ALEXANDER B., JR., ed. *The City Boss in America: An Interpretive Reader*. Pp. vii, 335. New York: Oxford University Press, 1976. $6.00. Paperbound.

CAREY, JAMES T. *Sociology and Public Affairs: The Chicago School*. Sage Library of Social Research, no. 16. Pp. 206. Beverly Hills, Calif.: Sage, 1975. $12.00. Paperbound, $7.00.

CHAFFEE, STEVEN H., ed. *Political Communication: Issues and Strategies for Research*. Vol. IV. Pp. 320. Beverly Hills, Calif.: Sage, 1975. $17.50. Paperbound, $7.50.

CHURCH, WILLIAM F. *Louis XIV in Historical Thought*. Pp. 127. New York: W.W. Norton, 1976. $6.95. Paperbound, $1.95.

CIPOLLA, CARLO M., ed. *The Emergence of Industrial Societies*. Vol. IV, Part I. Pp. 368. New York: Barnes & Noble, 1976. $19.50.

CIPOLLA, CARLO M., ed. *The Fontana Economic History of Europe: The Industrial Revolution, 1700–1914*. Vol. III. Pp. 624. New York: Barnes & Noble, 1976. $19.50.

CLISSOLD, STEPHEN, ed. *Yugoslavia and the Soviet Union, 1939–1973: A Documentary*

Survey. Pp. vii, 318. New York: Oxford University Press, 1975. $26.00.

CONGRESSIONAL QUARTERLY INCORPORATED. *Inside Congress*. Pp. v, 138. Washington, D.C.: Congressional Quarterly Incorporated, 1976. $5.25. Paperbound.

CONRADS, ULRICH, ed. *Programs and Manifestoes on 20th-Century Architecture*. Pp. 192. Cambridge, Mass.: MIT Press, 1975. $4.95. Paperbound.

COOK, CHRIS. *Sources in British Political History, 1900–1951*. Vol. II. Pp. 297. New York: St. Martin's Press, 1975. $16.95.

COOMBES, DAVID, ed. *The Power of the Purse: A Symposium on the Role of European Parliaments in Budgetary Decisions*. Pp. 393. New York: Praeger, 1976. No price.

COX, ARCHIBALD. *The Role of the Supreme Court in American Government*. Pp. vi, 118. New York: Oxford University Press, 1976. $6.95.

CUOMO, MARIO. *Forrest Hills Diary: The Crisis of Low-Income Housing*. Pp. vi, 209. New York: Vintage, 1974. $2.95. Paperbound.

DANIELS, NORMAN, ed. *Reading Rawls: Critical Studies of a Theory of Justice*. Pp. vi, 352. New York: Basic Books, 1975. $15.00. Paperbound, $5.00.

DAVIS, DAVID BRION. *The Problem of Slavery in the Age of Revolution, 1770–1823*. Pp. 576. Ithaca, N.Y.: Cornell University Press, 1975. $5.95. Paperbound.

DAVIS, JAMES W. and DELBERT RINGQUIST. *The President and Congress*. Pp. 224. Woodbury, N.Y.: Barron's Educational Series, 1975. $2.50. Paperbound.

DE CRESPIGNY, R.R.C. *This Century China*. Pp. vi, 299. New York: St. Martin's Press, 1975. $15.95.

DELLINGER, DAVE. *More Power Than We Know: People's Movement Toward Democracy*. Pp. 336. New York: Anchor Press, 1975. $3.95. Paperbound.

DEMAUSE, LLOYD, ed. *The New Psychohistory*. Pp. 313. New York: Psychohistory Press, 1975. $12.95.

DERRY, JOHN W. *Castlereach*. Pp. viii, 247. New York: St. Martin's Press, 1976. $15.95.

DE SOUSA, DANIEL. *Sociological Formalism and Structural Functional Analysis: The Nature of the "Social"-Reality Sui Generis? Form? System?* Pp. 148. Hicksville, N.Y.: Exposition Press, 1976. $7.50.

DODGE, DOROTHY R. and DUNCAN H. BAIRD, eds. *Continuities and Discontinuities in Political Thought: A Transitional Study*.

Pp. v, 314. New York: Halsted Press, 1975. $13.95. Paperbound, $7.95.

DOLBEARE, KENNETH M., ed. *Public Policy Evaluation*. Vol. II. Pp. 286. Beverly Hills, Calif.: Sage, 1975. $17.50. Paperbound, $7.50.

DOUGLAS, DAVID C. *The Norman Fate: 1100–1154*. Pp. 273. Berkeley: University of California Press, 1976. $22.50.

EHRLICH, PAUL R. *The End of Affluence: A Blueprint for Your Future*. Pp. 307. New York: Ballantine, 1974. $1.95. Paperbound.

ELDRIDGE, J.E.T. and A.D. CROMBIE. *A Sociology of Organizations*. Pp. 218. New York: International Publications Service, 1975. $12.50.

FAIRBANK, JOHN KING, KATHERINE FROST BRUNER and ELIZABETH MACLEOD MATHESON, eds. *The I.G. in Peking: Letters of Robert Hart Chinese Maritime Customs, 1868–1907*. Vols. I and II. Pp. vii, 1625. Lawrence, Mass.: Harvard University Press, 1976. $50.00 per set.

FARINA, AMERIGO. *Abnormal Psychology*. Pp. ix, 207. Englewood Cliffs, N.J.: Prentice-Hall, 1976. No price.

FEIRING, EVOLYN G. *Concatenation: Enoch's Prophecy Fulfilled*. Pp. 240. Long Beach, Calif.: Rocky Mountain Press, 1973. $3.00. Paperbound, $2.00.

FINGER, SEYMOUR MAXWELL, ed. *The New World Balance and Peace in the Middle East: Reality or Mirage?* Pp. 308. Cranbury, N.J.: Fairleigh Dickinson University Press, 1976. $12.00.

FLOUD, RODERICK. *An Introduction to Quantitative Methods for Historians*. Pp. xi, 220. Princeton, N.J.: Princeton University Press, 1975. $3.45. Paperbound.

FONTAINE, ROGER W. *On Negotiating With Cuba*. Pp. 99. Washington, D.C.: American Enterprise Institute for Public Policy Research, 1975. $3.00. Paperbound.

FRIEDMAN, BERNARD. *Smuts: A Reappraisal*. Pp. 222. New York: St. Martin's Press, 1974. $14.95.

GAYLIN, WILLARD. *Partial Justice: A Study of Bias in Sentencing*. Pp. xii, 244. New York: Vintage, 1974. $2.95. Paperbound.

GLENNERSTER, H. *Social Service Budgets and Social Policy: British and American Experience*. Pp. 272. New York: Barnes & Noble, 1976. $17.50.

GOLDMAN, MARSHALL I. *Environmental Pollution in the Soviet Union: The Spoils of Progress*. Pp. ix, 372. Cambridge, Mass.: MIT Press, 1972. $3.45. Paperbound.

The Great Ideas Today: 1975. Pp. 473. Chicago, Ill.: Encyclopedia Britannica, 1975. No price.

HANSOT, ELISABETH. *Perfection and Progress: Two Modes of Utopian Thought.* Pp. 219. Cambridge, Mass.: MIT Press, 1974. No price.

HARRIS, PETER B. *Political Realities: The Commonwealth.* Pp. vi, 168. New York: Longman, 1975. $9.00.

HEISE,DAVID R. *Causal Analysis.* Pp. vii, 301. New York: John Wiley & Sons, 1975. $15.95.

HENDEL, SAMUEL, ed. *Basic Issues of American Democracy.* 8th ed. Pp. vii, 443. Englewood Cliffs, N.J.: Prentice-Hall, 1976. $6.95. Paperbound.

HENDERSON, DAN FENNO. *Village "Contracts" in Tokugawa Japan: Fifty Specimens with English Translations and Comments.* Pp. vii, 234. Seattle: University of Washington Press, 1975. $10.00.

HENDON, WILLIAM S. *Economics for Urban Social Planning.* Pp. 314. Salt Lake City: University of Utah Press, 1975. $15.00.

HERENDEEN, JAMES B. *The Economics of the Corporate Economy.* Pp. ix, 262. Port Washington, N.Y.: Kennikat Press, 1975. $15.00.

HERMAN, VALENTINE and JAMES E. ALT, eds. *Cabinet Studies: A Reader.* Pp. ix, 302. New York: St. Martin's Press, 1975. $19.95.

HERMASSI, ELBAKI. *Leadership and National Development in North Africa.* Pp. 253. Berkeley: University of California Press, 1975. $3.65. Paperbound.

HIGHAM, ROBIN, ed. *Intervention or Abstention.* Pp. 221. Lexington: University Press of Kentucky, 1975. $14.75.

HOCHMAN, HAROLD M., ed. *The Urban Economy: Problems of the Modern Economy Series.* Pp. vii, 296. New York: W.W. Norton, 1976. $14.95. Paperbound, $3.95.

HOEHLER, RICHARD. *The Transcendentalists.* Pp. 432. Conifer, Colo.: Richard S. Hoehler, 1972. No price.

HOGAN, ROBERT. *Personality Theory: The Personological Tradition.* Pp. vii, 223. Englewood Cliffs, N.J.: Prentice-Hall, 1976. $5.95. Paperbound.

JACKSON, ROBERT. *South Asian Crisis.* Pp. 240. New York: Praeger, 1975. $12.50.

JENKINS, ROY. *Nine Men of Power.* Pp. vii, 231. New York: The British Book Centre, 1976. $17.95.

JONES, PETER, ed. *The International Yearbook of Foreign Policy Analysis.* Vol. II. Pp. 266. New York: Crane, Russak & Co., 1976. $15.00.

KARST, KENNETH L. and KEITH S. ROSENN. *Law and Development in Latin America.*

Pp. 758. Berkeley: University of California Press, 1976. $32.50.

KATZ, FRED E. *Structuralism in Sociology: An Approach to Knowledge.* Pp. viii, 218. Albany: State University of New York Press, 1976. $15.00.

KING, EDMUND J., CHRISTINE H. MOOR and JENNIFER A. MUNDY. *Post Compulsory Education II: The Way Ahead.* Pp. 200. Beverly Hills, Calif.: Sage, 1975. $12.00. Paperbound, $6.00.

KOBLIK, STEVEN, ed. *Sweden's Development from Poverty to Affluence, 1750–1970.* Pp. 380. Minneapolis: University of Minnesota Press, 1975. $16.50. Paperbound, $4.95.

KRICKUS, RICHARD. *Pursuing the American Dream: White Ethnics and the New Populism.* Pp. ix, 424. New York: Doubleday, 1976. $3.95. Paperbound.

KRUEGER, ANNE O. *Foreign Trade Regimes and Economic Development.* Vol. I. Pp. xiv, 339. New York: National Bureau of Economic Research, 1975. $17.50. Paperbound, $5.00.

LAPLACE, JOHN. *Health.* 2nd ed. Pp. vi, 652. Englewood Cliffs, N.J.: Prentice-Hall, 1976. $9.96. Paperbound.

Law and Development: The Future of Law and Development Research. Pp. 91. New York: International Legal Center, 1975. No price.

Legal Education in a Changing World. Pp. 94. New York: International Legal Center, 1975. No price.

LEHMAN, EDWARD W. *Coordinating Health Care: Explorations in Interorganizational Relations.* Sage Library of Social Research, no. 17. Pp. 252. Beverly Hills, Calif.: Sage, 1975. $12.00. Paperbound, $7.00.

LENZER, GERTRUD, ed. *Auguste Comte and Positivism: The Essential Writings.* Pp. xi, 505. New York: Harper & Row, 1975. No price.

LESSNOFF, MICHAEL. *The Structure of Social Science.* Pp.173. New York: International Publications Service, 1975. $10.50.

LEVITAN, SAR A., GARTH L. MANGUM and RAY MARSHALL. *Human Resources and Labor.* 2nd ed. Pp. vii, 631. New York: Harper & Row, 1975. $15.95.

LEVITAN, SAR A. and WILLIAM B. JOHNSTON. *Indian Giving: Federal Programs for Native Americans.* Pp. v, 83. Baltimore, Md.: Johns Hopkins University Press, 1975. $7.50. Paperbound, $2.25.

LEWIN, ROGER, ed. *Child Alive.* Pp. 240. New York: Anchor Press, 1975. $2.95. Paperbound.

LIPPIT, VICTOR D. *Land Reform and Economic Development in China: A Study of Institutional Change and Development Finance.* Pp. ix, 181. New York: International Arts and Sciences Press, 1975. $15.00.

LIPPMAN, THEO, JR. *Senator Ted Kennedy: The Career Behind the Image.* Pp. x, 296. New York: W.W. Norton, 1976. $9.95.

LOVINS, AMORY B. and JOHN H. PRICE. *Non-Nuclear Futures: The Case for an Ethical Energy Strategy.* Pp. ix, 223. Cambridge, Mass.: Ballinger, 1975. No price.

LUNDSTEEN, SARA W. *Children Learn to Communicate.* Pp. v, 457. Englewood Cliffs, N.J.: Prentice-Hall, 1976. $10.95.

MAI, LUDWIG H. *Men and Ideas in Economics.* Pp. v, 270. Totowa, N.J.: Littlefield, Adams, 1975. $3.95. Paperbound.

MANNING, C.A.W. *The Nature of International Society.* Pp. vii, 220. New York: Halsted Press, 1975. No price.

MARDER, ARTHUR. *Operation Menace.* Pp. vii, 289. New York: Oxford University Press, 1976. $18.75.

MARRIS, PETER. *Loss and Change.* Pp. 200. New York: Anchor Press, 1975. $2.95. Paperbound.

MATHIESON, R.S. *The Soviet Union: An Economic Geography.* Pp. vi, 342. New York: Barnes & Noble, 1976. $18.50.

MAXWELL, JAMES A. *Specific Purpose Grants in the United States: Recent Developments.* Research Monograph, no. 12. Canberra: Australian National University Press, 1975. $5.00. Paperbound.

MELLAFFE, ROLANDO. *Negro Slavery in Latin America.* Pp. 180. Berkeley: University of California Press, 1975. $11.50.

MENDELSON, MARY ADELAIDE. *Tender Loving Greed.* Pp. vii, 245. New York: Vintage, 1975. $2.45. Paperbound.

MEUNIER, ROBERT F. *Shadows of Doubt: The Warren Commission Cover-Up.* Pp. 165. Hicksville, N.Y.: Exposition Press, 1976. $7.50.

MICHAEL, FRANZ H. and GEORGE E. TAYLOR. *The Far East in the Modern World.* 3rd ed. Pp. v, 962. Hinsdale, Ill.: Dryden Press, 1975. No price.

The Middle East: U.S. Policy, Israel, Oil and the Arabs. 2nd ed. Pp. 144. Washington, D.C.: Congressional Quarterly, 1975. No price.

MITFORD, JESSICA. *Kind and Usual Punishment: The Prison Business.* Pp. vi, 373. New York: Vintage, 1974. $2.45. Paperbound.

MOHAN, RAJ and DON MARTINDALE, eds. *Handbook of Contemporary Developments in World Sociology.* Contributions in Sociology, no. 17. Pp. xviii, 493. Westport, Conn.: Greenwood Press, 1975. $25.00.

MURRAY, J. B. and EMILY MURRAY. *And Say What He Is: The Life of a Special Child.* Pp. viii, 232. Cambridge, Mass.: MIT Press, 1975. $8.95.

NANDA, B.R., ed. *Indian Foreign Policy: The Nehru Years.* Pp. vi, 279. New York: International Publications Service, 1976. $13.50.

NDETI, KIVUTO. *Cultural Policy in Kenya.* Pp. 70. New York: UNIPUB, 1975. $3.30. Paperbound.

NUTTER, G. WARREN. *Kissinger's Grand Design.* Pp. 111. Washington, D.C.: American Enterprise Institute for Public Policy Research, 1975. $3.00. Paperbound.

PASSIN, HERBERT, ed. *The United States and Japan.* 2nd ed., revised. Pp. v, 167. Washington, D.C.: Columbia Books, 1975. $4.00. Paperbound.

PELTZMAN, SAM. *Regulation of Automobile Safety.* Pp. 53. Washington, D.C.: American Enterprise Institute for Public Policy Research, 1975. $3.00. Paperbound.

PENNOCK, J. ROLAND and JOHN W. CHAPMAN. *Participation in Politics: No-Mos XVI.* Pp. vii, 300. New York: Lieber, Atherton, 1975. $12.95.

POLLACK, HERMAN. *Jewish Folkways in Germanic Lands, 1648–1806.* Pp. vii, 410. Lawrence, Mass.: MIT Press, 1975. $3.95. Paperbound.

POSTER, MARK. *Existential Marxism in Postwar France: From Sartre to Althusser.* Pp. vii, 415. Princeton, N.J.: Princeton University Press, 1976. $17.50.

Presidential Elections Since 1789. Pp. v, 170. Washington, D.C.: Congressional Quarterly, 1975. No price.

PRESSMAN, JEFFREY L. *Federal Programs and City Politics: The Dynamics of the Aid Process in Oakland.* Pp. 178. Berkeley: University of California Press, 1975. $10.95.

PRITCHETT, C. HERMAN. *The American Constitutional System.* Pp. v, 133. New York: McGraw-Hill, 1976. $3.95. Paperbound.

RECORD, JEFFREY. *Sizing Up the Soviet Army.* Pp. vii, 51. Washington, D.C.: The Brookings Institution, 1975. $2.50. Paperbound.

RICHARDSON, BRADLEY M. *The Political Culture of Japan.* Pp. 282. Berkeley: University of California Press, 1975. $4.25. Paperbound.

ROEBUCK, JULIAN B. and WOLFGANG FRESE. *The Rendezvous: A Case Study of an After-Hours Club.* Pp. v, 278. New York: The Free Press, 1976. $10.95.

RUBEL, MAXIMILIEN and MARGARET MANALE. *Marx Without Myth.* Pp. 368. New York: Barnes & Noble, 1975. $20.00.

RUBIN, VERA, ed. *Cannabis and Culture.* Pp. vi, 598. Chicago, Ill.: Aldine, 1976. $24.95.

RUNCIE, JOHN F. *Experiencing Social Research.* Pp. ix, 184. Homewood, Ill.: Dorsey Press, 1975. $5.50. Paperbound.

SCHNEIDER, MICHAEL. *Neurosis and Civilization: A Marxist/Freudian Synthesis.* Pp. v, 302. New York: The Seabury Press, 1975. $12.95.

SCHOENBERG, BERNARD et al., eds. *Bereavement: Its Psychosocial Aspects.* Pp. ix, 375. New York: Columbia University Press, 1975. $15.00.

SCOTT, WILLIAM F. *Soviet Sources of Military Doctrine and Strategy.* Pp. v, 72. New York: Crane, Russak & Co., 1975. $4.95. Paperbound, $2.75.

SHAFFER, ARTHUR H. *The Politics of History: Writing the History of the American Revolution, 1783–1815.* Pp. 228. Chicago, Ill.: Precedent, 1975. No price.

SINGER, H.W. *The Strategy of International Development: Essays in the Economics of Backwardness.* Edited by Alec Cairncross and Mohinder Puri. Pp. x, 248. New York: International Arts and Sciences Press, 1975. $20.00.

SINGLETON, FRED. *Twentieth Century Yugoslavia.* Pp. vii, 346. New York: Columbia University Press, 1976. $15.00. Paperbound, $5.95.

SOHNER, CHARLES P. *American Government and Politics Today.* 2nd ed. Pp. 376. Glenview, Ill.: Scott, Foresman, 1976. $7.50. Paperbound.

STADELMANN, RUDOLPH. *Social and Political History of the German 1848 Revolution.* Pp. vii, 218. Athens: Ohio University Press, 1975. $11.00.

STEDMAN, MURRAY S., JR. *State and Local Governments.* Pp. v, 419. Englewood Cliffs, N.J.: Prentice-Hall, 1976. $7.50. Paperbound.

STOOKEY, ROBERT W. *America and the Arab States: An Uneasy Encounter.* Pp. v, 298. New York: John Wiley & Sons, 1975. $6.95. Paperbound.

SUMPTION, JONATHAN. *Pilgrimage: An Image of Mediaeval Religion.* Pp. 391. Totowa, N.J.: Rowman and Littlefield, 1976. $15.00.

TAYLOR, IRVING A. and J.W. GETZELS, eds. *Perspectives in Creativity.* Pp. vii, 353. Chicago, Ill.: Aldine Press, 1975. $14.75.

TERRELL, JOHN UPTON and DONNA M. TERRELL. *Indian Women of the Western Morning: Their Life in Early America.* Pp. 200. New York: Doubleday, 1975. $2.95. Paperbound.

THOMLINSON, RALPH. *Population Dynamics.* 2nd ed. Pp. 653. New York: Random House, 1976. No price.

THOMPSON, LEONARD. *Survival in Two Worlds: Moshoeshoe of Lesotho, 1786–1870.* Pp. 389. New York: Oxford University Press, 1976. $24.00. Paperbound, $7.00.

THOMPSON, RICHARD. *Retreat from Apartheid: New Zealand's Sporting Contacts with South Africa.* Pp. vii, 102. New York: Oxford University Press, 1975. $4.50. Paperbound.

TIMPANARO, SEBASTIANO. *On Materialism.* Pp. 260. Atlantic Highlands, N.J.: Humanities Press, 1976. $15.50.

TINDER, GLENN. *Tolerance: Toward A New Civility Tinder.* Pp. 187. Lawrence: University of Massachusetts Press, 1976. $12.50.

THE UNION OF CONCERNED SCIENTISTS. *The Nuclear Fuel Cycle.* Revised Edition. Pp. vi, 291. Cambridge, Mass.: MIT Press, 1975. No price.

URBAN, G.R., ed. *Detente.* Pp. 368. New York: Universe Books, 1976. $20.00.

VAN CLEAVE, ALEXANDER MICHAEL. *Charles I's Lord Treasurer: Sir Richard Weston, Earl of Portland (1577–1635).* Pp. xii, 261. Chapel Hill: University of North Carolina Press, 1975. $21.95.

VON HIRSCH, ANDREW. *Doing Justice: The Choice of Punishments.* Pp. vi, 179. New York: Hill and Wang, 1976. $9.95.

WAKEMAN, FREDERIC, JR. and CAROLYN GRANT, eds. *Conflict and Control in Late Imperial China.* Pp. 352. Berkeley: University of California Press, 1976. $14.75.

WARNER, SAM BASS, JR., ed. *The American Experiment: Perspectives on 200 Years.* Pp. xi, 134. Boston, Mass.: Houghton Mifflin, 1976. $6.95. Paperbound, $3.95.

WAY, H. FRANK, JR. *Liberty in the Balance: Current Issues in Civil Liberties.* Pp. v, 128. New York: McGraw-Hill, 1976. $3.95. Paperbound.

WENDEL, THOMAS, ed. *Thomas Paine's Common Sense: The Call to Independence.* Pp. 176. Woodbury, N.Y.: Barron's Educational Series, 1975. $1.95. Paperbound.

WHISEHUNT, DONALD W. *The Environment and the American Experience: A Historian Looks at the Ecological Crisis.* Pp. 136. Port Washington, N.Y.: Kennikat Press, 1975. $6.95.

WHITESIDE, ANDREW G. *The Socialism of Fools: Georg Ritter von Schonerer and Austrian Pan-Germanism.* Pp. 414. Berkeley: University of California Press, 1975. $22.75.

WILLIE, CHARLES V. *Oreo: On Race and Marginal Men and Women.* Pp. 95. Wakefield, Mass.: Parameter Press, 1975. $3.95. Paperbound.

WILLRICH, MASON. *Energy and World Politics*. Pp. v, 234. New York: Free Press, 1975. $10.00.

WILSHER, PETER and ROSEMARY RIGHTER. *The Exploding Cities*. Pp. 238. New York: Quadrangle, 1975. $8.95.

WILSON, WILLIAM J. *Power, Racism, and Privilege*. Pp. vii, 224. New York: The Free Press, 1976. $4.95. Paperbound.

WINTERS, STANLEY B. and JOSEPH HELD, eds. *Intellectual and Social Developments in the Hapsburg Empire*. Pp. 304. New York: Columbia University Press, 1975. $14.00.

WIRT, FREDERICK M. *Power in the City: Decision Making in San Francisco*. Pp. 431. Berkeley: University of California Press, 1975. $14.95.

WOLFF, ROBERT PAUL. *About Philosophy*. Pp. iv, 305. Englewood Cliffs, N.J.: Prentice-Hall, 1976. $9.95.

WOLINS, MARTIN, ed. *Successful Group Care: Explorations in the Powerful Environment*. Pp. v, 463. Chicago, Ill.: Aldine-Atherton, 1974. $14.75.

World Communications: A 200 Country Survey of Press Radio Television Film. Pp. viii, 533. Murray Hill Station, N.Y.: UNIPUB, 1975. $21.00.

WRIGHT, DEIL S. et al. *Assessing the Impacts of General Revenue Sharing in the Fifty States: A Survey of State Administrators*. Pp. viii, 189. Chapel Hill: University of North Carolina Press, 1975. $4.00. Paperbound.

YOUNG, JAMES O. *Black Writers of the Thirties*. Pp. 257. Baton Rouge: Louisiana State University Press, 1974. $10.00.

ZWIEBACH, BURTON. *Civility and Disobedience*. Pp. v, 241. New York: Cambridge University Press, 1975. $10.95.

INDEX

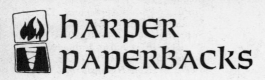

THE AMERICAN ACADEMY

announces publication of

THE 85th ANNIVERSARY CUMULATIVE INDEX OF THE ANNALS 1971–1975

Volumes 393–422, inclusive

Will be available in the Fall

$ 7.00 Paperbound
$10.00 Clothbound

This Index is not included in subscription to THE ANNALS. Members wishing to order now can use the form provided below.

INDEX ORDER FORM

85th

The American Academy of Political and Social Science
3937 Chestnut Street
Philadelphia, Pa., 19104

Please send:

.... Paperbound $ 7.00

.... Clothbound $10.00

☐ check enclosed

Add $1.00 for postage and handling

Name ....

Address ....

.... **Zip** ....

THE AAPSS

Cut on Dotted Line

286

Number
of Copies
P | C

Number
of Copies

P | C

Peace Settlements in World War II   P

Progress and Prospects of the United Nations   P & C

Social Implications of Modern Science   P & C

Belgium in Transition   P & C

Making the United Nations Work   P & C

The Netherlands during German Occupation   P & C

The Disabled Veteran   P

Postwar Jobs for Veterans   P

Adolescents in Wartime   P

International Frontiers in Education   P

Agenda for Peace   P & C

Higher Education and the War   P

Transportation: War and Postwar   P

The American Family in World War II   P

The United Nations and the Future   P

Our Servicemen and Economic Security   P

Southeastern Asia and the Philippines   P

Nutrition and Food Supply: The War and After   P

Labor Relations and the War   P

Winning Both the War and the Peace   P

The Press in the Contemporary Scene   P

Public Policy in a World at War   P & C

Defending America's Future   P & C

Billions for Defense   P & C

When War Ends   P

Marketing in Our American Economy   P

Government Expansion in the Economic Sphere   P

Frontiers of Legal Aid Work   P

Democracy and the Americas   P

Refugees   P

Appraising the Social Security Program   P

Ownership and Regulation of Public Utilities   P

Freedom of Inquiry and Expression   P & C

Present International Tensions   P

Social Problems and Policies in Sweden   P

Consumer Credit   P

Our State Legislators   P

Cut on Dotted Line

Number
of Copies

P | C

——	——	Revival of Depressed Industries P
——	——	The United States and World War P
——	——	Consumers' Cooperation P & C
——	——	Current Developments in Housing P
——	——	Improved Personnel in Government Service P
——	——	The American People: Studies in Population P
——	——	The Attainment and Maintenance of World Peace P
——	——	Education for Social Control P
——	——	Toward National Recovery P
——	——	Banking and Transportation Problems P & C
——	——	Social Insurance P & C
——	——	The Administration of Justice P
——	——	Prohibition: A National Experiment P & C
——	——	An Economic Survey of Australia P
——	——	Elements of an American Foreign Policy P
——	——	The Insecurity of Industry P & C
——	——	The Coming of Industry to the South P & C
——	——	The Second Industrial Revolution P & C
——	——	Real Estate Problems P & C

- P—Paperbound only; P & C—Paperbound and Clothbound
- Quantity and wholesales discounts cannot be applied to this special offer.
- Orders for 5 books or less must be prepaid.
- Orders for 6 books or more must be invoiced.
- All special sales are final.

Please send me the volumes as indicated above.

☐   Enclosed is $————— (add $.75 for postage and handling)
☐   Please bill me.   Postage and handling additional.

Name————————————————————————————————

Address—————————————————————————————————

City——————————————State——————————————Zip————

THE AMERICAN ACADEMY OF POLITICAL AND SOCIAL SCIENCE

3937 Chestnut Street   Philadelphia, Pa. 19104

Kindly mention THE ANNALS *when writing to advertisers*